Methods in Clinical Psychology

Volume 2
Prediction and Research

METHODS IN CLINICAL PSYCHOLOGY

Methods in Clinical Psychology

Volume 2
Prediction and Research

Robert R. Holt
Research Center for Mental Health
New York University

Plenum Press · New York and London

Library of Congress Cataloging in Publication Data

Holt, Robert R
  Methods in clinical psychology.

  Bibliography: p.
  Includes index.
  1. Clinical psychology. 2. Personality assessment. 3. Prediction (Psychology) 4.
Psychological research. I. Title. [DNLM: 1. Projective techniques — Collected
works. 2. Psychology, Clinical — Methods — Collected works. 3. Research —
Methods — Collected works. WM145 H758m]
RC467.H65   157   77-10429
ISBN 0-306-31124-0 (v. 2)

© 1978 Plenum Press, New York
A Division of Plenum Publishing Corporation
227 West 17th Street, New York, N.Y. 10011

Printed in the United States of America

Acknowledgments

The author and the publisher would like to thank the following for permission to reprint, with revisions and additions, the author's previously published articles in this volume.

American Psychological Association

Clinical and statistical measurement and prediction: How *not* to survey its literature [pp. 74–123], originally published in *JSAS Catalog of Selected Documents in Psychology*, 1975, *5*, 178, MS No. 837.

Clinical *and* statistical prediction: A reformulation and some new data[pp. 20–37], originally published in *Journal of Abnormal and Social Psychology*, 1958, *56*, 1–12.

Yet another look at clinical and statistical prediction: Or, is clinical psychology worthwhile? [pp. 55–72], originally published in *American Psychologist*, 1970, *25*, 337-349.

John Wiley & Sons, Inc.

A clinical–experimental strategy for research in personality [pp. 127–138], originally published in S. Messick and J. Ross, Eds. *Measurement in Personality and Cognition*. New York: John Wiley & Sons, Inc., 1962, pp. 269–283.

McGraw-Hill Book Company

Experimental methods in clinical psychology [pp. 139–186], originally published in B. Wolman, Ed. *Handbook of Clinical Psychology*. New York: McGraw-Hill Book Company, 1965, pp. 40-77.

Silver Burdett Company

Methods of research in clinical psychology [pp. 187–261], originally published in 1973.

Williams & Wilkins Co.

Clinical judgment as a disciplined inquiry [pp. 38–54], originally published in *Journal of Nervous and Mental Disease*, 1961, *133*, 369–382.

Preparation of Chapters 1, 4, 5, 7, 8, 9, and 10, as well as the reworking of the rest of the material for book publication, was supported by a United States Public Health Service Research Career Award, Grant No. 5-K06-MH-12455, from the National Institute of Mental Health, which is gratefully acknowledged.

Preface

This book presents my main writings on methodological issues, with one principal exception—a paper first published in 1962, which appears as the first chapter of the companion volume, on Projective Assessment. As I explain in the general preface to Volume 1, that chapter and the General Introduction were designed to set forth the premises and viewpoint of the work as a whole (which was originally planned as one very heavy book). Naturally, I hope that readers of this volume will want to read at least those introductory parts of the other one. Yet I feel that the ten chapters presented here are self-contained and can be understood and used without prerequisites.

But the issue that was central to that paper on individuality and generalization in the psychology of personality cropped up again in what came to be known as the controversy over clinical vs. statistical prediction. It took me some years to see beneath the tangled surface of that emotion-arousing conflict to the underlying methodological issues: Is a science of personality and clinical psychology possible? More specifically, is it possible to have a humane, nonmechanistic but scientific psychology? To do so requires working systematically and quantitatively with human judgments about meanings. Can that really be done? Can quantitative research models, first developed in the older, harder sciences, be applied to ideas, feelings, longings, life events, and subjective phenomena generally?

These questions arose, I now believe, because we have been going through a transitional time, during which an entire world view is being challenged and replaced by another one. The older outlook—much more than a model or a paradigm, it is a set of philosophical and methodological assumptions—has been described by many authors, notably Yankelovich and Barrett (1970), after Whitehead (1925), as scientific materialism, by Ackoff (1974) as Machine Age science, and by Mumford (1970) as the scientific aspect of the Myth of the Machine—the reductionistic, analytic, mechanistic, hyperobjective tradition in science. The newer and more adequate scientific world view takes as its basic model of reality not a machine but a living system; it is thus called organismic, or the systems view of the world. It is by no means to be confused with older antagonists of mechanistic science, such as vitalism or personalism; at its best it is a *synthesis* of such antagonistic pairs as holistic vs. atomistic, reductionistic vs. transcendental, global vs. analytic, behavioristic vs. Gestalt or humanistic, and clinical vs. statistical.

The series of papers in which I worked through the ins and outs of the controversy to these methodological issues therefore forms an appropriate introduction to the main part of this volume, which is devoted to a group of more detailed and practically oriented discussions of how to plan, carry on, report, and evaluate research on individual personalities and their disturbances. The initial section, which carries the short title Prediction, begins with an overview written especially for this book. It may surprise a good many people, who see me and Meehl as on opposite sides of the clinical vs. statistical Donnybrook, to learn that my position is a great deal more like his than it is different. I believe that any reader of the papers contained here who turns to Meehl's collection of his papers on psychodiagnosis (1973) will agree. In our different styles, we both have tried to integrate our commitments to clinical and scientific work, seeking to enrich each by the contributions of the other. Our differences are on the level Holton (1973) calls *thematic:* matters of basic assumption and presupposition that are neither empirical nor theoretical (in the narrow sense of theory as a body of propositions ordering and manipulating observations). I cannot imagine myself ever agreeing that "One would . . . like to be able to subscribe to the methodological dogmas of strict behaviorism and strict operationism" (Meehl, 1973, p. viii). I am not now, nor have I ever been, party to reductionism and positivism, as I understand those terms. To me, they are anachronistic survivals of nineteenth-century modes of thought which flourish in psychology partly because we do such a poor job of training our students in the history and philosophy of science and because most psychologists have never been aware that there was any other way to be rigorous and disciplined. One of my hopes for this book is to show such an alternative to both the simplemindedness of the behaviorist and the muddleheadedness of the undisciplined clinician.

The rest of this volume deals with research methods in clinical psychology (and also in psychiatry and psychoanalysis). As the preceding part is the most personally comprehensive in collecting everything I have written on the prediction problem, the final section is most comprehensive in its coverage of its subject matter. As a treatise on clinical research, it can compete pretty well with the other available general treatments of how to do and evaluate research in clinical psychology. At the same time, I am conscious of its shortcomings, and want to remind the reader that any skill as complex as scientific investigation must be learned by working along with a more experienced colleague over as long a time as one can reasonably arrange, perhaps a year as a minimum and preferably several. Indeed, the same caveat applies to the diagnostic skills that form the subject of the first volume.

In the preface to Volume 1 I have acknowledged debts of gratitude to the most important of the many people who have helped me to bring this book into being. Here I wish merely to reiterate my thanks and to repeat their names: Henry A. Murray, Robert W. White, David Rapaport, Martin Mayman, Roy Schafer, Paul Bergman, Margaret Brenman, Sibylle Escalona, Merton Gill, Louisa Howe, George Klein, Lester Luborsky, Daniel Horn, Jacob Cohen, Mark Fulcomer, Noel Dunivant, Fred Pine, Edwin S. Shneidman, Bettie Brewer, Mary Ann Dishman, Robyn Dawes, Irene Kaus, David Wolitzky, Joan Holt, and my sons Danny and Michael. I am also grateful to Barbara Sayres for her help in preparing the indexes to both volumes.

Robert R. Holt

New York

Contents

Contents of Volume 1

Other Methods

Prediction

1

The papers in this section deal with several aspects of a major controversy in psychology during the decades of the 1950s and 1960s, usually known as "clinical versus statistical prediction." In two ways they are a bridge between the first and the second (present) volume of this work. Much of clinical prediction is an application of the diagnostic and assessment skills treated in Volume 1, put to the test in a series of more or less controversial research designs; and the two volumes of the work represent somewhat overlapping but chronologically successive periods of my own work, which began as largely diagnostic, and became primarily investigative as an outgrowth of my first major research involvement (Holt & Luborsky, 1958), which took me into the thick of the struggle. Moreover, the attempt to come to grips with this controversy, which would not die, taught me a great deal about research methods.

In one way, Chapters 2–5 do not make full sense out of their context, being only one half of a running argument—usually with Paul E. Meehl, most recently with Jack Sawyer, but more generally with a whole school of thought represented by such other psychologists as Hoffman (e.g., 1960), Sarbin (e.g., Sarbin, Taft, & Bailey, 1960), Kleinmuntz (e.g., 1967), and Goldberg (e.g., 1968b). In this chapter, therefore, I want to try to give the reader at least some idea of how the controversy developed[1] and what the other side's major points have been. Since I have been one of the most active voices on the clinical or judgmental side of the argument, I can hardly be expected to give a fair and disinterested account of my opponents' contributions though I shall try to do so. Caveat lector!

A Historical Survey of the Clinical-Statistical Prediction Controversy

Shortly before World War II, Paul Horst and a group of co-authors (1941) published a monograph, *The Prediction of Personal Adjustment,* summarizing the status of research on not only the prediction of marital adjustment and the success of prisoners released on parole, but also of vocational and

---

[1]In the first part of this chapter I have drawn freely on Chapter 7 of Holt and Luborsky (1958).

educational selection and achievement. They showed the logical similarity of the scientific problems in all these disparate fields, and outlined the major steps of method and specific kinds of difficulties that have been encountered in many researches since then. Vocational selection (chiefly in industry) had received its first big impetus with the development of group intelligence tests in World War I together with interviewing and trade tests guided by job descriptions to help find the right man for each of hundreds of jobs. Another legacy of military psychology to industry was the personality inventory. Though it began as an attempt to measure adjustment by means of a self-administered psychiatric interview, it soon grew into a variety of measures of various traits, just as the Army Alpha fathered a brood of tests to measure a differentiated array of abilities. All of these instruments, and the related inventories of occupational interests which were invented shortly after the war, lent themselves to large-scale administration, quantitative scoring, and statistical processing. They were used to predict performance on various kinds of jobs and in educational contexts, and their success could be measured by the handy correlation coefficient and the related method of predicting by linear regression.

Meanwhile, another approach to predicting important things about people had developed in the life insurance business—the actuarial method. It was applied with impressive success to forecasting marital success and the success of parole for prisoners. Actuaries had noticed that people with different objective demographic characteristics tended to live to different ages, and having many cases available and no trouble with their clear-cut criterion, they proceeded to study the joint effect of several predictors taken in combination. To apply the method to predicting violation of parole, a researcher like E. W. Burgess (1928) first collects data on a large number of cases, including such facts about each released prisoner as his age, sex, marital status, ethnic origin, type of crime committed, etc., and also the crucial criterion—whether or not he violated parole after a given period of time. Next he cross-tabulates each of the personal characteristics against the others, making up all possible types of prisoners (e.g., young-male-single-Irish-embezzlers; middle-aged-female-divorced-Yankee-murderers; and so forth). If he uses many characteristics and does not have thousands of cases, some of the cells in the resulting grid will have few or no cases in them, so classifications must be made grosser, or the sample increased in size, or both. Finally, the maker of an actuarial table computes the success-frequency for the prisoners in each cell of the grid and can immediately use it predictively. If you know that 35% of 200 young-male-single-Irish-embezzlers violated parole within a year, the best prediction about another prisoner of that description is that he will *not* violate parole. Such a table is useful only if the proportion of "successes" differs considerably from cell to cell; it may be necessary to add some kinds of information and discard others that do not discriminate until substantial differences are obtained. Finally, the researcher has to try it out on a new group, making predictions and then checking them. If the proportion of success remains about the same as before in each cell, predicting the violation of parole thereafter is extremely simple. Any clerk can do it merely by entering the table with all of the required information about any particular prisoner.

The main alternative to the actuarial or statistical approach when Horst and his colleagues were summarizing the field was the case study method. The product of a clinical tradition, it approached the forecasting of any kind of behavior from a highly contrasting position; instead of working from a few objective facts about many people, it meant amassing many facts about a few people considered one at a time. Clearly, that is how a psychoanalyst works, and Freud's influence as well as that of such psychiatrists as Adolf Meyer and the psychologist Gordon Allport, opposed though they were in many ways, convinced workers in many disciplines that human behavior was too complexly determined to be predictable unless one made an intensive study of each subject's unique personality and life history. Though their own expertise was in the statistical tradition, Horst *et al.* were sympathetic to this point of view, pointing out various ways in which careful analysis of individual cases helps in predictive research. They were willing to suspend judgment on the comparative merits of the two types of method until more research should come in, and maintained a more cooperative than competitive outlook.

But even in the early 1940s, there was no dearth of spokesmen for the competitive position. Murray *et al.* (1938) began a highly influential report of his theory of personality and the cooperative research (emphasizing the study of individual lives) it had given rise to at the Harvard Psychological Clinic by throwing down the gage. Psychologists are divided, Murray said, "into two large classes holding opposite conceptual positions. One group may be called *peripheralists,* the other *centralists.*" He goes on to characterize the former group as "objectivists," who are positivistic, mechanistic, or given to physiological explanations. They emphasize the stimulus as the principal governor of behavior and look on personality "as the sum total or product of interacting elements rather than a unity which may, for convenience, be analyzed into parts." By contrast, the centralists (of whom Murray counted himself one) speak of organizing and directing processes inside the person, in the brain or in the unconscious mind. They are (in his terms) conceptualists, totalists, intuitionists, and dynamicists, believing in the emergence of holistic properties unpredictable from a knowledge of separate parts, and in abstract, hypothetical forces within the organism that require a sensitive observer as a measuring instrument to gauge them.

Clearly, this is a schism between two major outlooks in psychology. The tough-minded, empirically-oriented, pragmatic and (so it is alleged) characteristically American tradition in psychology has been behavioris-

tic; it has been interested in elements rather than in wholes; and at first
sight it fell in love with operationism. Its traditional enemy has been (to
use William James' dichotomy again) tenderminded, not unwilling to flirt
with intuition and the direct examination of phenomenal experience. In
the second camp, the personality as a whole is an object of value, almost
of veneration, and its warriors have had a deep distrust of attempts to
fractionate the individual, even conceptually. This feeling has been
matched by the suspicion in the opposing group of anything that
smacked of the occult, mystical, or otherwise nonscientific. (Holt &
Luborsky, 1958, Vol. 1, p. 94)

Friendly enemies though they were in so many respects, Murray and his
colleague at Harvard, Gordon Allport, agreed in opposing the behavioristic
majority, which surrounded them and set the tone of American psychology
for many decades. Predictably, the followers of Watson, Thorndike, and
Skinner found the actuarial and statistical approach to predicting behavior
much more to their liking than the study of individual cases, which the two
Harvard rivals both taught. Allport went a step further than Murray had a
few years earlier, stating:

> The only way to make a certain prediction of effect from cause is to study
> the life in which the causes operate, and not a thousand other lives. This
> is not to deny that actuarial prediction has its place (in dealing with
> masses of cases); it is good so far as it goes, but idiographic prediction
> goes further. . . . Studies should be made of the relative success of
> actuarial and case study predictions. (1942, pp. 157, 160)

At about the same time, Lundberg (1941) spoke from the other side of
the widening gap, claiming that there was no underlying difference between
the two methods, let alone anything so fundamental as Allport's claim of a
fundamental methodological distinction between idiographic and nomothetic approaches (see Volume 1, Chapter 1). All prediction was statistical, he
argued, based on the simple idea that what had frequently occurred would
occur again; it was just that the case history proponents did not recognize the
actuarial basis of their predictions.

The next major development came about again as a result of war. The
statistical techniques of multiple correlation were not new, but were highly
developed and applied to the prediction of such tasks as learning to pilot an
airplane. The invention of the correlation coefficient had been comple-
mented by the test of intelligence, which enabled educators to predict
freshman college grades with a validity of about **.50**. The actuarial table,
however, made it possible to take into account patterns of several predictive
variables simultaneously instead of only one, but it was hampered by the
sheer cumbersomeness of many boxes if predictors were more finely graded
than being split into two or three categories. A great deal of the information
in the many-valued score like the IQ was lost if it was introduced into an

actuarial table. Multiple correlation made it possible to make full use of the differentiation in continuous scores and in the proliferating tests of more precisely delimited abilities and traits, to predict either dichotomous or continuous criteria. And in order to make full use of this statistical resource, various teams of psychologists (largely in the Air Force) worked out an ingenious and effective technology.

The result was a five-step process, which I describe in slightly different ways in Chapters 2 and 4.

> Detailed studies were made of what a pilot does, what a student of flying has to be able to learn. Next, psychologists tried to figure out what abilities a person had to have, what tempermental characteristics he should possess, etc., in order to do this job. A large number of tests was assembled, including already standardized measures of some of the abilities in question and a good many new ones. Then large samples of flight trainees were given these tests, and their progress through training was watched. A statistical measure (biserial correlation) was then computed between each test score and the pass-fail criterion [successful completion of the program vs. "washing out"]. At this point, many tests proved worthless and were discarded. The tests that predicted well were repeatedly cross-validated—tried out on new groups—until a stable result had been achieved. (Holt & Luborsky, 1958, Vol. 1, p. 88f.)

Some test scores might appear to be good, stable predictors, yet not be worth retaining because of redundancy—the information they provided was already present in other test scores. Multiple regression methods made it possible to find the smallest battery of tests to predict the criterion most efficiently.

> Moreover, the tests were subjected to constant study and revisions. With each successive sample of students, the most promising of the originally selected tests were retained, others were modified to . . . [assess] qualities not yet well measured, new ones were added, and all were again correlated with each other and the criterion to find the most efficient group of tests with the smallest overlap. After this process had been repeated with a few thousand airmen, an efficient battery of reasonably reliable, objective and easily scorable tests were finally worked out. Thus, a very good level of validity (r = .6) was reached and held through repeated trials. (*Ibid.*, p. 98)

During the decade that followed the throwing down of the challenge, a fair amount of research began to accumulate: much of it, like the Air Force work, proceeding from the statistical-actuarial tradition, some from the clinical tradition (notably Murray's work in selecting spies for the OSS, 1948), and some comparing the two. But the controversy did not come into the view of most psychologists and the evidence was largely unknown before the book by Paul E. Meehl (1954), *Clinical vs. Statistical Prediction.* He examined the issues in a thorough and compelling way, and made a valuable collection of available evidence which he presented with expert comments on its limitations and strengths.

Most of the book is given over to Meehl's discussion of the theoretical issues involved in the controversy, which is too subtle and complex to be easily summarized or reduced to easily remembered formulas. As a result, it has been less influential than it deserves. He did, however, effectively refute the claim of Sarbin (1943, 1944) that all prediction is essentially actuarial in structure—the Lundberg argument. He showed, first, that clinicians do not operate just by ordering a case to a class of similar cases, predicting by the known frequency of the criterion behavior in that class. Instead, they use their data to formulate a structural-dynamic hypothesis about the personality or a theory of how that person operates, which can be used to generate predictions of his behavior under given circumstances. Moreover, actuarial systems ideally do not involve judgment, while clinicians have latitude to adjust their predictive systems as they see fit at any stage. This freedom enables the clinician to operate more flexibly, adaptively, and creatively, but it is also a freedom to make many kinds of errors. It is therefore an empirical question whether by and large clinicians can profit from their freedom or whether actuarial systems excel because they are constrained from making many kinds of mistakes.

Therefore, though he tried to mediate the dispute and to find the proper spheres within which clinicians and statisticians might operate, Meehl ended up treating the score of studies he examined as if the question were simply to compare two different approaches, clinical versus statistical prediction. And in that collection of researches, the palm easily went to the statisticians.

It is safe, I think, to say that Meehl's book made a sensation in psychology. It was very widely reviewed and praised, becoming one of the most frequently cited books of its time. The year after it was published, the annual invitational conference of the Educational Testing Service was devoted to the controversy, which waxed hotter than ever (Humphreys et al., 1955). Meehl was a central figure in that conference and in a symposium on clinical and statistical prediction published in 1956 by the Journal of Counseling Psychology, the same year that he (Meehl, 1956b) published a challenging paper presenting the work of his student Halbower, closely followed by several other empirical and conceptual contributions (Meehl, 1957, 1959; Meehl & Dahlstrom, 1960). In 1961 he was elected president of the American Psychological Association. This honor was richly deserved, for he had made many other diverse contributions to psychology, but none of them had given his name the wide currency of his book and papers on clinical and statistical prediction.

Recall that Meehl's book appeared less than a decade after the end of World War II, a period of extraordinary, force-fed growth of clinical psychology. What had been a minor insignificant branch of applied psychology, attracting very few graduate stduents and not taught as such in more than a tiny handful of universities, suddenly became the most popular specialty in graduate psychological education. The American Psychological Association first stimulated the spread of specialization and then set up accreditation for the resulting spate of programs to produce Ph.D.s in clinical psychology. There were rational bases for distrusting the soundness of this sudden growth in response to social need and available money, and plenty of irrational ones as well. The academic, largely experimental and behavioristic establishment in American psychology grew uneasy, suspecting that the influence of psychoanalysis on the burgeoning branch of the family tree was unhealthy and fearing that it might become so large as to unbalance the whole. In this climate, a book by a practicing clinician with psychoanalytic training who was also a respected contributor to methodology and to the traditional psychology of rat learning, which presented evidence damning to the pretensions of clinicians while maintaining a balanced, ambivalent orientation, was bound to find an audience.

Like many others who had been trained in the old clinical tradition before the flood, I found myself in a position of considerable conflict. Because of my identity as a clinical psychologist, I felt a strong tendency to identify myself with the new wave of younger colleagues, to feel happy in the prospect that ours was becoming an important and powerful voice in organized psychology as we were attaining something approaching (but never achieving) parity of status with psychiatrists in hospitals and clinics, and to plunge into the task of organizing graduate education of clinical psychologists to help make it as good as possible. Yet at the same time, I was repelled and taken aback by much of what I saw in this brash emergent. Too many people were being pushed through too rapidly to attain a doctoral level of expertise in either research or clinical work, let alone both. It was simply not possible simultaneously to maintain high standards and to grow exponentially. The push behind the growth was easily available public money for training and job opportunities for graduates; granted the nature of our culture, that proved an easy victor over the more idealistic desires for a small—or at least slowly growing—profession of experts with first-class minds, nurturant motivation, and a high level of personal maturity.

In this setting, I saw the actuarial attack on clinical judgment as yet another assault on the quality of my profession. Naively, I thought that I could do what Meehl had failed to do, with my paper of 1958a (reprinted here as Chapter 2): mediate the dispute with a balanced approach, stop the attack on the very aspects of clinical work that required long, slow training, and puncture the irrational self-glorification of some of my colleagues. Instead, I was immediately assimilated to the clinical side of the battle; like Meehl's my attempt to analyze and redefine the issues was ignored. The other chapters of this section were originally a further series of efforts to get psychologists to stop fighting and think about what matters of substance and theoretical import were really at stake. I am reminded of a *Peanuts* cartoon strip in which Charlie Brown, being chased by a group of angry big kids, escapes unharmed—how? "Suddenly, he organized a discussion group," we are told. It is funny precisely because it is preposterous. When a fight is going on, the regressive pressures on participants and audience alike are enormous, and any attempt to get the antagonists to become colleagues in a sublimated intellectual inquiry is futile outside of a small and highly controlled setting. My quixotic attempt has been met with probably deserved ridicule; for example:

> Long ago two broad integration possibilities were distinguished: actuarial (or statistical) and subjective (or "clinical"). When they are pitted against each other repeatedly, as in a cockfight, neither manages to kill off the other in a clean enough manner so that all of the betting money changes hands. Most psychologists have come to agree with Meehl (1971), who long ago set up the gaming regulations. On the other hand, Holt (1970a) has always objected to these very rules, and thus he sporadically confesses his refusal to pay up. The major unresolved problems today (other than persuading Holt to do some research instead of exhorting others to do it for him) include, on the actuarial side, a specification of the sort of prediction functions that are most appropriate for today's measures, and on the subjective side, a specification of the optimal meld of empirical data with informed intuition. (Goldberg, 1974, p. 359f.)

The author is right that I have from the beginning tried to get the rules changed, so that we could stop fighting or gambling and start learning something more useful. The attentive reader of the following chapters will, I hope, see in them something more than an indirect and disguised attempt to get other people to do my research for me.

During the 1960s, a couple of other surveys of the literature appeared (notably that of Gough, 1962, and Sawyer, 1966) with conclusions similar to Meehl's, and one (Korman, 1968) with sharply diverging conclusions favoring clinical prediction. More empirical studies were published; Meehl (1965) noted briefly that his collection of relevant researches numbered 50, only one of which he then considered a clear success for the clinicians (Lindzey, 1965). Even that conclusion was sharply attacked by a new recruit to the anticlinical side, Goldberg (1968a).

The latter is a productive empiricist much of whose work has questioned the utility of clinical and other forms of subjective judgment. The situation has a number of features in common with a controversy of about a century earlier, that between vitalism and mechanism. Both views about the nature of life were wrong, the vitalists' claim that living organisms contained something unknowable by the scientific method—an *élan vital* or entelechy—as well as the mechanists' debunking retort that organisms were just fancy machines and nothing more to it. Yet, as Rapoport (1962) wisely pointed out, the latter camp ended up making the more valuable contributions to biology even though they never succeeded in their reductionistic aim, because they clung to the scientific method. Goldberg and such colleagues at the Oregon Research Institute as Hoffman and Dawes have adopted a set of working assumptions that make their research irrelevant to most of clinical psychological practices (as I have argued in Chapter 5); yet these same assumptions, plus their assiduous empiricism and good scientific method, have enabled them to carry out a lot of interesting and probably valuable research, not all of it unfavorable to judgment. They have shown, for example, that the vaunted method of empirical keying used in constructing the MMPI has no advantage over "rational" keys based solely on clinical judgment, in terms of ability to predict independent criteria (Hase & Goldberg, 1967; Ashton & Goldberg, 1973). By an empirical test, they have shown how difficult it is for clinicians to profit from experience in learning the meaning of MMPI profiles (Goldberg, 1968b), how much better clinicians are at devising diagnostic schemes—as always, using MMPI profiles—than at applying them to a series of cases, as compared to a computer (Goldberg, 1970), and how fruitless, so far, has been the search for any proof that elaborate configural methods can predict any available criterion better than a simple linear combination of quantitative predictors (Goldberg, 1968b). Moreover, the linear model has been strikingly effective in simulating or reproducing the predictions of professional decision-makers in various fields, despite introspective reports that they were using complex, variable, and configural methods of integrating data.

Goldberg's conclusion, which was independently reached by several other workers whom he quotes, is that "when acceptable criterion information is available, the proper role of the human in the decision-making process is that of a scientist: (a) discovering or identifying new cues which will improve predictive accuracy, and (b) constructing new sorts of systematic procedures for combining predictors in increasingly more optimal ways" (Goldberg, 1970, p. 423). I believe that the evidence tends to support him under the following conditions, which have held in the research he bases his conclusion on: the predictors are quantitative scores or simple, objectively ascertainable classifications of people like sex; and the predictions must be made on a large number of subjects. Confronted by the creative challenge of devising a new method of predicting something, a person's motivation is likely to be sustained by the very existence of obstacles and difficulties, as is his attention; but faced with the task of applying his resulting theory or technique and his skill over and over again to a series of normally varying cases, the main obstacle becomes boredom with a repetitive task, which inevitably interferes with attention and concentration. Consequently, if the judgmental task is susceptible to being modeled by a computer, the machine is likely to make so many fewer careless errors than the man as to cancel out the latter's occasional exercise of originality in coping with a new pattern of predictors.

Where I remain unconvinced, however, is that such a finding has any direct bearing on most clinical judgment, or that it has clear implications for either clinical practice or the appropriate training therefor. My reasons for these reservations are spelled out in the papers that follow, particularly in Chapters 4 and 5.

Looking back on the history of this controversy, I am not discouraged by the fact that many textbooks now tend to treat it as a war of attrition which has been just about won by the proponents of the actuarial and statistical tradition. There have been some real gains, which will probably outlast the assimilative oversimplifications of the secondary sources. There has been a small resurgence of respect for human judgment, a recognition that creativity cannot yet be modeled or automated, and some improvement in our knowledge about how to assess research and to review a body of literature. Once Glass' (1976) important contribution to this last endeavor has had a chance to penetrate and be absorbed by psychologists, I believe that we may hope to see no more essay-reviews like those of Meehl (1954), Gough (1962), and Sawyer (1966), but instead meta-analyses that may be much more informative (see Chapter 9).

However ingeniously such a meta-analysis is carried out, however, it can be no better than its materials. No matter how impressively high it is piled, garbage remains garbage. I have felt for a long time that there was some fundamental error in the formulation of the problem that made the accumulating evidence irrelevant to the conclusions people wanted to draw from it, and I put forward several hypotheses about what might be the matter in Chapter 3. Let me make one final attempt.

The classical research design pitting clinical against statistical predictions—the "gaming regulations" Goldberg (1974) refers to—makes one silent assumption which is difficult to see because it pervades most of modern psychology. That is a commitment to a strictly analytical methodology. All of the essential information about any topic can—nay, must—be expressed, in this view, in terms of separate bits of information and independent analytical measurements of part-processes and part-structures. It assumes, further, that clinical judgment must operate by dissecting reality and then putting the pieces together somehow to make predictions of behavioral outcomes— performances of such a kind that they make satisfactorily predictable criteria, which Levy (1963) calls the *bounded class* of predictions. Everything else the clinician does that does not fit this procrustean bed is simply neglected. Once a clinician has granted these assumptions, the rest follows inevitably; the five-part predictive technology, the powerful analytical resources of mathematics, and the fast reliable processing of data by computers combine to defeat him sooner or later.

If, however, any substantial part of a working clinician's job consists of tasks in Levy's *unbounded class*—e.g., to size up and take action concerning such systems as families in a social structure, or persons living in the real world of their everyday lives, the above research model is seriously lacking. Not only are most of his data semantic, plastic (figural or presentational), and behavioral rather than symbolic, but they are nonanalytical, and his task is rarely to do with them anything like predicting an objective, quantifiable criterion. No doubt the familiar fallibilities of clinical judgment continue to operate when they are difficult to measure or demonstrate—lapses of attention, intrusions of personal conflict or preoccupation, idiosyncrasies and unreliabilities of all kinds in the intake and processing of information, and so forth. Nevertheless, there is simply no available substitute for judgment in the actual professional situation![2]

I do not mean to argue that clinicians have been systems theorists all along or even that many of them would agree with the above statement of the problem. Many advocates of clinical judgment who have been unconvinced by the weight of the accumulated evidence (which has caused Meehl to accuse them of remaining untroubled in their dogmatic slumbers) have tended to accept an earlier approximation of the systems outlook—the approach of Gestalt psychology. They have felt opposed to systematic dissection or measurement of part-functions because of a frequently intuitive and ill-articulated recoil, a repugnance grounded on the emotional conviction that the dead hand of such cut-and-dried procedures would wither human reality. Because the partisans of clinical and of statistical prediction have contrasting thematic, ideological, and identity commitments, making contrasting assumptions that are not testable on the contingent, x-y plane of Holton (1973), the controversy continues without conclusive resolution. Indeed, when seen as a "horse race" (Cronbach, 1956), which means not so much a scientific proceeding as an adversary (or zero-sum) contest, in which one party is simply right and the other wrong, it can lead to nothing but a hardening of positions.[3]

---

[2]Levy (1963, pp. 173–174) takes a very similar position: "The formal approach to psychodiagnosis, yielding as it has information of an essentially quantitative nature, would seem best suited to the bounded problem. . . . It is, for example, only a matter of patience and ingenuity to find the best combination and weighting of variables to predict academic success, recidivism, or likelihood of benefiting from shock therapy. . . . On the other hand, in accounting for the day-to-day behavior of a patient or as a guide in determining the course of a psychotherapeutic interview, the information forthcoming from a purely formal psychodiagnostic evaluation would be of minimal value. . . . [In such unbounded decision-making] psychological interpretation, by passing new dimensions through the data, may help to generate new insights not otherwise possible."

[3]" . . . the adversary method for the settlement of disputes about the truth . . . is ascientific not only in its procedure, but in its greater commitment to victory rather than to truth" (Hammond & Adelman, 1976, p. 391).

The needed redefinition of assumptions is, I believe, provided by the approach of general systems theory. From that perspective (for which I refer you to Weiss, 1969), cooperation instead of competition becomes rational as well as agreeable, for both analytic and holistic approaches are necessary to complete the task of science. It also suggests that the clinician needs to redefine his task, not only to stop trying to process analytical measurements by judgmental processes if he has been conned into accepting that as the way to be more scientific, but to refine and discipline his judgment and empathic perceptions.

To give Meehl his due, I want to call attention to the striking last chapter in his recent book (Meehl, 1973), where he gives repeated demonstration of his own devotion to the development of his clinical judgment and skill in detecting subtle whole-qualities of persons for diagnostic purposes (e.g., the "schizophrenic float"). If my position on the limitation of the kind of clinical judgment I am talking about to a few experts seems elitist, wait until you read his! We are actually a great deal more alike than different in most of our professional values.

The challenge to our profession and science, then, is not to show that there are clinicians who can predict some criteria better than a formula under some conditions, nor to specify "the optimal meld of empirical data with informed intuition" in making predictions. Rather, it is to find better ways to inform the clinician's intuition and to help him cope with the intrinsic threats to the validity of his judgment. Notice Goldberg's choice of that word "intuition"—a vague and fuzzy-sounding term (as is another favorite adjective of the anticlinical camp, "global") used by the exclusively analytically minded to describe any nonanalytical process, which the blinders of their own cognitive style force them to conclude must be less differentiated or less realistic than their own way of thinking. Actually, such "intuitive" processes as paying attention to the properties of the presenting system as such are in no way mystically transcendental or preanalytically diffuse, but are characteristic of common sense. Clinicians (a general term I use to refer to diagnosticians and psychotherapists of all kinds including psychiatrists and social workers as well as to clinical psychologists) need to learn and use what they can of analytical technology, but not at the cost of losing their common sense. And we need to direct research efforts to the problem of learning how to discern the appropriate systemic level where order can be found in any situation, and how to systematize and improve on common sense as a guide to observing important nonreducible properties of total systems. Then, I believe, we will make some progress in a useful understanding of clinical judgment—even wisdom—and may be able to contribute more to good clinical work than all the predictive research ever done or contemplated, no matter how sophisticated the method by which its literature is assembled and integrated.

What I have been opposing all these years is not formal methods (statistical and actuarial methods of predicting, or systematic and controlled procedures) but attempts to denigrate and eliminate judgment. Some of the formalists may protest that they have only wanted to expose the excesses of those who relied on judgment too much and at the wrong points, but I fear that the result has been to intimidate and discourage many a practicing clinician in the necessary exercise of his judgment. Medical practice, for example, does not consist solely in administering standard treatments to clearly differentiated cases of single diseases. Most patients, even nonpsychiatric ones, do not suffer from classical illnesses for which there are clearly optimal treatments. Attempts to computerize diagnosis in internal medicine have been going on for some years, but they still fail to yield definite results in many cases, so that the physician still has to fall back on his judgment. If that judgment is constantly derogated and if the prevailing ethos urges him to restrict its exercise as much as possible, will he be able to accept the responsibility of using it when it is most needed?

Further, if the change in ethos which we already see happening continues, and if it is necessary for clinical practice and research that one be at home with mathematics and computers, it seems likely that the kind of person attracted to medicine, psychology, and other clinical professions will change. More humanistic, intuitive-empathic people might be repelled, and the technologically minded attracted, which would have the effect of further increasing the tendency to technicize and automate what are currently judgmental practices. Where, then, would the innovators come from? Perhaps it is a sentimental attachment to a stereotype that was never typical, to foresee mournfully the demise of the kindly old family doctor; perhaps the average level of medical care for most people most of the time would improve in the hands of clean, cool technicians. I still feel that this is not the kind of world I want to live in. And I am bothered by the thought that if few people strive to sharpen their intuition, if doctors are no longer urged to treat the person, not the symptom, and if diagnosis and therapy are cast in terms of an exclusively analytical orientation, then it will be difficult to make certain kinds of progress, the kind that begins with poorly articulated, tacit, but nevertheless accurate knowledge. Much of what we now know in fairly precise and analytical form began as hunches. If hunches go out of style, where will the hypotheses come from that will help researchers find new parts of the undiscovered truth?

Yet we must also consider the unanticipated consequences of ignoring the advances that have been made in systematizing aspects of judgment. As Elstein (1976, p. 700) puts it, "the more it is insisted that a clinical situation cannot be analyzed in terms of risks and likelihoods, estimated however roughly, the more investigation in these terms is discouraged." He points out the fact that "psychological research on human judgment and decision-making has had little impact on medical practice" (*ibid.*, p. 696), quite possibly because it is so threatening. To the practitioner, dealing every day with life-and-death decisions, the message of much of the work is, "Your judgment is not nearly as good as you think it is," which is a threat to the security, self-esteem, and even the professional identity of many clinicians. Small wonder that they find it easy to ignore work that lies largely outside their field, seems of dubious relevance, and clearly is still embroiled in controversy. That is no prescription for getting the needed research done, either.

I have not been able to formulate an answer that I find fully satisfactory. It was a mistake ever to have delineated as a controversy or competition (clinical versus statistical) what should have been an integrative and cooperative enterprise from the beginning; but there is no turning the clock back. Meehl still does not seem to agree that his 1954 book, by its very title, set in motion the forces that stereotype him as anticlinical and make inevitable the experiences he reports finding so annoying—that students are astonished to find that he spends a great deal of his time doing psychoanalytic psychotherapy and teaching a traditional kind of intuitive and judgmental, clinical approach to diagnosis. I have a hunch, still untested, that it might help to start graduate students out with a theoretical paradigm that is integrative rather than reductionistic—general systems theory instead of behaviorism, psychoanalysis, or some amalgam of the two (such as Meehl apparently uses). We must find ways of fostering their ego development generally and their cognitive maturation specifically to the point where they can think and work in integrative ways; I'm pretty well convinced that we are not currently doing an optimal job of it by conventional graduate programs. And then we have to bring about change to modes of professional practice that will make progress possible.

The old pattern, inherited from the Middle Ages, allowed only slow and uncertain growth of professional skill. Wise master clinicians could pass along what they had learned from their teachers plus any personal increment (in which error was always mixed with truth) only slowly and inefficiently to their apprentices. All too often, the legendary exploits of great clinicians left behind nothing more than a wondering memory—at times perhaps because the tacit component of personal knowledge (Polanyi, 1958) cannot be made explicit, but surely at times because no one knew how to or even tried to do so. Since corrective feedback comes so slowly in the practice of clinical psychology, error and especially irrelevancy tends to be discovered only falteringly and occasionally. (By irrelevancy I mean the essentially untestable propositions of "deep dynamics" or metapsychological efflorescence to which many clinical experts devote all too much of their time, incidentally causing people like Meehl and me to stay away from case conferences. It is not easy to discriminate the irrelevant from the truly abstract or unconscious, categories that are notoriously difficult though not impossible to test, as irrelevant propositions are.)

Surely little progress results when clinicians whose own education, scientific and clinical alike, was superficial attempt to follow the traditional model of professional practice and education. Pressures to keep graduate education short enough to be humanly possible, coupled with a lack of the professional controls that might guarantee the attainment of requisite skills in postdoctoral training, create a situation in which we are not even preserving and transmitting the level of skill attained in the past, not at least in those dying arts, diagnostic psychological testing and multiform personality assessment (Holt, 1967g).

The newer, post-1954 tradition attempts to substitute cookbooks for the trained diagnostic eye, objective and self-administering tests for interviews and projective techniques, and a general reliance on psychometric and statistical method in coping with clinical problems. In practice, I find the results distressingly superficial, the tools inadequate to most real clinical problems, and people who have been trained this way clinically clumsy and insensitive.

Whichever the tradition in which clinical psychologists are trained, the conditions of practice continue to insulate them from the consequences of their decisions. Technical incompetence is easily masked by an authoritative, scholarly, or charismatic manner, and by institutional routines that make it difficult to confront the persons responsible for clinical errors with late-developing consequences. The kinds of changes Meehl (1973) advocates in his concluding pages would help; so would a general professional commitment to following up each case. Finally, I think that there are some models for a new kind of professional practice that will combine rigorous procedure and humane sensitivity, and will make it possible both for clinical discoveries to be made (which the actuarial tradition makes difficult) and for them to be disseminated (which the old clinical tradition made difficult).

I am pinning part of my hopes on a synthetic approach known as decision theory or decision analysis. Like much of modern systems theory, it began with operations research in World War II, an approach that attempts to look at practical problems as broadly as possible, and to record, objectify and even quantify (where possible) rules for assessing them, for generating as wide a range of alternative solutions as possible, and for evaluating the solutions. Another important ancestor was game theory. Decision theory is not new (Wald, 1950; Girshick, 1954; W. Edwards, 1954); it has been used for some time in personnel selection (Cronbach & Gleser, 1957), and is currently being applied to medical decision-making (see Elstein, 1976, for a review and sources) and in various kinds of evaluative research (W. Edwards, Guttentag, & Snapper, 1975), and in sociopolitical problem-solving (Hammond & Adelman, 1976). It does not insist that everything be quantified; it not only accepts the role of value judgments in decisions but insists that they not be omitted—all that are relevant; where objective and empirical data on the probabilities of various relationships are not available, it encourages the substitution of subjective likelihoods; and in as many ways as possible, it tries to include everything that persons of excellent judgment would draw on in making difficult decisions. It appears, then, to be a realization of the kind of "sophisticated" integration of clinical and statistical traditions for which I called in 1958.

The road to progress in the realm of clinical judgment does not lie in continuing, destructive attacks on all manifestations of what is most human about the ways in which clinicians and other experts approach problems. We have to find ways of helping clinicians without threatening them. Doubtless the approach will be more effective if it conveys the message, "Here is a way I believe I may be able to assist you with some of the most difficult and agonizing aspects of your practice," rather than, "Research shows that you are deceiving yourself and harming your patients by acting as you do—change your ways!" Since decision analysis makes it possible to use the observing eye, the feeling heart, and the wisdom of the good clinician as well as whatever can be contributed to decisions from formulas, actuarial tables, and the like, it holds out the hope of continued progress. It may take an extraordinary and creative person to see that a previously neglected aspect of a patient's total situation is relevant to helping him, but once that step has been taken and embodied in a new decision rule, it is available to any workaday practitioner. As long as the door is open to such innovations, clinicians will be motivated to sharpen and exercise their judgmental and intuitive capacities, without having to rely on them alone.

2

At the time when the Menninger School of Psychiatry was conceived, shortly before my arrival in Topeka in 1946, David Rapaport proposed to Karl Menninger and Robert Knight that they do research on this bold new venture in the large-scale training of psychiatrists. When they designed the procedure for assessing and selecting among applicants, they built in a plan for gathering data to study the effectiveness of those procedures.

All of this was under way when Dr. Rapaport recruited me for a job at the VA Hospital in Topeka and hastily but intensively trained me in diagnostic testing, then the main function of clinical psychologists. But in the summer of 1947, he decided that he could no longer carry the main burden of the selection research himself and took me on to the staff of the Menninger Foundation half-time to work on it, very shortly to be joined by Lester Luborsky. Somewhat later, William R. Morrow came to us from the Berkeley team that had produced The Authoritarian Personality, *and the three of us worked intensively for several years gradually reshaping and completing the project, which was funded originally by the Veterans Administration and the Menninger Foundation, at its end by the New York Foundation. When David Rapaport left Topeka in 1948, Sibylle K. Escalona took over the supervison of the project as the Foundation's new Director of Research.*

This is not the place to try to tell the full story of that research project, most of which may be found in the two volumes we finally produced (Holt & Luborsky, 1958). We started out naively, knowing very little about selection research or any controversy about how to do that kind of work and full of confidence that the clinical methods of personality assessment we had learned under the name of diagnostic testing would do the job. The data had all been gathered and partly analyzed when I left the Menninger Foundation in the fall of 1953 to direct the new Research Center for Mental Health at New York University, but I continued to work with Dr. Luborsky and the project staff for the next few years, with many visits back to Topeka.

We were well into the writing of our book when Meehl (1954) published his bombshell. It caused me to see our work in a new light, partly reflected in the published form of the book and more succinctly in the following paper, which appeared almost a year before the full monographic report. Although my view of some of the issues has changed considerably, I have decided to reprint it with only a couple of minor corrections; the sequence of chapters and Chapter 1 show how my ideas have developed.

Clinical *and* Statistical Prediction: A Reformulation and Some New Data

The controversial discussions started a few years ago by Meehl's tightly packed little book, *Clinical vs. Statistical Prediction* (1954), still continue—especially among graduate students in psychology, most of whom have to read it. Clinical students in particular complain of a vague feeling that a fast one has been put over on them, that under a great show of objectivity, or at least bipartisanship, Professor Meehl has actually sold the clinical approach up the river. The specific complaints they lodge against the book are, in my opinion, mostly based on misinterpretations, wishful thinking, or other errors, yet I have felt for some time that there was something valid in the irrational reaction without knowing why.

What I propose to show here is that clinicians do have a kind of justified grievance against Meehl, growing out of his formulation of the issues rather than his arguments, which are sound. Finally, I want to offer a slightly different approach to the underlying problems, illustrated by some data. It may not quite make the lion lie down with the lamb, but I hope that it will help us all get on with our business, which is the making of a good science and profession.

THE ISSUES RESTATED

Meehl's book contains a review of the controversy, a logical analysis of the nature of clinical judgment, a survey of empirical studies, and some conclusions. I am not going to go into his treatment of the logical issues and his psychological reconstruction of clinical thinking; for the most part, I agree with this part of the book and consider it a useful contribution to methodology. I want to focus rather on his conception of what the issues are in the controversy, on his treatment of the evidence, and on some conclusions.

Many issues make better reading when formulated as battles, and the field of the assessment and prediction of human behavior has not lacked for controversy-loving gauntlet-flingers. The sane and thoughtful voices of Horst and his collaborators (1941), urging compromise and collaboration, have been shouted down by the war cries of such partisans as Sarbin (1943) on the actuarial side and Murray *et al.* (1948) on the clinical or (as they put it) organismic. Meehl approached the problem with a full awareness of the feelings on both sides and apparently with the hope that the therapeutic ploy of bringing them all out into the open at the beginning would enable him to discuss the issues objectively.

In a recent discussion of the stir his book has raised, Meehl (1956a) has expressed surprise and dismay that his effort to take a balanced and qualified position has led so many people to misunderstand him as claiming that clinical prediction has been proved worthless. Yet he is not blameless; by posing the question of clinical versus statistical prediction, he has encouraged two warring camps to form. This in turn makes it appear all the more compellingly that there are *two* clear-cut types of prediction to be compared.

The root difficulty, I believe, lies in Meehl's acceptance of *clinical* and *actuarial* as concepts that can without further analysis be meaningfully applied to a variety of predictive endeavors of an experimental or practical sort. Accepting them as valid types, he can hardly do anything other than pit one against the other and try to decide what is the proper sphere of exercise for each. But the terms in this antithesis mean many things; they are constellations of parts that are not perfectly correlated and can be separated.

The issue cannot therefore be sharply drawn so long as we speak about anything as complex as "clinical prediction" or "the clinical method." Rather, I think the central issue is the *role of clinical judgment in predicting human behavior.* By clinical judgment here, I mean nothing more complicated than the problem-solving or decision-reaching behavior of a person who tries to reach conclusions on the basis of facts and theories already available to him by thinking them over.

Let us make a fresh start, therefore, by examining the logical structure of the predictive process with an eye to locating the points where clinical judgment may enter. The following five-step process is idealized, and in practice some of the steps are more or less elided, but that does not hurt this analysis.

First, if we are to predict some kind of behavior, it is presupposed that we acquaint ourselves with what we are trying to predict. This may be called job analysis or the study of the criterion. Perhaps those terms sound a little fancy when their referent is something that seems so obvious to common sense. Nevertheless, it is surprising how often people expend a great deal of time and effort trying to predict a kind of behavior about which they know very little and apparently without even thinking that it might help if they could find out more. Consider the job of predicting outcome of flight training, for example. Many attempts to predict passing or washing out have been made by clinicians without any direct experience in learning to fly, without any study of flight trainees to see what they have to *do* in order to learn how to fly a plane, or of the ways they can fail to make the grade (see Holtzman and Sells, 1954).

There is a hidden trick in predicting something like success in flight training, because that is not itself a form of behavior. It is an outcome, a judgment passed by someone on a great deal of concrete behavior. The same is true for grades in college, success in any type of treatment, and a host of other criteria that are the targets in most predictive studies. Because it is hidden by the label, there is a temptation to forget that the behavior you should be trying to predict exists and must be studied if it is to be rationally forecast. In the highly effective pilot selection work carried out by psychologists during the war, careful job analyses were an important step in the total predictive process and undoubtedly contributed a good deal to the over-all success.

This first stage is hardly a good point at which to try to rely on clinical judgment. The result is most likely to be that guesses, easy and arbitrary assumptions, and speculative extrapolations will attempt to substitute for real information. And no matter how remarkable clinical judgment may sometimes be, it can never create information where there is none.

The *second* logical step is to decide what intervening variables need to be considered if the behavior is to be predicted. As soon as we get away from the simplest kind of prediction—that someone will continue to act the way he has been acting, or that test behavior A will continue to be correlated (for an unknown reason) with criterion behavior B—we have to deal with the inner constructs that mediate behavior and the determining situational variables as well. You cannot make a rational choice of the kind of information you will need to have about a person to make predictions without some intervening variables, though they may remain entirely implicit. At this point, judgment enters—always, I think, though it may be assisted by empirical study. The best practice seems to be to give explicit consideration to this step, and to supply judgment with as many relevant facts as possible. This means studying known instances, comparing people who showed the behavior in question with others who in the same situation failed to.

All too often, when the problem of intervening variables is considered at all, it is handled by unaided clinical judgment. For example, in the Michigan project on the selection of clinical psychologists (Kelly & Fiske, 1951), a good many personality variables were rated, but there was no previous work highlighting the ones that might be related to success as a clinical psychologist. It was left up to each judge to form his own conception (from experience, theory, and guess) about what qualities mattered most. Again, this puts a greater burden on clinical judgment than it should reasonably be asked to bear. Yet some clinicians seem to have the mistaken notion that they are being false to their professional ideals if they stir from their armchairs at this point; nothing could be further from the best in clinical tradition, which is unashamedly empirical.

Third, it is necessary to find out what types of data afford measures or indications of the intervening variables, and can thus be used to predict the criterion behavior. If a good job has been done of the preceding step, it may be possible to rely entirely on judgment to make the preliminary selection of appropriate means of gathering predictive data. For example, if a job analysis and study of persons who have done well at the performance in question both suggest that verbal intelligence and information of a certain type are the main requisites, it would be easy to make good guesses about appropriate instruments to provide the predictive data. I use the word "guesses" deliberately, however, to emphasize the fact that judgment can do no more than supply hypotheses; it cannot substitute for an empirical trial to see whether in fact and under the conditions of this particular study the likely looking instruments do yield data that predict the criterion.

Notice that almost any actuarial predictive system presupposes carrying through this step. If there is to be an actuarial table, one has to collect great numbers of cases to determine the success frequencies for each cell in the table; if a regression equation is to be used, there must be a preliminary study to fix the beta weights. Unfortunately, it is possible to work clinically *without* first getting an empirical check on one's hypotheses about likely seeming instruments. At the risk of boring you, I repeat: there simply is no substitute for empirical study of the actual association between a type of predictive data and the criterion. Just as judgment is indispensable in forming hypotheses, it cannot be used to test them.

Perhaps this caution seems misplaced. Do I seem to be urging that you should first *do* a predictive study before embarking on one? I am. That is exactly what happens in actuarial prediction: the formula or table being pitted against judgmental prediction is typically being *cross*-validated, while in none of the studies Meehl cites were the clinical predictions under test being cross-validated. This alone is a major reason to expect superior performance from the actuarial predictions, and again it is a disadvantage under which the clinician by no means has to labor.

The next step, the *fourth* one, is to gather and process the data to give measures of the intervening variables. Meehl clearly recognizes that at this point clinical judgment either may play a large role or may be minimized. At one extreme, the data-yielding instrument may be a machine, a gadget like a complex coordination tester, which automatically counts errors and successes and makes a cumulative record of them. The resulting numbers may be directly usable in a regression equation without the intervention of anyone more skilled than a clerk. At an intermediate level, scoring most psychological tests requires a modicum of clinical judgment, though a high degree of reliability may be attained. At the other extreme is the interview; a great deal of clinical judgment is needed to convert the raw data into indices of the constructs the interviewer wants to assess.

It is easily overlooked that judgment needs the help of empirical study in this phase of the work too. The clinician's training supplies this empirical base in large part, but when he is using a familiar instrument to measure unusual intervening variables, or when he is working with an unfamiliar instrument, judgment grows fallible, and it is no more than prudent to piece it out by careful study of the same kind of predictive data on known subjects on whom the intervening variables have been well assessed independently.

The *fifth* and final step is the crucial one: at last the processed predictive data are *combined* so as to yield definite predictions in each case. The job can be done by clinical judgment, or it can be done by following a fixed rule (an actuarial table or regression equation) in a mechanical way. That much is clear; indeed, this is the locus of Meehl's main interest. I am taking it as granted that a clinician often integrates data in a different way than a statistician—as Meehl says, by performing a creative act, constructing a model of the person from the given facts put together with his theoretical understanding and thus generating perhaps a new type of prediction from a pattern he has never encountered before. We are all curious to know how well good clinicians can do it, and wonder if actuarial combination of data can do as well or better.

But it now seems plain that Meehl has been *too much* interested in this last stage, and as a result has neglected to pay enough attention to the way the earlier aspects of the predictive process were handled in the studies he has reviewed. Here I want to state my main critical point: *If two attempts to predict the same behavior differ significantly in the role played by clinical judgment as against actual study of the facts in one or more of the four earlier parts of the predictive process, a comparison of the successes of the two attempts can tell us nothing definite about the effectiveness of clinical judgment at the final, crucial stage.* For this reason, in none of the 20 studies Meehl cites were the comparisons pertinent to the point. Particularly at the vital third step, the predicting statisticians have had the advantage of having previously studied the way their predictive data are related to the criterion; the clinicians have not.

If your reaction is, "So much the worse for the clinicians; nobody stopped them," I am afraid you are thinking about a different question from the one Meehl has raised. If the issue were whether some clinicians have made themselves look foolish by claiming too much, then I should agree: these studies show that they have, and unhappily, they have brought discredit on clinical methods generally. But the studies cited by Meehl and more recently by Cronbach (1956) in the *Annual Review of Psychology* unfortunately have too many flaws at other points to tell us what clinical judgment can or cannot do as a way of combining data to make predictions. It is as if two riflemen were having a target match, but one took a wrong turn on the way to the shoot, never showed up, and lost by default. He demonstrated himself to be a poor driver, perhaps, but we never found out how well he could shoot, which is what we really wanted to know.

The other point I want to make in connection with the five-step analysis of the predictive process is this: since there are so many ways in which clinical judgment can enter, for better or worse, it makes little sense to classify every attempt to predict behavior on one side or the other of a simple dichotomy, clinical versus statistical. There can be many types of clinical and actuarial combinations, and many are in fact found in Meehl's mixed bag.

For purposes of exposition, I should like to suggest an only slightly extended typology. Extracting from the best actuarial studies those parts of their procedure during the first four steps that are simply the application of common sense and the scientific method, I propose that we can make it quite plain that these can be separated from actuarial prediction at the final step by creating a third type. Thus we should have:

Type I. Pure Actuarial: Only objective data are used to predict a clear-cut criterion by means of statistical processes. The role of judgment is held to a minimum, and maximal use is made of a sequence of steps exemplified in the most successful Air Force studies in selecting air crew personnel (job analysis, item analysis, cross-validation, etc.).

Type II. Naive Clinical: The data used are primarily qualitative with no attempt at objectification; their processing is entirely a clinical and intuitive matter, and there is no prior study of criterion or of the possible relation of the predictive data to it. Clinical judgment is at every step relied on not only as a way of integrating data to produce predictions, but also as an alternative to acquaintance with the facts.

Type III. Sophisticated Clinical: Qualitative data from such sources as interviews, life histories, and projective techniques are used as well as objective facts and scores, but as much as possible of objectivity, organization, and scientific method are introduced into the planning, the gathering of data, and their analysis. All the refinements of design that the actuarial tradition has furnished are employed, including job analysis, pilot studies, item analysis, and successive cross-validations. Quantification and statistics are used wherever helpful, but the clinician himself is retained as one of the prime instruments, with an effort to make him as reliable and valid a data-processor as possible; and he makes the final organization of the data to yield a set of predictions tailored to each individual case.

If we now re-examine the studies cited by Meehl and Cronbach, we see that most of them have pitted approximations to Type I actuarial predictive designs against essentially Type II naive clinical approaches. It seems hardly remarkable that Type I has generally given better results than Type II; indeed, the wonder should be that the naive clinical predictions have done as well as they have, in a number of instances approaching the predictive efficiency of actuarial systems.

Other studies cited have come closer to comparing Type II with Type III—naive versus sophisticated clinical prediction instead of clinical versus statistical. For example, the prognostic studies of Wittman (1941) compared predictions of reaction to shock treatment made in a global way at staff conference with a system she devised. But her system used highly judgmental predictive variables, as Meehl himself points out (ranging from *duration of psychosis* to *anal erotic versus oral erotic*), and they were combined using a set of weights assigned on judgmental, not statistical grounds.[1] What she showed

---

[1]It is true that the weights were applied in the same way for all cases; in this respect, the system deviates from the ideal Type III.

was that a systematic and comprehensive evaluation of the 30 items in her scale (all based on previous empirical work) made better predictions of the outcome of shock treatment than global clinical judgments not so organized and guided. A study of movement in family case work by Blenkner (1954) came to a very similar conclusion with somewhat different subject matter. When social workers rated an initial interview according to their general impressions, they were unable to predict the outcome of the case, whereas when their judgments were organized and guided by means of an outline calling for appraisals of five factors which had been shown in previous studies to be *meaningfully,* not statistically related to the criterion, then these judgmentally derived predictive variables, combined (like Wittman's) in an a priori formula, predicted the criterion quite well. Yet both studies are tallied as proving actuarial predictions superior to clinical.

Meehl's conclusion from his review of this "evidence" is that clinical prediction is an expensive and inefficient substitute for the actuarial method, and one that keeps clinicians from using their talents more constructively in psychotherapy or exploratory research.

The evidence available tells us hardly anything about the relative efficacy of clinical judgment in making predictions. The weight of numbers should not impress us; as long as the studies don't really bear on the issue, no matter how many are marshaled, they still have no weight. Remember the *Literary Digest* poll: many times more straw votes than Gallup used, but a faulty sampling principle, so that piling up numbers made the conclusion less valid as it got more reliable. Moreover, the studies tallied are so different in method, involving varying amounts of clinical judgment at different points (in the "actuarial" instances as well as the "clinical" ones), that they cannot sensibly be added together.

What is fair to conclude, I think, is that many clinicians are wasting their time when they try to fall back on their clinical judgment in place of knowing what they are talking about. They have been guilty of over-extending themselves, trying to predict things they know nothing about, and learning nothing in the process of taking part in what Cronbach calls "horserace experimental designs," in which clinicians and statisticians merely try to outsmart each other. A multiplication of such studies will not advance clinical psychology.

One kind of comparative study might teach us something even though it would be hard to do properly: simultaneous attempts to predict the same criterion from the same data by clinicians and statisticians *who have gone through the same preliminary steps.* As the statistician studies the original group to determine the critical scores for his multiple cutting-point formula (or whatever), the clinician will study the configurations of these scores in individuals of known performance. Then we will see how their respective predictive techniques work.

Does it really make sense, however, for both to use the same data and predict the same criterion? A second possibility would be for two otherwise equally sophisticated methods to predict the same criterion, each using the kind of data most appropriate to it. Or, third, the more clinical and the more statistical methods would not predict the same criterion, but each would undertake to predict the kind of behavior it is best suited to, using the most appropriate kind of data.

Doesn't this third proposal abandon experimental controls necessary for intelligible results? To some extent, yes; but one may have to give up some control to avoid absurdity. As long as clinician and statistician are trying to predict the same criterion, the clinician is likely to be working under a severe, though concealed, handicap. The study will usually have been designed by the statistician; that is his business. He will naturally choose the kind of criterion for which *his* methods seem best adapted; indeed, the nature of his method makes it impossible for him to choose the kind of predictive task that would be most congenial to the clinician, such as drawing a multidimensional diagnostic picture of a total personality, or predicting what a patient will do next in psychotherapy. Thus, the statistician takes advantage of the foolish boast of the clinician, "Anything you can do, I can do better," and plans the contest on his own grounds. The clinician ends up trying to predict grade-point average in the freshman year by a "clinical synthesis" of high school grades and an intelligence test. This is a manifest absurdity; under the circumstances, how could the clinician do other than operate like a second-rate computer? If clinical judgment is really to be tested, it must operate on data that are capable of yielding insights. Moreover, it makes hardly any more sense to expect it to grind out numerical averages of course grades than to expect an actuarial table to interpret dreams.

For reasons of this kind, McArthur (1956) called for studies of the third type just listed and maintained that there have as yet been no studies in which the clinician has been given a chance to show what he can do on his own terms. I want therefore to present briefly some results from one such attempt: a study in which clinicians tried to predict criteria of their own chosing, using clinical types of data—interviews and psychological tests (mainly projective techniques).[2]

VALIDATING NAIVE AND SOPHISTICATED CLINICAL PREDICTIONS: SOME NEW DATA

The project was an effort to improve the methods by which medical men were selected for specialty training in the Menninger School of Psychia-

---

[2]This study is presented at length in Holt and Luborsky (1958); the research was carried out with the collaboration of Drs. Wm. R. Morrow, David Rapaport, and S. K. Escalona.

try. It was begun by Dr. David Rapaport, together with Dr. Karl A. Menninger, Dr. Robert P. Knight, and other psychiatrists at the Menninger Foundation at the time the Menninger School of Psychiatry was founded 11 years ago. In the late summer of 1947, Dr. Lester Luborsky and I jointly took on major responsibility for the project although quite a number of other people have made important contributions.

Our work consisted of two predictive studies. Following the terminology suggested above, one used a naive clinical method, while the other was an attempt at a more sophisticated clinical method. The naive clinical design was simple: psychiatrists and psychologists used their favorite means of assessing personality to forecast the level of future performance of psychiatric residents at the time when they applied to the School. The applicant came to Topeka after some preliminary correspondence, having survived a rough screening of credentials and application forms. He was seen by three psychiatrists, each of whom interviewed him for about an hour, rated his probable success as a resident on a ten-point scale, and made a recommendation: Take, Reject, or Doubtful. The psychologist made similar ratings and recommendations after analyzing results of a Wechsler-Bellevue, Rorschach, and Word Association test. In addition, both psychologists and psychiatrists submitted brief qualitative reports of their appraisals of the man's positive and negative potentialities. All of the data (except test protocols) and predictions were turned over to the Admissions Committee, which made the final decision to accept or reject each applicant.

During the years of the project, from 1946 through 1952, six successive classes of residents were chosen. The first 456 applicants who went through this procedure formed our experimental population (excluding small numbers of Negroes, women, and persons from Latin-American and non-European cultures, since these minorities offered special problems of assessment). A little over 62% of these applicants were accepted by the Committee, but only 238 actually entered the School; 46 changed their minds and went elsewhere. Nevertheless, we kept in touch with them and the 172 rejectees by a mail follow-up questionnaire for several years, so that we have data on certain aspects of their subsequent careers.

The clinicians making the predictions had in some cases had considerable experience in training psychiatric residents, but there was no explicit job analysis or preliminary study of criterion groups. They simply fell to and made their predictions and their decisions.

To test the validity of these clinical decisions, let us use as a criterion, first, whether or not a man passed the certifying examination of the American Board of Psychiatry and Neurology—the criterion set up by the specialty itself. We have this information on all subjects from the lists published by the Board. The Admissions Committee's decisions had a good deal of validity as predictors of this criterion: 71% of the men they voted to accept had passed the Board examination in psychiatry by the end of 1956, while only 36% of the rejected candidates had done so. This difference is significant at better than the .001 point. The recommendations made by interviewers (taking them all as a group) and the recommendations of the psychological testers to accept or reject likewise were highly valid predictors of this criterion, significances in both cases also being beyond .001.

It is interesting that the Committee decisions were slightly *better* at predicting both staying in psychiatry and passing the certification examination of the American Board of Psychiatry and Neurology—better than either the psychiatric interviewers or the psychological testers. It is possible, however, that much or all of this apparent superiority is due to the fact that rejection by the committee did discourage a few applicants from seeking training elsewhere.

Data of this kind are encouraging to the people trying to run a school of psychiatry but hard to interpret in a larger context. Who knows but that an actuarial table based on objectively ascertainable facts like grades in medical school, marital status, age, etc., might not have done just as well? We never took such a possibility very seriously, but we did try out a few such objective predictors in our spare time, just out of curiosity. None of them showed any particular promise as a predictor of any criterion taken alone, though it is possible that patterns of them such as an actuarial table uses might have operated a little better than chance.

The criteria on which we spent most time and labor were measures of competence in psychiatric work during the last two years of the three-year residency. Whenever a resident completed a period of time on a particular service, we would interview the staff men, consultants, and others who had directly supervised his clinical work, and get them to rate it quantitatively. The resulting criterion measure had a coefficient of internal consistency above **.9**[3] (for the last few classes), and we have every reason to think it has a great deal of intrinsic validity. We also got the residents to rate each other's work. The reliability of their pooled ratings of over-all competence is also **.9,** and this criterion (which we call "Peers' Evaluations") correlates from **.66** to **.78** with Supervisors' Evaluations.

These criterion judgments enable us to test the validity of the predictive *ratings*. The validity correlations are not exciting, though for the entire group of residents in the Menninger School of Psychiatry they are all significantly better than zero at the 1% point. Taking the *mean* of the ratings given by the psychiatrists who interviewed an applicant, this predictor is correlated **.24** with Supervisors' Evaluations. The predictions of the psychological testers were not significantly better: the validity coefficient is **.27.**

[3]Correlations in bold type are significant at the 1% point, those in italics, at the 5% point. One-tailed tests are used throughout to test the null hypothesis that the predictor is not correlated *positively* with the criterion. [I no longer use one-tailed tests, but do not have access to the data of this study to re-evaluate all the tests, so have let them stand with the caveat that the reader should not be overly impressed with significance levels anyway.]

There was some fluctuation from class to class, the *mean* interviewers' validities varying from exactly .00 to .52, the tester's validities from .12 to **.47.** Likewise, the validities of ratings made by individual clinicians vary over the same range: psychiatric interviewers from .01 to **.27** ($N = 93$) or .47 (significant at only the 5% point because N was only 13), and psychologists from .20 to **.41** ($N = 40$). At the same time, those individual clinicians all did much better in making the basic discrimination: recommending acceptance of men who actually became psychiatrists.

These correlations are nothing to get excited about, and nothing to be ashamed of either, particularly in view of the restriction of range in this selected, accepted sample. They show that the naive clinical method depends a good deal on the ability of the particular clinician doing the predicting, and that—at least in this study—a pooling of judgment helped make up for the deficiencies of individuals.

Let us turn now to the second experimental design, which I have called a *sophisticated clinical* type of prediction. I shall have to skip lightly over many complicated details, and make things look a little more orderly than they actually were. The design included a job analysis of the work done by psychiatric residents, which was broken down into a few major functions (such as diagnosis, psychotherapy, administration of wards) and 14 more specific aspects of work. Then we attempted to specify attributes of personality that would facilitate or hinder a man in carrying out such work, first by collecting the opinions of persons who had had long experience in training psychiatrists, psychotherapists, or psychoanalysts. The second way we went about it was to make an intensive study of a dozen excellent residents and a dozen who were rated at the bottom by their supervisors. We went over all the original assessment data on them, interviewed them and tested them extensively, trying out many novel approaches and then seeing what discriminated these known extreme groups. Thus, we learned what personological constructs differentiated good from poor residents, and what tests and test indicators gave evidence of these constructs. Hoping to guide clinical judgment in the use of interviews and projective tests, we used the data from these small samples of extremes to help us write detailed manuals on the use of the interview, TAT, Rorschach, and other techniques in the selection of psychiatric residents. The manuals listed discriminating cues, both positive and negative, which were to be summed algebraically. We then made preliminary cross-validations of these manuals (as many as we could) with encouraging results (Luborsky, Holt, & Morrow, 1950) and revised them after studying predictive successes and failures.

As a last step, we set up another predictive study to submit our manuals to a final cross-validation on a group of 64 subjects and to accomplish several other purposes at the same time. Four psychologists served as judges; each of them scored tests or interviews according to our manuals and also made free clinical judgments based on increasing amounts of data. Two of the judges made such predictive ratings after going through an entire file of assessment data: credentials, intellectual and projective tests, and a recorded and transcribed interview.

How did we make out? Considering first the manuals, only indifferently well. Of the six, two proved worthless (TAT Content and a special projective test); the other four all showed more or less promise, but there was none that yielded consistently significant validities regardless of who used it. Reliability, in terms of scorer agreement, was on the whole not very good, for a good deal of clinical judgment was still demanded. Consider, for example, one TAT cue that worked well for one judge (validity of .26 against Supervisor's Evaluations of Over-all Competence). This cue called for judgments of the *originality* of each TAT story, obviously a matter on which psychologists might fairly easily disagree: scores by Judges I and II correlated −.04. The validities attained by the manuals for the Interview, Rorschach, Formal Aspects of the TAT, and Self-Interpretation of the TAT were on about the same general level as those from our first, naive clinical design—mostly in the .20s.

Now for the free clinical predictive ratings. When the judge had only one test or an interview to go on he usually added little by going beyond the manual and drawing on his general experience and intuition. Some judges did slightly better with free ratings than with manual scores, some a little worse. At this point, you may wonder at all this exposition for so small a result: barely significant validity coefficients, about the same size as those from a naive clinical approach, despite the attempt to create a sophisticated clinical predictive system that involved many actuarial elements. I believe that the lesson of our findings up to this point is simple. *With an inadequate sample of information about a person, no matter how sophisticated the technique of prediction, there is a low ceiling on the predictive validity that can be attained.* In our experience, even a battery of two or three tests (if exclusively projective), or an interview and a couple of projective techniques, does not give an adequate informational sample to enable clinicians to make very accurate predictions of complex behavioral outcomes over a period of three years.

Look next at the results when experimental judges made their predictions from as complete a body of information about a man as could be assembled at the time he applied. The hard-headed statistical expectation *should* be that validities would at best remain at the same level, and more likely would decline. The widely read preliminary report of the Michigan project on the selection of clinical psychologists (Kelly & Fiske, 1950) reported declining validities as increasing amounts of information were made available to judges (in a design which, for all its complexity, was essentially a naive clinical one). Not so many people have read the full final report (Kelly & Fiske, 1951), where this issue is not discussed; it is necessary to pore over many tables and tally numbers of significant correlations at various stages to find out for oneself that with the final criteria there was a

Table 2.1. Some Validities from Systematic Clinical Assessment of Applicants for Residencies in the Menninger School of Psychiatry

| | Validities of Predictors Against Criterion Evaluations of: | | | | | | | | | |
| Predictors: | Overall Competence | | Competence in Psychotherapy | | Competence in Diagnosis | | Competence in Management | | Competence in Administration | |
	Sup.[a]	Peer[a]	Sup.	Peer	Sup.	Peer	Sup.	Peer	Sup.	Peer
Predictive Ratings										
Judge I: PRT[b]	.26	.23	.12	.26	.13	.21	.31	.00	.20	.10
Judge II: TAT	-.10	-.02	-.16	-.01	-.05	.20	-.08	.01	.04	.11
Judge I: All data	.57	.52	.48	.55	.58	.42	.52	.36	.55	.42
Judge II: All data	.22	.48	.15	.36	.24	.42	.13	.24	.24	.27
Liking Ratings										
Judge I: PRT	.29	.34	.16	.35	.24	.36	.15	.17	.19	.16
Judge II: TAT	-.02	.13	-.08	.15	.00	.30	-.17	-.02	-.14	.10
Judge I: All data	.58	.64	.45	.58	.51	.52	.52	.52	.50	.46
Judge II: All data	.25	.49	.20	.47	.21	.56	.10	.30	.18	.30

[a]Sup. = Supervisors' Evaluations; Peer = Peers' (Sociometric) Evaluations.
[b]PRT = Picture Reaction Test, a specially devised projective test similar to TAT.
Numbers of cases: For Judge I—Supervisors' Evaluations, PRT: 63, all data: 37
Peers' Evaluations, PRT: 45, all data: 30
For Judge II—Supervisors' Evaluations, TAT: 63, all data: 64
Peers' Evaluations, TAT: 45, all data: 46

slight *rising* trend in validities of clinical predictions as the amount of information available to the predicting judge was increased.

The same thing is true of our results, but in a dramatic and unmistakable way (see Table 2.1). Considering only the two judges who went through the entire mass of material, their final free clinical ratings of Over-all Competence were correlated **.57** and *.22* with Supervisors' Evaluations and **.52** and **.48** with the sociometric Peers' Evaluations. In considering these correlations, remember that they are attenuated by a significant restriction of range, since all subjects had successfully passed through an Admissions Committee screening which had considerable validity. They have not been corrected for less than perfect reliabilities, either.

An incidental finding is even more remarkable. The predictive analysis was made approximately a year after the assessment data had been gathered. The judges went right through the entire series of cases, making their ratings in a *blind* analysis; names and other identifying data were concealed, and there was no direct contact with the subjects. Nevertheless, judges formed rather vivid impressions from the material, including a feeling of how well they would like each candidate personally. For control purposes, they were required to rate this feeling of *liking*. When we undertook to correlate the liking rating with predictors and criteria so as to partial out this possible source of error, we found that it was the best predictor we had! These ratings of liking by Judges I and II are correlated highly with their predictive ratings, but even more highly with Supervisors' Evaluations (**.58** and *.25*) and especially with Peers' Evaluations (**.64** and **.49**).[4] A study of these liking ratings suggests to us as the most plausible explanation that they differed from our intentional clinical predictions in being somewhat more irrational, affective—perhaps intuitive—reactions to the same data.

In all of the correlations I have been citing, you will perhaps have

---

[4]One consequence of the delay between the gathering of the data and their analysis was that some of the *S*s who entered the Menninger School of Psychiatry became known to the predictive judges, raising the possibility of contamination of their predictions by criterion-relevant knowledge. Despite the fact that the analysis of the assessment material was done "blind," identifying data having been removed or concealed, Judge I fairly often recognized the identity of *S*s at the final stage of analysis. He therefore did not make predictive ratings in such instances, which is why his *N*s are so low for this stage. There were a few borderline instances of partial or questionable recognition, however, in which Judge I (four cases) or II (two cases) had some information or misinformation about the subject. If these cases are eliminated, Judge II's validities go up more often than they go down, the range being from a decrease of .16 to an increase of .15. Judge I's validities against Supervisor's Evaluations are negligibly affected, the range of effects extending from a loss of .08 to a gain of .20. Most of his validities against Peers' Evaluations were more seriously affected, however, especially at the final (all-data) stage of analysis, where losses of up to 28 correlation points occurred. On the whole, however, even a very conservative handling of the problem of possibly contaminated cases does not change the essential import of the results: It was still possible for Judge I to obtain four validities of **.50** or higher, and for Judge II to obtain two validities of **.36** or higher. (For a fuller discussion of the problem of contamination in these results, see Holt and Luborsky, 1958.)

noticed that one judge consistently did slightly better than the other. This is certainly to be expected. When clinical judgment is the main technique of processing data, there are bound to be differences due to the skill of clinicians in doing this particular job.

Are we justified in citing these few high validities as evidence of what the sophisticated clinical method can do in a study where it is given a chance to prove itself on grounds of its own choosing? I believe that we are. The psychologists who were our Judges I and II were considered to be good but not extraordinary clinicians, certainly no better than the best of the psychologists and psychiatrists who made the "naive clinical" predictions. They differed principally in that they had an adequate sample of data and had been through all the preliminary stages of studying the criterion in relation to the predictors in earlier groups of subjects. Moreover, they used systematic methods of analyzing the data, attempting to record all inferences and working with a set of intervening variables—personality constructs which were directly inferred from the test and interview data, and from which in turn the behavioral predictions were made. In a true sense, their clinical ratings were not naively based on unguided and uncontrolled judgment; they constituted a cross-validation of a whole structure of hypotheses about the determinants of psychiatric performance based on intensive prior study. Even so, our study left a great deal to be desired as a model of the sophisticated clinical approach—particularly on the scores of (a) a better job analysis, (b) a more broadly based, configurational approach to the design of manuals, and (c) a better stabilized criterion (see Holt & Luborsky, 1958).

By way of contrast, a few more data before a final summing up. You remember that the battery of tests used in the first naive clinical predictive design consisted of the Wechsler-Bellevue, Rorschach, and Word Association tests. (The Szondi was also given, but was usually ignored; and the Strong Vocational Interest Blank was also routinely given, but was never scored in time to be used in the actual assessment for the Admissions Committee). The Rorschachs we gave were of course scored in the conventional way as well as by our special manual, and we thought it might be fun to see how some of the usual Rorschach scores would be related to the criterion. So we tried 14 scores and simple indices (like A%) with one class, and were surprised to find some rather high correlations. We decided therefore to see how a straight statistical-actuarial method of using the Rorschach would perform. Scrutinizing the table of intercorrelations between the Rorschach scores, we chose five of them that promised the greatest chances of success: DR%, number of good M, new F+%, F%, and Stereotype% (scored after Rapaport, Gill, & Schafer, 1946)—the last two because they looked as if they might be good "suppressor variables." A multiple regression equation was worked out to give the best linear combination of these variables to predict Over-all Competence; R for this Class was .43 ($N = 64$). We noticed, however, that in the regression equation only the first two scores seemed to be playing any appreciable part, and in fact the multiple correlation using only percent of rare details and number of good M was also **.43**. The other three were dropped from the formula, which was then tested on the Rorschach scores and criterion ratings of the first three classes. As expected, the correlation dropped out of sight on being cross-validated; with the new group of 116 subjects, it was .04.

The Strong Vocational Interest Blank, which (with an intelligence test) gave the best validities in the Kelly-Fiske study, likewise failed to yield any good predictor of competence in psychiatry. Even the special key ("Psychiatrist A") produced by Strong from a statistical analysis of thousands of blanks filled out by diplomates in psychiatry (Strong & Tucker, 1952) failed to predict any of our criteria at a statistically significant level: no r's as high as .2. This last finding deserves emphasis, because Strong's key was the product of a highly developed statistical technology, had an adequate numerical base, and had every opportunity to show what a pure actuarial method could achieve.

We made a further attempt to combine the best-predicting scores from the tests used in the standard battery into a regression equation. The R between Verbal IQ (Wechsler-Bellevue), Lawyer key (Strong VIB), DR% and No. Good M (Rorschach), and Over-all Competence was **.56** on the original group of 64; cross-validated on 100 cases, it dropped to .13.

SOME PRACTICAL IMPLICATIONS

If we had concentrated on an actuarial rather than a clinical approach and had come up with a simple, objective procedure that had a high and stable level of validity in predicting psychiatric performance, it could have been misused. It might have tempted many psychiatric training centers to adopt a single mold from which would have been cast a generation of psychiatrists, who would have had to meet the problems of the future with a standard set of resources derived from the past. The more successful we are in finding objective, impersonal, and statistical methods of selecting members of a profession in the image of its past leaders, the more rigid will be the pattern into which it is frozen.

For a concrete example, consider Strong's Psychiatrist A key again for a moment. It expresses the pattern of interests held in common by men who were diplomates in psychiatry at the end of the war, most of whom must have trained fifteen to twenty years ago. It should hardly be surprising that residents whose interests most closely approached this pattern tended to have skills as administrators and diagnosticians rather than as psychotherapists. If they had happened to achieve a high correlation with our over-all criterion, it might have helped populate American psychiatry of the 1960s and 1970s with near-replicas of the old state hospital superintendent.

It might be argued, however, that a similar result could have been expected if we had succeeded in providing explicit methods of clinically analyzing other types of data to select psychiatric residents. They too would have been based on a study of men who were successful at one time in history, and would have suffered the same danger of getting out of date. The answer is that even sophisticated clinical prediction never gets quite that rigid. Changes creep in; the result may be that validities gradually regress, or the drift may be determined by valid appraisals of newly important variaɒ:es. Clinical methods are more flexible than their actuarial counterparts; they *can* be more readily modified by new studies based on observations of developing trends in the criterion. Moreover, valid clinical impressions can be obtained from an intensive study of a few known cases, while it takes large samples to set up or revise an actuarial system. There can be no guarantee that clinical methods *will* be kept up to date, of course, nor that the attempt to do so will not spoil their validities. Any predictive system needs constant overhaul and revalidation.

By sticking with the only capriciously accurate, sporadically reliable, and eminently flexible method of clinical judgment in selecting trainees, psychiatry will at least be able to keep in touch with developments in a growing and changing profession. Moreoever, it will be able to maintain a healthy diversity within its ranks. There are many jobs to be done in psychiatry, requiring quite different kinds of men. There must be thoughtful men who like to sit in deep chairs and analyze patients all day long. There must be activists to organize new institutions and give inspirational leadership to groups of colleagues. Psychiatry needs many more men than it has whose main interest is in research and teaching, others to work with broad preventive programs in public health, group therapists, specialists in somatic treatments, and many more varieties of the general species. If the pure actuarial approach were to be seriously applied to psychiatry, it would be necessary to develop a formula for each of many different types of practice and to revise it constantly as new developments created needs for new types of practitioners. To do so would be impossibly expensive and laborious. Psychiatry is well-off, therefore, sticking with a basically clinical approach to assessment and prediction in selecting its members, but trying constantly to make it more scientific.

The important issue, however, is not what method of selecting its members is best for any particular profession, but the relative inertia of actuarial predictive systems and the maneuverability introduced when the generating of predictions is done by clinical judgment. This freedom is a source of weakness as well as strength; it enables the clinician to fall into errors of many kinds (to which statistical predictions are less subject) and also to adapt himself sensitively to all kinds of changing circumstances. When clinical methods are given a chance—when skilled clinicians use methods with which they are familiar, predicting a performance about which they know something—and especially when the clinician has a rich body of data and has made the fullest use of the systematic procedures developed by actuarial workers, including a prior study of the bearing of the predictive data on the criterion performance, then sophisticated clinical prediction can achieve quite respectable successes. I hope that clinicians will take some heart from our results, but I urge them to refine their procedures by learning as much as possible about statistical prediction and adapting it to their own ends.

To summarize. Meehl failed in his aim to mediate the statistical-clinical quarrel because he defined the issues in a way that perpetuates competition and controversy. The real issue is not to find the proper sphere of activity for clinical predictive methods and for statistical ones, conceived as antithetical ideal types. Rather, we should try to find the optimal combination of actuarially controlled methods and sensitive clinical judgment for any particular predictive enterprise. To do so, we must strike the right balance between freedom and constraint, a balance which may shift a good deal in one direction or the other depending on the nature of the behavior being predicted. But we can find such balances only if clinically and statistically oriented workers give up contentious, competitive attitudes and seek to learn from each other.

3

The following paper was written at the Center for Advanced Study in the Behavioral Sciences in Palo Alto, where I was a Fellow during 1960–1961. I presented a brief version at a symposium on clinical judgment at the Twenty-fifth Psychological Research Conference of the San Francisco Bay Area, Palo Alto Veterans Administration Hospital, in April 1961. The main stimulus for the paper, however, was the opportunity the Center afforded me to get informally acquainted with colleagues from a wide variety of disciplines, for "the behavioral sciences" were interpreted broadly enough so that historians, linguists, philosophers, a literary critic, and others who had not always thought of themselves as scientists were included in a yeasty community. Common elements of method began to strike me, and I did some reading in the methodologies of these other fields as well as discussing the issues with such keen thinkers as Abraham Kaplan, Edmund Leach, Henry Nash Smith, and Silvan S. Tomkins, most of whom kindly read and commented on an early draft of the paper, along with my friend Merton M. Gill, who was then living across the bay. It is a pleasure to repeat here my thanks to them and to the Center for its pleasant working conditions and for all that interdisciplinary stimulation.

Clinical Judgment as a Disciplined Inquiry

In the beginning was the Clinician. And the fogs of mysticism lay heavy upon the land. And the people suffered greatly, and cried out to the Clinician, Woe is unto us! But tell us, wise one, what kind of woe is unto us, and how can we escape therefrom? And the Clinician opened his mouth and spake large words, and great was the obscurity thereof. But behold, in the generations of those that sought righteousness, a prophet did come, and Pearson was his name. And his disciples did turn upon the seed of the Clinician, and smote them grievously, yea, even unto the loss of their grants. Now it came to pass that a judge arose in the land, and Meehl was his name. The Clinicians and Statisticians did congregate before him, saying, Tell us, oh master, which among us hath righteousness. Blessed are the peacemakers, said the judge Meehl, and he uttered his judgment. Whereupon the battle waxed more furious than ever, and the Statistician did seek to cut off the Clinician's third ear with his mighty formula. And the Clinician did seek to laugh his adversary to scorn, but his laughter was troubled, and hollow the sound thereof.

38

Verily, he that held forth alone in the beginning was hard pressed at the end, for the Statistician respected not the Clinician's gray hairs.

The clinician did, of course, come first. Long before statistical and actuarial method was invented, people tried to figure things out as best they could, and those who were good at predicting future events were hailed as prophets. Fearing the unknown, man has always given great respect to those who claimed to know the future, and has held them in awe. It is understandable, therefore, that an aura of mysticism attached to the intuitive pronouncements of the clinician, who often honestly did not know how he knew what he knew, and who attributed his successes to all kinds of irrelevancies.

Later came the statistician, bright with arrogance, and haughty in the knowledge of his powers. Where the clinician relied on his fingertips and the seat of his pants to assess intangibles like intelligence, the statistician set about building objective tests to measure them. Steadily the frontiers of the statistician have advanced, often at the expense of the clinician's domain. Mathematics has drained the swamps and burned off the fogs of mystery in many indisputable cases. Small wonder, then, that the minions of the actuary and the statistician are becoming a little swollen with pride and ambition, and threaten the clinician with utter rout.

I trust I have used enough metaphors to convince you that I am, in fact, a real live clinician, and probably a soft and fuzzy thinker. Nevertheless, I want to make it clear, before going any further, that I applaud the efforts of people like Meehl (1954) to clear away the haze, and look forward to the day when the mysteries of clinical judgment may be wholly laid bare. My sympathies are not with those of my colleagues who glory in their own inability to analyze or understand the processes of inference and judgment, even though I believe that, when the analysis is finished, many differences in kind will be found between the cognitive processes of the clinician and the procedures of the statistician. It can only help the clinician to have the processes of clinical judgment and inference made as clear and explicit as possible.

Further, it is good to focus close attention on the process of clinical judgment, because the issues involved are significant far beyond the purview of psychology—they get us into methodological questions hotly debated in many of the behavioral sciences and, indeed, in the humanities.

Let me begin by restricting the meaning of the term. In contrast to the view of Hoffman (1960), I would exclude from clinical judgment the very operations he studies: the combination of quantitative data. If the issues are defined as they are framed in Hoffman's paper, it is a foregone conclusion that the clinician is going to be left to choke on the dust in the wake of the formula. I have too much respect for the formidable powers of modern statistics and high-speed computers to think that the cleverest and most experienced clinician is going to be able to excel at predictions based solely

on quantitative data. In practice, however—that is, except in the special
context of experimental studies—clinicians do not make any substantial use
of such predictions. True, a good deal of the literature on the analysis of the
Rorschach, the MMPI, and the scatter of the Wechsler subtests would give
one such an impression; clinical judgment might seem to be a matter of
mulling over numbers representing scores on these tests and various deriva-
tives of them (ratios, differences, and what not). One sees statements that a
larger number of M than average may indicate creative imagination or
delusional thinking, depending upon the configuration of other scores. In
practice, however, the relevant configuration is almost invariably one of
meanings, not quantitative scores—in this example, qualitative aspects of
responses that indicate the presence of a thinking disorder, or even a context
of presenting symptoms or aspects of clinical history. Again, I would not
deny that I have seen impressive virtuosity on the part of people who
describe a personality after just seeing an MMPI profile, a Wechsler scatter-
gram or a Rorschach psychogram; but these are largely stunts, rarely systematically validated, and not a major device of clinical reasoning in everyday
practice. And a computer could doubtless be programed to digest such
configurations of numbers and their behavioral correlates, thereafter performing even greater prodigies of pattern analysis than any expert.

Instead, I believe that the essence of clinical work lies in dealing with
verbal meanings—discursive symbols, if you prefer Langer's (1951) term. This
is the essence of free associations, dreams, autobiographies, social histories,
TAT stories and other projective test data. To a lesser extent, clinicians work
with presentational symbols such as figure drawings and expressive behavior,
too. These kinds of material cannot be used at all without the interventions
of a trained intelligence. For this very reason, those who wish to demonstrate
the superiority of actuarial and statistical predictions try to define things so
that both parties to the competition deal only with numbers. Indeed, unless
some such proviso is made, it is impossible to set up a direct comparison of
two different methods of predictively analyzing the *same* body of data. So
much the worse for the comparisons; I agree with Lee Cronbach that little of
scientific value emerges from such horse races.

As soon as we leave behind objective tests, demographic variables like
age and length of hospitalization, and miniature situations yielding quantitative measures of performance, we are getting onto admittedly marshy
ground. It is fair to say that no other field has solved all the problems of
method involved in the interpretation of symbols. Langer calls it "a field
which usually harbors a slough of despond for the philosopher, who ventures into it because he is too honest to ignore it, though really he knows no
path around its pitfalls. It is the field of 'intuition,' 'deeper meaning,' 'artistic
truth,' 'insight,' and so forth. A dangerous-looking sector, indeed, for the
advance of a rational spirit!" (1951, p. 92). Titchener stood with the early
behaviorists in getting rid of the messy problem of meaning by excluding it
from the province of scientific psychology. Meaning has made a modest

comeback among modern behaviorists since the development of such techniques as Osgood's semantic differential, which gets us to the comfortable realm of numbers again. By taking note of the fact that speech is a form of behavior, the superobjectivists have been able to include language and even thought in their theories of behavior. Note, however, that such psychologists stay as far as possible from interpreting verbal texts themselves; that is left to the subject, his response being taken as the operational definition of meaning.

I am not so negative toward such research as the tone of these remarks may imply; on the contrary, I use "objective" methods myself. It is clear, however, that the clinician uses meanings in quite a different way. When he makes a clinical prediction (and any assessment of personality or psychotherapeutic intervention is at least implicitly a prediction), he looks directly at the verbal texts[1] themselves and *interprets* them. In doing so, he follows in a long tradition of human scholarship, a tradition which in fact antedates science. Historians, anthropologists, sociologists, political scientists and also biblical scholars, philosophers, literary critics, and other scholars of the humanistic disciplines are the clinician's brothers-in-arms in relying every day on the interpretation of meanings from verbal texts. On the hunch that there might be something to learn about the interpretive aspect of clinical judgment by forays into some of these other disciplines, I began work on this paper by reading some literary criticism,[2] history, and anthropology, noting the methods the authors were using on verbal texts. What follows grows out of these observations, out of some methodological reading, and out of my own clinical work, particularly interpreting the TAT and trying to teach such interpretation.

METHOD OF ANALYZING VERBAL MEANINGS

In dealing with verbal texts, the disciplined worker (in the sciences and the humanities alike) can perform a number of operations on the particular message itself, which we may call internal analysis, and others by reference to

[1] Most of the time, clinicians *listen* to what the patient says, in an interactive context of participant observation. It may not appear obvious, therefore (though I believe it to be true), that the mental operations performed by the listening psychoanalyst or psychiatrist are substantially identical with those of the diagnostic tester, reading and reflecting on his protocols. In this paper, I have deliberately disregarded the analysis of nonverbal data, which may play a large role in psychotherapy. [See Chapter 5, below.]

[2] Specifically, I undertook to discern the analytic operations performed by Henry Nash Smith (1958) in his brilliant introduction to Mark Twain's *Huckleberry Finn*, and relied further on a similar reading of Auerbach (1953), as well as on psychological and other sources from the behavioral sciences. I owe a particular debt to Lerner (1958) (especially the contribution by Erik Erikson). It is less easy to specify the many ways in which my thinking about these matters has been influenced by two years of work in content analysis, under the tutelage of D. P. Cartwright and A. A. Campbell.

other materials—external analysis. Since I have deliberately left vague the boundaries that define a "message," the distinction between internal and external is pretty arbitrary, and I attach little significance to it.

Internal Analysis

At least six kinds of internal analysis may be distinguished:

1. The content of meanings may be *summarized*. The analyst gets rid of the redundancy by a process of abstraction and selection. Eliminating redundancy implies the ability to perceive identities or similarities of meaning despite apparent differences; eliminating irrelevancy or the unimportant implies the ability to conceptualize—to recognize a meaning as an instance of a generalization—and it brings into play *standards* of importance which must derive from some theory. Summaries thus use two complementary aspects of conceptual thinking: the formation of generalizations or abstractions from a realm of particulars, and the particularization of an abstraction.

Like all the other analytic procedures to be described they require the use of some theory, explicit or implicit.

2. One may *collate* a verbal message, examining it for internal consistency and inconsistency. The mental operations involved here are essentially the same as the ones just described. Such inconsistencies may be important cues to the historian or literary critic in his efforts to establish the authenticity of a document; to the therapist, they may be the very points at which to direct his interpretive efforts.

3. The analyst of verbal messages *interprets* or translates their content. In that case where he wishes to substitute sentences in one language for sentences in another, he follows a set of rules, most notably a dictionary, to tell him how to transform or replace individual words, and a grammar to tell him how to put the words together to make acceptable sentences. When he interprets a dream, some of the steps the psychotherapist goes through are logically identical with those of the linguist: he, too, has sets of rules that enable him to substitute a superficially very different text for the one originally presented. As Wittgenstein once said, "The internal similarity between things which at first might seem to be entirely different . . ."—for example, a sheet of music and the sounded notes—lies "in the fact that there is a general rule by which the musician is able to read the symphony out of the score" (quoted by Langer, 1951, p. 79). Thus, the task of interpretation requires the development of such rules for decoding encoded information. This type of analysis implies, of course, that human communications often or typically have more than one layer of meaning. A verbal discourse may transmit one set of ideas in its manifest content encoded according to one set of rules, but there may simultaneously be encoded, by a different set of rules, another (latent) which may be recovered by the application of these rules.

What is the relation between interpretive translation and conceptualizing? Both would be examples of Sarbin's "instantiation of modules" i.e., classifying something as an instance of a general category; Sarbin, Taft, & Bailey, 1960). In conceptualization, we subsume something under a general conceptual category, generalizing a particular; in translation, however, we substitute an instance in one frame of reference for an instance in another, without subsumption or generalization. The simplest case, translating a message from one language to another, involves such fixed procedures that it is today possible to program a computer to carry them out with moderate success.[3] But in the kind of symbolic translation that the clinician does, in analyzing dreams or projective test data, the rules are less fixed and must be applied more flexibly. A cigar may have oral or even anal significance as well as phallic; and sometimes it is only a cigar. How then, does one tell which meaning to substitute, if indeed one should translate at all? The rules help by specifying occasionally in terms of context: thus, if the cigar is mentioned along with an emphasis on its color, dirtiness, and smelliness, and if it is one of several examples of similarly dirty and smelly things that do not share its oral and phallic implications, then the anal interpretation is to be accepted as the most likely hypothesis. The ultimate criterion to decide whether to translate or not and, if so, how, is internal consistency. If we make the substitution, does the interpretation as a whole make sense, or not? That is, is it self-contradictory, does it fit into a larger context? "Fitting in" goes beyond just the ascertaining of logical contradiction; it involves also judgments of congruence and the formal elegance of the total structure that results. (See discussion of evaluation, below.)

At this point, many clinicians may object that there is a considerable difference between translating a single symbol and interpreting a whole style of life. In the former instance, the model of translation seems a good deal more applicable. It is true, I think, that the larger the body of verbal material being interpreted, the more judgmental the process, and the less obvious it is that translation is involved at all. Yet the psychoanalyst, reflecting back over many hours of the patient's production, and noting the emergence of a general pattern, let us say, of self-destructive rebellion, uses a number of individual translative steps in subsuming many superficially different episodes under the general category, which emerges in his mind as the one abstraction that expresses something true about all the incidents the patient has related. Each incident may have given rise to several possible interpretations, so that these clusters of possibilities affect one another by cancellation and reinforcement, the most recurrent ones then acting as a readiness later to perceive new episodes in terms of the emerging hypothesis. This, in turn, may be only one element in a constructed pattern; the finished "interpretation" involves other steps beside the one here called interpretation—notably, causal discerning and synthesis. (See below.)

[3] [I realize now that this is a highly oversimplified account of translation.]

4. The interpreter may analyze not the content but the formal and *structural* properties of the text. This may be done in a number of ways in different disciplines. The literary critic, for example, may apply a conceptual apparatus containing rhetorical and stylistic categories: the text is prose, a myth, it is anaphoric, paratactic, and so on. The anthropologist, interested less in style than in patterns of content, may find in a set of myths a recurrent pattern of binary opposition involving a balance of paired elements, each of which is dichotomously subdivided (Levi-Strauss, 1955; Leach, 1961). The clinical psychologist may note the brevity of a TAT story, the simple sentence structure, the stereotyped repetition of phrases, and the presence of circumstantial description, leading him to the inference of depression (Rapaport, Gill, & Schafer, 1968).

Note that the last two types of analysis involve what the content analyst calls *coding:* identifying an aspect of a communication (of its form or of its content) with a concept or category in an analytic outline, conceptual system, or code. The discussion so far has carried the implication that, in either case, this is a procedure of typing or categorizing. But a second type of operation is often involved in either case: quantitative *rating* or scaling. The raw data are examined for their congruence with a concept, and a number is assigned representing the frequency with which a kind of instance occurs, the degree to which the fit is exact, or the intensity of its expression. Thus, for example, one may look for anger, and count all its manifestiations in a text, or rate the degree to which a given statement approximates an ideal statement of "pure anger," or (conceiving of anger as a variate ranging from mild irritation to blind fury) rate the intensity of anger in a given bitter statement. According to Lazarsfeld and Barton (1951, p. 155) "There is a direct line of logical continuity from qualitative classification to the most rigorous forms of measurement, by way of intermediate devices of systematic ratings, ranking scales, multidimensional classifications, typologies, and simple quantitative indices. . . . One way to develop social science measurement is to *systematize* these commonly performed research procedures, by codifying exactly what successful researchers [read here, clinicians] do in carrying out these simpler forms of measurement and exploring their logical implications."

5. One may analyze a verbal message by reacting to it, and observing one's own reaction. This method, described by Murray *et al.* (1938) as *recipathy,* is a vital part of the clinician's kit of tools, especially in therapy. If the psychotherapist finds himself beginning to get angry at the client, he may well infer that the message being transmitted includes provocation. As Erikson (1958, p. 84) has said, "The evidence is not all in if he does not succeed in using his own emotional responses during a clinical encounter as an evidential source and as a guide in intervention, instead of putting them aside with a spurious claim to unassailable objectivity."

6. An important procedure in analyses of verbal materials is the *discerning of causal relations.* There has been a good deal of discussion and contro-

versy over the legitimacy of causal analysis in history, for example (Social Science Research Council, 1954), and the traditional view of linear causality has been widely rejected on philosophic grounds, being replaced by a view of events as part of a nexus of functional relations from which no single cause or effect can be extracted. Nevertheless, such sophisticated models may be built up out of old-fashioned observations of single causal relations, and these in turn are *not* exclusively Humean inferences on the basis of statistical contingency.

Following the Gestalt psychologists (e.g., Köhler, 1947), Michotte (1946) and Heider (1958) have made experimental demonstrations and analyses of the perception of cause: people do react to single events with a certain kind of structure by *perceiving* that A causes B. In such an instance, A and B may have not only a certain temporal sequence, but may also share common meanings, move in specifiable ways, or involve elements that stand to each other in the relation of an intelligible transformation (e.g., homologous shapes, but B' is smaller than B: the observer perceives that the intervening event A causes B to shrink). This kind of discerning of causal relations plays a critical role in all science in the setting-up of hypotheses and the interpretation of findings. (See below.) There has been no such experimental work that I know of in the realm of verbal materials, but I believe that the cognitive processes involved are basically the same as in the realm of nonverbal events. To some extent, there must be added another cognitive operation: from the verbal text, the analyst reconstructs images of events in which causal relations occur. (For another type of causal analysis, see below, discussion of *comparison*.)

External Analysis

An approximately equal number of techniques of external analysis may be listed also:

First, the text under consideration has been *selected* from some larger population of possible data; the technique of selection is an easily overlooked contributor to the ultimate interpretation, and a mode by which clinical judgment is exercised. If the message in question is the statements of a patient in a therapeutic hour, various external factors bring about the selection, which is thus not obvious. If it is a historical document chosen for study among myriad such materials, it is plain that the historian has selected and that his principles of selection will vitally affect his conclusions. One has to ask: is the sample of verbalization a sufficient basis for the further analysis proposed? Did the method of selection insure representativeness of the population sampled? In history, the selection is made on more or less explicit theoretical grounds. Moreover, "the documentary method of historians is reflected in the quoting or citing of statements to illustrate the pros & cons of moot points" (Social Science Research Council, 1954, p. 130). "Citations are selected in terms of their relevance to the thesis," not in accordance with some sampling procedure. Thus Sellars (1960) cites and analyzes toasts, personal correspondence and schoolboys' essays for evidence in support of his thesis that slavery was a conflict-ridden moral problem for the South; but the historian never proceeds by *systematically* sampling all such material and then extracting all themes relevant to slavery. Instead, the historian makes a case, trying to avoid the self-deception that results from the systematic ignoring of contrary evidence. In anthropology and sociology, the method varies: at the most sophisticated extreme there are content-analysts like Lazarsfeld, who take considerable pains to take a probability sample when analyzing, say, the newspapers of a country to extract its basic values. At the other extreme are workers who are unaware of the problem, and sample simply according to convenience and availability: thus, the one tribesman who can speak English may become an unwary anthropologist's informant, and provide a seriously biased sample of information about customs. In clinical psychology, diagnostic assessment usually develops its own data, and the diagnostician uses them all, overlooking the fact that he too is sampling. Has he given enough tests? Has he given the appropriate ones? Has he supplemented them with the most advantageously chosen interview questions? Here, however, the principle of random sampling has but narrow relevance; selection (like summarizing, which it closely resembles) must be guided primarily by relevance to a theory.

A second form of external analysis consists of reconstructing the chain of circumstances that brought about the verbal message itself, or the real events it refers to (if any). This *genetic* analysis obviously plays a large role in history, in literature, in political science and in many other disciplines beside clinical psychology. Central to it is the method of discerning causal relations. (See above.)

A third—and most important—type of external analysis is *comparison* with other, similar texts, bringing out similarities and differences of content or structure, especially in conjunction with other known facts about the verbal samples compared (cf. collation). This is obviously J. S. Mill's joint method of similarity and difference. Tomkins (1947) was the first to demonstrate the applicability of Mill's canons to the interpretation of the TAT. (This might just as well have been called a method of internal analysis, but one story may be taken as context for another, as well as one *S*'s TAT as context for another *S*'s whole TAT.) Henry's (1956) concept of "negative content" is relevant here: one may use knowledge of what usually occurs in a series of similar communications to help one notice what is significantly *not* present in the text under analysis. Such comparisons may aid almost any of the kinds of internal analysis mentioned; the central principle here is that of statistical inference. This method is obviously central to literary criticism and related fields, such as hermeneutics and the anthropologic analysis of myth. It is also closely related to two other methods of external analysis I want to mention.

The fourth such method is to examine a verbal message in relation to *other types of data* from the same source, looking for common elements. Thus, in a paper referred to above (Sellars, 1960), the historian sought common elements in different types of documentary materials as well as (implicitly) considering, for example, an after-dinner toast in relation to what is known about the genre. To take an example from psychology, one approaches the analysis of a projective test from the standpoint of other kinds of information about the patient, such as the affect and other nonverbal behavior accompanying the responses, demographic characteristics, presenting complaints, objective test profile; the clinician seeks generalizations that will cut across or at least not be inconsistent with all types of information.

Fifth, a message may be considered in relation to a set of external (usually *evaluative*) standards. If it is literature, the critic may, in elucidating various aspects of its structure, adjudge them more or less good in an esthetic sense; if it is a letter written by a historical figure, the historian may cite it as an example of the man's military relevant bravery; if it is a TAT story, the psychologist may rate its genuineness or creativity. All of these are basically value judgments, and they may play a role in the work of scientific as well as humanistic disciplines. A nonevaluative instance of this type of analysis is clinical diagnosis, in which the results of preliminary (or primary) inferences from the raw data are compared with a set of ideal types: the standard diagnostic syndromes. The person who produced the verbal messages being analyzed may then be categorized ("pigeon-holed"), or he may be characterized by the degree to which he approximates various diagnoses and the particular characteristics he shares with them.

According to the methodologists of the *Geisteswissenschaften,* a critical point of difference between natural and "cultural" or social sciences was the central role of the concept of value in the latter (see Holt, 1962b [Volume 1, Chapter 1]). Even so clear a thinker as Max Weber considered this to be a basic differentiation. How, then, can it be said that value judgments play a role in natural science? [See also Chapter 10, below.] First, it is obvious that much of the subject matter of social sciences is made up of values, unlike the natural sciences; anthropologists and sociologists are much concerned with the evaluative premises and systems (ideologies, religions, and so on) of various groups of people. Yet as long as a value is treated as a fact worthy of study, like a myth, dream, or superstition, it can be studied objectively and no methodologic difference emerges. Second, value judgments are used every day in the natural sciences in much the way described above. The scientist is constantly evaluating his work in terms of pragmatic values. Does an experimental approach pay off? Does an instrument work? And he evalutes his theory against sets of standards like simplicity and elegance. The physicist's assumption of parity, that nature has no preference for right- or left-handed rotation, grew out of essentially esthetic or formalistic reasoning. In mathematics and theoretical physics, the facts are considered to make most sense, the elements of a theory fit together best, if organized in an esthetically pleasing fashion.[4] Thus, esthetic criteria of evaluation are important in these highly advanced scientific disciplines, where they are usually referred to as elegance. Simplicity (parsimony), balance, and clarity of organization are component values of elegance. Finally, theory is used in all sciences in an essentially evaluative way, in decisions about scientific *importance.* The decision that a phenomenon is worthy of investigation because of its bearing on a theoretical issue is an easily overlooked value judgment.

The final step in either the internal or the external analysis of clinical data—both discursive and presentational symbols—is *synthesis:* bringing the pieces together into a coherent verbal formulation capable of being grasped and used by another human being, in the sense that a therapeutic interpretation, or a case formulation in a few prose paragraphs, is more understandable and memorable than a Q-sort. This function requires clinical judgment of the broadest grasp, guided by logical considerations of internal consistency, to a very minor degree by empirical rules, and largely by theory. For an excellent example, which respects the complexity of real clinical situations, see Erikson's account (1958) of how he interpreted a patient's dream. In it, he demonstrates how the clinician can examine a verbal message simultaneously from many points of view and in a number of relevant contexts, including an empathic assessment of the patient's affective condition, and can pull the pieces together in a strategic verbal intervention requiring clinical judgment of the highest order. This synthetic phase involves a good deal of what I have called *secondary inference* [Volume 1, Chapter 2]: the drawing of conclusions on the basis of primary inferences from the data (cf. Colby, 1958 on "1st and 2nd order inference"). Though I have been speaking only in terms of clinical psychology (and related disciplines like psychoanalysis) in discussing this final, synthetic step, it obviously enters into the analysis of verbal materials in the other scientific and humanistic disciplines as well.

SIMILARITIES OF PROCEDURES IN ALL DISCIPLINED INQUIRY

So far, I have tried to draw occasional parallels to procedure in other behavioral sciences and humanities that use the interpretation of verbal information. Does the fact that meanings are discerned put the cognitive operations of these workers on a different methodological plane from those of scientists who are not dealing with verbal materials? The German philosophers of half-a-century ago who made an ill-starred attempt to develop a special and separate methodology for the cultural sciences thought that the

[4][Each of Einstein's early papers "begins with the statement of formal asymmetries or other incongruities of a predominantly aesthetic nature (rather than, for example, a puzzle posed by unexplained experimental facts), then proposes a principle . . . which removes the asymmetries as one of the deduced consequences. . . ." (Holton, 1973, p. 168).]

use of meanings was a fundamental point of difference [Volume 1, Chapter 1]. It is not, because the grasp of linguistic meaning (including values) is a special form of perception, and all science involves perceptions of human observers, followed by cognitive manipulation of symbols.

The basic observational operation in physics is said to be pointer-reading. A machine performs a measurement, but the experimenter has to receive the information generated and process it. Of course, there are now automatic machines for processing data, even in psychology: you can hook S into a polygraphic setup, and the electrical impulses will be automatically measured, graphed, correlated, and factor analyzed. Yet ultimately, E has to enter, to receive and decode or interpret the information—no matter how sophisticated the machine that generates it, no matter how far removed it is from the elementary operation of laying a meter stick on something, what E does is essentially the same. He must recognize the congruence of two discriminable entities (cf. recognition of verbal meanings). In the simple situation of measuring length, he recognizes the identity of the end of what is to be measured with a corresponding point on the meter stick (the other ends having been aligned—also an operation involving discrimination and recognition); in reading a pointer, he must discriminate and recognize the location of the pointer at a numerical position on the scale. If the measuring machine is much more complicated and automated, he still has to be able to discriminate and recognize the output, whatever it is.

Discrimination is a selective process, really quite complicated. E has to know where to look; he has to direct his attention there, not being distracted by the surround; he has to be physiologically capable of distinguishing figure from ground (pointer and numeral from dial-face; end of object from the physical context in which it is embedded). Ordinarily, in full illumination and with the kinds of examples that come most readily to mind, such discrimination is so smoothly and effortlessly performed that we overlook it or think it radically different from discriminating verbal meanings. Yet suppose you want to measure the length of a cloud or some other object without obviously demarcated boundaries; the operation of discriminating the end of the object from its surround will be extremely difficult, and the measurement approximate and inexact (unreliable). If you seek to measure a nematode, like a dead vinegar eel, against a ruled glass scale in a microscope, the lack of contrast may make the discriminative operations frustratingly difficult to an untrained microscopist. The point is that even the elementary operation of distinguishing the basic items of information from their contexts may differ considerably from one situation or example in natural science to another, and not infrequently is as tricky and judgmental a business as the discrimination of verbal meanings. Both involve separating information from noise.

Logically, however, it is conceivable that E discriminates the necessary discriminanda, but does not recognize them. Surely it happens a great deal in scientific work that E can and does see differences between phenomena but ignores them or considers them outside the realm of his interest because they do not correspond to anything of importance (i.e., relevance to his scientific aims). Recognition is the operation of establishing correspondence between something perceived and something conceived, between discriminated sense-data and a concept stored in E's memory. In certain kinds of aphasia, pathology nicely separates these two phases: the patient can discriminate, let us say, a chalk mark on a blackboard, but has no idea of what it means; he cannot recognize it.

Failures of recognition can occur in several ways. There can of course be a failure of the presupposed *sine qua non,* discrimination. Discrimination can occur, but E may not have the requisite concept in his memory: he is ignorant of a distinction, untrained in recognizing something of importance. Both of these requisites may be present, yet something may block the scanning process by which the memory is made available for checking against the perceptual process for degree of fit. (In the above example, organic lesions may interfere; fatigue, drug-effect, illness, emotional upset and other adventitious sources of mental inefficiency, or noise may also prevent this process; the discrimination may be too fragmentary or incomplete to make the process fully possible; E may be too rigid to perform the scanning operation, or have some other such defect of personality as a cognitive style (Klein, 1956) of demanding too exact a degree of correspondence, or of accepting even gross partial identity as a satisfactory fit—sharpening versus leveling, or something like it; the memory traces of the relevant concepts may be insufficiently well differentiated or too poorly established: E may not have a good grasp of what he is looking for, may not fully understand the concept.) In some situations, the discrimination may be difficult and the concept not very precisely definable, e.g., in reading X-rays: can precise criteria for the recognition of an ulcer crater be set down, since every duodenum is shaped differently from every other, no two ulcers occur in precisely the same spot, and no two are visualized in precisely the same manner? It takes training, with a lot of ostensive definition supplementing the basic conceptual one, before the young radiologist develops fully usable capacities to discriminate the relevant shadows *and* to recognize a crater when he sees one.

The hypothesis I am proposing is that many of the operations performed by analysts, clinical psychologists, anthropologists, linguists, sociologists, and scholars in a number of other behavioral sciences *and* disciplined humanities are exactly analogous or even homologous to discrimination and recognition as described above. Obviously, all such disciplines involve the selection of data (discrimination), and focusing on particular objects of study; they also involve conceptualization: the application of concepts having operational definitions to the discriminated data (recognition). The other operations used—classification, abstraction, discerning of relationships (e.g., cause or functional dependence; contradiction or inconsistency; similarity or

partial identity; meaningful implication)—may be viewed as more sophisticated forms of these two. They certainly are used in the natural sciences as
they are in the behavioral ones.

Physicists and other experimenters in the "hard" sciences have a great
deal of respect for what they call intuition. By this term they do not mean
anything supernatural like revelation; but they do not mean unrecognized
statistical inference, either. Intuition in this sense refers to the creative
process by which new theories and experimental ideas arise. If we look at it
more closely, we will find that it involves many of the operations described
above for dealing with verbal texts: discerning of causes not through statistical association, but by meaningful congruence; the manipulation of theoretical ideas by means of analogies and constructions to form new propositions;
judgments of the probability of payoff and of relevance of facts to
hypotheses. The nuclear physicist Deutsch (1958) writes, "The decisive
intuition of the experimenter is really the ability to *recognize relevance* in the
evidence presented by the experiment." This statement points to another
phase of the work (besides that of hypothesis-formation) when judgment
plays a large role: after the experimental data have been presented. In the
discussion of results, *E*s discern causal relations, look for what makes sense,
seek internal consistency, or consistency with a theory. In all sciences, there is
this phase of reflection on the data obtained, which may even get pretty
speculative; and I want to point to the methodological identity of these
cognitive operations with those of the clinician, literary critic, or behavioral
scientist in interpreting meaningful discourse.

The implicit goal of those who glorify statistical prediction seems to be to
exclude intuition and judgment from science entirely, replacing it by cookbook rules, logical analyses, or mathematical formulae solved by electronic
computers. But: "There is no recipe, no rule of procedure which will permit
the unimaginative experimenter to consider all of these [i.e., the necessary
and the relevant] possibilities by applying systematic logical analysis to all
aspects of his apparatus" (Deutsch, 1958). Again, this is an experimental
nuclear physicist who is speaking about investigation in his own field. No—
imagination, creativity, and intuition will always remain essential qualifications for scientists of any kind, including the purest mathematicians. We had
best, therefore, try to understand this phase of scientific work, instead of
minimizing it as if it were something to be ashamed of.

THE ROLE OF PREDICTION

It is sometimes said (e.g., Sarbin, Taft, & Bailey, 1960) that the hallmark
of science is its use of prediction; to establish the utility of its propositions,
clinical judgment (like the unscientific humanities) has only the inferior
criterion of internal consistency at its disposal. Let us begin a consideration

of relations between clinical judgment and prediction by examining these criteria.

Internal consistency is no stranger to science; it is used in all sciences at the stage of constructing theory. Much of what Einstein contributed to physics was of just this sort: he had the capacity to educe generalizations or to abstract in a way that brought out the internal consistency of phenomena and concepts long thought unrelated or even contradictory. On a homelier level, any intelligible thought whatever requires some attention to internal consistency, for the secondary process gives way to the primary when contradiction is tolerated, and logical conclusions cannot be reached.

When contrasted to internal consistency, predictive validity seems at first sight to be a very different kind of criterion of truth. But is it? One forms a hypothesis on the basis of one body of data (or on the basis of a theory, when there is at least indirect reference to the data involved in its development), predicts that this state of affairs will continue to hold in a new sample of data, and tests the prediction. But *the test of predictive validity is nothing more than establishing the degree of internal consistency within the combined body of (1) the data (and theory) on which the prediction was based, and (2) the newly obtained data.* Logically, there is no difference between the two criteria; therefore, what looks like prediction can be converted into a search for internal consistency, and vice versa.

Thus, the clinician can and should accomplish something like a cross-validation by dividing the data within the sample available to him: predictions based on the Rorschach may be tested in the TAT, and it is even possible to form hypotheses on the basis of responses to one card or picture and to test them on the immediately following material within the same test. After every interpretation or other intervention, the patient's subsequent behavior enables the therapist to test his hypotheses. Moreover, routine clinical work offers opportunities to collect different kinds of data to verify predictions: hypotheses based on a diagnostic study may be checked in the course of therapy; finding signs of an unsuspected brain lesion, the testing psychologist may suggest a neurologic examination which in turn verifies his diagnosis.

While there is no essential difference between internal consistency and predictive validity, there are certain practical advantages to formal cross-validation or predictive study. The predictive experiment generally uses a sample of Ss different from the ones on whom the prediction was based, and involves gathering data at a different time and possibly in different ways. The true cross-validation is in this way superior to splitting the data gathered at one time and treating the halves as replicates of the experiment: subtle sampling biases that affect the latter are not so likely to affect cross-validation, and any other unknown parameters of the original result are less likely to be repeated (Campbell, 1957). The clinician can rarely go beyond what amounts to cross-validation, though some of the data available to the clinician who has a battery of tests and some interview material are so different in kind that the prediction from one such source of data to another must be mediated by the same processes of constructing and operating a theoretical model that are involved in the design of good original experiments. And, granted an adequate theory, the clinician may predict phenomena not previously observed: his investigation may thus not be merely a cross-validation.

Granted the need to supplement the disciplined analysis of a body of data by predictive verification, are there any differences between the processes of clinical and statistical predicting beyond the differential amounts of error they may contain? Yes—despite the arguments of those who claim that clinical predictions are only unsystematic and therefore faulty actuarial predictions (Lundberg, 1941; Sarbin, Taft, & Bailey, 1960). I agree with Meehl (1954) that the clinician generates many of his predictions (not all; some are actuarial) by means of a creative cognitive act. "Essentially the judge constructs a model of a personality and deduces the appropriate kind of behavior from that model. This means that he must take data of whatever kind he can get and put together a total picture of a personality that would have produced such data" (Meehl, 1954, p. 210).

Like any other kind of creative thinking, the thought processes of the predicting clinician may involve regression in the service of the ego: in creating new ideas, new forms, new theories, we can use primitive, illogical, even magical kinds of thought-processes in flexible alternation with more rational ones. An N of 1 is obviously not a reliable base for a hypothesis, yet the hypothesis may prove true. And the fact that the primary process often disregards logic and reality does not mean that it necessarily leads to error; it means only that hypotheses must be tested. No analysis of the process can settle the question of how "credible" clinical inferences are, no matter how dubious their major premises; only the outcome of the predictions can tell us about their truth.

By contrast, the method of statistical prediction is formed on the model of the secondary process—reproductive, not productive thought. Statistical methods can never create anything new, and thus can predict only recurrences of old patterns of behavior. (Since so much of behavior *is* repetitive, statistical prediction works quite nicely most of the time; that is not the point, in this argument.) I am not saying that *statisticians* cannot create anything new; on the contrary, many of them are highly creative. But as the statistician devises new theories, new techniques, new types of formulas, he does not use actuarial procedures. He does not limit himself to the approaches used successfully by Pearson, Fisher, and other statistical innovators of the past, applying them in a mechanical way to his new problems; he knows perfectly well that he would get nowhere that way. Instead, he proceeds just as intuitively as the clinician or the physicist: he daydreams about his work, mulls his problems over, sleeps on them, works by fits and starts of inspiration. He just says nothing about that phase of his work in symposia on clinical judgment.

Though I freely concede the need for clinical judgments to be subjected to the test of prediction, I very much doubt that this is the way to refine or improve the process of judgment itself. Some clinical psychologists have perhaps been too much impressed by the principles of test-construction, too ready to generalize them to the status of guides for other ways of obtaining and dealing with data. The statistical study of reliability and validity (the latter through predictive studies) can be helpful in letting you find out where you are, but it offers precious little aid to your efforts to get further ahead. I have come to this view from a rather disillusioning experience. When Luborsky and I (1958) were engaged in our final predictive study of methods for selecting psychiatric residents, we decided to make many specific predictions on the basis of interviews and projective tests and verify them, in the hope that we might learn more about how to improve clinical judgment. But when our criterion data were in and the predictions were tested, we found that the numbers told us very little: judgments from a single test, let us say, were slightly more valid in this area than that, but how we went astray or why we could at times make correct predictions remained obscure.

Murray *et al.* (1938) once wrote that the clinical mind of the research worker was "psychology's forgotten instrument," one that could produce greatly if we could only learn how to use it. Perhaps so little progress has been made in refining this instrument because most of the effort to do so has mistakenly treated the clinical judge as if he were a test, and because psychologists have neglected to study the ways their fellow-scholars in other fields have attempted to discipline their analyses of verbal meanings: to carry them out in a systematic, orderly, and reproducible fashion.

SUMMARY

Clinical judgment is the informal application of the creative, inquiring intelligence to human problems as principally conveyed through words. The methods it uses are in large part different from those of statistical prediction, although they are not by that token mysterious, unanalyzable or sacrosanct: they are the operations used in all sciences and in all kinds of disciplined human inquiry as hypotheses are formed or as the scholar reflects on the meaning of what he has found. The clinician should make every effort to test his hypotheses by generating concrete predictions and verifying them on new samples of data. But he should also strive to understand, to discipline, and to improve the analytic and synthetic processes of clinical judgment. In doing so, he can get more help from studying the methods of other disciplines that deal with verbal meanings than he can from predictive experiments themselves.

4

During much of the decade of the 1960s I was working on psychoanalytic theory and other problems at a considerable remove from clinical and statistical prediction. I had said my say and wished that the controversy would simmer down. It did not disappear, however, no matter how hard I looked in the other direction. When Gough's (1962) and Sawyer's (1966) reviews appeared, I was slow to read them. Indeed, it took the stimulus of having to write a new assessment of personality assessment, in the final chapter of my section of Janis, Mahl, Kagan, and Holt (1969), to get me to reconsider the old controversy.

My 1958 paper had originally been presented at a graduate colloquium at Yale in 1957. When I was asked to address a Yale colloquium just ten years later, I thought it appropriate to revisit the old problem; the first draft of the following paper (based on Chapter 41 in Janis et al., which became Chapter 10 of Holt, 1971c) was presented under the title, "Good grief! Another look at clinical and statistical prediction?" For a more stately occasion, when I had to give an address as recipient of the Great Man of the Year Award of the Society for Projective Techniques and Personality Assessment (on September 1, 1969, during the Washington, D.C., convention of the American Psychological Association), I toned down the title somewhat. The slightly peevish tone remains in the text, however, I fear.

Yet Another Look at Clinical and Statistical Prediction: Or, Is Clinical Psychology Worthwhile?

Recent years have seen a series of retreats by the once proud legions of personality assessment in general and of diagnostic testing with projective techniques in particular. Interest in the diagnostic function of the clinical psychologist has lagged; the general level of university training in clinical assessment has gone steadily down, and along with it probably the average level of competence in assessing personalities. Nonclinical psychologists increasingly take a patronizing attitude to the clinical assessment enterprise, implying if they do not state outright that it is a quixotic pursuit for a first-rate person since it has allegedly been proved to be unreliable and invalid.

The main evidence cited against the diagnostic tester—thrown into his face might better capture the emotional tone of many exchanges—is the rout of clinicians by exponents of statistical and actuarial prediction. For it is the impression of most psychologists, I believe (though I have no hard survey data to back me up), that clinical prediction has so consistently failed to match the achievements of statistical prediction that the exceptions may be neglected.

It is high time for a counterattack! We psychodiagnosticians do not have to hang our heads, and we ought to speak up for ourselves so forcefully that our nonclinical colleagues begin to realize that we do indeed have a valuable discipline with a great deal to contribute to psychology. A strategic place to begin is the familiar dispute over prediction, which is what I am considering today. I will begin by reviewing the current status of the controversy, critically evaluating recently published surveys of evidence and exposing their serious biases. Along the way I will consider the generalizations and implications that have been drawn from the evidence, often with little regard for elementary standards of scientific reasoning. I will end with a review of the issues that have been at stake in the controversy and attempt to say what can be concluded about them.

SURVEYS OF THE EMPIRICAL EVIDENCE

I believe that it is safe to assume that everyone here knows the general contents of Meehl's (1954) famous book, *Clinical vs. Statistical Prediction,* though his survey of empirical evidence is probably better remembered than his subtle and perceptive discussions of some of the issues. He found: "16 to 20 studies involving a comparison of clinical and actuarial methods, *in all but one of which the predictions made actuarially were either approximately equal or superior to those made by a clinician*" [p. 119].

The next major relevant publication was by Gough (1962). This is a thoughtful and useful paper despite its faults, some of which I shall allude to below. He brought out the long history of the controversy and its various subproblems, reviewing many specific predictive studies but not attempting a comprehensive survey or any simple overall summary. I will not, therefore, consider it in any detail. The general tone of his paper may be seen in two of his conclusions: "Although statistical modes of prediction at the present time seem to have surpassed the clinical ones in accuracy, neither procedure has done very well" and "no fully adequate study of the clinician's forecasting skills has been carried out." The second of these judgments seems to me more justified than the former.

Meehl (1965) reported that his tally of relevant studies had reached a total of 50, but he gave no bibliography and his conclusions cannot be checked. The one positive finding favoring clinical over statistical prediction in his 1954 survey, he now said, had disappeared on closer examination: the apparently significant finding had been attributable to an invalid use of statistics; but its place was taken by Lindzey's (1965) demonstration that a couple of expert clinicians could reliably distinguish homosexual from heterosexual TATs whereas an actuarial system based on previous experience failed. Still, the weight of numbers seemed to him rather crushing to hopes for clinical methods.

The most recent and in many ways most systematic survey was published by Sawyer (1966). He reported finding only 45 relevant studies despite the fact that he broadened his purview to take in comparisons between clinical and statistical *measurement* as well as prediction. Meehl had distinguished between psychometric and nonpsychometric data, but then had concentrated on what he—as well as Gough—considered the most important and interesting part of the predictive process, the final step in which data of whatever kind are combined to yield the actual predictions. If any kind of cut-and-dried or "mechanical" procedure was followed, prediction was called actuarial or statistical by all of the surveyors, and clinical if the processing was carried out by a person using his head in some way that could not be specified exactly in advance. Sawyer adduced several convincing arguments that the neglected issue of how the data were gathered needs to be considered simultaneously with the type of prediction. Again, the distinction is similar: clinical measurement requires special training (e.g., in interviewing or projective testing); mechanical measurement, as by self-administering tests, can be carried out by any reasonably competent clerk.

Since data can be collected in either of these two ways or by both of them, and can be combined either clinically or statistically, six "prediction methods" result, in addition to which Sawyer describes two types of synthesis: in *clinical synthesis*, the clinician has not only the raw data but the actuarial prediction itself which he can try to improve on; in *mechanical synthesis*, the clinician's prediction is fed into a master formula along with other quantitative predictors.

The 45 studies Sawyer abstracts yield 75 comparisons. These were tallied according to whether the clinical or the mechanical method was superior, or they were "equal" (by criteria that will be discussed below). Sawyer summarizes:

> the present analysis finds the mechanical mode of combination always equal or superior to the clinical mode; moreover, this is true whether data were collected clinically or mechanically. Clinical combination actually predicts less well with data collected by both modes than with only mechanically collected data, and clinical combination that includes a mechanical prediction is inferior to the mechanical composite alone. [I cannot forbear interpolating that this conclusion is *not* supported by his

own data.] . . . nonetheless, clinical skills may contribute through data collection, by assessing characteristics that would not otherwise enter the prediction [pp. 192–193].

This last conclusion stems from the fact that by Sawyer's overall summary measure, the best method seems to be the "mechanical composite," in which data collected both clinically and mechanically are combined in a statistical or actuarial way. In the end, then, the clinician is conceded to have some uses, if he will confine himself to being a sensitive measuring instrument and will not presume to put data together in the form of a prediction.

McReynolds (1968) published an overview of the current status of psychological assessment. Among the nine major trends he listed was the following:

> The issue of clinical vs. actuarial prediction continues to be an active research area. . . . It is essentially the question of whether a . . . prediction from given data is more accurate when made in a global, judgmental manner [note the linkage of terms] by a skilled clinician, or when made on the basis of the best statistical formulae and actuarial data. Most of the comparative studies favor the actuarial over the clinical method, but there is some doubt that the clinical approach has been adequately represented [p. 8].

That year also saw the publication of the only survey I know of in which the weight of the evidence ends up on the clinical side—a review by Korman (1968) of over 40 attempts to predict managerial performance. He concludes:

> Perhaps the most intriguing finding that emerges from this review is the relative usefulness of the "judgmental prediction" methods, as exemplified by executive assessment procedures and peer ratings. While allowance must be made for the generally small samples involved and for the general paucity of research overall, it would seem that there is no basis for assuming any superiority of the "actuarial" over the "clinical" method at this time. In fact, the evidence is to the contrary [p. 316].

It may seem astonishing that the papers of Sawyer and Korman, coming to opposite conclusions after reviewing approximately the same number of studies, could be approvingly cited by the same authors, but Owens and Jewell (1969) manage to do so in their chapter in the *Annual Review of Psychology*. Sawyer's summary is called "very informative . . . an admittedly selective but excellent review" [pp. 439, 440]. Korman's paper is called "an extensive survey" and his conclusion is characterized as "unexpected . . . at variance with Sawyer's findings." Owens and Jewell do seem a bit inclined to believe Sawyer's more "expected" outcome, commenting that Korman's "may be a function of predictor-criterion parallelism" [p. 441].

CRITIQUE OF THE SURVEYS

Such are the results. Now what can we make of them? In order to evaluate the findings of the studies so as to know just what lessons clinical psychology can learn from them, we must first examine them critically. But in attempting to do so, I find myself a little embarrassed: many of the criticisms I would make of Gough and Sawyer are the same as the points I raised, principally against Meehl, over a decade ago (Holt, 1958a; [Chapter 2]), and I want to do something more than simply repeat myself. Is it that my contribution sank like a stone wholly unnoticed? No; it is just about the most quoted and most reprinted thing I have written. Have my arguments been rebutted? Not to my knowledge; indeed, I must confess that when Gough and Sawyer do refer to me they do so respectfully and without taking issue with me on any of my specific points. Gough even went so far as to endorse one of my complaints—that most of the comparisons were not fair to the clinical method. I can only conclude that either I failed to make myself clear, or else it has seemed better to ignore objections that could not be met.

Let me then summarize my older critique, briefly noting its applicability to the recent surveys. I rejected as misleading the dichotomous classification of studies as clinical or statistical, on the grounds that the central issue is the role of clinical judgment, which may enter the predictive process at any one or more of five points (today I distinguish six). Let me review now, therefore, these six steps and make some remarks about the role of clinical judgment in each.

First comes the analysis of the criterion—"job analysis," or the study of what is to be predicted. In what I have called naive clinical designs, this first phase is skipped or done simply by guesswork; that is why it is naive, *not* why it is clinical. Actually, the study of criterion behavior cannot be carried out without the steady exercise of a great deal of judgment, in deciding what is the most meaningful measure of what you are trying to predict, which in turn presupposes an understanding of the behavior in question and the circumstances under which it shows itself.

An easily overlooked but major aspect of studying the criterion is to find out to what extent it is determined by intrapersonal as against extrapersonal or situational factors, to get an idea of how much weight should be given to the former. Very few workers have made much study of the criterion from this standpoint. Rather, it seems to be almost universally assumed that since we cannot know what the situational determinants will be, we might as well concentrate on developing intrapersonal predictors, hoping that the external, press determinants will be distributed randomly or else will be constant for all subjects. Sometimes, as in the Kelly-Fiske (1951) study of clinical psychologists, these assumptions have been grotesquely inapplicable: their criterion data were grades in all universities then having clinical training programs, and ratings in a great variety of Veterans Administration installations all over the country, given by an enormous number of raters with all conceivable varieties of standards that existed within the profession of clinical psychology. Moreover, the clinicians who attempted to predict the future competence of the trainees assessed in that study had no idea how, when, where, or by whom competence would be evaluated. Yet all of the well-known "results" of the Kelly-Fiske study, which have done so much to create a nihilistic picture of the value of clinical assessment, were based on such indefensible criteria.

The work of Stern, Stein, and Bloom (1956) stands in refreshing but lonely contrast. Their book is mostly devoted to demonstrating the importance of making careful analyses of the criterion to be predicted, with as much emphasis on an analysis of the situation in which the subject's behavior will occur as on clinical assessments of personalities. It is a fatal error, they argue, for a psychologist to assume that he knows what the criterion *ought* to be, and to predict that; he should find out what criterion judges really look for in a student, for example, and delineate a model of the ideal student in *their* terms. In several studies of this kind, they were able to predict faculty evaluations of students in several different kinds of schools on the basis of intensive multiform assessments, with uncontaminated r's as high as .70. But their samples were very small ($N = 10$ for the correlation just given), and they did not compare "clinical and statistical predictions," so their important contribution to method has not received sufficient attention, and the book is not cited in any of the surveys.

The second step in prediction is discovering the situational *and* intrapersonal *intervening variables* that need to be measured in order to predict the criterion. In any predictive system there is undoubtedly some analysis of this kind even though it may not be recognized as such. A statistician trying to predict which prisoners will violate parole will waste a tremendous amount of time in constructing an experience table if he does not at least have some hunches—based on an implicit set of intervening variables—about what sorts of predictors to look for. Again, judgment plays an important role in directing the search for good predictors in either a predominantly clinical or a predominantly actuarial design. The issue again is not whether judgment is involved but whether it is used intelligently in the study of known criterion groups in their realistic settings.

The third step is to choose one's specific measuring instruments. A neglected but important question is how *appropriate* the instruments are to the task. If the preceding steps have been carried out properly, so that we know what constructs we need to be able to measure, the choice of techniques can be made rationally. All too often, in both the clinical and the actuarial traditions, the choice has been made on the basis of prejudice, sheer familiarity with one set of possibilities and ignorance of others, or vague hunches. Once again, we see that judgment and subjectivity *must* be used, and that the prospects for successful prediction are better to the extent that such judgment is disciplined.

In the fourth step, the predictors that have been selected are given a first empirical trial on a sample, with the same criteria and the same types of subjects as in the ultimate target situation. In the best kind of prediction, this step is vitally necessary. As I noted 12 years ago, there is nothing about clinical methods that precludes this step, even though the studies that have been tallied as clinical have almost never included it. For that reason alone, they are at a severe disadvantage and are not logically comparable to good actuarial studies.

This brings us to the point where what has been learned so far is applied in a cross-validation study. Here two more steps may be distinguished: in the fifth, data are gathered and processed or scored. If explicit use is made of a set of intervening variables, as in a sophisticated clinical design, quantitative estimates of these variables are the outcome of this step. Judgment typically plays a minimal role in a pure actuarial system at this point, the processing being such a routine matter that it is done by subprofessionals or by a computer program. Even so, prudence dictates that such data as objective-test answer sheets be inspected for evidence that they have not been filled out in a capricious or other obviously invalid way. In addition to this level of judgment, in any study that uses meaningful data such as TAT stories, qualitative observations, or drawings, a higher order of specifically trained judgment goes into the processing: scoring and the rating of traits.

The last step is the one that has mainly interested most writers. The scores, ratings, or what have you are combined to make the final predictions, which are statistically related to the criterion. Note that a study may have been clinical in the sense of requiring a high level of trained judgment at *every* preceding step, but if the processed data are combined according to any uniform procedure, even when the rules are *not* actuarially derived, then Meehl or Gough immediately classified it as actuarial, Sawyer as "mechanical composite." For there to be a clean test of the relative effectiveness of clinical judgment and actuarial procedures at this supposedly crucial point, *all of the preceding steps would have to be substantially the same for both the clinician and the actuary.* This is not so much a plea for justice as an elementary application of scientific method! It strikes me as something worth pondering that psychologists possessed of the highest intelligence and the most sophisticated grasp of scientific method fail to reject the great majority of the comparisons on the grounds of gross failure to control major sources of variance.

In order to test the efficacy of clinical judgment at the final stage, research would have to follow this design: after studying criterion behavior, choosing meaningful and appropriate criterion measures, and selecting the necessary intervening variables and techniques to measure them, a psychologist would use all his clinical skills to assess the intervening variables as sensitively as possible, thereafter making his predictions of the criterion for this preliminary sample. These would be tested against the criterion, and hits and misses would be identified. Then, while he was restudying all his data in an attempt to learn from his successes and failures so far, the clinician's estimates of the intervening variables would be turned over to the statistician, who would correlate them with the criterion and come up with, let us say, a multiple regression equation. Finally, the critical test with a cross-validation sample: the statistical prediction would be provided easily by having the new set of trait ratings entered into the regression equation by a clerk who could do simple arithmetic. The clinician would make his predictions in the same way as before, and both sets would be correlated with the criterion.

Unfortunately, I know of no such study. But from a partial approximation to it in some data from the old research on selecting psychiatric residents by Holt and Luborsky (1958, Vol. 2, pp. 382–386), I should not be at all surprised if statistical predictions were as good as the clinical ones, or possibly even better. You see, I have a great deal more confidence in the intrinsic validity of those trait ratings than I do in the clinical predictions, because clinical psychologists are trained specifically in assessing personality, *not* in making predictions of behavioral outcomes!

You may feel that I have suddenly given up the fight and have conceded the crucial issue too soon. Far from it; I only wish to dramatize how far from crucial I feel this final phase to be as a test of the utility of clinical judgment in a predictive undertaking. If Sawyer's conclusion were in fact correct, and the best kind of predictive system were of the kind I have just outlined, with the ultimate predictions being made by means of some actuarial formula, we would see the victory of something that was overwhelmingly clinical up to the final touch. It would be impossible to operate such a system without a great deal of expensive clinical time, a fact that would convince an *administrator* quickly enough that it was a clinical enterprise rather than a primarily statistical one he was supporting.

So much for the replay of my 1958 critique; now let us consider the most recent of the would-be comprehensive surveys, that of Sawyer (1966). Elsewhere (Holt, 1975a [Chapter 5, below]) I plan to publish a detailed dissection and rebuttal of this paper, which I will only briefly summarize here.[1] Just how good are the 45 researches Sawyer brings together, tabulates, and uses as the basis for a series of sweeping generalizations about clinical procedures? In brief, most of them have very little evidential value. Five miscellaneous types of error flaw the great majority, in addition to several other deficiencies.

---

[1][To avoid duplication of what is more thoroughly covered in Chapter 5, I have slightly condensed the following critique. I have let stand the numerical assertions such as "In 15 of the 45 studies . . ." since, where necessary, the changes are made and explained in the next chapter. There, not five but 13 types of flaws in the presentation and use of evidence are discussed.]

1. *Criterion contamination of un-cross-validated formulas.* In 15 of the 45 studies, clinical predictions of some kind are compared with statistical predictions (usually involving multiple regression) that use weights based on the same sample to which they are applied.

It is a commonplace that multiple correlations shrink when applied to a new sample, since they must by their nature capitalize on every chance variation in the original data. Perhaps I take this issue more seriously than Sawyer because I have had the experience of getting my hopes up when Verbal IQ, the Strong Lawyer key, the number of good M responses, and percentage of all rare details in the Rorschach gave a multiple R of .56 on a sample of 64 psychiatric residents (against supervisors' ratings of overall competence), only to see all that crumble away to .13 in a cross-validation sample of 100. True, when samples are very large the danger of shrinkage diminishes markedly, but only two of the offending studies tallied were adequately protected in this way.

2. *Inadequate criterion measures.* In five studies, the criteria used had some type of inadequacy. Actually, in rejecting only five studies because of inadequate criteria, I am bending over backward to be conservative, for Sawyer included only a dozen papers in which the criteria are of the kinds clinicians are ordinarily concerned with. As in other surveys, most studies of clinical and statistical prediction do not concern *any specifiable behavior* of the subjects. Meehl, for example, notes that the researches he collated "all involve the prediction of a somewhat heterogeneous, crude, socially defined behavior outcome." In practice, this means that what is predicted from the study of one person is mostly the behavior of *other* people, *not* studied, who give him grades, promote him, raise his salary, discharge him from a hospital or from some course of treatment, or otherwise *evaluate* his behavior in unforeseeable future situations, or even rate what they believe his behavior to be, which itself may be more of a prediction than an observation. To a clinician whose idea of predicting behavior is anticipating patients' responses to psychotherapeutic maneuvers, the kind of prediction tested in the published research is more like prophecy. As Meehl (1954) demonstrates, the criterion in a typical predictive study is so complexly determined, being the cumulation of so many individual acts, that

> in order to predict this outcome by clinical understanding it would be necessary to formulate an extremely detailed conceptual model of personality structure [and of the situation, or press]. . . . Now it is obvious that in none of the studies cited did the clinician have an opportunity to "formulate the personality" or to determine the *press* in anything like the detail indicated [p. 123].

But instead of concluding that the researches in question were not therefore reasonable tests of the clinician's ability, Meehl indicates only that the latter should have refused to try to make a nonactuarial prediction. He may be right, but judgment about when to cooperate and when to refuse is of a different order from that involved in combining data to make predictions, and the two should not be confounded.

One of Sawyer's bases for deciding whether to include a study or not was that it should predict a behavioral outcome and *not* the assessment of traits, the very type of work (along with therapy) for which clinical psychologists are primarily trained. Whether or not a predictive system gets set up and validated is largely determined, not by the psychological significance or clinical relevance of the behavior predicted, but by extraneous social considerations among which the economic bulk large. Consequently, in Brunswik's phrase, the ecological validity of the sampling of possible criteria is of necessity poor.

3. *Misleading classification of judges as "clinicians."* If the criteria were rarely clinical, the same is true of the persons Sawyer labels as "clinicians." He admits that psychologists or psychiatrists made the "clinical" measurement and/or prediction in only 22 of the 45 studies he included. In others, the so-called clinicians were military officers or enlisted men, graduate students, sports writers, and the subjects themselves. "Thus," Sawyer comments with a detectable trace of understatement, "the level of experience in psychological assessment is by no means uniformly high." Conservatively, serious question should be raised about the relevance of at least 15 studies to clinical measurement and prediction because judges lacked relevant training or experience, or both.

4. *Insufficient power to detect differences.* The published surveys have been made by psychologists whose competence was more statistical than clinical, so one would expect at least that good psychometric standards would have been applied to the evidence. Yet in two of Sawyer's 45 studies the number of subjects is wholly inadequate to support generalization (N's of 3 and 8, respectively), while in six others it is so small (from 30 to 47) that there is insufficient power to establish any but the grossest differences; not surprisingly, in most of these small studies no significant differences were found.

5. *Use of quantitative data only.* In six of the 45 studies, the only data are MMPI profiles. I realize that for Meehl, Hoffman (1960), Kleinmuntz (1967), and others, a comparison of a formula and an expert interpreter of the MMPI is ideally clean, for both predictors have exactly the same data, and only the method of reaching predictions differs. But I cannot conceive that any clinical judge could do anything in principle other than apply an informal actuarial method when confronted with nothing but a string of numbers. Only someone addicted to the Minnesota Multiphasic would consider mulling over a quantitative profile to be an exercise of clinical judgment. No, if clinical judgment is to be given a chance to show what it can do, it has to have meaningful, *qualitative* data to work with (though it need not be restricted to such data exclusively).

Aside from these deficiencies in the studies themselves, several of the procedures Sawyer used in presenting, summarizing, and tabulating the evidence are biased in favor of mechanical measurement and prediction: differential treatment of best clinicians and best tests; the arbitrariness of Sawyer's criteria for what constitutes a difference, and his inconsistency in applying his own criteria; and a number of logical errors.

I have already mentioned the fact that there exists another survey, Korman's, covering as many studies as Sawyer's, in which clinical predictions were superior to actuarial ones most of the time. True, Korman published two years later (1968), but only ten of the researches he reviewed were too recent to have been included by Sawyer. It is rather remarkable that, except for the fact that both cited Meehl's book, there is no overlap whatever in the two bibliographies! It would take me too far afield to criticize or expound Korman's survey any further; let me simply point out the fact that he did bring together attempts to predict *one reasonably homogeneous criterion:* the performance of business managers, and remind you of the caution and reasonableness of his conclusions.

The suspicion of bias in Sawyer's selection of evidence grows when we notice that he fails to include in his survey the two studies reported by Gough as demonstrating that clinicians can add valid variance to predictions made by a regression equation, though it is clear that he must have known of them. It is equally clear that he must have known of another comparison of clinical and actuarial predictions contained in an article with an obvious title, because he cites the paper but fails to make any mention of the "new data" its title promises. (Gough, incidentally, did the same thing.) That paper is, of course, my own (1958a). In it, I refer to three attempts to develop actuarial predictions of the overall competence of psychiatric residents using various scores taken from the battery of tests given applicants before their acceptance, each of which failed on cross-validation, while the routine, naive clinical predictions had a low but significant and useful level of validity. Now it is true that these studies are quite sketchily described in the article, so that it might be argued that there are insufficient details for them to be very critically examined; but the paper refers the interested reader to the book by Luborsky and myself where the information is laid out (Holt & Luborsky, 1958, Vol. 2, Appendices 12.2, 13.3, 13.6, 13.7). Does it not seem curious that none of the surveys has *even alluded* to these attempted comparisons of clinical and statistical prediction?

A selection of evidence is biased if it results in the inclusion of the irrelevant as well as the exclusion of the relevant. Sawyer seems to have added to his pile any study in which the statistical prediction of anything that could be remotely considered a behavioral outcome is compared with a nonstatistical prediction, as long as the latter (the supposedly "clinical" prediction or measurement) did not surpass the former. The result is a lopsided jumble constituting a sample of no intelligible population, from which it is literally meaningless to try to generalize. It seems amazing how little attention we psychologists usually pay to this elementary point about the logic of inference; perhaps the trouble arises from our habit of accepting generalized terms without examining them carefully. Does it really make sense to ask questions about *prediction,* qualified only as clinical or statistical? Have we learned nothing about the great specificity of behavior? Today, virtually none of us would accept unchallenged any attempt to generalize about "aptitude," especially if tests of all kinds of abilities were indiscriminately lumped together. Similarly with prediction: we must ask what kind of behavior is being predicted, by whom, under what conditions, and by what means, etc., before our questions can start to become meaningful. It is an absurd non sequitur to assume that because clinicians use judgment in making predictions, the results of *any* study in which *anybody* uses judgment to predict *anything* are relevant to the ordinary functioning of clinicians. It is bad enough that clinical assessors have occasionally put their reputations for competence in jeopardy by attempting to predict grades in college or some other nonclinical criterion about which they have no technical knowledge; it is intolerable to have the inept attempts of nonclinicians to do the same thing cited as evidence that clinical assessment is worthless.

Clinical psychologists do not after all try to predict any and all kinds of behavior; why not examine what they *do* predict? Note that you would have to sample clinicians in some rational way in order to generalize about them. Just do this as a thought experiment, and then compare how good an approximation you have in the data amassed by Meehl, Sawyer, *et al.;* it quickly becomes evident that the fit is so absurdly bad that generalizations about clinical psychologists or the discipline of clinical personality assessment are wholly unwarranted.

THE ISSUES

Let us examine what are the issues being tested in all this work and how the empirical studies bear on them.

The methodological or epistemological issue. Are there idiographic methods that afford a unique access to truth? This issue was injected by Allport (1942), whose exaggerated ideas about what the clinical method of studying unique individuals could accomplish were not derived from studying personalities at first hand, for he was no clinician and never wrote a case study, but from studying German philosophy. He was convinced that individual behavior could be predicted only from qualitative case studies and put forward the notion that there should be research to demonstrate the superiority of this approach over the actuarial. Such notions can hardly be tenable any more. Whatever else one may think about the evidence, it has been clearly established that statistical prediction *is* applicable to unique individuals and that it can do as good a job as that done by trained clinicians, at least for many socially important kinds of "behavior." Yet this claim was refutable on logical and philosophical grounds alone, which I have done elsewhere (Holt, 1961b [Chapter 3, above], 1962b [Volume 1, Chapter 1]; see also the theoretical sections of Meehl, 1954). The theoretical position on which the hypothesis was based is not held by many clinicians, and demolishing it in no way undermines the logic of clinical assessment.

The cognitive issue: is clinical inference only informal statistical inference? This problem, most clearly associated with the name of Sarbin (1943; see also Sarbin, Taft, & Bailey, 1960), is as little related to data as the first. Sarbin contends that the clinical assessor can in principle predict *only* by statistical inference. He rejects the claim that building a theoretical scheme is a genuinely creative act, and holds that any expectation of the future can be nothing more than extrapolation from past experience. Since in his original experiment (Sarbin, 1943) the clinicians did in fact not do any better than systematically accumulated and statistically manipulated experience, he believed that his point was proved. Meehl (1954) adequately demonstrated that this was a non sequitur, and that even when they are incorrect, clinical predictions do not necessarily consist only of informal statistical inferences, guesses, and speculations.

Yet a cognitive-epistemological issue remains, a sophisticated modern version of this older one. It can be stated operationally. To what extent can the processes of clinical judgment be programmed for a computer? Notice, first, that this formulation is quantitative, not all-or-none, for it is certain that at least some routine aspects of the clinician's cognitive activity *can* be taken over by a computer. In general, we know that the limit of what the computer can do is set by our ability to specify the processes in detail. If Sarbin were right, automation would be relatively straightforward. You would store in the machine's memory a complete set of inferential rules, of the following general type: if R is greater than 35 and $F + \%$ is greater than 40 and M is greater than 4, print out the statement, "He is likely to be more creative than average." The machine would scan the numerical input and, on recognizing the specified set of data, would output the inferential conclusion. Such a rule is capable of considerable sophistication and refinement in terms of pattern; machines can be just as configurational as clinicians when dealing with quantitative scores. Piotrowski (1964) has developed this type of computer program for analyzing the Rorschach, though I should add that I made up the example. Quite a few persons have written similar programs for interpreting MMPI profiles [e.g., Kleinmuntz, 1963].

But, I hope you are objecting, most clinicians work to only a small extent with purely quantitative data; more typically, personality assessors rely on verbal texts (like TAT stories or interviews), on graphic data (like figure drawings), and on direct impressions from observation and interaction with the subject, with a large emphasis on empathy and recipathy (Murray *et al.*, 1938—inferring the subject's state by observing one's own affective reaction to him). I have listed these three classes of data in order of increasing difficulty for the computer: it can already do a good deal with verbal texts; pattern recognition programs have progressed far enough to open up at least the theoretical possibility of even such an odd hybrid as computerized graphology, though not very soon. But to the best of my knowledge, no one has even claimed that a machine might ever be able to duplicate the processes of empathic observation.

Even the computer analysis of verbal texts is limited, so far, to the counting of specified words and phrases. Since words can be preclassified into psychologically meaningful rubrics, computer programs can perform subtle and interesting analyses. This is a low level of judgment, however, as compared to interpreting a dream or even scoring a Rorschach—processes that require the clinician to comprehend at least whole paragraphs at a time. In any event, such an enterprise is only remotely connected with the making of predictions. Surely, comparisons of clinical and statistical prediction have little to contribute to the cognitive issue in its modern reformulation.

The conceptual issue: are the clinician's concepts and theories any good? While this issue has not been explicitly posed by many writers on clinical and statistical prediction, it may well underlie a good deal of the interest that has been generated. Clinical psychologists tend to overlook the influence of the *situation* in determining behavior, and among determinants within the individual they tend to be most interested in unconscious needs, conflicts, fantasies, defenses, pathological trends, identifications, and the like. Since such variables are usually assessed by means of indirect clinical inference, and by use of methods (like projective techniques) that lack the usual psychometric credentials of demonstrated reliability and validity, many nonclinicians look askance at the whole enterprise of clinical assessment. They often feel that common sense, plus the application of the laws of learning, would probably do a much better job of psychodiagnosis and psychotherapy, and the simple, nontheoretical approach of actuarial prediction appeals to them.

The ultimate test of the usefulness of any theory is whether or not it can be demonstrated to contribute to knowledge and man's ability to manage his world and his life more effectively. Yet there are too many other possible sources of error in the failure of any particular set of clinical predictions for it to constitute a rigorous test of the clinician's theories. This need not imply that his concepts have too little relevance to reality, either. The concepts may be good, bad, or indifferent, but if the measuring instruments are ineptly applied by a poorly trained person, or if the latter lacks good normative information about how his tests operate in the population being predicted, or if he makes incorrect assumptions about the situations in which future behavior will take place, or if he lacks information about some critically important ability—to give just a few examples—he may predict very badly. It is impossible, therefore, to conclude anything about the value of clinical theories from the results of the prediction surveys.

The theoretical issue: the role of prediction in science. Several authors (e.g., Gough, 1962; Sawyer, 1966) have traced the importance of deciding whether clinical or statistical predictions are more accurate to the allegedly fundamental role of prediction in science. According to Sawyer, "it underlies explanation." As I see it (following Polanyi, 1958), the aim of science is explanation through understanding. Though prediction is surely the best way to verify that your understanding is valid and not self-deceptive, it is a means and not an end in itself. It is perfectly possible to predict and control without understanding, a state of affairs that leads to empiricism rather than science. Anyone can predict about as well as a pharmacologist can what will happen when a headache sufferer takes an aspirin, for the mechanism of the drug's reaction is not yet understood. Once it is, the door will probably be open to the development of even more effective drugs with fewer side effects; that is what has happened often in pharmacology. Indeed, in other fields it is commonplace that the scientific process has *begun* with an empirically observed regularity or rule of thumb, which incidentally makes prediction possible but—more to the point—stimulates the curiosity of a scientist to find out how it works.

This is one reason that clinicians have been fertile producers of theories to aid our understanding of personality. Psychometricians, and in fact most behavioristically and positivistically trained psychologists, tend to downgrade the importance of understanding as a scientific goal. Indeed, the logic of statistical prediction does not require understanding of the behavior in question. All that is needed is some measurable predictive variables that are correlated with the criterion. The statistician's interest ceases once he has found the most efficient and stable formula that combines scores to predict the criterion. Yet this is the point at which a psychologist should become really curious and start investigating the reasons for the observed regularity! No wonder statistical prediction has made such a small contribution to psychology; it will continue to do so as long as we do not see that prediction is a scientific means, not an end in itself. Whether you agree with this analysis or not, you will concede, I feel confident, that this theoretical issue will never be resolved by tallying relative successes of different predictive systems.

Lurking in the background, and never made fully explicit, is another essentially philosophical issue—the role of objectivity in psychology. This is an extremely important question and one that cannot be adequately discussed in brief. I should do no more than indicate my belief that it is one of the hidden motors that keeps this controversy churning. I hope that I do not need to detail the argument that no empirical box score is going to settle such fundamental matters as phenomenology versus positivism.

The practical issue: if you need to be able to predict something, how should you go about it? There is evidential support as well as a strong a priori case for the proposition that the sort of sophisticated, six-stage predictive system I outlined earlier is better than a causal, thoughtless, unanalytical one. Just how great a role, if any, should clinicians be given in such a system? That depends on a balance of many factors, including how big the job is, how much the behavior seems to depend on central rather than peripheral factors in the personality, and the resources available. There is no automatically correct answer.

A large enough group of researches dealing with educational selection have accumulated by now so that it might be possible to begin to make some cautious generalizations about that domain. I think it has been pretty well demonstrated that academic grades (in which most of the variance is attributable to cognitive abilities well measured by psychometric tests) are best predicted by actuarial means using previous grades and relatively objective test scores. In the field of vocational selection, as soon as we get away from academic types of criteria from early stages of training and into more socially significant measures of success after some years on the job, the weight of evidence begins to swing over toward predictive systems employing clinical judgment at several stages, particularly in professions and managerial positions in which success depends to an appreciable degree on nonintellectual aspects of personality.

The main issue, the emotional one: is clinical psychology any good? Since the studies of clinical and actuarial prediction do not adequately sample clinical psychologists, and since the criteria predicted only occasionally have direct relevance to clinical work, the collations of research done to date are a highly inappropriate basis on which to evaluate the profession or its assessment function even if the surveys were not so demonstrably biased in their selection and handling of evidence. Moreover, the controversy tends to concentrate attention on horseraces between clinicians and statisticians at the expense of studies designed to evaluate clinical assessment most directly and appropriately. The main importance of the controversy is that the failure of clinicians to predict such complex social outcomes as school grades and success on parole any better than actuarial methods has been used as a stick to beat clinical psychology with. Because personality assessors could not surpass statisticians on the latter's territory, they have been accused of incompetence in their own domain and have been called smug and complacent when they fail to present convincing quantitative evidence that clinical assessment (and psychotherapy) are valid and effective.

The controversy has been going on during a time when clinical psychology has come under increasingly critical scrutiny. Recall, for example, Eysenck's (1965) attack on the effectiveness of psychotherapy, the threat of Division 3 to withdraw from APA because of Central Office's activities on behalf of clinicians, and the attacks on clinical programs from within university faculties.

These and similar developments have generated a good deal of pressure on clinical psychologists to demonstrate the validity of their diagnostic and therapeutic techniques by the usual kinds of experimental evidence, or else to give up clinical teaching and practice. It just happens that there is hardly a research task within psychology more complex and difficult than evaluating assessment and treatment. In the judgment of most qualified members of the profession, there has never been a truly adequate study of either; to do so properly would take great resources of money, time, personnel, subjects, statistical sophistication, and research creativity. The working clinician himself, spending most of his time trying to understand and to help people in distress, could hardly be expected to take careful stock of his theories and practices under these circumstances. Despite some of Meehl's claims, good research data can rarely be accumulated during clinical practice. The research that has been published, therefore, has tended to be either what could be done as a sideline by clinicians, or else projects set up by persons who knew much more about experimental design than about the nature of clinical assessment and how it might be studied meaningfully.

Against this background, it is understandable how even such excellent scientists as Meehl greatly overgeneralized the results of the surveys of research on clinical and statistical prediction and overlooked some of the data reviewed above. Indeed, Meehl (1954) admitted that his well-known conclusion—that the clinical psychologist should turn from diagnostic assessment to concentrate on therapy and research—"is my personal hunch, not proved by the presented data or strongly argued in the text" [p. vii].

SUMMARY

The vast majority of the issues that underlie the continued interest in structuring and maintaining such an artificial dichotomy as clinical versus statistical prediction turn out to be incapable of being resolved by tallies of successes and failures for the antagonists. What *can* be concluded from the surveys of these empirical studies? Five statements can be made. (a) When the necessary conditions for setting up a pure actuarial system exist, the odds are heavy that it can outperform clinicians in predicting almost anything in the long run, *if* both sides have access *only* to quantitative data, such as an MMPI profile. (b) A complete six-step predictive system is almost always better than a more primitive one, and even when it seems to be entirely statistical it requires the exercise of a great deal of subjective judgment to work efficiently. (c) Disciplined, analytical judgment is generally better than global, diffuse judgment, but is not any the less clinical. (d) To predict almost any kind of behavior or behavioral outcome, one does better to assess the situation in which the behavior occurs in addition to assessing the actors' personalities. (e) Granted such knowledge and a meaningful criterion to predict, clinical psychologists vary considerably in their ability to do the job, but the best of them can do very well. That is, they *do* have skills in assessing personality by largely subjective but partly objectifiable procedures, making use of theories that permit a deeper and more valid understanding of persons than anything the statistician can provide.

I am sure I do not surprise anyone by concluding, finally, that clinical psychology in general and the assessment of personality and psychopathology in particular *are* very much worthwhile. Indeed, I believe that psychology as a whole would be much poorer without psychodiagnosis and clinical assessment. There are powerful forces within psychology working to bring about this impoverishment in the name of science. The final irony comes when the enemies of clinical psychology try to use the tallies of published successes and failures of what *they* call clinical and statistical predictions as evidence from which to generalize about the inadequacies of clinical methods. For in doing so, they forsake scientific standards of evaluating evidence and generalizing results, and let their prejudices blind them to the irrelevancy of the published surveys to the judgments they wish to make.

5

Since I had committed myself in my 1970a paper (the preceding chapter) to publish a full-scale critique of Sawyer's review, I pecked away at the job during the next few summers. If the resulting paper (particularly in its opening section) is tedious to read, it was even more so to write, and I could never get excited enough about it to give it a high priority on my work schedule. Nevertheless, it did seem necessary to set the record straight in detail, if only to back up the assertions of my preceding paper by citing chapter and verse. The Psychological Bulletin *has an honorable tradition of publishing rejoinders to its reviews, so I fancied that the editor would be eagerly awaiting my manuscript, which I finished in the fall of 1973. (I am grateful to Dr. Mark Fulcomer, who was then a colleague, for reading the manuscript and making a number of helpful suggestions.)*

To my chagrin, however, it came back not many weeks later with a negative judgment: too much, too late, not without error itself, and probably counterproductive. The editor hoped that the problem could be laid to rest, the questions having been wrongly put; he feared that publishing the paper would only prolong the fruitless controversy. Nevertheless, I decided to go ahead and find another outlet and submitted it to the APA's Journal Supplement Abstract Service *in February 1974.*

After it had been accepted a couple of months later, I belatedly realized that I had an obligation to Jack Sawyer to let him see it before publication. I sent him a copy, therefore, asking him to give me the chance to eliminate errors of fact or interpretation of his work. Even before he had had a chance to study it, he sent me a copy of the rejoinder to my 1970 paper that he had submitted to the American Psychologist, *the editor of which had unfortunately rejected it. Unfortunately, because it would seem only fair for him to have had a chance to defend himself against my attack. But the subsequent events convinced me that it was better, after all, for us not to have been allowed to carry on a discussion in print. I prepared a rebuttal of Sawyer's rejoinder, and he came to see me in the summer of 1974 to discuss the whole thing. When we had the chance to size one another up as human beings, our dialogue became a great deal more friendly and productive than it would have been in the letters column of a journal, where I would probably have succumbed to the temptation to score off him as much as possible—to no good purpose. As it was, he helped me see that my tone in a number of passages was needlessly hostile, as well as correcting a few factual points which I have acknowledged in footnotes.*

It is a special pleasure to acknowledge his help. His admirably frank, open, and nondefensive manner in our discussion convinced me that the errors detailed here, even the apparently systematic ones, are attributable to insufficient care with details and not to any malice or anticlinical intent on Sawyer's part. Indeed, he expresses chagrin that his paper has been used as a weapon against clinical psychology, and in his unpublished rejoinder to my 1970 paper he exclaims: "clinician-beaters, please lay off."

Clinical and Statistical Measurement and Prediction: How *Not* to Survey Its Literature

The review article by Sawyer (1966) has, in subsequent years, been frequently and approvingly cited as if it were a reliable and relatively definitive treatment of its topic, clinical and statistical measurement and prediction (e.g., Donelson, 1973; Fiske, 1971; Goldenberg, 1973; Hoch, 1971; Owens & Jewell, 1969; Wiggins, 1973). Yet the paper contains so many errors and flaws of almost every kind that its usefulness as a secondary source must be severely challenged. This critique will begin by provisionally accepting Sawyer's own procedures and standards, showing the many respects in which he applied them inadequately, and will then challenge much of this framework, point by point.

ERRORS IN APPLYING ANNOUNCED PRINCIPLES

Misapplication of the Eightfold System of Classifying Predictions

In his Table 1 (reprinted here), Sawyer presented a scheme for ordering the multiplicity of predictive systems or methods reported in his bibliography. With the exception of methods 7 and *8*, the definitions are relatively straightforward and easy to apply; the clinical and mechanical syntheses are more internally heterogeneous than the other types, as Sawyer points out. Essentially, however, a method is classified as *7* if a clinician is given a mechanically produced set of predictions and attempts to improve on it, by the use of clinically and/or mechanically gathered raw data; it falls under *8* if a clinically generated prediction is used in a formula (or some other "mechanical" predictive system) along with mechanical data and/or quantified clinical data.[1] Though it has certain other inadequacies, which I shall

[1]Repeatedly, Sawyer alleges that what he calls "clinical synthesis" is the same as my description of a sophisticated clinical predictive system, which does *not* include the critical defining characteristic of his Method 7—the availability to the clinician of a prediction produced by mechanical combination. He seems to have come to his false conclusion by taking one incidental particular of the example I offered of a sophisticated clinical prediction and assuming that it was central and essential. In the final phase of the study Luborsky and I (1958) conducted at the Menninger

discuss later, this scheme is a distinct advance over the cruder classifications used by Meehl (1954) and Gough (1962). In applying it, however, Sawyer makes at least 16 errors.[2]

a. In two studies (Doleys & Renzaglia, 1963; Westoff, Sagi, & Kelly, 1958), Ss' own estimates of themselves or statements of intention, *not* based on any specified batch of data and improbably based to any extent on "mechanical" data, were classified *5* (clinical combination of both types of data) instead of *1* (clinical combination of clinical data). In Westoff *et al.*, the alleged "clinical prediction" was an engaged couple's statement of the number of children they wanted to have; since this is not a prediction, combining it with some test scores and biographical items does not produce a mechanical synthesis *(8)* but a mechanical combination *(6)*.

b. In his treatment of Doleys and Renzaglia, Sawyer classifies the total score from the SCAT, which he explicitly describes as "one score only," not as *4* (where quantitative test scores are usually properly put) but as *6*, implying that it is in some way a mechanical combination of clinical and mechanical data.

c. A problem affecting his classification of the predictive methods in several studies arises with respect to biographical data. By the latter, Sawyer means objective facts like age, sex, marital status, education, etc., which are readily obtainable from many Ss by means of a biographical inventory or are collected by a clerk using simple interviewing techniques that do not presuppose clinical training. Such data are heavily relied on in many actuarial predictive systems, for example that of E. W. Burgess (1941) for predicting violation of parole, and the resulting predictions are properly classified as *4*. Consider, however, the typical situation of psychiatric diagnosis: the psychiatrist's data are his direct observations, the qualitative semantic data he elicits by interviewing the patient (and sometimes the latter's relatives), and the miscellaneous information in the case folder, which often will include notations of age, sex, etc., recorded on admission, sometimes by a clerk, but usually by a clinically trained person. Should the latter be considered mechanical data? If so, real-life clinical situations will never give rise to

---

School of Psychiatry, we included a procedure Sawyer classifies as a mechanical combination of data—the clinical judges added up what we called "cue sums" from checklists applied to interviews, TATs, and the like for one predictor, and then made free clinical predictions based on the same data. Sawyer failed entirely to grasp the defining property of sophisticated clinical prediction, which is that it should be based on a complete, five-stage predictive system. [Readers who do not have a special interest in Sawyer's paper or the literature it surveys are invited to skim or skip to p. 84 (Failure to include important literature . . .).]

[2]"At least," because this evaluation does not attempt to be definitive. I have not located and reread each of the primary sources, and I have corresponded with only a few of their authors. Such correspondence has, however, turned up errors I could not have known about otherwise, so ideally all authors should have been asked for commentary on Sawyer's treatment of their data. It became evident that the partial information available to me was sufficient to raise such serious questions about the review that a complete job was unnecessary.

Table 5.1.   Classification of Prediction Methods

| Mode of Data Collection | Mode of Data Combination | |
	Clinical	Mechanical
Clinical	1. Pure clinical	2. Trait ratings
Mechanical	3. Profile interpretation	4. Pure statistical
Both	5. Clinical composite	6. Mechanical composite
Either or both [a]	7. Clinical synthesis	8. Mechanical synthesis

[a]Plus, for the clinical synthesis, the prediction of Method 2, 4, or 6; or, for the mechanical synthesis, the prediction of Method 1, 3, or 5. [From Sawyer, 1966, p. 181.]

predictions classifiable under *1* (pure clinical); only in the artificial atmosphere of special studies will it be possible to provide clinical judges with nothing but the kind of information that requires clinical judgment to gather it.

It seems to me, therefore, that except when some particular emphasis is laid on the use of nonclinical methods to gather objective biographical facts, the inevitable obtaining of such data by an interviewer should not be considered a sufficient basis to classify his method as *5* instead of *1*. Sawyer did in fact classify clinical predictions by a psychiatrist as *1* in the case of Schneider, Lagrone, Glueck, and Glueck (1944) though he specifies the data as "bio, int;" yet in five other studies[3] (Borden, 1928; Dunham & Meltzer, 1946; Glaser, 1954; Glaser & Hangren, 1958; and Gregory, 1956) where the specification of data is exactly the same, he uses the classification *5*. All of these should, I believe, be called *1, except* Schneider *et al.*! For, to quote Meehl's summary of the latter, the psychiatric diagnoses "were based on many sources of data, such as FBI and police reports, data from service records, questionnaires filled out by employers, [and many others], hospital reports, Red Cross social histories, and interviews by the psychiatrists and psychologists" (Meehl, 1954, p. 113).

d. Gregory (1956) used a regression technique to combine mechanical data (test scores and grades) and clinical data in the form of ratings on the basis of interview and references. According to Sawyer's Table 2, these do not seem to have been predictions, yet the combination is classified *8* instead of *6*, which seems more plausible.

e. In his brief presentation of Hamlin (1934), Sawyer gives a misleading impression of the data, predictions, and findings, as well as misclassifying

[3]The only one of these I have been able to check directly is the paper by Dunham and Meltzer, who say nothing about the kinds of information available to the psychiatrists who made prognostic ratings. In his third footnote, on p. 185, Sawyer acknowledges helpful comments from both Meltzer and Glaser, so it *may* be that he had sufficient information to justify his classification. This evidence is not a sufficient basis for confidence, however, since he made a similar acknowledgment to Trankell, but distorted the latter's study (see below).

them. Here is an excerpt from his Table 2, giving his summary of Hamlin's findings:

Prediction method and data	Clinician	Mechanical combination	Validity
5. (6), int	Psychiatrist		.28
6. 100 bio, tests		Not combined	.25–.35
8. (6), pred (5)		Unit weights	.55

(Footnotes indicate that the validities are contingency coefficients, and that the range given is for "20 best items of 100.") Translated, this seems to say that the basic data were a group of 100 objective items, some of them test scores and some biographical data, which if that were so should have been called *4;* but the reader mystified by Sawyer's *6* (implying mechanical combination of clinical and mechanical data) would presumably shrug it aside, noting that no conclusion was drawn except that *8* was superior to *5.* The latter seems to be a psychiatrist's attempt to predict the criterion (adjustment in a reformatory) on the basis of all the objective items plus his own interview. Method *8,* to conclude the translation, combined the clinical prediction with the 20 best objective items.

The facts, however, are rather different. Hamlin explored the validity of *over* 100 items, mainly the kind of thing Sawyer succinctly characterizes as "bio," but they also included a good many clinical ratings, judgments, and predictions, one of them called "Prognosis for institutional adjustment, psychiatrist's estimate." This is, of course, the prediction classified as *5;* and it hapens to be among the 20 best items, ranking 13th. Moreover, the first two ranks are occupied by "Original assignment in reformatory" (about which Meehl comments that it was "presumably based on some kind of human judgment by an administrator, but the author does not explain it" [1954, p. 105]) and "Prognosis for future behavior, psychiatrist's estimate." Finally, the mechanical prediction with a validity of .55 happens to be based on 15 items (not 20 or 100) and though it includes the just-cited prognosis of future behavior it does *not* include the one Sawyer says it does.

f. For unknown reasons, in summarizing the study by Harris (1963), Sawyer classifies the combination of football scores by a formula as *2.* The combination is mechanical, to be sure, but it is news to me that it requires clinical training to obtain the scores in a football game. The appropriate classification, of course, is *4.*

g. Sawyer's summary of Pierson (1958) classifies high school grades, averaged to make a predictor of college grades, as *4.* Ordinarily, one would agree; but in this study, grades were being compared with other ratings made by many of the same high school teachers, including a prediction of "General ability to do college work," classified as *1.* Pierson does not specifically discuss the data on which the ratings were based, but it is clear that they were essentially the same observations and performances on which the teachers based their grades. Thus, if the ratings are construed as clinical combination of clinical data, then the average grades should be construed as mechanically combined clinical data, or 2. Actually, however, methods 5 and 6 fit the facts better, since both ratings and grades were undoubtedly based in part on test scores.

h. Sawyer gives the false impression that Trankell (1956) combined five test scores in an un-cross-validated R of .84, which he classified as *4* and treated as equivalent to the "clinical composite" *(5)* of the same tests plus interview and observations. Actually, "The multiple correlation mentioned by Sawyer does not refer to the five test instruments but to the *assessment variables*. They were fourteen . . . and represent another way of reordering the diagnostic interpretations made by the psychologist. . . . Comparing the correlation of .88 for the 'subjective overall score' with the multiple correlation of .84 for the 'subjective assessment variables' only confirms that . . . the psychologists were able to make use of their own assessments with results that slightly surpassed the results of an application of a statistical formula constructed by means of the results of the selection when the criterion is already known. . . . The test prediction in my first paper never had the size of .84. No value [i.e., no multiple correlation of test scores with criterion] was determined because it would have provided for a comparison with the psychologists' assessments [that was] unfair to the statisticians. I tried to make this clear to Sawyer when he worked with his survey. . . . He seems to have grasped only partly what I meant and has distorted the meaning of some of my figures in such a way that he could include my study and discuss it in his terms." (Personal communication from Arne Trankell; emphasis in original.)

The comparison was thus one of methods 5 and 6, and by a statistically more appropriate technique than the one Sawyer used (see below), the clinical composite was superior to the mechanical composite. As a matter of fact, this study turns out to be the closest approximation yet to the design I sketched in my 1970a paper (p. 341 [Chapter 4, p. 61f.]) for a test of the efficacy of clinical judgment at the final stage of the predictive process, except that there was no cross-validation. In the same letter quoted above, Trankell writes that he did not pursue it to that point because the clinical versus statistical "fight is concerned with an artificial problem and the dichotomy is meaningless. . . . After having met, year after year, the stubborn denials and biased misinterpretations made by those psychologists who belong to the cluster of mechanical technologists, I have felt it as an aimless task to devote more time and energy in trying to convince them."

Misapplication of Criteria for Evaluating Differences

After classifying validities of predictive systems according to his eightfold scheme, Sawyer next applies a set of explicit criteria for deciding when a difference is to be considered large enough and reliable enough to conclude that one method is superior to another. His explicitness here is to be applauded. He begins by adopting the conventional .05 alpha (two-tailed), and disregards differences of whatever size if they are insignificant by this criterion, usually accepting the significance test presented by an author. With one exception, validities are presented in one of two ways: as some type of correlation coefficient between predictor and criterion, or as a percentage of hits.[4] In the case of percentages, he says that the smallest difference construed as favoring one method over another was 12% for 1000 Ss, "while the largest difference indicating equality was 13% for 30 Ss" (p. 190; the first study is E. W. Burgess, 1941, the second is Lindzey, 1965). This statement appears to be true, and the amount of overlap tolerated seems justifiable in terms of the numbers of Ss.

When it comes to correlations, however, Sawyer claims that "the largest difference thus judged as indicating equality was .13 for 232 Ss" (p. 190). He does not say which piece of research he is alluding to, for Table 2 contains no study with $N = 232$ nor any with a difference in correlations of .13. But a difference of .18 (between the validities he cites for methods 4 and 6, reported by Parrish, Klieger, & Drucker, 1954) he calls no difference though the $N = 1000$! He continues with a mildly puzzling statement: "In addition, five other differences—all smaller than .13—were also called equal, even though their large number of Ss (averaging over 2000 each) made them statistically significant." I cannot find five such differences in his table. Presumably he meant to include Conrad and Satter (1945; $N = 3246$, $\Delta_r = .09$, conclusion: $4 = 5$), and Bobbitt and Newman (1944; $N = 1900$, $\Delta_r = .07$, conclusion: $4 = 5$; $\Delta_r = .05$, conclusion: $5 = 8$; $\Delta_r = .02$, conclusion: $4 = 8$—undoubtedly justified). The next largest study of this kind is Parrish et al. (1954; $N = 1000$, $\Delta_r = .11$; conclusion: $2 = 4$), but even including the .02 difference from Bobbitt and Newman, which is probably not reliable, that would make the average N for these five comparisons 1989, which to my clinician's eye does not seem to be "over 2000."[5] Sawyer goes on: "All other statistically significant differences—the smallest being .18—were considered as indicating inequality for the two methods." This statement is wrong on two counts: he actually treated three differences smaller than .18 as indicating inequality, and the difference of .18 as of indeterminate significance, but as most likely not reliable. Two of the small differences taken as real come from Parrish et al. (1954). Four validities are cited from that study—two for

---

[4]This appealing simplification seems to be an advantage until one digs into the details of the research being summarized. Chapter IX of the OSS assessment book (Murray et al., 1948) is strongly recommended for its careful demonstration of the ways in which such summary coefficients can seriously misrepresent the efficacy of predictions in messy, real-life situations.

[5]In another personal communication (July 22, 1974) Sawyer explained to me that this statement dates from an early draft of his paper, when he was including a second small but reliable difference from Conrad and Satter's study, with $N = 3500$. After eliminating the latter, he simply neglected to change the statement.

method *2* (.35, .40), method *4* (.29), and method *6* (.47). Sawyer reaches three conclusions: that *2* = *4* (Δ_r = .06, .11), that *6* > *2* (Δ_r = .07, .12!), and as we have just seen, that *4* = *6*.[6] By reference to Drucker (1957), however, we find that the validities Sawyer cites are corrected for restriction in range; the uncorrected validities are: method *2* (.20, .24), method *4* (.29), and method *6* (.34). Now we can see that *2* = *4* (Δ_r = .05, .09), and that *4* = *6* after all (Δ_r = .05, not .18); but in both of the comparisons of methods *2* and *6*, the differences are still smaller than .18 (.14 and .10). The larger of these differences might be taken as support for the conclusion that *6* > *2*, since it is reliable and larger than .13; but in that case, Sawyer should *also* have concluded that *6* = *2*, on the basis of the smaller difference. The other difference smaller than .18 construed as an inequality comes close: in Pierson (1958), the validity of teachers' predictive ratings was .48, that of averaged grades .65 (Δ_r = .17; N = 228). The difference of .18 taken as interpretable comes from Halbower (1955), which will be discussed below; in this study, N = 8.

Errors and Bias in the Use and Citation of Statistics

Another type of error pervades Sawyer's treatment of correlational findings. Notice that he states his criteria in terms of differences between pairs of correlation coefficients, regardless of their size. One would expect a postdoctoral fellow in a department of statistics to be well aware of the metrical peculiarities of r, which are such that a constant Δ_r has a highly variable meaning up and down the scale, as far as its predictive efficiency is concerned. Since in the present context our interest in correlation coefficients is precisely what they can tell us about the accuracy of prediction, it would seem much more reasonable to set up a criterion in terms of the coefficient of alienation, $\sqrt{1 - r^2}$, or better, $1 - \sqrt{1 - r^2}$, which is the amount of reduction in the error of estimate. There are no conventional standards for this last measure with the comforting familiarity of .05 for alpha, but one might argue that a reduction in the error of estimate of 5% would not be negligible—this corresponds to the gain when we abandon one predictor with a validity of .20 for another with a validity of .37.

Let us see what difference it might make if we adopt this criterion. To begin with, we could not accept a statement like Chauncey's (1954) that two validities were both in "the .60's" as indicating that they were equivalent, for the difference in predictive efficiency between r's of (for example) .60 and .66 is greater than 5%. Thus, no conclusion could be drawn from this

---

[6]Sawyer (personal communication) has informed me that these were clerical errors, which he has corrected in two reprintings of his article (in *Studies in Personnel Psychology*, Vol. 2, No. 2, Oct. 1970; and in Richard I. Lanyon & Leonard D. Goodstein, eds., *Readings in Personality Assessment*. New York: Wiley, 1971). There, he concludes that *4* = *2, 6* > *4*, and *2* = *6*, and he modifies his later tables and text accordingly.

anecdote. In re Cliff (1958), Sawyer's conclusion of no difference between two validities of .83 and .79 might have to be changed to $8 > 4$ (if the difference were significant; but see below). Sawyer also concluded that there was no difference between predictive methods in three other studies, *in each of which clinical predictions happened to surpass mechanical ones* by relatively small Δ_r's; but by the criterion of the coefficient of alienation (a), these differences are all substantial: Grebstein (1963), $1 > 2$, $\Delta_r = .12$, but $\Delta_a = 9\%$; Husén (1954), $2 > 4$, $\Delta_r = .10$ but $\Delta_a = 6\%$, $5 > 4$, $\Delta_r = .12$ but $\Delta_a = 7\%$; Trankell (1956), $5 > 6$, $\Delta_r = .04$ but $\Delta_a = 8.5\%$! (True, Grebstein reported that the difference between his correlation coefficients was not reliable, but see below.) This change in criteria alone would affect the total tallies enough so that the apparent superiority of 4 over 2 would disappear and 4 versus 5 would be nearly a dead heat.

With respect to three studies, Sawyer's treatment of the statistics should not be called erroneous, but his statistical judgment in selecting findings to present is at least arguable and seems to show a consistent anticlinical bias. It is interesting to compare his reporting of Bobbitt and Newman (1944; $4 = 5 = 8$) and of Dunlap and Wantman (1944; $4 = 6 = 8 > 1$) with that of Meehl (1954): the latter is probably not vulnerable to the charge of being biased against statistical prediction, but he cites both these studies as having trends in the clinical direction, albeit insignificant ones.

Both Meehl and Sawyer fail to note, in their summaries of Blenkner (1954), that the apparent success of the "actuarial" prediction (classified 2 by Sawyer; $r_{bis} = .52$, which should have been reported instead of .62, which is not cross-validated) vanishes if we notice that Blenkner also computed its validity in the form of a plain old Pearson r: .22.[7] The apparent significance of the coefficient goes from well beyond the .01 level to poorer than .05 (with 45 degrees of freedom, $r_{.05} = .288$). Which then is the more appropriate statistic? Blenkner's criterion was, unfortunately, badly distributed: she used a scale with more than seven steps to rate the degree of movement in casework records, but found *zero* movement in 74% of the cases. Of the others, 3% showed downward, 23% upward movement of some degree. The problem with the criterion is that it provides too little differentiation of the cases; but the biserial r differs from its Pearsonian parent in that it reduces the criterion to a dichotomy, thus throwing away most of the scanty information available! Sometimes it is justifiable to do so when a significant increase in reliability can be achieved, but the reliability of the extended movement score was .86, which is adequate, and that of the dichotomy (positive movement versus nonpositive) is not reported. It is quite evident that using the biserial approximation, with the additional assumptions it requires, resulted in a loss of meaningful discrimination, not only from the fact that the validity

---

[7]In his Table 2, Sawyer says: "Unless otherwise noted . . . decimals represent product-moment correlations with the criterion." He neither reported Blenkner's product-moment r nor "otherwise noted" that the figure given was a biserial.

coefficient changed so greatly but also from a qualitative analysis of the most discrepant cases which Blenkner provides. Thus vanishes one of Sawyer's and Meehl's prize exhibits of the superiority of "actuarial" over "clinical" prediction.[8] (See also the section below on failure to consider intercorrelation of predictors.)

Errors in Summing and Manipulating Data

Sawyer says that the 45 studies yielded 75 comparisons, though it is not clear how he arrived at that precise number. At any rate, after the above corrections have been made (*except* for the ones involving a *change* in correlational criteria), Sawyer's Table 3 can be reconstructed. It does not seem worth the space it would take to insert here the corrected figures; the seeming import is the same—damning to both clinical measurement and clinical prediction. Likewise with his Table 4. The correct summary figures differ from his by more than 1% in five of the eight cells, but his errors seem to have canceled one another out for the most part except for methods 2 and 5. Sawyer's Table 4 presents "the percentage of the comparisons in which the method was superior, plus one-half the percentage of the comparisons in which it was equal" (p. 192). This summary figure for method 2 was 43% according to Sawyer, 50% according to a more scrupulous following of his own criteria; for method 5, he had 26%, I get 30.5%.

Let us look now at what Sawyer does with his Table 4. His first observation is that, "Within each mode of data collection, the mechanical mode of combination is superior by margins of 23, 25, 49 and 25%" (p. 192). These differences now become 30, 24, 41, and 23%, respectively. This array "replicates Meehl's (1954) conclusion," Sawyer adds; but since many of the studies covered by the two surveys are the same, it is claiming too much to call this a replication. (Sawyer draws conclusions from 43 studies, of which 21 were covered by Meehl.)

Sawyer's fourth observation involves further manipulation of the (by now highly derivative) figures: he claims that "the clinical composite . . . is about 24% lower than the other seven values would indicate in the absence of interaction." The method is to compare the difference between clinical and mechanical modes of combining data within modes of collecting data, row by row, and assume for any one row that the percentage difference should be the same as the mean percentage difference for the other three rows. Clearly, there is a great deal of opportunity for the cumulation of errors. The discrepancy is actually only about 15%; but the apparent size of differences in numbers of studies is greatly exaggerated by their having been converted into percentages, and there is no way of evaluating the significance of such differences.

Nevertheless, Sawyer plunges right on to interpret his illusory finding:

[8]I must plead guilty to equally misleading summaries and interpretations of the Blenkner study in my 1958a and 1970a papers [Chapters 2 and 4, above].

"Thus, when combination is mechanical, it is better to have both kinds of data than either alone; but when combination is clinical, having both kinds is little better than having only clinically collected data and not as good as having only mechanically collected data." He seems to be talking about concrete researches, but is actually generalizing on the basis of differences between pairs of figures indirectly derived from comparisons of all kinds of studies. From his own Table 3 (or from the corrected figures), the last assertion just quoted is untrue: when data were combined "clinically" to make predictions, it made little difference whether the investigators surveyed had both kinds of data or mechanical alone, but the worst situation to be in was to have clinical data only. Moreover, he seems to be making it a general conclusion that either method 5 or 7 is approximately equal to method 1 —yet in his own Table 2 (as well as in my reconstruction) there was not a single comparison of 1 with either 5 or 7. He also concludes that method 3 is superior to either 5 or 7; it happens that there were three such comparisons, in all of which he himself judged the methods of equal validity. Moreover, a couple of paragraphs on, he reiterates this misleading claim: "Clinical combination actually [sic] predicts less well with data collected by both modes than with only mechanically collected data."

Likewise, in his fifth conclusion from Table 4, Sawyer made more of the same kinds of logical errors. He took the artificial and unstable composite percentages of his grand summary table, which are based on as few as six comparisons, as a suitable basis for generalizations that seem to refer to concrete researches: "The clinical synthesis . . . surpasses the clinical composite"—i.e., 7 > 5? His table 2 admits that no difference was found, the two times these methods were directly compared. He goes on: "The mechanical composite . . . is better than either, and is not improved by adding to it the clinical prediction." That is, he says that 6 > 5, 6 > 7, and 6 = 8. Methods 6 and 7 were never compared in the literature Sawyer surveyed, yet he repeated his contention: "clinical combination that includes a mechanical prediction is inferior to the mechanical composite alone." There is a shred of evidence to back up one conclusion, however, for in one study 6 was found superior to 5 (though in two others they were equivalent). Notice that here (as in several other places and with respect to clinical synthesis) when Sawyer discusses mechanical synthesis he assumes that it rests on both kinds of data—that methods 6 and 8 differ only in that the latter adds the clinical prediction. In point of fact, however, it is not so defined, and in only one of the two comparisons between 6 and 8 does his description apply (no difference was found in either study).

In order to reach such a conclusion, about what the results would be if methods were directly compared, by recourse to the manipulation of figures in his Table 4, he has to assume that each method has been compared to a random sample of all others. Tallying the actual comparisons he has to work with, however, quickly shows a highly nonrandom state of affairs. Consider methods 5 and 6 (clinical and mechanical combination), for example; 5 was compared 12 times with 4, 6 only three times; but 6 was compared four times with method *1* and *5* never was. In fact, in the studies surveyed, method *1* was *never* pitted against another clinical predictive system (*3, 5,* or *7*), whereas method *2* was compared with each of the other types of mechanical combination (*4, 6,* and *8*). Indeed, Sawyer calls attention to the fact that many types of comparison have been slighted for certain other favorite designs, but it did not occur to him that this situation invalidated many of his detailed conclusions. Moreover, he must assume that errors in the various studies are random and thus cancel one another out, whereas there are in fact many systematic and cumulative errors.

He must assume, also, that the percentages in Table 4 are based on roughly equal numbers of experiments equivalent in evidential value. Actually (as we shall shortly see), the researches differ greatly in their worth as evidence, also in sample size, size of effects, significance of results, and in the probable stability versus shrinkage of findings, all of which are excellent reasons not to treat them as equally useful. Sawyer ignores most of these issues, in particular not attempting to assess the utility of the evidence provided by most studies. Even when he makes a gesture in this direction he goes ahead and tallies up the findings anyway (with the sole exception of Sydiaha's). And the numbers of available comparisons range from 6 for method *7,* 12 and 15 for methods *3* and *6,* to 28 and 42 for methods *5* and *4.* It is obvious that percentages based on such small numbers are highly unstable—a fact vividly exemplified by the contrast between his summary figures and mine, based on the same studies and using the same criteria.

A preliminary conclusion, thus far, must be that Sawyer applied his own framework in a careless and at times arbitrary fashion. A more serious indictment is the fact that his method of marshaling the evidence implied and required *either* uniformity of studies in their value and cogency as evidence *or* a method of weighting them, neither of which was true.

Failure to Include Important Literature on the Topic

But far and away the most important assumptive failure remains to be mentioned, one that makes all the criticism so far dwindle in importance to minor cavils. When anyone surveys and collects together the evidence on a topic and attempts to reach conclusions that go beyond the specific studies discussed, he must obey the logic of survey research, the fundamental principle of which is *unbiased sampling.* A survey of empirical evidence is ideally complete within the area delimited by the subject matter as explicitly defined. If the area is too vast, a random sample is an acceptable substitute; a biased sample is never scientifically acceptable (useful though it is as a means of intellectual combat). As I put it earlier:

> Sawyer does delimit his area adequately, even if he does not stick rigidly to his boundaries, but he fails to cover the ground he has staked out. In drawing his conclusions, Sawyer makes a great point of "the remarkable

consistency of these studies: *not one single conclusion directly opposes another*—that is, there is no pair of methods for which one study found one method better while a second study found the other method better" [p. 191]. [Actually, even within his collection, the unanimity vanishes when the corrections listed so far are made.] This unanimity depends for its impressiveness entirely, however, on the unbiased comprehensiveness of the collection of studies (Holt, 1970a, p. 343).

In an approximately contemporaneous paper to Sawyer's, Meehl made a very similar point:

> Monitoring of the literature yields a current bibliography of some fifty empirical investigations in which the efficiency of a human judge in combining information is compared with that of a formalized ("mechanical," "statistical") procedure. . . . The current "box score" shows a significantly superior predictive efficiency for the statistical method in about two-thirds of the investigations, and substantially equal efficiency in the rest. . . . It would be difficult to mention any other domain of psychological controversy in which such uniformity of research outcome as this would be evident in the literature. Since Professor Lindzey's (1965) paper is the first and only empirical comparison of the relative efficiency of the two methods showing clear superiority for the clinical judge, it is deserving of special attention (Meehl, 1965, p. 27).

In discussions with colleagues, when I have brought up some of my objections to the majority of the studies covered by Sawyer, Meehl (1954), Gough (1962), and others of their persuasion, on the grounds of their evidential inadequacies and irrelevancy to clinical psychology, the rejoinder has usually been to brush aside these objections because of the 'overwhelming weight of the evidence,' unsatisfactory though it might be. For some time, I was unable to counter with an impressive list of positive, proclinical data. True, Gough did mention two studies (Coyle, 1956; Trankell, 1959; as we shall see below, Gough's characterization of Trankell's findings is not quite accurate) demonstrating that clinicians can add valid variance to predictions made by a regression equation, which were silently ignored by Sawyer.[9] I

[9] In a rejoinder to my 1970a paper submitted to the *American Psychologist* (and unfortunately rejected), the text of which he has kindly made available to me, Sawyer notes that "Trankell's [1959] study in fact included no regression equation or other mechanical combination with which to compare clinical judgment, and was excluded for this reason. [But see below, pp. 95–96.] . . . I should have included Coyle's dissertation; the abstract . . . noted that adding counselor ratings to objective data increased the multiple correlation with college success from .415 to .525." In the same unpublished paper, he indicates that he chose not to include the Holt-Luborsky studies because they "say little that is definitive about the comparative validity of clinical and statistical methods." In particular, he criticizes us for not providing clear-cut comparisons between actuarial and clinical predictions on exactly the same samples. The point is valid; yet what remains striking is the contrast in his standards here and when applied to far less relevant studies, from which incidental findings that happen to favor nonclinical methods are included despite methodological deficiencies that make them far less useful evidence than our Topeka exercises.

have always felt a bit hesitant in advancing my own data, because the three attempts Luborsky and I made to develop actuarial predictions of the overall competence of psychiatric residents were not specifically designed as clinical-statistical horse races (partly because they were carried out before we read Meehl) and because they have certain other inadequacies as evidence. Nevertheless, they were a good deal better evidence than many of the studies included by Sawyer and were certainly known to him, and to Meehl (by 1965).

The most dramatic indication that Sawyer had not met the assumption of unbiased comprehensiveness of his survey, however, was the publication only two years later of Korman's (1968) review of research on the prediction of performance of business managers. He covered as many studies as Sawyer,[10] including only ten published too late to have been found by Sawyer, who ignored this entire literature.

I cannot undertake here to evaluate the research on executive assessment centers and similar work surveyed by Korman, nor does it seem necessary to establish the point. Judging by the eight studies I was able to locate without major effort, the average quality of the work Korman reviewed was at least as good as that reviewed by Sawyer. The issue, however, is that Sawyer wrote as if he had covered the relevant literature, and it is now evident that he failed to do so and should have made no claim of comprehensiveness.

This fact alone is enough to invalidate much of his review paper and its conclusions. Nevertheless, I shall continue with the task of critique—not because of the paper's intrinsic importance, nor even because I seriously

---

[10]In his rejoinder (see footnote 9), Sawyer says: "In reality, Korman had 28 studies and I had 45." It is true that Korman's tables cite only 28 studies, but in the text Korman discusses data from ten more. That is a total of only 38, which is five fewer than Sawyer's 43—not 45, since he (correctly) drew no conclusions from Sydiaha's (1959) irrelevant research and since he counts Lindzey (1965) twice because the latter reported similar studies on two different samples. But by this last token, Sawyer overlooks the fact that the majority of the sources cited by Korman gave separate findings from more than one sample; indeed, the total number of samples in the studies that Korman surveyed was 123! Sawyer's unpublished rejoinder goes on to claim that "only 9 of his included both 'judgmental' and 'psychometric' methods in the same study. Of these . . . 3 were published after mine was submitted and 3 others were military reports not widely available. I had in fact considered the remaining three but excluded them because they failed to include mechanical combination. The superior judgmental performance that Holt mentions is based upon comparing the set of studies that use judgmental methods with the set of studies (some the same, most of them different) that use psychometric methods." Comparisons that confound different samples with different methods are, of course, suspect, but they are not devoid of evidential significance. Moreover, by my count, 15 of Korman's references, not 9, contained comparisons of the kind Sawyer was looking for, and the number of separate samples was 34. Three of them were published in 1965, two in 1964. As to his point about the failure to include mechanical combination, it should be noted that Sawyer did include researches in his survey in which the "mechanical" predictions were based on single scores—when the latter were superior to "clinical" predictions.

believe that I can undo the damage done by widely disseminated and quoted reviews of which it is only one and perhaps not the most influential. It is, however, useful as a take-off point for an attempt to learn how to do a very important job: critically surveying, collating, and drawing conclusions from a body of psychological research on a particular topic. There is all too little published discussion of how to do this task, the urgency of which to all psychologists is only beginning to be appreciated. We are at the edge of an advancing tidal wave of psychological literature, already so vast that only those who are working on highly circumscribed or novel topics can hope to read all the primary reports of relevant research. So far, the response of psychologists to this crisis has been primarily to turn to the computer experts (on information storage and retrieval) for answers. Yet even the best computer systems available can do no more than provide bibliographies, the comprehensiveness of which depends on authors' (or abstractors') including certain key words. Read through the titles in Sawyer's bibliography, and you will quickly see that a minority of them include any machine-recognizable fragment or transform of "clinical vs. statistical measurement and prediction." Even putting together an unevaluated bibliography requires a great deal of human ingenuity and judgment, but that is the merest beginning of the task. Much of what appears relevant from title or abstract turns out not to be, and a central part of the job is applying standards of good research design and execution. As I shall argue at more length below, an even more neglected but vital final component is applying good standards for drawing conclusions and implications from research data.

Perhaps it is well for me to emphasize the fact that I have learned a good deal from writing the present critique, and that I do not consider all of the points that follow self-evident, or matters that any well-trained psychologist should have known about. I think it quite likely that if I had been doing the job Sawyer undertook over a decade ago, I would have fallen into many of the same errors. My wish is not to hold him up to a scorn I do not feel, but to help us all get on with the immensely difficult task of evaluating psychological research.

THE EVIDENTIAL VALUE OF SAWYER'S COLLECTION OF DATA

I shall continue, therefore, beginning to go beyond Sawyer's own ground rules by taking up the important question of how one assesses the quality of evidence. It is necessary to continue to accept provisionally his definition of the problem as comparing clinical and statistical measurement and prediction.

Most of the evidential weaknesses and other kinds of critique focused on specific studies are summarized in Table 5.2. Let us consider, first, six issues of basic inadequacy as scientific evidence.

Table 5.2.   Ways in Which Studies Cited by Sawyer Are Inadequate as Evidence

1. Barron (1953b): partial criterion contamination; insufficient power (N = 33); inadequate sample of judges (N = 8); data base unrepresentative (MMPI only); different treatment of judges and tests[a]

2. Blenkner (1954): criterion contamination (Sawyer reports invalid result when valid, cross-validated result is available); inadequate sample of judges (N = 2); predictive systems of unequal sophistication; different treatment of judges and tests[b]

3. Bloom & Brundage (1947): criterion contamination (lack of cross-validation; but N = 1000 or more); inadequate sample of judges (N = 1)[c]; judges not clinicians[d]; remote, negligible relevance to clinical practice; data base unrepresentative[e]; different treatment of judges and tests[b]

4. Bobbitt & Newman (1944): criterion contamination (fact that weights were based on sample used for validation was not reported by Sawyer); inadequate sample of judges (N = 2)[c]; remote, negligible relevance to clinical practice; data base unrepresentative[e]; predictive systems of unequal sophistication; different treatment of judges and tests[b]

5. Borden (1928): criterion contamination (lack of cross-validation noted by Sawyer); inadequate sample of judges (N = 1); missing data; partial, arguable relevance to clinical practice

6. Burgess, E. W. (1941): criterion contamination (lack of cross-validation; but N = 1000 or more); inadequate sample of judges (N = 2); partial, arguable relevance to clinical practice; different treatment of judges and tests[a]

7. Burgess, E. W., & Wallin (1953): criterion contamination (lack of cross-validation noted by Sawyer); inadequate sample of judges (N = ?); judges not clinicians (graduate students); partial, arguable relevance to clinical practice; different treatment of judges and tests[b]

8. Chauncey (1954): inadequate sample of judges (N = 3); judges not clinicians (student personnel administrators); remote, negligible relevance to clinical practice; systems apparently of unequal predictive sophistication; different treatment of judges and tests[b]

9. Cliff (1958): criterion contamination (lack of cross-validation noted by Sawyer); inadequate sample of judges (N = 1); judges not clinicians (naval officers); remote, negligible relevance to clinical practice; different treatment of judges and tests[b]

10. Conrad & Satter (1945): criterion contamination (lack of cross-validation noted by Sawyer; but N = 1000 or more); inadequate sample of judges (N = 1)[c]; judge not a clinician (an "interviewer," level of training not given in original); remote, negligible relevance to clinical practice; different treatment of judges and tests[b]

11. Doleys & Renzaglia (1963): criterion contamination (lack of cross-validation noted by Sawyer); judges not clinicians (college freshman Ss); remote, negligible relevance to clinical practice; different treatment of judges and tests[b]

12. Dunham & Meltzer (1946): different criterion for each prediction; inadequate sample of judges (N = 1?)[c]; missing data; predictive systems of unequal sophistication; different treatment of judges and tests[b]

13. Dunlap & Wantman (1944): criterion contamination (lack of cross-validation noted by Sawyer); inadequate criteria; insufficient power (N = 26–69—total 208); inadequate sample of judges (N = 3); judges not clinicians (three-man teams: psychologist plus two military men); remote, negligible relevance to clinical practice; data base unrepresentative[e]; different treatment of judges and tests[a]

14. Glaser (1954): criterion contamination (unit weights, which may have been based on the same sample used for validation); inadequate sample of judges (N = 2); one judge not a clinician (sociologist and psychiatrist); partial, arguable relevance to clinical practice; predictive systems of unequal sophistication[f]; different treatment of judges and tests[a]

15. Glaser & Hangren (1958): criterion contamination (unit weights, which may have been based on the same sample used for validation); inadequate sample of judges (N = 1); judge

Table 5.2.   *(continued)*

not a clinician (probation officer); partial, arguable relevance to clinical practice; predictive systems of unequal sophistication[f]

16. Grebstein (1963): insufficient power ($N = 30$); inadequate sample of judges (three groups of five judges each; Sawyer properly reports only data from the five who were experienced clinical psychologists); data base unrepresentative (Rorschach scores only); predictive systems of unequal sophistication; different treatment of judges and tests[a]

17. Gregory (1956): criterion contamination (lack of cross-validation noted by Sawyer); inadequate sample of judges ($N = 2$); judges not clinicians[d]; remote, negligible relevance to clinical practice; different treatment of judges and tests[b]

18. Halbower (1955): insufficient power ($N = 8$); inadequate sample of judges ($N = 2$—5); data base unrepresentative (MMPI and four biographic items); predictive systems of unequal sophistication; different treatment of judges and tests[a]

19. Hamlin (1934): criterion contamination (fact that weights were based on sample used for validation not reported by Sawyer); inadequate sample of judges ($N = 1$); partial, arguable relevance to clinical practice; different treatment of judges and tests[b]

20. Harris (1963): inadequate criterion; inadequate sample of judges ($N = 2$); judges not clinicians (sports writers); no relevance whatever to clinical practice

21. Hovey & Stauffacher (1953): insufficient power ($N = 47$); inadequate sample of judges ($N = 1$); data base unrepresentative (MMPI only; judges spent less than 3 minutes per S to make ratings on 14 traits); different treatment of judges and tests[b]

22. Husén (1954): criterion contamination (not reported by Sawyer); inadequate criteria (superior's rating; may be at least partly a prediction); inadequate sample of judges ($N = 1$ per S, but many judges must have been used); judges not clinicians[d]; remote, negligible relevance to clinical practice; different treatment of judges and tests[b]

23. Kelly & Fiske (1950); criterion contamination (not reported by Sawyer); insufficient power ($N = 53$–93); partial, arguable relevance to clinical practice; different treatment of judges and tests

24. Lepley & Hadley (1947): inadequate sample of judges ($N = 2$); judges not clinicians (aviation psychologist and flight surgeon); remote, negligible relevance to clinical practice; data base unrepresentative[e]; predictive systems of unequal sophistication; different treatment of judges and tests[b]

25. Lewis & MacKinney (1961); criterion contamination (lack of cross-validation noted by Sawyer); inadequate sample of judges ($N = 6$); judges not clinicians ("counselors"); partial, arguable relevance to clinical practice; data base unrepresentative (test scores, grades, seven biographic items); different treatment of judges and tests[b]

26. Lindzey (1965): criterion contamination (not reported by Sawyer); insufficient power ($N = 40$); inadequate sample of judges ($N = 1$)

27. Lindzey (1965): criterion contamination (lack of cross-validation noted by Sawyer); insufficient power ($N = 30$); inadequate sample of judges ($N = 2$); different treatment of judges and tests[a]

28. Meehl (1959): judges not all clinicians (15/21 "psychologists" were graduate students); data base unrepresentative (MMPI only); different treatment of judges and tests[b]

29. Melton (1952): insufficient power ($N = 35$); inadequate sample of judges ($N = 1$); judges not clinicians (psychology graduate students); remote, negligible relevance to clinical practice; predictive systems of unequal sophistication; different treatment of judges and tests[a]

30. Oskamp (1962): data base unrepresentative (MMPI only); predictive systems of unequal sophistication[f]; different treatment of judges and tests[b]

31. Parrish, Klieger, & Drucker (1954): inadequate sample of judges ($N = 1$+); judges not clinicians (Army NCO and Officers); remote, negligible relevance to clinical practice;

(continued)

Table 5.2.   (*continued*)

predictive systems of unequal sophistication[f]; different treatment of judges and tests[b]

32. Pierson (1958): criterion contamination (only partly reported by Sawyer); sample of judges perhaps inadequate; judges not clinicians (high school teachers); remote, negligible relevance to clinical practice; predictive systems of unequal sophistication[f]; different treatment of judges and tests[b]

33. Polansky (1941): insufficient power (N = 3); some judges not clinicians; predictive systems of unequal sophistication; different treatment of judges and tests[b]

34. Rosen & Van Horn (1961): inadequate sample of judges (N = 1[committee]); missing data; judges not clinicians (scholarship award committee); remote, negligible relevance to clinical practice; predictive systems of unequal sophistication

35. Sarbin (1943): criterion contamination (partial lack of cross-validation noted by Sawyer); inadequate sample of judges (N = 5); remote, negligible relevance to clinical practice; predictive systems of unequal sophistication; different treatment of judges and tests[b]

36. Schiedt (1936): inadequate sample of judges (N = 1); missing data; judge doubtfully a clinician (prison physician); partial, arguable relevance to clinical practice; predictive systems of unequal sophistication

37. Schneider, Lagrone, Glueck, & Glueck (1944): inadequate sample of judges (N = 1); missing data; partial, arguable relevance to clinical practice; predictive systems of unequal sophistication

38. Sydiaha (1959): criterion contamination (alleged by Sawyer, but see text); inadequate criteria; inadequate sample of judges (N = 1); judge not a clinician (personnel officer); remote, negligible relevance to clinical work

39. Trankell (1956): criterion contamination (lack of cross-validation noted by Sawyer); inadequate sample of judges (N = 3); partial, arguable relevance to clinical practice; different treatment of judges and tests[b]

40. Truesdell & Bath (1956): criterion contamination (lack of cross-validation noted by Sawyer); inadequate sample of judges (N = 9); judges not clinicians ("counselors"); remote, negligible relevance to clinical practice; data base unrepresentative (test scores, grades); different treatment of judges and tests[g]

41. Watley & Vance (1964): possible criterion contamination; remote, negligible relevance to clinical practice; data base unrepresentative (grades, test scores, biographic items); different treatment of judges and tests[f]

42. Westoff, Sagi, & Kelly (1958): criterion contamination (lack of cross-validation noted by Sawyer); judges not clinicians (Ss themselves); no relevance whatever to clinical practice

43. Wirt (1956): inadequate sample of judges (N = 8); data base unrepresentative (MMPI only); predictive systems of unequal sophistication

44. Wittman (1941): sample of judges perhaps inadequate; different treatment of judges and tests [g]

45. Wittman & Steinberg (1944): sample of judges perhaps inadequate; different treatment of judges and tests [b]

[a]Data on performances of individual judges available but suppressed by Sawyer.
[b]Data on performances of individual judges not in original source (when I could check it).
[c]Clinical prediction was made for each S by one judge, but there were so many Ss that many judges must have been used.
[d]Judge was an "interviewer," not clear whether level of training and experience were given in original report (not checked by me).
[e]The only qualitative data (i.e., only data other than test scores plus a few objective biographical items) were interviews of 5 to 30 minutes.
[f]Point seems to be applicable, but I did not study original source.
[g]Data on individual judges' performances are available; Sawyer suppresses them, or includes but averages them in drawing conclusions.

Criterion Contamination

At least 22 of the 45 studies are affected by some degree of criterion contamination, in 11 instances to such an extent that at least one of the conclusions listed by Sawyer is invalidated.[11] Sawyer showed a curious ambivalence about this issue, most clearly indicated perhaps in the instance of Sydiaha (1959). He presented the study in his Table 2 in the same way as all the others, but added the following footnote: "The same officer who interviewed a man and made [predictive] Q sorts also determined whether he was accepted [the criterion]; because of this contamination, no decision is assigned." It is difficult to understand why the study was included at all. Its presence serves only to give some readers a misleading impression that the author was thorough in searching out even remotely relevant studies and scrupulous in evaluating them, plus the unjustified impression of Sydiaha's incompetence as a researcher. Actually, Sydiaha's intention was not to compare clinical and statistical predictions, using acceptance-rejection as a criterion, but to compare two models of assessment in an effort to find out what the acceptance-rejection judgment was based on. The results clearly show that this judgment was much more a function of the kinds of personal traits measured in a Q-sort based on an interview than it was of the quantitative biographical and test data available to the judges. It was only by twisting Sydiaha's data to a use for which he did not intend them[12] and for which they are obviously unsuited that Sawyer managed to include—and then exclude—this study.

If he had been as concerned as he seemed in this instance to refrain from reaching conclusions when the predictor is affected by knowledge of the criterion or vice versa, Sawyer should have withheld judgment about most of the comparisons in which, as he admits in a footnote, the mechanical combination by means of (usually multiple) regression equations was not cross-validated. Indeed, he comments disapprovingly: "Multiple regression, more often than not in these studies, employed weights derived from the same sample on which the validity was assessed; consequently, it overestimated the replicable relation—to an extent varying directly with the number of variables and inversely with the number of subjects" (p. 190)—and, he should have added, varying directly with the size of the pool of variables from which those in the actual regression equation were drawn. Yet he not only included and tabulated them, he made no effort to adjust his evaluative standards to the inevitable inflation of apparent validity. Consequently, in

---

[11]Elsewhere (Holt, 1970a), I gave the figures as 15 instead of 22 and 13 instead of 11. The changes result from further opportunity to study the evidence.

[12]"It should be understood that the validity of the decision making models developed in this study was not investigated . . . a followup is being planned in which the clinical and statistical scores will be correlated with criterion measures . . ." (Sydiaha, 1959, p. 400).

seven of the comparisons he tallied, the indication that mechanical prediction is superior is spurious, and four others indicate an equivalence of
mechanical and clinical predictions that is questionable. When a "clinical
prediction," typically not the product of a sophisticated predictive system, is
compared with a non-cross-validated R, the only outcome that is not moot is
the unlikely one that the former is decisively larger.

Moreover, in at least six instances, he failed to report that a "mechanical"
prediction was of this contaminated type. In the case of the Blenkner study,
he cited a contaminated validity (without so labeling it) even though the
original paper gives an only slightly shrunken cross-validation figure. Of the
main prediction in the Hamlin (1934) paper, Meehl says explicitly: "this
score . . . was not cross-validated." A subtler instance of criterion contamination occurs in Sawyer's treatment of the Kelly-Fiske (1950) data, which is
logically equivalent to presenting an R without cross-validation. For each of
12 criteria he compares the median correlation of many clinical ratings,
made without benefit of any previous study of the relation between the data
the clinicians had to the criteria being predicted, to the median of the *best* 12
correlations of 101 test scores with the criterion. Thus, after knowledge of
the results, the test scores that happened to be most highly correlated with
the criteria were selected, which is in effect giving them unit weights and all
other scores zero weights, while clinical ratings are all weighted alike.

Strictly construed, the criterion-contamination objection holds for part
but not all of the actuarial predictions of a couple of studies, for example that
of method *8* (mechanical synthesis) in Pierson (1958), not so noted by
Sawyer. The issue of criterion contamination is not very important, however,
in an attempt like Pierson's to see if adding a clinical prediction to a superior
nonclinical predictor can increase the latter's validity. If, as Pierson found,
the best that can be done by multiple regression is to add .02 to the statistical
validity correlation, it seems wholly implausible that cross-validating on a
new sample would make a real difference grow where there was none
before. In none of the studies surveyed was method *8*'s validity cross-
validated; when he claimed superiority for *8*, Sawyer did note this fact in
every instance except that of Pierson, and when he concluded a failure to
achieve a significant raising of the validity, only once—in his summary of
Sarbin (1943)—did Sawyer note that it was not cross-validated.

Another piece of research in which Sawyer failed to note the contaminated status of one actuarial prediction is that of Lindzey (1965). From
previous statistical studies of the association of certain TAT signs with overt
homosexuality, Lindzey tried out a list of 20 such predictors on a sample of
40 male undergraduates, half of them homosexual. Most of the signs held
up, ten of them significantly discriminating the homosexuals from the
heterosexuals; but three signs tended to discriminate in the opposite direction from the one indicated. Unfortunately for his own point, Lindzey did
not cumulate the data with those signs pulling against cross-validation suc-

cess, though that would have given the appropriate vaidity against which to compare the dazzling 95% success of his clinical prediction.[13] Instead, he used afterknowledge of the criterion to make the best linear combination of his 20 items, explicitly stating that "This involved reversing two variables"; even this overfitted result could achieve only an 85% success. Doubtless that seemed sufficient to make his point, that a skilled clinician who *had* had the opportunity to study the TAT's of known homosexuals and heterosexuals in other samples could extract more valid information on this distinction in a cross-validation than the best formula, uncontaminated or not. Lindzey also tried to improve on the actuarial prediction by means of a configural scoring system, which gave exactly the same validity; Sawyer does report that *this* prediction is criterion-contaminated.

Inadequate Criteria (3 Studies, 10 Conclusions)

In Harris (1963), the criterion—the winning team in a set of football games—was unreliable. In two studies, the criterion ratings were made so soon after the predictions they were to validate that they are hardly more than predictions themselves. The criterion rating of "post-training pilot *potential*" in Dunlap and Wantman (1944) is in fact stated as a prediction. As I put it earlier, the other was

> the celebrated attempt to predict performance in clinical psychology (Kelly & Fiske, 1951). Famous and expert clinicians assessed Veterans Administration trainees, attempting to predict their future performance as clinical psychologists; a preliminary set of "validities" was published in the *American Psychologist* (Kelly & Fiske, 1950) using as criteria ratings by professors and Veterans Administration supervisors after the subjects had had no more than a couple of years of graduate work! Even the final report only a year later relied on similar ratings made while the subjects were still in graduate school (Holt, 1970a, pp. 341–342).[14]

I neglected to make it clear that Sawyer used only data from the *earlier* of these two publications. The reason, I suspect, is that the data presented in

---

[13]At the time when Goldberg's (1968a) critique of his paper was submitted to the *Journal of the Experimental Study of Personality*, Lindzey was offered an opportunity to rebut, and kindly persuaded the editor to pass it on to me. I then wrote Lindzey, pointing out this deficiency in his reporting and asking him if he could extract from the original data the numbers of hits and misses for the total list of 20 signs, without any reversals. Unfortunately, he did not have access to the data. Unlike Sawyer, Goldberg does point out the fact that the actuarial validity in Lindzey's first study is un-cross-validated and therefore spuriously high, but he does so only in an inconspicuous note to his table, and writes in his text as if this were not the case. Actually, as many as nine of the 36 hits for the formula may have been affected, in which case the difference would be one of 25%, $p < .01$.

[14][In the interest of cutting down duplication, I omitted the above passage when making the paper into Chapter 4; the same is true of other quoted passages from my 1970a paper.]

the final report look less damning to clinical predictions. It is also noteworthy that Sawyer made no mention whatever of the only report from this same research that gives correlations with posttraining criteria: Kelly and Goldberg (1959). This sobering monograph shows that *not one of the many predictors,* whatever their degree of approximation to either the clinical or the mechanical ideal of measurement or prediction (i.e., combination of data), *had any replicated validity.* One likely hypothesis for this failure is the fact that one of the two samples of Ss was assessed after they knew they had been accepted for graduate training, and the other was more or less successfully given the impression that the assessments, which took place prior to acceptance, would affect the Ss' chances of being admitted. The consistent failure of the Strong Vocational Interest Blank's scores to have usable validity in actual selection use stems from the same weakness: Ss present themselves for assessment with markedly greater caution, attempting to "fake good" in various ways, when they believe that some important outcome is at stake than when they are not so threatened (as in the testing on which scoring keys are based). It is possible that this criticism might be made of other validities cited by Sawyer, since the point is often neglected by psychometric researchers.

As I pointed out above (footnote 2), I have not made an independent evaluation of all the studies listed by Sawyer. Please note, therefore, that all of the figures cited here on evidential inadequacies are *conservative.* (Elsewhere I report a total of five instances of inadequate criteria, but it now seems more appropriate to characterize what Sawyer calls the criterion in the study of Sydiaha, 1959, as contaminated, and to treat the nonbehavioral criterion of Westoff, Sagi, & Kelly 1958, as clinically irrelevant.)

Insufficient Power (8 Studies, 13 Conclusions)

In one instance where Sawyer concluded "*4 > 3,*" Halbower (1955; consistently called "Hallblower" by Sawyer) used only eight Ss, obviously a flimsy basis on which to generalize. The finding, celebrated in Meehl's (1956b) "Wanted—a good cookbook," is a difference between two mean Q correlations, each relating a predictive Q-sort of 154 items to a criterion sort (averaged across from two to five predictive judges and across the eight patients). One of the vexing properties of Q-technique is the logical difficulty of applying the usual significance tests to differences in Q correlations, for the latter are extremely sensitive to the nature and number of items. Moreover, mean Q correlations may be unstable regardless of the number of items if small numbers of judges and subjects are used, as was the case in the (still unpublished) Halbower dissertation. Sawyer was, accordingly, running a considerable risk of a Type I error in concluding that Halbower had found a significant difference.

Where obtained differences of moderate size go in the clinical direction, however, Sawyer becomes quite conservative. In interpreting the researches of Grebstein (1963), Hovey and Stauffacher (1953), and Lindzey (1965), in each of which there was a substantial difference favoring clinical combination of data which failed to be very significant because of small N (from 30 to 47), Sawyer concluded every time that no difference had been found. (See discussion below of the problem of correlated predictors.)

There is an intrinsic dilemma of power in clinical research. When the issue concerns the predictive performance of which clinicians are capable, it cannot be meaningfully tested unless good clinicians, working with good data, have enough time to consider the data carefully. To satisfy such requirements implies that the research will be slow and expensive, properties that militate against large numbers of Ss. With small N's, however, statistical power is slight and one is likely to get results that do not quite make it to the conventional .05 level. The larger and more statistically adequate the sample, the more necessarily superficial must be the assessment of each case; or else Ss must be accumulated over a long time in an unusual work setting that provides the necessary controls and financial support.

Trankell (1956, 1959) seems to have found such a setting in selecting pilots for the Scandinavian Airline Service. In six years of work, he managed to accumulate a total of 363 Ss (out of 780 applicants, all of whom already knew how to fly); 29 of them were dismissed during or subsequent to training "due to inability to fly in SAS." This uncontaminated criterion was predicted with the astonishing validity (for such a large N) of .75 by a clinical combination of what Sawyer would call both clinical and mechanical data. Scores from five objective tests administered to these Ss had validities ranging from $-.07$ to .42. Two points are noteworthy about the 1959 report: the omission of multiple regression as a way of combining the test data cannot be attributable to ignorance or oversight, since in an earlier report with a smaller N, Trankell (1956) did report using multiple correlations as a way of combining judgmental ratings. Even if we make the unlikely assumption that the tests have zero intercorrelations, the *maximum* R obtainable from the zero-order r's reported by Trankell (1959) is less than .64; and a cross-validation on the available 172 Ss would necessarily have been lower than that (thus, much lower than the clinical validity). Second, Sawyer does not cite the later study, using only the earlier report (which was published in Swedish in a far less accessible source) with a smaller N and an inflated (criterion-contaminated) validity estimate for the statistical prediction; and he called the two methods equivalent.

Trankell (1959) makes an incidental comment concerning his criterion which is worth pondering. During the first years when he was selecting pilots and co-pilots for SAS, the psychologist's final recommendations were not always followed; thus, a few Ss were accepted with low scores on the clinical prediction. But then as the excellence of the psychologist's recommendations began to become evident, fewer men were accepted against his advice, and thus the range on the predictor was greatly restricted. This natural consequence of success means that it becomes difficult to add to the original statistics. Indeed, failures must necessarily begin to occur for reasons *other* than those implicit in the clinical assessments, and the correlation with the prediction must necessarily (but misleadingly) fall. This fact alone is enough to account for the decline in validity from .88 (in 1956) to .75 (in 1959). If it were possible to get comparable criterion information on rejected Ss, of course, this problem would not occur; but in the real world of commercially applied psychology, such data are hardly ever available.

Because of all these difficulties in the way of getting good clinical validities on large samples, there is an a priori likelihood that when clinical prediction is good, samples are likely to be too small to attain conventional levels of significance. If a survey uncovers several such studies, but rejects their evidence by the mechanical application of a decision rule that would be appropriate for a single study, the chances of Type II error multiply. In his survey, Sawyer includes 8 N's under 100. Only once (Barron, 1953b) was the trend in a direction favoring statistical combination ($4 > 3$), while in four studies the trends favored clinical prediction (Lindzey, 1965, $1 > 2$, $1 > 2$; Grebstein, 1963, $3 > 4$; Hovey and Stauffacher, 1953, $3 > 4$); the remainder of the conclusions of no difference involved comparisons among types of statistical or among types of clinical predictions, respectively.

Inadequate Sample of Judges (39 Studies, 63 Conclusions)

Despite the fact that Brunswik's (1956) celebrated monograph is given lip service by many psychologists, one of his basic points—that it is just as important to sample objects adequately as to sample subjects—seems almost entirely ignored. In our context, the "objects" include the persons making predictions. Only very exceptionally (a study of the performance of an outstanding expert is the only one that comes to mind) are we content to learn how well a single judge, or a small group of judges, did the task of clinical prediction; surely, to Sawyer they are of interest only as representatives of the larger population of clinicians. But if we take representative design seriously, it is necessary both to have a decent *method* of sampling judges and a large enough *number* of judges to meet minimal standards. It is safe to say that the literature surveyed by Sawyer pays no attention to the necessity of random or otherwise representative sampling of judges (and only exceptionally, of Ss either). In 16 studies, conclusions are drawn on the basis of "clinical predictions" by single individuals, and in only five studies were there from 12 to a maximum of 42 judges. There was also a sixth (Doleys & Renzaglia, 1963) in which the 183 college freshmen served both as Ss and as "clinicians." If we make the charitable assumptions that the (usually unspecified) sampling methods and the skimpy sample sizes of these six studies are adequate, we are still left with serious inadequacies in the overwhelming majority of the studies and extremely shaky bases for virtually all of Sawyer's conclusions.

Inadequacy of Reporting of Primary Data (1 Study, 1 Conclusion)

Although quite a few of the reports cited by Sawyer have minor deficiencies and omissions in reporting, this point applies primarily to the study attributed to Chauncey. From Sawyer's bibliography, we find that the prime publication of this study is a single paragraph in Meehl (1954, p. 112f.), described as based on personal correspondence. The account is altogether too brief and summary to be independently evaluated; for example, we are told nothing about the clinical training of the persons who allegedly made clinical predictions about the future grades of entering Harvard freshmen, and nothing about the critical issue of whether or not they had opportunities to study the types of data used to evaluate scholastic promise on cases with known outcome before attempting to make predictions. As was indicated above, the validities are not given except in a crude way ("All four of the resulting validity correlations were in the .60's, the statistical validity ranking second"), and one must take it on faith that an appropriate statistical test was used to reach the conclusion that the differences found were not significant. We know nothing about the meaningfulness of this difference in terms of predictive efficiency, and there is no way of telling whether the statistical test took into account the correlation between predictors (see below)—a frequent omission in this field of research, and one not discussed by Meehl in his critique of other studies where it did in fact apply.

It could be argued, in Meehl's defense, that his pioneering survey of the evidence found few relevant studies altogether, so that he should be forgiven for including *all* research that bore on the issue of clinical versus statistical prediction even though it had not been published. Why, then, did Meehl *not* include the following?

> When Meehl was first bringing together the results for his book, I wrote him of a case in which "clinical" prediction (in his sense) was better than statistical prediction: at Wesleyan the then Director of Admissions used to predict grade point average for everyone admitted and his correlations ran around .80 with actual grades because he knew the schools the boys came from and the Wesleyan situation very well. The best actuarial multiple correlation came to about .64. Meehl never included this result, nor has anyone ever referred to it . . . (personal communication from D. C. McClelland, 8 July 1968; see also McClelland, 1951, p. 99).

Does this constitute an adequate counterbalance to the Chauncey "findings"? *It is impossible to say, because the lack of adequately reported prime publications makes the two studies' evidential value moot.* Whatever Meehl's reasons for including one acecdote and not the other, Sawyer should have omitted this type of "evidence."

Results Indeterminate Because of Missing Data (5 Studies, 5 Conclusions)

Meehl calls attention to an important deficiency in a number of published studies—the failure to make predictions and/or gather criterion data on a sizable group of cases. In some studies, predictive judges were permitted to omit predictions on cases about which they felt doubts, while mechanical formulas were not usually allowed this luxury: Sawyer takes no note of this problem though Meehl points it out in relation to Borden (1928) and Schiedt (1936). Sawyer handles the issue in relation to E. W. Burgess (1941) by making simplifying assumptions of unknown applicability which allowed him to conclude that a 12% difference in favor of an un-cross-validated actuarial validity justified the concusion, $8 > 5$.

Crucial data are omitted in at least two other studies, in one of which Meehl, who calls attention to the problem, refuses to draw any conclusion though Sawyer is nothing loath. Schneider, Lagrone, Glueck, and Glueck (1944) report results in terms of percentage of success in identifying military offenders. Meehl comments:

> No indication of the false positive rate is given for either method. Since general experience with statistical screening devices in such situations suggests that many are screened who are not considered diagnosable upon closer psychiatric study, it is particularly important to know the false positive rates for the Glueck tables versus the psychiatrist. Since we lack this information, the present study can only be classed as indeterminate . . . (1954, p. 114).

I thoroughly agree. Sawyer concludes that $1 = 6$. Similarly, he includes the paper by Rosen and Van Horn (1961), in which the cross-validation of clinical and statistical methods is given solely in terms of the proportion of the highest 40% on the predictors who received at least B averages. If the authors had reported anything about the numbers or rates of false negatives or true negatives, meaningful hit rates could be computed; but as it is, no valid conclusion can be drawn. Sawyer's Table 2 says $3 = 4$.

Failure to Consider Intercorrelation of Predictors in Evaluating Differences in Validity

The level of statistical sophistication in the literature surveyed by Sawyer is, to be charitable, uneven. One common[15] error is not to take into account

---

[15]In none of the 16 studies I have read was this factor taken into account. It is possible, of course, that some of the others paid appropriate attention to it in testing the significance of differences. Because of this lack of differentiation, the point is not included in Table 5.2.

the correlation between pairs of predictors when comparing their correlations with some criterion, despite the fact that standard texts such as NcNemar's (1949) lay plenty of stress on the need to use different formulas when predictors are independent and when intercorrelated, whether the method involves differences between proportions or differences between correlations. A method like chi square (used by both Lindzey, 1965, and Goldberg, 1968a, in evaluating the former's data) assumes independence of predictors and is clearly not appropriate, systematically underestimating the significance of the difference obtained. In this particular instance, Lindzey does not report his findings in a way that makes it possible to use the standard test for nonindependent proportions (McNemar, 1949, p. 56 ff.), but even if the clinical prediction had been as highly correlated as possible with the criterion-contaminated best actuarial predictions, the p-value for the difference would have been only about .06.

Here is what Sawyer has to say about this problem:

> For both correlations and percentages, significance tests were based upon the assumption of zero correlation between the two methods, since the actual correlation is rarely available. If, however, the corelation between methods within a study is in fact positive, *which seems likely*, the significance of the observed differences is underestimated (p. 191; emphasis added).

It does indeed seem likely that when two sets of predictions of the same criterion are made with respect to the same Ss, on the basis of partly or wholly identical sets of data, the correlation between methods must be positive. Sawyer's procedure thus produces a systematic tendency toward Type II errors and makes suspect all of his conclusions of no difference between pairs of methods except when obtained differences were of negligible size, in an absolute sense. Since the majority of the studies with a trend judged insignificant favor clinical prediction or measurement, Sawyer's apparently conservative stance actually worked to minimize the clinical showing.

Consider, for example, Grebstein (1963), who compared a formula and small groups of judges with varying degrees of clinical training as predictors of IQ from the Rorschach psychogram. The cross-validated validity of the multiple regression formula was .56; that of the most sophisticated group of clinicians and of the best single judge was .68—a very substantial difference when correlations are this high. Grebstein and Sawyer conclude, however, that the methods are equivalent, and Grebstein presents no data on the correlation between the clinical and statistical predictions. He does however include the following passage:

> Individual multiple regression equations derived from each judge showed that the more experienced judges frequently used the same four

variables $(M, Z, F+\%,$ and $RC)^{16}$ as the competitive equation. The multiple regression coefficients associated with all the judges ranged from $+.84$ to $+.98$ ... (Grebstein, 1963, p. 130).

If the correlation between the *general* regression prediction and the experienced judges' predictions were as low as .8, the p-value for their superiority in validities over the formula would be less than .01 (my calculations).

The next group of considerations to be discussed approaches the issue of what constitutes acceptable evidence on the clinical-statistical questions from a different standpoint—that of relevance. If a study compares apples and oranges, it can offer no pertinent evidence on the relative juiciness of peaches and pears, though it may give excellent information about the topic it is concerned with. It is necessary, therefore, in considering the value of research as evidence, to ask what generalizations are to be made; *for relevance must be defined in terms of the inferences we want to draw from a body of evidence.*

As I have argued elsewhere [Chapter 4], the main conclusions that have been drawn from the clinical-statistical surveys have been derogatory to the practice of clinical psychology, particularly to clinical methods of assessing personality and psychopathology. It could hardly be otherwise, because the very denomination of the topic points to clinical psychology: one antagonist is variously known as statistical, or actuarial, or mechanical, but the other is almost invariably called *clinical* measurement and/or prediction. To be sure, a medical man will probably not interpret that last term as a reference to APA's Division 12, but the vast majority of the readers of the *Psychological Bulletin* are undoubtedly psychologists and it would be disingenuous to pretend that a term like "clinical inference" makes most psychologists think about the behavior of a pathologist in a medical lab, or of a stockbroker, or of an admissions officer of a private college. (These examples are three of the four with which Goldberg, 1970, begins a paper on "clinical" inference; the other one, his first, is the behavior of a psychologist in a Suicide Prevention Center.)

Since his title as well as a good deal of his discussion indicates that Sawyer did intend conclusions to be drawn about clinical psychological practice on the basis of his survey, one might expect that he would have been at some pains to demonstrate the relevance of each piece of research. To qualify, the measurements and predictions called "clinical" should have been made by clinicians, using clinical data, and directed toward the kinds of behavior with which practicing clinicians are usually concerned. Most of them, we shall see, were not.

---

[16]RC stands for Range of Content.

Judges Not Clinicians

From seven to 25 of the 45 studies used as judges (called "clinicians" by Sawyer) persons to whom such a label is more or less inappropriately applied. By any reasonable standards, army officers, sportswriters, high school teachers, scholarship committee members, and miscellaneous lay persons serving as subjects cannot be considered clinicians. I am not raising any question about 20 studies in which the judges were all psychologists or psychiatrists, even though in a number of them no evidence was given that all of the psychologists had clinical training. (Moreover, not every clinical psychologist would like his level of competence to be estimated from the predictive abilities of psychiatrists!) That leaves a gray area of 18 studies in which more or less serious questions can be raised about the judges. Three experimenters used students of psychology as predictive judges; one can hardly generalize about the capacities of professionals from studies of those who are still in training. My inclination is to question also the inclusion of four studies in which the alleged clinicians were identified only as "military 'interviewers' (probably enlisted men)," Sawyer remarks, of unspecified training and experience. True, we do not know until we compare clinicians with different levels of training and experience whether these variables count for anything, and five studies did use groups of judges who were mixed in this way, incuding some persons who were clearly not clinicians but at least one professional psychologist or psychiatrist. They may be considered marginal, as may seven pieces of research using professionals who, though not psychologists, may be nearly as allied as psychiatrists are: caseworkers, counselors, a probation officer, personnel officer, and prison physician. In *every* case, however, Sawyer classifies these judges as "clinicians," conceding only that "the level of experience in psychological assessment is by no means uniformly high." (I cannot make my figures for the subgroups match with his, but it is not very important.) It seems likely that this purely residual definition of a clinician (someone who does *not* use a statistical or other mechanical method of predicting) is not deliberately meant to be insulting, but that it probably grows from ignorance about clinical training and methods.

Criteria Irrelevant to Clinical Psychology

Again, relevance is not an all-or-none matter; the criteria being predicted were clearly and directly relevant to clinical practice in only 14 studies (with 14 conclusions), however. In 11, I judge the relevance partial and arguable (six studies of criminal behavior, usually violation of parole; plus adjustment in a reformatory, ratings and exam performance of clinical psychology students, job satisfaction of engineers, a marriage success score in a sociological study, and pilot retention in an airline[17]). In 18 pieces of research, the criterion had remote or slight relevance to clinical work, being a measure of success or failure in some kind of school, mainly military or undergraduate college (in six instances, freshman grades). The two criteria of no relevance whatever have already been mentioned: the winning team in football and the number of children a couple have in 20 years.

Data Base for Predictions Not Representative: Purely Quantitative or Otherwise Inadequate

In six studies the only data available to the predictive judges were MMPI profiles (occasionally with a couple of biographical items), and in four others the data were exclusively quantitative (Rorschach scores; or other test scores, grades, and a few biographical items). In addition, in at least two and possibly five studies (all of which were criterion-irrelevant anyway), the clinical data consisted solely of a brief interview (less than half an hour), and the "clinician" seems to have had little time to evaluate the data carefully. I shall not repeat here my argument (Holt, 1970a) that these studies are not representative of most routine assessment practice—much less, of *good* practice—in which test scores are always supplemented by substantial amount of qualitative, meaningful data. Rather, I would like to advance an argument based on Guilford's Structure of Intellect model.

Summarizing several decades of work from his highly productive laboratory, Guilford (1967) has proposed a three-dimensional model to account for the many independent factors of ability. He has shown that it is possible to generate and test predictions with the model, both predictions about previously undiscovered abilities and what might be called diagnostic predictions about the probable factorial structure of various kinds of tasks and performances. Let us try to see, in terms of this framework, what are the intellectual processes in "combining data to make predictions." The first dimension, *operations*, comprises cognition, memory, convergent production, divergent production, and evaluation—a major aspect of judgment. Predicting is not a matter of the acquisition of information, nor of its storage and retrieval, but it is a kind of problem-solving in which there is one best answer to be attained, so it seems to be mostly convergent production (with, of course, some creative—divergent production—and evaluative aspects). In terms of the second dimension, *products* (which include units, classes, rela-

---

[17]See discussion of Trankell studies. Pilot retention in SAS sounds superficially like pass-fail in basic flight training, a criterion in one other study described in Table 5.2 as only remotely relevant, but it is actually quite different.

Sawyer now agrees with this criticism. In his unpublished response to my 1970a paper, he writes: "Evaluating clinicians on their ability to predict such criteria not of their own choosing or their liking now appears to me to constitute an important bias I should have considered more seriously."

tions, systems, transformations, and implications), making predictions is again far from factorially simple, but implications and transformations must be among the major products of the convergent production.

Finally, the third dimension treats the nature of the data, which Guilford calls *content*. He has discovered four types: figural (e.g., figure drawings, Bender-Gestalt), symbolic (e.g., sets of numbers, like an MMPI profile), semantic (e.g., TAT stories, interview data), and behavioral (e.g., observations of interpersonal skill, or empathic assessments of facial expressions of emotion). I have chosen examples from the data of multiform personality assessment to indicate that clinical psychologists often work with all of these kinds of data.

Guilford's important discovery is that the many specific abilities formed by the cubic intersection of his three dimensions are to an impressive extent *factorially independent*. That conclusion is not universally accepted, to be sure, and it may be questionable over the entire range of human ability; but it is most likely true for the restricted range that concerns us—the abilities of professionals and scientists. It is an elegant way of expressing the common observation that one psychodiagnostician is excellent with the Rorschach and life-history materials but cannot seem to get the hang of working with graphic materials, while another is an expert interpreter of test profiles but misses all the behavioral cues his colleagues find so telling. The central implication for us is that statistical prediction is limited almost entirely to symbolic data, whereas clinical prediction typically involves all four types but most importantly semantic and behavioral content.[18]

If this analysis is correct, then, we cannot generalize from a person's performance on a task of convergent production of transformations of symbolic data—even when done entirely nonmathematically, in his head—to his probable performance at convergent production of transformations with *any* other type of content. Thus, when Goldberg (1968b, 1970) and his colleagues set out on their broad program of research, restricting their Ss to MMPI profiles, the hope that they could reach conclusions about clinical inferences and judgment in general was doomed to disappointment. Moreover, the ideal form of the clinical-statistical contest, as described by Meehl (1954), in which both parties are limited to precisely the same data, inevitably limits the possible conclusions to an artificially narrow corner of the clinician's usual professional world.

If we take these last three considerations together, 31 of the 45 studies have at least one serious count of irrelevance against them, plus six others vulnerable to the charge that the criterion being predicted was less than optimally relevant. I shall return to this issue of relevance again, below.

The issues of relevance just covered may be looked on as evidence of an

---

[18][It does *not* necessarily follow that allowing a clinician nonquantifiable data of these kinds will improve his performance over what he can do with (symbolic) quantitative measurements.]

implicit anticlinical bias, since in each case the effect was to include studies in which the largely unsuccessful nonstatistical predictions were treated as though they were just as cogent as others—a rapidly diminishing handful—in which criteria, judges, and data all bore a reasonable resemblance to what corresponds to them in actual clinical work. Sawyer's failure to include numerous studies in which the results are favorable to judgmental assessments, and systematic errors in his application of his own evaluative scheme, which exaggerate the apparent superiority of mechanical measurement and prediction in the studies surveyed, may also be put under this heading. At any rate, the next three points are clearly sources of anticlinical bias in the research (and to some degree, the survey).

Failure to Compare Predictive Systems of Equal Degrees of Sophistication (14 to 20 Studies, 17 to 25 Conclusions)

This point, which I have made repeatedly in previous publications, has been given lip service only, misinterpreted, or ignored. Sawyer cites my 1958a paper, but neither mentions the point—not even in suggestions for future research—nor argues against it. Methodologically, it is important, for it amounts to a confounding of important sources of variance. If one predictive method incorporates the benefits of past experience with the predictors, criteria, and their relationship, while the other does not, then it is fallacious to ascribe any resulting differences in their efficiency to different methods of combining data to form predictions. And surely it is trivial and unnecessary to demonstrate again that knowledge is superior to ignorance.

I have tried to tabulate studies in this respect conservatively, not citing this point against them if the statistical prediction was not cross-validated, even though the latter may have had the benefit of a more complete predictive system than the "clinical" predictions in other respects. Also, I have *not* included studies like those of Meehl (1959) and Wittman and Steinberg (1944) in which the statistical prediction was a real cross-validation while the clinical predictions lacked the benefit of any prior formal study of predictive successes and failures, because of the presumption that the allegedly experienced clinicians had learned to make the prediction in question from previous experience. Goldberg (1968b) has shown how dubious this generous assumption is when it comes to psychologists' ability to learn much from experience with MMPI profile data, even with immediate feedback.

Blenkner's (1954) study is a good example of an inadvertent failure to be fair to clinical prediction. Available cases were split into two samples, and an actuarial method of combining clinically judged aspects of the initial interview was worked out on the first group, cross-validated on the second. It would have been easy to have given the clinical judges an opportunity to learn from their successes and failures on the first sample, also, then seeing if they could improve their "nil" performance on the second sample; but that was apparently not considered.

On the other hand, it is quite noteworthy that in the few studies where it is explicitly stated that predictive judges did carry out all or most of a complete six-step predictive system [Chapter 4], the "clinical' ' predictions had a rather high absolute level of efficiency and tended to be better than the actuarial (Hovey & Stauffacher, 1953; Lindzey, 1965; Trankell, 1956; see also Trankell, 1959). Note, also, that there are *no* instances of studies in which the clinical predictions had the advantage of a more sophisticated predictive system than the actuarial ones, just as there are none in which the apparent validity of clinical predictions was maximized by knowledge of the criterion in a way that would parallel the failure to cross-validate a multiple correlation or its equivalent.

Failure to Give Data on Best Judges (35 Studies, As Many As 47 Conclusions)

Though it happens that in ten instances, Sawyer does not present data on the performances of individual judges even though they are available in the paper cited, the much more usual state of affairs is that such data are not available. The issue of unfairness is complicated here, and the researches Sawyer surveyed differ considerably in their handling of it. When it comes to mechanical predictions, there is rarely any question but that the most effective predictor should be the one tested. Meehl (1954), in commenting on the studies he assembled, often criticizes them for having used a less than optimal method of generating statistical predictions but never makes the parallel point concerning clinical predictions. Strictly speaking, to give "clinical prediction" an equal shake with mechanical prediction, one should examine the performance of individual judges, and compare *best* predictors of one kind with best of the other; or else compare the average performance of several clinicians with the average performance of several mechanical predictive procedures—a design that has seldom been followed.[19] The reason is simple: its pointlessness is apparent, much more so than the meaninglessness of averaging the predictive performance of a small group of available "clinical" judges who do not consitute a sample of any definable population.

The logic of the situation is slightly different depending on what kind of conclusions you are interested in drawing. If your concern is pragmatic, you want to be able to answer the question: "Given a particular predictive problem, what is the cheapest and easiest way to solve it with available resources?" Then it is possible to argue that the nonmechanical predictions should be made by a sample of the judges available to do the job in question,

---

[19][In a personal communication of April 20, 1976, Robyn M. Dawes called my attention to the fact that "The comparison of the average judge with that of the 'average performance of several mechanical predictive procedures' was in fact what Corrigan and I did" (referring to Dawes & Corrigan, 1974) " . . . although we did it for a different reason. The average procedure out-predicted the average judgment. . . ."]

while the best obtainable mechanical predictor should be used. The presumption is that while better clinicians might exist, they cannot practically be found and imported as easily and inexpensively as the best actuarial system. Most studies seem to be designed in this way. Even in terms of this formulation, however, it is still highly likely that if there is more than one judge available there will be considerable variance in their predictive performances, and the possibility is worth investigating that the best judge with one sample will continue to be superior with another. Yet there is no evidence that Sawyer ever considered such a possibility; if any such study was done in any of the researches he assembled, he does not report it. Meehl (1954), by contrast, has a sensible discussion of this issue and presents the data on individual judges when they are available. Goldberg (1968a) correctly points out that one should be guarded in drawing conclusions from a single-sample predictive performance by an individual judge, no matter how brilliant. It is the same point as the need to cross-validate multiple regression formulas or best test scores from a pool of potential predictors: any and all predictors must be cross-validated!

The other kind of question that is often implicit in psychologists' interest in the clinical-statistical contests is less pragmatic: "Is it possible for *any* clinical judge to predict a given criterion as well as or better than an optimal mechanical system?" Such a question clearly calls for the comparison of best single performances of both kinds, and, of course, it implies the need for cross-validation just as much as the preceding one. (And let me repeat the point that any such comparisons are uninterpretable if the predictive systems being compared are not comparable in degree of sophistication.)

Whatever the design, therefore, the predictive efficiencies of individual judges should be reported,[20] and at least the range of such performances should be presented in a survey like Sawyer's. He is quite inconsistent in this respect, in one instance (his presentation of Glaser, 1954) giving validities separately for two judges, but otherwise presenting only averaged figures regardless of the number and level of training or experience of the judges. At worst, he gives the median validity of a large number of judges against 12 criteria and the median of the *best* correlations of 101 test scores with the

---

[20]In many researches, especially those with samples exceeding a hundred or so, any one "clinical" prediction was made by a single judge, but the single validity figure reported pools the performance of numerous judges each working with a different subsample. The exigencies of research, particularly in ordinary institutional settings, usually make it impossible to assign Ss randomly to judges, and both the sizes and the makeup of the resulting subsamples of Ss may differ considerably. That was the case with the "rule-of-thumb" predictions made by psychiatrist interviewers in the Menninger research and the large differences we found among their individual validities were surely not attributable entirely to abilities and other intrapersonal factors. Nevertheless, it seemed prudent to recommend that an interviewer with a sizable *negative* validity be dropped, and to make maximal use of the one with the best validity. My memory (unfortunately, it is fallible and can no longer be checked) is that the validity of the interviewers' pooled predictions went up afterward.

same 12 criteria (his summary of Kelly & Fiske, 1950). That is, for each of a dozen criterion scores, he computed the *average* performance of all clinicians but selected the test validity that happened to be *highest,* then presented the medians of these two sets of 12 figures each. I should add that Sawyer drew no explicit conclusion (except that $3 = 5$), but the reader is bound to get the impression that tests and clinicians perform equally well (or poorly). And even in the case of the Glaser paper, his conclusion ($6 > 5$) is correct with respect to the psychiatrist but not for the sociologist (for whom $6 = 5$); the conclusion is obviously based on the average of the two "clinical" validities.

Most of the time, it is difficult to know how the failure to present individual judges' validities affects the conclusions. In Halbower's study, Meehl (1956b) tells us clearly enough that no one of the 25 clinicians and students performed as well as the "cookbook," so the conclusions are *not* affected. Usually, however, we simply do not know enough from the published paper to be able to tell—a fact that, in itself, indicates how inconclusive many of them are as evidence against the claimed predictive powers of "clinicians."

Sawyer's treatment of this issue is curiously self-contradictory. In his discussion, he notes the point made by Holt and Luborsky (1958) that clinicians differ greatly in their ability to do the job of prediction, but adds: "It should not be necessary, however, to validate each clinician separately" despite the fact that we reached the opposite conclusion on the basis of actual data. He goes on: "Variables like type of training, amount of experience and personality may identify groups of clinicians, who, in particular situations, can predict more accurately" (p. 196f.). We thought so too, investigated, and found that no such variables could identify the clinicians who were best predictors. As a matter of fact, Sawyer goes on to cite Taft (1955), and Sarbin, Taft, and Bailey (1960) to the same effect—but this does not cause him to reconsider the position he had predicated on this false assumption, which would have meant presenting the data available on individual clinicians.

"Clinical Predictors" Did Not Have Access to Most Relevant Data (2 Studies, 9 Comparisons)

Here is another logically very tricky issue, which comes up as soon as the persons who make predictions by different methods have different data. Clearly, if A has access to datum d and B does not, *and* if d has enough relevance to the criterion, then that fact alone will tend to put a ceiling on the possible validity attainable that is lower for B than for A—another instance in which the design confounds something else with the variable under investigation: the "clinical" or "mechanical" method of combining data to yield predictions. This is one of the main reasons for the widespread opinion that the ideal design should limit "clinician" and statistician to the same body of data, which (because of the nature of actuarial methods) in practice are almost entirely numerical. That design's limitations have already been pointed out above (p. 102f.).

The Lindzey (1965) study illustrates another design, only a slight departure from Meehl's ideal: there is one body of data, here the TAT, which is treated in two ways. On the one hand, researchers try to isolate reliably scorable "signs" or rateable variables, intended to extract the predictive kernels from the chaff of the total protocol, and to derive formulas or other mechanical rules to combine them to predict something. On the other hand, clinicians process the entire set of stories—not just the ratings, or as in this instance not including the ratings and scores—using whatever they can get out of them to help them predict the same criterion. If the clinician has more data, there is also the chance that he is exposing himself to more irrelevancies; and if he does better than the formula, an industrious, actuarially-minded researcher can still search the protocols for predictive information not yet incorporated in the mechanical system with some possibility of finding and using it.

All too often, differences in predictive method are even more confounded with even greater differences in data. A fair number of the comparisons tallied by Sawyer are of this type (some of those in Cliff, 1958; Doleys & Renzaglia, 1963; Dunlap & Wantman, 1944; Glaser & Hangren, 1958; Gregory, 1956; Husén, 1954; Lewis & MacKinney, 1961; Parrish, Klieger, & Drucker, 1954; Rosen & Van Horn, 1961; Watley & Vance, 1964; Westoff, Sagi, & Kelly, 1958; Wittman, 1941; and Wittman & Steinberg, 1944). In many of these, the predictive efficiency of some test scores is compared with that of an interviewer based mostly on his direct impressions, followed by a combination of the two, and the kind of question being asked is something like: "Can an interviewer add anything to a mechanical predictive system, regardless of the kind of data available?" Such a question may have a degree of practical utility in some settings, but research so directed cannot meaningfully be tallied up in the same column as research aimed in an entirely different direction.

In two studies, however, the "clinical predictors" did not have access to highly relevant predictive data. Both (Dunlap & Wantman, 1944; Gregory, 1956) were attempts to predict criteria of achievement in military training programs, to which cognitive and other abilities are obviously highly relevant; in both, "clinical predictions" were made by interviewers who were not allowed to see test measures of these abilities, though their judgments were being compared with predictions that incorporated the test scores in question. Surely such research can teach us nothing. When it is well known that a criterion like college grades is rather well predicted by previous grades and cognitive tests, but there remains reliable yet unpredicted variance in the criterion, you are unlikely to be able to find out whether nonintellectual measures of whatever kind can predict that residual variance by zero-order correlations of proposed predictors with the criterion. But if a clinician were presented with a group of Ss known to have the same actuarially predicted level of achievement, he might conceivably be able to make different predictions for some of them based on assessments of other aspects of their personalities—particularly if he were first given the opportunity to study his assessment data on other Ss whose subsequent criterion performance was known (e.g., overachievers and underachievers). Why aren't studies of this kind more popular? In part, no doubt, because their designs don't seem to yield evidence directly comparing "clinical" and mechanical predictions. Here is one way in which a conventionally accepted formulation of a problem has an unfortunate steering effect on the kinds of research that gets done.

Note, incidentally, that when naive clinical predictions are compared with a reasonably good statistical predictive system, the cross-validation design of the latter protects it against including irrelevant data, and the lack of prior study of predictor-criterion relationships by clinicians leaves them unprotected against the real possibility that they will be asked to do a job in the absence of important relevant information. The well-known paper by Holtzman and Sells (1954) has been widely cited in discussions of clinical and statistical prediction even though it contains no explicit comparison of two kinds of predictions (which is doubtless why Sawyer did not include it), partly because it follows the just-suggested model in part. Nineteen well-known psychologists, most of whom had had extensive clinical experience, some in military settings, were asked to pick which Air Force trainees had been eliminated from primary flight training because they had developed overt personality disturbances, in a group all of whom had similar and adequate scores on basic aptitude tests. In a number of ways, it seems a fair test of clinical prediction: the data were personality tests, mostly projective, which had been administered before the training began; the criterion was overt psychological disturbance of a kind clinicians are presumably used to working with, and the authors made an effort to describe the "population and the case histories of unsuccessful cadets and . . . the critical requirements for success. . . ." I was asked by Holtzman and Sells to participate, but refused mainly because of two flaws in the design: the tests had all been modified or specially designed for use with this population, so general previous experience with Rorschach, for example, was applicable to an unknown degree with their group ink-blot test; but more important, there was no opportunity to see how other comparable Ss who had succeeded or failed looked on this particular battery of tests. Further, I was not sure that I could be wholly uninfluenced by certain data (such as a group Szondi test and a modified Figure-Drawing test) from which I was pretty sure that I would get only confusion. For these reasons, I felt no confidence that I would be able to do the job, and no surprise when I read the report that no one who did participate had been able to predict significantly better than chance. The paper also includes a footnote indicating that empirical scoring keys had been developed with some promise of validity for three of the tests, but not for the Szondi, the drawing test, or the psychosomatic inventory. Fully half of the battery, then, contributed only noise; and it is as unfair to clinicians to supply them with irrelevant information as it is to deny them access to relevant data.

I must confess that it is easier to produce something like my Table 5.2 than it is to prescribe exactly how considerations of the kind cited there should be used by a person who undertakes to evaluate and integrate the findings from a body of published research. A single criticism of one study, for example, may be enough to destroy its utility, while another paper may still have some evidential value despite several weaknesses. It comes down to a matter of judgment, which cannot easily be reduced to the equivalent of a computer program. In all too few universities are psychologists given systematic training in how to read the literature—how to consider the many dimensions of design, execution, analysis of data, generalization from findings and relevance to practical and theoretical issues, in deciding how much credence to give reports of research. It is surely not enough for a surveyor merely to bring the reader's attention to certain flaws in a piece of research if they make the findings equivocal; he must accept the responsibility to make a final judgment about each paper's relevance and adequacy, and to disregard its purport if it does not come up to a reasonable level of quality. To be sure, men of good will differ in where they set the cutting points, but that does not mean that the author of a review paper may be allowed to use *any* standards he likes, with *any* degree of consistency. Ultimately, the editor and his surrogates, the referees, must monitor (among other things) the author's standards and cutting points. The fact that a paper contains much that is thoughtful and useful—as Sawyer's paper does, despite all my criticism— must not be allowed to outweigh its failure to do an adequate job of weighing the quality of evidence provided, study by study.

CRITICISMS OF SAWYER'S FRAMEWORK

The preceding sections have presented some of the reasons for my judgment that, even granted his own framework of assumptions, definitions, and procedures, Sawyer's survey was so badly executed as to be not merely lacking in cogency in reaching his conclusions but positively misleading. Let us look now at that framework itself, for it has grave deficiencies as well.

Definition of the Problem

"Clinical vs. statistical *prediction* is only half the problem. . . . The prior problem, largely neglected, is clinical vs. mechanical measurement. . . ."

Thus begins Sawyer's abstract of his paper; and throughout he repeatedly asserts that by widening the scope of his survey to include modes of measurement, he is conducting "a comprehensive evaluation": "the general purpose of this paper is . . . to provide a framework for the fair and complete comparison of all" methods.

The aim of comprehensiveness is a praiseworthy one, but Sawyer has let the good become the enemy of the better by assuming that just supplementing modes of combining data to make predictions by modes of measurement is all he needs to do to provide a sufficiently broad framework. My 1958a paper attempted to reformulate the question posed by Meehl in 1954 by providing a broader "framework for the fair and complete comparison" of methods in the area he had staked out. Of course Sawyer was under no obligation to adopt my analysis; but he might well have discussed it. The evidence is, however, that he failed to understand it. Otherwise, it is hard to see why he would have implied in the paper's second paragraph that I neglected "the measurement part of the problem," when in fact the paper he cites (Holt, 1958a) includes measurement as one of five steps in the predictive process, in which I now (Holt, 1970a, 1971c) distinguish six steps. This analysis is not original; I got the basic ideas from Horst *et al.* (1941), and Cronbach (1960) presents a five-stage analysis of prediction research in almost exactly the same terms. There is hardly any excuse, therefore, for Sawyer's posture of having made a great leap forward by discovering the importance of one additional step in addition to the final one, while neglecting to deal with three or four others which have been discussed in relevant literature for at least 25 years: job analysis or more generally the study of the criterion, conceptual analysis (locating the variables to be measured), preliminary trial of methods, and processing data to obtain measures of the intervening variables.

Choice of Problem

Whether the focus be on measurement, prediction, or all aspects of predictive systems, why is it of interest or value to compare the clinical and the mechanical? Sawyer considers this question briefly; his reply is, "for the same reasons that prediction itself is important—theoretically, because it underlies explanation, and practically, because it permits individuals, groups and societies to operate more effectively." These sweeping propositions are presented as if self-evident, which I do not believe them to be.

In what sense can prediction be said to "underlie" explanation? It often empirically precedes it: the ancient astronomers observed many regularities in the movement of heavenly bodies and could predict them long before they could understand and thus explain them. In this sense, prediction has the relatively trivial meaning of defining a phenomenon for scientific study, which has little or nothing to do with the clinical versus statistical horse races, and cannot substitute for a genuine analysis of what if any real theoretical issues are testable by such comparisons. (For such an attempt, see Chapter 4.) My experience is that the more earnestly I have tried to locate such theoretical issues, the less do tallies of comparative successes appear relevant to them.

And as to the practical issue, I have argued repeatedly that it is most meaningfully formulated *not* as "Is clinical or statistical prediction generally more efficient/effective/cheaper/better?" but "How can we best go about solving particular predictive problems?" The former way of putting it implies that somehow all predictive problems are alike *solely by virtue of our having classified them as predictive.* Here is the fallacy of reification, with which psychologists ought to be familiar enough to be wary of it if not to avoid it completely. Behavior is disconcertingly specific to situations; the fact that a predictor (clinical or mechanical to any degree by any criterion) works in one setting with one population gives us little assurance that it will work equally well when these parameters are changed. But the procedure of tallying together any and all predictive researches just so long as they contain comparisons that can be forced into the procrustean dichotomy implicitly assumes that there is no problem of validity generalization.

Neglect of the Situation

The just-mentioned fact—the dependence of behavior on the situation in which it occurs—gets surprisingly little attention from Sawyer. His scheme for classifying and analyzing research contains no explicit place for situational determinants of the behavior being predicted, since his focus is limited to modes of measuring aspects of persons and modes of combining those data. Only in the final section of the paper, when he is making recommendations for future research, does he include a section on Conditions, with this disarming opening statement: "The answer to any comparison also depends strongly on the particular conditions under which it is made. As Table 2 shows, these conditions vary widely; their variation constitutes the most conspicuous reason why the results of the 45 studies cumulate less than they might." That, incidentally, is the only hint that there is any problem about their cumulating, and it is not developed any further. The term "conditions" turns out, however, to comprise not only the criterion situation but "the data, the sample of subjects, the clinician, and the statistical method": and Sawyer has only one paragraph to say about the criterion situation—less than about any of the other conditions. That paragraph is exclusively concerned with the problem of predicting different criteria within the same situation, and whether a different "balance of clinical and mechanical modes" might be needed to predict, for example, science grades and other course grades in a college.

It should hardly be necessary to make a case that what we often call "the stimulus" (press, behavior settings, environmental determinants) cannot be ignored if one is interested in predicting behavior. Yet, oddly enough, even psychologists who are most ideologically committed to an S-R position seem to be quite content with predictions that take no account whatsoever of situational variables, just as long as they are in some statistical or "mechanical" format.[21] To be sure, clinical psychologists are justifiably notorious for being too exclusively focused on "intrapsychic" properties of people, and they are easily as likely as their actuarially minded brethren to neglect the situations in which predicted behavior is to occur. One reason for this failure may be the fact that most of their contact with the people they study intensively is in carefully controlled situations. Intuitively, most therapists feel that it is important to carry out treatment in a constant setting in which the impact of as many exciting stimuli as possible is minimized. Similar control and constancy of press is the rule in diagnostic work also. Perhaps for this very reason, clinicians easily come to overestimate the importance of nonsituational determiners of behavior. The result may often be that the effects of a valid set of intrapersonal predictors are overwhelmed by more important external determinants, since the predicting clinician typically assesses only the subjects' personalities.

Isn't the actuarial predictor equally limited, if he works only with measures derived from the subjects? I doubt it. If the external determinants of the criterion do not vary unpredictably but tend to recur for most Ss, an actuarial system is more likely to find a means to combine intrapersonal measures in a way that respects the impact of press even when they are not measured as such. Consider, for example, the possibility that grades in a certain college are determined to a considerable extent by the responses of the teachers to the physical attractiveness of the students, which is not measured because neither the clinician nor the actuary suspects its relevance. Given the same data, like intelligence test scores and previous grade-point average, clinicians are likely to weight IQ too heavily; while a regression equation developed on a previous sample in the same college will hug the mean more closely and thus make fewer large errors. Experiences of just this kind led Stern, Stein, and Bloom (1956) to make what might be considered "clinical" studies of behavioral settings and the actual criterion as against the theoretical one to which the faculty give lip service, with highly successful results.

Sawyer should, therefore, have scrutinized the relevant research with an eye on the amount of attention paid to the criterion situation and particularly

---

[21][Goldberg (1972) has pointed out a new trend in personality assessment, following in the wake of Cronbach's (1957) influential call for trait-by-treatment interactional research design, Mischel's (1968) polemical reassertion of situationism, and the growth of interest in social learning theory (Rotter, 1954). That is an attempt to create more situationally specific tests of traits (e.g., Endler, Hunt, & Rosenstein's inventory of anxiety-by-situation interactions, 1962). Goldberg comments, "It is only in the area of scholastic prediction . . . that psychologists have begun to develop measures to predict trait-by-treatment interactions effects. . . . The road has proved incredibly rocky. Recent reviews . . . have revealed very few replicated effects."]

any differences between competing predictive systems in their access to or the amount of attention they paid to situational information. Second, he should have explicitly considered the degree of homogeneity in the criterion situation as a determinant of the ceiling on predictability, study by study. I have little doubt that a major reason the clinical predictions of in-training success were so much better in the Menninger study than in the Michigan study is that all the Ss in the former (Holt & Luborsky, 1958) were in one school, the Menninger School of Psychiatry, which was well known to the most successful predictive judges, whereas in the latter (Kelly & Fiske, 1951) the students were scattered over all the doctoral programs in clinical psychology then extant and all the VA installations accepting trainees—in addition to which, the predictive judges had no information on what the criterion situation was to be or even when the criterion evaluations were to be made, during or after graduate school.

Finally, Sawyer should not have attempted to summarize and compare predictive researches except within a realm having some degree of situational homogeneity. Despite the differences among universities just alluded to, it is at least arguable that studies of educational selection are comparable, particularly if one considers military training schools in a separate subgroup, and there has been enough research to make it worth while to focus in this way. Moreover, if Sawyer had chosen that modest objective, he would have had a manageably delimited universe of literature, which he might have hoped to search with some chance of being comprehensive. For the literature on clinical versus statistical prediction and/or measurement is not self-identifying; a computer scan of any existing data base with even a large number of descriptors would miss much of what Sawyer found (though it would turn up some obvious studies he omitted). The entire universe of behavior is too large a purview for any kind of comprehensive searching strategy, and the research literature on it is by no means comprehensively covered by the *Psychological Abstracts*.

Ineffective Deliminations

Sawyer did make some attempt to limit his purview, and my only objection to most of his announced principles for doing so is that they did not exclude enough to create a manageable realm. First, he eschewed three related considerations: (a) the nature of the data as viewed from Coombs's (1960) perspective, (b) the process of clinical inference, and (c) detailed statistical technicalities. Second, he decided to concentrate on studies using more than one predictive variable, and on "the prediction of behavioral outcomes, rather than assessment of traits" or diagnosis. His reasoning for the last exclusion cannot be appraised since it is not given. Grudgingly, he made an exception for "Six studies with assessment-like criteria . . . because they are either well-known or otherwise of particular interest" (p. 185), an ambivalent procedure that left plenty of room for bias in selection. I imagine that he tried to exclude diagnostic and assessment studies because they inevitably use criteria that are themselves based on clincial judgment. Mirroring the power relationships of the two professions, diagnostic "predictions" of clinical psychologists are usually validated against the judgments of psychiatrists. In the case of measurements of other personality attributes, we are up against the fact, surely embarrassing to many a nonclinician, that the best available (most face-valid) criterion is a consensus of clinical judgments made by a team of experts after intensive, multiform assessment. Accepting that kind of criterion raises the unpleasant possibility that any success of clinical predictions will be in part spurious, because the predictor and criterion share substantial amounts of irrelevant variance.

Probably for such reasons, Sawyer excluded most of the kinds of predictions clinical psychologists actually make in their daily practices: virtually all of diagnosis and assessment, and all of the predictions in therapy on which clinicians make their reputations (e.g., in supervising someone else's work, going out on a limb about what the client is going to say or do in the next few treatment hours, and being right). Consequently, then, a survey that purports to present a comprehensive comparative evaluation of clinical and mechanical measurement and prediction *excludes* the very kinds of predictions clinicians are explicitly trained to make, and which make up something like 95% of their actual, everyday predictive work. Instead, clinical psychology as a whole is put on the defensive by the poor performance of alleged clinicians even the best of whom were expected to predict criteria about which they knew too little on the basis of data that were unfamiliar, largely irrelevant, or both.

Problems in the Definition of "Clinical"

At each of the five or six steps of a total predictive system, clinical judgment may play a *greater or less* role, as I have repeatedly demonstrated. In one remark, Sawyer gives evidence of some awareness that the relevant reality is not binary: "Meehl (1954) established a dichotomy. . . . For present purposes, however, it is appropriate to recognize that there exists a continuum of the amount of clinical participation . . ." (p. 183). After that tip of his hat, he proceeds nevertheless to dichotomize everything into clinical or mechanical, depending on whether a clinician must be involved.

In his first footnote, Sawyer thanks me along with seven other persons "for helpful comments on an earlier version of this paper." So far as I can determine, the recognition (just quoted) of a continuum of clinical participation is the only thing he got from my letter to him of November 26, 1960, of over five single-spaced pages. In it, I complained that he was

> using a dichotomy in a situation more nearly resembling continuous variation. If you think only of self-administered "objective" tests on the one hand and sensitive interviewing or the skilled administration of

projective tests on the other, the dichotomy does not seem to be forced; but that's true in any similar situation if one considers only the extremes. Actually, the Rorschach would be considered by most people a "clinical" method of gathering data; yet it may be administered by a nonclinician, or by a poorly trained clinician. Does the MMPI become "nonmechanical" (or clinical) when the questions are asked by a clinician who simply checks off the responses in the precoded catagories? Does the Szondi test change from one end to the other of your dichotomy depending on whether the person who gives it has been certified by ABPP or not?

There are two issues here, I think. One is the degree of skill required to obtain the data. The other is the nature of the data themselves. The first issue is a tricky one, since one could argue quite reasonably that almost any test works better when well administered—that is, when given by a clinically trained person who is skilled in gaining rapport, getting the subject to take the test seriously, and to answer the questions conscientiously. Here the issue is not whether the method of gathering data is clinical or mechanical, but whether it is adequate or not. It is not so easy to lay down flat generalizations about adequacy, since a lot depends on the problem, the particular instrument being used, the nature of the subject, the setting, and the like. If the subject is being tested in a sufficiently impressive institution so that he approaches his tasks seriously, and if a sober, intelligent group of subjects are being used, then you might get perfectly good autobiographies by simply handing out a printed slip of instructions. To call that mechanical . . . would be to overlook the most important considerations in getting good data.

As I noted, the other dimension of variation here is the nature of the data themselves. I think for your purposes you might express that in terms of the degree to which the data obtained from the subject need to be predigested (i.e., scored, content-analyzed, interpreted) before they can be worked with statistically. Consider the interview again, for a moment. If you are using it in the manner of the interaction chronograph and are concerned only with timing utterances, then you will need someone who handles the stopwatch well to work over the data before they can be processed statistically. [It can now be done automatically by machine.] Let's say that you are interested in the degree of positive or negative opinion on certain topics about which the interviewer was instructed to ask; that will call for a relatively simple content analysis, such as can be carried out by any bright college sophomore after a few hours of training. Or you may be after something much subtler, requiring expert, highly trained clinical judgment. With this example, I have tried to point out the complexity of this second dimension, for it varies with the interest of the person analyzing the data. If you are simply going to count words in a typescript, then an interview requires a clinician no more than does an MMPI; yet the interview remains qualitatively different, in that it does lend itself to a greater variety of judgmental analyses than the MMPI.

These issues are too widely ignored, especially by the technologically minded, to whom it would probably come as a surprise to learn that the validity of an "objective" test like the MMPI may depend to a very large extent on its *not* being handled as a device for mechanical measurement. When a test is as obviously fakeable as this one, it is imperative that a relationship of trust and rapport be established with the subject if he is to give true answers rather than merely self-serving ones (see Lovell, 1967).

There is a second difficulty in defining "clinical," at the point of prediction. Two overlapping and often confounded, but logically separate criteria exist for defining a prediction as clinical: individualization and judgment. Clinical$_i$ means that a separate kind of prediction is made for each individual, based on study of him not just as a particular instance of a generalization but as to some extent a unique configuration of general laws. By this criterion, statistical prediction would assign values to an individual just on the basis of group membership. Clinical$_j$ means that the prediction is the product of human judgment applied to data concerning the persons whose behavior is being predicted. By this criterion, statistical prediction is the product of rules arrived at by mathematical means, as a result of quantitative, relatively objective research.

It is easy to demonstrate that these two definitions are independent, for all four of the logically possible combinations exist, exemplified by published research. We might denote a study as "clinical$_{i,j}$" when each case is studied by a clinician, who analyzes such semantic data as interview and TAT by principally judgmental means, constructing a "theory" of each particular case and attempting to derive predictions from that theory. A study is "clinical$_i$, statistical$_j$" when each individual is studied over time and statistical, relatively objective associations are found between psychometric assessments and his behavior—e.g., Cattell's P-technique. Note that clinical judgment's role is minimized, but the focus is on the study of the individual as a more or less unique behavioral system. The most sharply contrasted case is "statistical$_i$, clinical$_j$"; here the predictions are made according to a general rule for all cases, which however is arrived at not by statistical but by clinical-judgmental means. The two papers by Wittman (1941; Wittman & Steinberg, 1944), cited by all reviewers as strong evidence for "statistical" as against "clinical" prediction, are good cases in point: she drew up a set of predictive indicators of which schizophrenics would profit from shock treatment, largely from a review of the clinical literature, almost all of which were judgmental ratings on such variables as "oral versus anal personality traits," based on the largely semantic, nonquantitative data found in hospital case folders. A simple sum of these judgmentally derived cues was the predictor; what made it "statistical$_i$" was the fact that there was one "theory" of prognosis applied to all cases. Finally, there is no problem in recognizing "statistical$_{i,j}$"; that is the common case of a study in which general rules are derived from quantitative studies of groups and are applied to further groups, without individualization or much use of judgment.

All of these complexities, regrettable but realistic, are overlooked or sacrificed by the expedient of the procrustean dichotomy. It is easy to make a theoretical case that any simplifying assumption throws away information; the hard issue is whether the gain in practicality outweighs the loss in fidelity. My reading of the evidence here is that much more was lost than gained by Sawyer's handling of the subtle problems of defining "clinical."

CONCLUSION: THE PROBLEM OF DRAWING CONCLUSIONS

Let us first see what Sawyer himself concluded from the data he collected and processed. There is an interesting contrast between his abstract, which admits that "Grossly uncontrolled differences . . . in clinical training, subjects, criteria, etc., prevent definitive conclusions" and the paper itself, which lacks any such appropriate cautions. He made a beginning at least once (on p. 190), admitting that in most of the studies the "clinicians" lacked clinical training or experience, and calling it "a problem that will be relevant later in evaluating this summary," but he made no reference to this or any other such "problem" on pp. 192–193, where he presents his main conclusions, under the heading "Combined Results."

True, that section begins with some appropriately cautious paragraphs; he says, for example, "we do not fully know under just what conditions one prediction method surpasses another." As soon as he starts talking about his Table 4, the "Summary of Conclusions from 45 Clinical-Statistical Studies," however, Sawyer's declarations are qualified only by such nonspecific language as "it seems likely that . . .," never by any indications of the populations to which his statements apply, nor to the real possibility that errors in the studies being manipulated are not random but systematic and cumulative. It is as if he were wholly innocent of any acquaintance with sampling theory and its relevance to the process of making inferences.

I am using the terms "populations" and "sampling" here in the broad sense encouraged by Brunswik (1956). He was the first to point out the fact that any experiment contains a sample not only of Ss but of "objects," too, usually a very small sample selected without any consideration of its representativeness. Thanks to Brunswik it is possible to see that the logic of sampling subjects applies sweepingly to *all* aspects of any empirical investigation. Correspondingly, we can generalize only within the sampling constraints that apply to the research providing our data base.

It is certainly not sufficient to avoid these issues by speaking exclusively in abstract and general terms, which is mostly what Sawyer does (for example, "the valid portion of clinical judgment is largely duplicated by mechanical prediction;" p. 193). To fail to state the narrow and peculiar limits within which such a statement can reasonably be said to apply is to invite the reader to believe that there are no such limits. However conventional such writing may be, it is none the less irresponsible.

Sawyer, like others before him, set up an explosive situation, left matches lying around, and walked away as if innocent. If someone else misuses his survey, it surely isn't his fault, is it? Didn't he after all modestly say, at the end of his section of conclusions: "The present analysis, though it compares a larger number of studies more comprehensively than any prior treatment, by no means firmly resolves the various questions of 'clinical versus statistical prediction'"? As Meehl discovered before him, such general disclaimers are wholly ineffective in restraining psychologists who have an ax to grind from using a survey of this kind to their own ends. It is part of a scientist's responsibility, I believe, to consider the use that others are likely to make of his work and to be particularly cautious not to encourage inappropriate generalization by such a choice of terms as *clinical* (instead of judgmental) prediction. By referring to anyone who made a prediction by any nonstatistical means as a "clinician," Sawyer encouraged his readers to believe that his conclusions could be generalized to clinicians at large, and in particular to the professional competence of contemporary clinical psychologists. It is not only bad logic and bad science to do so, but the long-run consequences for psychology may be ominous.[22]

As I have tried to indicate, the particular target of this critique is not especially unusual in neglecting all sampling considerations when he drew his conclusions; it is the exceptional psychologist who resists the temptation to write as if his little fragment of data allowed him to speak out on the laws of behavior, with hardly any further qualification. Yet this particular paper *is* unusual in such matters as carelessness with facts and figures and biased selection of evidence, matters that are usually monitored by referees and editors. Not having subjected other contemporaneous review articles to a comparably intensive scrutiny, I cannot make the last statement with certainty, but I strongly suspect that the editor liked the anticlinical purport of the paper so much that he was blinded to its faults. Once a "fact" becomes generally accepted, especially when it makes a comfortable fit with one's prejudices, it is extremely difficult to get people—including psychologists—to re-examine the evidence. Nevertheless, I hope that the passage of time will

---

[22]In his unpublished rejoinder, Sawyer complains with some justification that in my earlier critique (Holt, 1970a) I gave the impression that he had not pointed out the diversity of occupations and training among the predictive judges in the research he was summarizing, whereas he had made considerable point of it. True, there are a couple of paragraphs calling attention to the diverse background and education of the "clinicians," and I surely do not wish anyone to think that Sawyer is unaware of this limitation on the utility of his evidence. Perhaps the central fault of the survey, however, is the failure to follow through to their logical conclusion the implications of just such limitations as Sawyer was aware of. He could have weighted the studies; he could have divided them into sets for separate consideration, depending on their relevance and freedom from faults in design and execution; he could have qualified his conclusions; and no doubt there are other ways to take the flaws of the various studies into account, The way Sawyer chose seems the weakest of all: make the point early, before processing the results, and neglect it completely thereafter except for some highly general caveats at the very end in the abstract.

have helped us all to take a second and more dispassionate look at the shoddiness of the case against clinical methods.

Elsewhere (Holt, 1973a, [Chapter 7, below]), I have urged a distinction between *conclusions* and *implications* when we come to those final sections of scientific papers in which we try to take a broad perspective on our findings or those of the literature just surveyed and say what it all means. Such an attempt inevitably goes beyond the information given, in the narrow sense; we are only rarely interested in the particular sample of information collected, for its own sake.

> Let us say that when the careful investigator surveys the subjects and objects used in his study and induces their common properties on the *lowest* (most conservative) applicable level of generalization, he is drawing conclusions. That is, he is stating what he found in a form that is somewhat generalized, but he does not consider as established any proposition that ventures above the level that just characterizes all of his experimental subjects and objects. . . . When he extends his generalizations to classes of subjects or objects that do include those of his study but a good many others, let us call that drawing implications. (Holt, 1973a, p. 36)

And let us try to underline the distinction by using the declarative voice only for conclusions, reminding the reader by the explicit tentativeness of formulation that implications are only possibly true.

In this spirit, let me go beyond the immediate task of this critique to address the general clinical versus mechanical antithesis again and attempt to frame a conclusion and a few speculations. I believe that one point has been conclusively established: there is no magic in clinical intuition that enables a clinician to predict a criterion about which he knows little, from data the relationship of which to the criterion he has not studied, and to do so better than an actuarial formula based on just such prior study of predictor-criterion relationships. In retrospect, it seems absurd to have expected that it could have been done. The cockiness and naive narcissism of some clinicians were nourished by a fallacious conception of the nature of science given respectability and wide currency by Allport. Today, it can surely be of little further interest that a person without an expert's level of ability, training, or experience cannot surpass a good actuarial formula, and usually does worse. Let us therefore flog this dead horse no longer.

For me, the heart of the matter is still the role of judgment versus reliance on "objective" or mechanical procedures. Is judgment best limited to the choice of appropriate statistics, the rejection of erroneous or contaminated data, and the like; or is there any need to train psychologists to understand and analytically reconstruct personalities, applying judgment to strictly psychological as opposed to general scientific types of issues? To be sure, it would be a simpler and easier task to train clinical psychologists if we could in good conscience adopt the "empty organism" point of view, and treat personalities exactly like rats, pigeons, or any other behaving organisms. By this one stroke, we would eliminate any need for empathy or intuition in our future human engineers; a thorough training in general research methods, objective psychometrics, and techniques of modifying behavior by schedules of reinforcement would do the trick. Indeed, it is alarming to notice that many clinical doctorate programs today seem to be adopting just such an approach. I have no general brief against behavior therapies; so long as they work, as some seem to do very well with many cases, let us find out their indications and proper sphere of application and let them take their rightful place in the clinician's therapeutic toolkit. And I am thoroughly in favor of good research and of training clinical psychologists to do it, also, At the same time, I find it not only foolish but irresponsible to train clinical psychologists without giving them the kind of contact with the inner complexity of human lives that intensive—clinical—personality assessment reveals.

Do we really know that such revelations are veridical and not self-deceptive? A good clinician works, I believe, by carefully weighing a great deal of evidence, each bit of which has many implications, and deciding among them on the basis of convergence. A very noisy signal is usable if you have enough of them. I think of the manifold indicators in a battery of clinical tests as being like the separate oscilloscope scans of the cortical consequences of a sensory input: any one has a low validity, a poor signal/noise ratio. Average a good many of them, however, and the signal begins to come through clearly, as in an average evoked potential. Bad research overlooks that process and considers the issue of validation closed once a validity coefficient has been obtained expressing the average co-occurrence of a single sign and any one of the many aspects of personality or psychopathology it may indicate. In terms of such research, clinical psychologists are trying to operate with hopelessly invalid test indicators, and the fact that they continue to do so is explained away by a variety of uncharitable assumptions. Of course, such bad research is easier, cheaper, and quicker to do and publish than research that respects the nature of clinical assessment. Therefore, the weight of the evidence will always seem to be heavily on the anticlinical side—*unless the research is carefully evaluated* before it is added up. Unfortunately, there is no scientific prestige to be obtained by doing the slow, grubby, expensive, theoretically uninteresting evaluation of the validity of personality assessment. Fortunately, however, the status of research on psychotherapy is improving rapidly, and its efficacy is no longer so easily scorned.

Finally, some speculations least directly related to data. The ultimate importance of the clinical-statistical issue stems from the two opposed, underlying conceptions of what psychology is all about. The polar extremes may be labeled mechanistic and humanistic, and it must be no secret that I am one of those who believe that psychology should be one of man's few bastions of humanistic yet scientifically disciplined learning. We desperately need to keep our grip on common sense, and not to let ourselves be carried away by technological fantasies of wholly automated systems of diagnosing human problems or predicting human behavior. Many psychologists are afraid of the subjectivity of human judgment, and cling to the false ideal that science is or could be wholly objective (see Polanyi, 1958, and Holton, 1973). Judgment is fallible, and the subjective processing of semantic and behavioral data cannot be made free of error—too bad; but some error can be tolerated, indeed is inescapable. Wherever we find ways to reduce or eliminate sources of error in our work, we must do so; we need to use machines to help us handle data, for example, for they can save us much time and labor. But we must not expect the computer to provide more than semiprocessed material for the exercise of trained, sharpened, disciplined but still very human judgment. Let us not forget that machines are fallible, too, and are capable of making greater mistakes than people by several orders of magnitude. A person balancing his checkbook is likely to make more errors than a machine in the first three columns from the right, but a computer is quite capable of making errors absurdly greater than the total amount in the entire account. Computers are, and will remain, sharply limited in their capacity to deal with semantic data, and wholly unable to deal with what Guilford calls behavioral data, which should be the true province of the clinical psychologist. As long as psychologists cling to the vain hope that the hard, slow, error-prone, but peculiarly psychological procedure of getting to know and understand other people can be short-cut by mechanical procedures, we shall probably continue to witness many dreary reruns of meaningless contests billed as clinical versus statistical prediction.

It is a great pleasure to be able to add that, in his unpublished rejoinder of 1970, Sawyer aligns himself with me on the conflict within psychology over the possibility of its being a wholly objective, value-free science. He goes on to endorse and enlarge on my point that "Whether or not a predictive system gets set up and validated is largely determined, not by the psychological significance or clinical relevance of behavior predicted, but by extraneous considerations among which the economic bulk large" (Holt, 1970a, p. 342). Sawyer then points out the fact that what was predicted in almost all of the 45 studies he surveyed was of interest and value for the sponsoring institution, and that such institutional bias often operates not only against the best interests of the clinician but against those of the subjects themselves.

At this point we should take careful note of the fact that the nature of the argument is significantly changing. Sawyer and I are not contending that mechanical procedures of selection are intrinsically opposed to the interests of the persons about whom predictions are made while clinical procedures must be disposed toward their interests. Clearly, given such a setup as prevails in most graduate programs for clinical psychology, with many more applicants than places, whichever method actually selects the applicants who will make the best students operates for everyone's best interests. Our objection is to accepting the silent assumption that educational resources must always be scarce relative to need or that it is natural for job-seekers to outnumber jobs, and therefore that a major task for psychology is to find the most efficient ways to select people rather than to achieve the best fit between the needs and capabilities of individuals and institutions that should help them maximize their potentialities for self and for society.

Sawyer and I agree, I believe, that outside the context of therapy, predictive systems of whatever kind are very rarely set up in an attempt to help people find ways to be more fully effective and happy. Rather, most of the predictive enterprises he, Meehl, and others have surveyed have made the silent assumption that people are either sheep or goats, and the job is to find and eliminate the goats: those who will violate parole, or not perform up to institutional standards in some school, or not profit from some available treatment program. They are the disposables, of no further interest once they have been spotted and weeded out. Whatever the methods used, whatever their degree of validity, the question Sawyer raises is whether psychologists want to spend their professional lives quietly supporting that kind of approach to human beings. Neither of *us* wants to, and we both believe that this controversy will have served some useful purpose if it helps to make more psychologists aware of the underlying issues and to reconsider their personal value commitments.

Research

6

Shortly after my arrival at the Center for Advanced Study in the Behavioral Sciences in the late summer of 1960, Silvan Tompkins asked me to participate in one of the Educational Testing Services's invitational conferences (held at Princeton, N.J., on October 13, 1960). The first thing I did during that year, therefore, was to write the following declaration of faith, following the prescription described in the opening paragraph.

Despite the occasionally combative tone of my voice and the hopes of the conveners for a lively fight, my presumptive opponent and old friend Raymond Cattell gave a moderate paper. His nondogmatic, sensible advocacy of factor analysis gave me few openings (though at the time, armed with the hostility of ignorance, I was a great deal more negative toward his strategy than I am today), and he refused to attack me. So the exchange was more amicable than acrimonious, and I dare say none the less edifying.

The paper remains a general statement of position concerning research in clinical psychology and personology to which I still adhere and is thus a suitable opener for this final section of papers on research methods.

A Clinical-Experimental Strategy for Research in Personality

I have been asked to state an alternative position to Dr. Cattell's on the strategy of research and theory-building in the field of personality. He is presenting the unorthodox proposals; so I find myself cast in a novel and somewhat uncomfortable role: the proponent of the status quo, the voice of conservatism. I lay no claims to originality in these matters, either; therefore, I can only summarize here my version of an approach that seems to me quite widely accepted.

Conservatism connotes dogmatism to me; therefore, let me start by arbitrarily enunciating ten principles of faith.

1. The subject matter of personology is human lives, in all their multitudinousness, and in all aspects from the secret and shameful to the trivial and banal.

2. To save itself from being choked by the abundance of its subject matter, personology must concentrate its best efforts on those aspects of lives that appear crucial or critical to the understanding and the prediction, ultimately, of the important events of life. This statement is of course riddled with value judgments like "crucial" and "important." So:

3. Some general theoretical orientation is vital to the study of personality to give guidance and orientation through the bewildering thickets of phenomena. Everyone, of course, has his theoretical orientation; most people today would agree that it is desirable to make it explicit. Mine is freudian with an ego-psychological slant derived largely from Rapaport (e.g., 1960) [since considerably revised].

4. From this vantage point, among the crucial variables to be dealt with are motivations—especially unconscious ones; inward, implicit and reluctantly revealed behaviors like fantasies, dreams, aversions, fears, and hopes; structural parameters of most behavior such as enter into the best diagnostic formulations (e.g., defenses), but including also such conflict-free matters as coping resources (L. Murphy, 1960) and style of cognitive control (Gardner, Holzman, Klein, Linton, & Spence, 1959); pathological tendencies, whether the S is recognized as a patient or not; and the S's view of and feelings about himself in all their social and somatic embeddedness, which I prefer to call *identity*, following Erikson (1959), but which is less comprehensively conceptualized as self-concept, or body-image.

5. The fact that many of these critical variables cannot today be measured with highly satisfactory reliability does not mean that they should be neglected; personology must forge ahead as best it can, muddling through if necessary but never taking its eye off the main chance.

6. Since many of the crucial phenomena of lives are kept secret the researcher cannot elicit them merely by means of a bland smile and assurance that all data will be kept strictly confidential, nor by the apparent anonymity of an objective test (factored or factorable), research in personality cannot do without two highly suspect types of data: those provided by projective tests and those that emerge from the psychotherapeutic interview—the first a technique to circumvent the S's wariness, the second to meet it head on and offer it a good reason for being abandoned. But breadth requires eclecticism, and the contributions of objective testing methods must not be eschewed, either.

7. The uncoordinated explorations of psychotherapists and psychoanalysts incidental to their therapeutic practice are a vital source of discoveries about personality.

8. In the total program of personology, such exploratory research must be followed up by more formalized investigations aimed at the verification of precisely formulated propositions. The latter type of research must have a design that is essentially experimental, though it need not take place in a laboratory.

9. Even when an experiment has been set up to test a specific proposition as rigorously as possible, it is essential that the E take every advantage of his opportunities to learn something new: to form new hypotheses, to observe unexpected parameters, and to ascertain the embeddedness of the phenomena under scrutiny in the personalities of his Ss by means of multiform assessment of them.

10. Finally, the attempt must be made continually to confront the guiding theory with experimental fact, to develop small-scale theories that may be consistent with the larger model, and to modify or reject concepts when repeatedly found wanting.

Probably I could think up some more dogmatic dicta if I tried, but here is a decalogue, which ought to be enough for an investigatory credo. There remains little but to expand, expound, and examine these statements, perhaps also exemplifying them if your tolerance for alliteration can be extended that far.

Let me go back to the beginning, then. Clearly, I follow Murray *et al.* (1938) and White (1952) in defining the subject matter of personology as human lives. Personology is scientific biography, and the genetic method can hardly be dispensed with even when the aim is just to understand a contemporary cross-section of a man. This principle entails or implies several of the others: the plenitude of data that accumulate in the life even of a college freshman; the necessity of getting at the inner, long-term directing goals and structures, by indirect methods as well as direct ones—that is, by multiform assessment. From this perspective, even the carefully standardized biographical inventory (which strives to make life-history data objectively measurable and which can be highly useful) obviously cannot provide all the necessary data for the illumination of the unique life: at a minimum, the autobiography and structured interview must be added,

I trust that I am belaboring the obvious when I point to the danger the student of personality runs of becoming overwhelmed by the quantity of data that can be obtained on a single case, let alone on a sample. [The sociologist, Robert Freed Bales and I, when students in Allport's seminar on personality, made our first case study together on a cooperative volunteer.[1] Within a week, he had dug up years of diaries, the baby books his mother kept, reams of correspondence (including her fond collection of every letter he had ever written her), themes written in college, a scrapbook containing every word or picture that had been published about our man, and an autobiography. In a few weeks, we added to this pile a dozen tests, objective and projective, a map of S's native city with many supporting sociological data, and reams of notes on interviews. We were able to digest all of this to some degree and get the study written up on time only because of two blessed deficiencies: neither of us had any idea about what to do with the

[1][A sampling of the raw data and an integrative analysis may be found in Holt (1971c).]

projective test data, and the tape recorder had not yet been invented.] A moderately exhibitionistic, deferent, abasive, or verbally fluent S can easily fill a file drawer with material for any E who has anything of the collector's bent.

Faced with this embarrassment of riches, many a personologist makes simplifying assumptions to prevent drowning in data. Some decide that a single test (typically the Rorschach, but sometimes the MMPI or TAT) measures the total personality, and concentrate on that. Others exclude all data that are not measured with specifiable and respectable reliability and validity, which cuts the task down enormously. Still others decide that only the patient's own words, uttered from a horizontal position and filtered through a trained therapist, really mean anything. It might be fruitful to look at the problem from the standpoint of Miller's (1960) list of strategies for coping with an overload of informational inputs; I am sure they would all be exemplified in the working practices of the various students of personality.

My own Guide for the Perplexed, as I confessed already, is psychoanalytic theory. Whatever its faults—and it has them in generous supply—it has the great virtue of having been based on prolonged contact with people who were willing to talk about themselves (many sides of themselves in addition to their masturbation fantasies, despite popular impression to the contrary), for *many* hours, nay, years. Such a quantity of direct contact with its subject matter, human lives, is unparalleled in this field, and gives psychoanalysis the same kind of advantage that the diagnosing internist of today has over his pre-Victorian antecedent who never got a chance to take an unobstructed look at the suffering body.

Under my fourth point, I have listed or alluded to the principal classes of variables with which I think personologists must deal. The list is intended to indicate a minimum, not to exclude other variables from consideration, and is more miscellaneous than it should be, containing concepts on all levels of abstraction. Likewise, when it comes to specifying the particular variables to be assessed under each of my half-dozen major headings, there are no guidelines that enable us to list coordinate and cleanly differentiated concepts. We must work with a variety of uneasy compromises: variables that overlap, that approach behavior on different conceptual levels, and that differ in degree of specificity. Some of the ones I use are derived rather directly from theory (e.g., primary and secondary process and their components), others are frankly empirical and commonsensical (e.g., breadth of interests, hostility toward the opposite sex); still others derive from psychologists' common heritage (e.g., vividness of imagery, social sensitivity); some own to a few factor analysts on their family trees (e.g., variables of ability and of cognitive control).

Does this disorder not demand the factor analyst's ministrations? No, because of my fifth commandment. It would be unwise and hardly feasible to factor the variables we work with at the Research Center for Mental Health, because so many of them are necessarily measured with such poor reliability and on such small samples. All the more reason for a stern psychometric purification? I don't think so. To state my position as briefly as possible: factor analysis and the other tools of the psychometrician are splendid for certain purposes, but not for all. When ratings of personality have been factored, they have sometimes yielded variables with so little intuitive meaning that they could not be rated directly, and not measured in any other way either.

It is good to know something about the redundancy in your conceptual equipment, but not to eliminate all of it. Measuring personality is in part a communicative process, and it is by now well established that a certain amount of redundancy is vital to efficient communication. When the only way we can get hold of an aspect of personality quantitatively is to rate it, I believe that we ought to do our best to rate it well. Raters are human beings and are seldom able to make use of a set of factor loadings as the definition of something to be extracted from a mass of rich, qualitative data. What is to be rated has to be defined in such a way as to make rating possible and to make it as reliable as is feasible. With the proper conceptual and practical training, raters can perform prodigies, but there is the question of diminishing returns: for any given research, is it worth the enormous investment of time to train raters to quantify something that doesn't make intuitive sense or something that cannot be rather directly inferred from the data available? Such practical issues have a lot to do with the particular set of variables you actually end up with.

As I hope I have made clear, theoretical issues require the retention of some variables that cannot be quantified with any elegance whatsoever. Doubtless there are many who will disapprove of the determination to keep up the struggle to use refractory concepts. Let them reflect on the history of medicine: if physicians of the nineteenth century—an era when on the whole the medical profession did more harm than good—had given up the attempt to cure diseases they could do nothing for, and if instead they had stuck to what they did have demonstrable success with, their patients would have undoubtedly been happier and healthier in the short run, but *we* would not be today. Modern scientific medicine developed only because the old, primitive doctors stuck at it and kept plugging as best they could. Similarly, in psychology if we turn our faces away from the attempt to measure unconscious motives, for example, because of the fact that it cannot be done today with demonstrable reliability or validity, this vitally important area of personality will be neglected. The psychoanalysts cannot be expected to provide such measures, and the factor analysts working with pencil-and-paper tests surely will not. As our science progresses, we should hope to see ratings progressively supplanted by tests or other objective techniques, but for the immediately foreseeable future, the researcher on personality will have to cope with many variables as best he can by means of rating scales.

The dangers of my position are not to be denied or burked. The personologist must not forget that many of his conceptual tools are in constant need of replacement or overhauling as soon as possible; he runs the danger of fooling himself that he is really measuring something like the superego or the sense of identity just because he is making the effort to do so. We have to be on the lookout constantly for unwanted consequences of conceptual redundancy (as in getting too excited by a string of significant findings involving a group of variables that essentially measure the same thing), and must at least try to *measure* that redundancy so that we can be aware of and allow for it (and here I welcome the aid of factor analysis). In general, my formula for tolerating the ambiguity and disrespectability of concepts and measuring devices is to be as fully aware of their defects as possible—preferably by means of measurement—and to avoid self-deception in their use.

Coming now to the sixth point of faith, the necessity to use such questionably quantifiable data as are provided by projective tests, personal documents, and interviews, much of what I have just said is applicable. The worker with these slippery instruments needs to *know* psychometrics and the standards of good test construction, even if he doesn't always put it all into practice. If the APA Test Standards were rigorously applied to the Rorschach and TAT, these indispensable diagnostic tools would have to be abandoned; but the alternative is not to say that such standards are wholly inappropriate to projective techniques and to go our merry way without restraint or responsibility. No, I think that any user of these tests who is not content to be a mere technician, doing what he was taught in a routine way, ought to be rather continually aware of the test standards and to strive toward them. Likewise for personality measurement generally: it needs a set of rigorous ideals, not to plunge its practitioners into despair but to guide them onto higher, firmer ground from which they will be able to get better leverage for work on their major problems of human lives.

Another aspect of the sixth point is a metric catholicism, which in itself is a safeguard. Here is another fruit of redundancy—using many simultaneous methods of measuring personality, one gains security from the overlap of findings. Thus, for example, in a study on reality deprivation Goldberger and I did (Holt & Goldberger, 1959) we found a pattern of positive adaptation to the unusual experimental demands (mostly, to perceive and do nothing for 8 hours) to be correlated with clinical ratings of effeminacy *and* with objective test measures of it (Grygier's DPI); with esthetic sensitivity as measured by pencil-and-paper instruments like the Allport-Vernon-Lindzey Study of Values, and by an objective technique like the Barron-Welsh Art Scale (of the Welsh Figure Preference test), as well as by the clinical ratings.

Such comforting consensus increases one's faith that the clinical ratings based on qualitative data have some reliability and that the objective instruments have some validity.

When we come to the seventh point, about the necessity of exploratory research, we approach the most exciting and creative aspect of work in personology. I cannot think of a single major discovery or hypothesis in this field that did not come out of exploratory and often quite informal investigation, rather than from rigorous verification of propositions. By the very nature of the scientific process, it is hard to lay down rules about how insights and researchable hunches are to be obtained; one can only expose a prepared and curious mind to an extended opportunity to observe important phenomena. Statistical inquiry is as unpromising a context of discovery as clinical work is a context of verification. The statistical manipulation of a set of data can occasionally line up a set of points that leads one's extrapolative sight beyond those data, but usually discovery is confined to the narrow circle described by the numbers one manipulates, even factor-analytically. By contrast, it would be hard to improve on the intensive study of individual cases in diagnostic or therapeutic practice, as a source of ideas about how people are put together, fall apart, or manage to function. It brings the clinician into intimate contact with the emotionally central facts of existence, many of which are so thoroughly concealed that we nontherapists are likely to overlook or forget about them.

True, psychoanalysts and other clinicians have been mining these rich lodes for many years and have not been loath to speculate freely in print about what they have observed. We are very far from exhausting the suggestions for more systematic inquiry in the writings of even one man, Sigmund Freud. Yet many important discoveries remain to be made by the clinical method. One has only to reflect that Erikson's clinical observations and theorizing and his exploratory research on identity (see Erikson, 1959) date from the recent past, to realize that testable new insights will continue to issue from the consulting room for years to come.

I stress testability to usher in point eight, the necessity to make the transition from the clinic to the laboratory. It is doubtless unnecessary to convince this audience that the psychoanalyst's form of clinical research, done as an incident to therapeutic practice, can hardly be used to verify or disprove propositions. But the design and execution of experiments that test propositions ready-made by the clinician is far from being all that is implied by this eighth commandment. Let me list a few other kinds of help we can get from the exploratory researcher. A very simple form consists of the experimenter's borrowing concepts from the clinician (e.g., separation anxiety, narcissism) and applying them directly in the assessment of personality via ratings. Or concepts may simply suggest an area, which the laboratory researcher proceeds to explore with his own methods; an example would be the work of Fisher (e.g., 1954), Luborsky and Shevrin (e.g., 1956), and our own laboratory (Klein & Holt, 1960) in the area of preconscious cognitive phenomena. When we carried out our first study of this sort (Klein, Spence, Holt, & Gourevitch, 1958), we wanted to use the masking phenomenon, or metacontrast as it is sometimes called, simply as a way of seeing what happens to a cognitive process when it goes on without awareness; since then, we have worked our way into a number of problems in the subliminal field that have no direct contact with the concept of preconscious mental processes, a term we no longer use in conceptualizing these experiments.

Another major focus of our work illustrates a third way in which concepts deriving from exploratory clinical research may be put to work in more formalized laboratory investigations (which are not yet true tests of propositions). This method is to take a psychoanalytic concept with empirical referents, make those explicit (that is, give it an operational definition) and then explore the phenomena concerned in new contexts or with methods different from those used in the work that generated the concept. One such concept Freud (1900a) called the primary process; from his clinical studies of his own and his patients' dreams, he found he had to postulate an intervening variable, the primary process, to account for the transformations of the latent dream thoughts into the manifest, reported dream. After a study of his theoretical writings on dreams and those of other, more recent ego-psychologists (particularly Hartmann, e.g., 1950), I arrived at an operational definition of a two-fold character: primary-process ideation is wishful, and it has certain formal properties which Freud described for the dream and dream work [see Volume 1, Chapters 8–11]. Armed with this definition, I set up a system of scoring categories to pick up manifestations of the primary process in Rorschach responses (Holt, 1959e). We are also using the definition in direct rating of primary process in TAT stories (Eagle, 1964), free verbalizations of Ss kept in perceptual isolation (deprivation of meanings) (Goldberger, 1961), and the productions of Ss who had been given LSD-25 (lysergic acid diethylamide; Barr, Langs, Holt, Goldberger, & Klein, 1972), in addition to dream protocols. It has made possible the exploratory study of the limits of thinking that show the hallmarks of the primary process in a variety of circumstances that tend to distort and disorder thinking. We have also been able to do some modest testing of hypotheses. The reason for the sudden outbreak of modesty is that the hypotheses we have tested so far have had more of the earmarks of empirically derived hunches than propositions rigorously derived from psychoanalytic theory.

Which brings me to another point about the testing of psychoanalytic propositions: it is difficult to make this theory yield testable propositions, and a lot of theoretical work must go on before anything like a critical test of the theory is possible. Why? First, because psychoanalytic theory has never been fully formalized or systematized and does not exist in neat, propositional form. You have to dig to find anything that sounds like such a proposition. Once you have found it, the chances are that it is not what it seems; it may not be a theoretical statement at all, but an empirical generalization. Thus, for example, Freud has been quoted as saying that the Oedipus complex is universal. Fine, that can be tested; a single exception will prove it sorely. But it is merely a rash statement by a man who loved to state his ideas in striking, sweeping terms, introducing qualifications and delimitations later (in passages that rarely get quoted; see Holt, 1965d); a pure empirical generalization, it has no theoretical content and may be disproved (*if* you can satisfactorily define the Oedipus complex) without touching the fabric of the theory. Or if the statement you propose to work with is *not* such a generalization, it is almost certain to be hard to understand out of context. This means that it must be carefully rephrased by someone who knows the corpus of psychoanalytic theory and its historical development. Few experimenters, even those trained in the psychology of personality, have had the patience, motivation, and specialized knowledge to do so.

Let me exemplify again. Consider the following quotation from *The Outline of Psychoanalysis* (Freud, 1940a), which is pretty clearly a theoretical proposition:

> . . . we speak of cathexes and hypercathexes of the material of the mind and even venture to suppose that a hypercathexis brings about a sort of synthesis of different processes—a synthesis in the course of which free energy is transformed into bound energy.

I recently had occasion to make a close study of this and related passages in Freud's writings (Holt, 1962a) and can assure you that here he is asserting a relation between the degree of consciousness and the degree to which thinking is rational—that is, follows the rules of the secondary rather than the primary process.[2] You will grant me that this last proposition in my rewording is not obvious in what Freud wrote, and that it sounds more testable. It can be quite rigorously tested, in fact, and a study from our laboratory has verified it in a limited way. The specific proposition tested in this experiment by Bach (1960) was that when Ss were asked to look at a card with a word written on it and then to write down a list of words, these "associations" would be logically related (according to the secondary process) to the meaning of the word on the card when the latter was clearly visible (in

[2]The key to the translation is that hypercathexis, which does the binding, is the construct Freud coordinated to attention and consciousness, and free and bound energy characterize the primary and secondary processes. [What I failed to realize at the time is that nothing much is gained by tracing a connection between the prediction and a theoretical passage. The experiment does not verify the theory, which is only the empirical observation dressed up in physicalistic language. The poverty of metapsychology appears here in the vagueness of everything except the theoretical nouns; the processes by which hypercathexis "brings about *a sort of* synthesis," or by which energy "is transformed" are not only left entirely unspecified, they have all the earmarks of arbitrary, ad hoc postulation. Indeed, Freud did not pretend that he was doing anything more, when he modestly said "venture to suppose" instead of trying to imply that he had in some way deduced the proposition.]

Freud's language, hypercathected), but that associations would be related by means of symbolic transformations when the word was too faint to be visible (could not be hypercathected). The findings with a small sample tentatively verified the predictions.

Even in this last case, which looks like a direct test of a theoretically derived proposition, I have to confess that the theoretical derivation was supplied only after the experiment was completed, the problem having been arrived at by a rather different route, as a test of an empirical generalization (thought processes that go on without awareness tend to have more characteristics of the primary process than when they go on with full awareness). I am not sure that I have made clear the difference between this idea stated empirically and theoretically, but I hope you agree that the test of an empirical generalization has the less relevance for the theory. Clearly, it is not easy to extract a good theoretical proposition and to test it by experiment, but when you do, you feel you are getting somewhere.

One reason you are getting somewhere is that, if as in this case the proposition is verified, you can start making parametric studies. That is, in a controlled way, you can close in on and define the specific conditions (parameters) under which the relation in question holds. Consider this last example for a moment longer: common sense argues that, even though in general thinking may approximate the picture of the primary process more when it goes on outside awareness, there are clearly exceptions. Thinking produced in awareness may be (apparently) quite crazily crammed with primary process—for example, the speech of schizophrenics, or of people who have taken enough of certain drugs, or the productions of many modern poets and other artists (who are able to regress, not crazily but adaptively). On the other hand, after the posing of a problem, thinking may go underground, so to speak, and emerge with answers that could hardly have been arrived at in any way other than rationally—for example, the solution of mathematical problems during sleep (Hadamard, 1945). Therefore, we must set about finding the limits of our original result by varying different aspects of the experiment. When we find these limits, they will enable us to make a direct contribution to the theory of cognition, a contribution that will help to make it sharper, more specific, and more empirically applicable.

I have left myself little time to cover my last two points. The ninth is just a reminder that to test a hypothesis is not to make discoveries, but that any piece of research offers opportunities for discovery, for the formation of hunches and the obtaining of insights, if you keep your eyes open to everything that is going on, *not* just whether the statement tested was confirmed or disconfirmed. Following my teacher, Henry A. Murray, I have found that it is a valuable adjunct to experimental research to study the personality of each subject, quantify it in ratings, and then statistically explore the relations between laboratory findings and assessments, or make qualitative comparisons of extreme cases. For example, in the study on reality deprivation (Holt & Goldberger, 1959) cited above, Goldberger and I got valuable leads about the role of the passivity required by the experiment (a requirement that is probably far more stressful to certain somatotonic Ss than any homogeneity of sensory stimulation you may be able to achieve), from the assessement data on our Ss.

By way of elucidating my final, summary statement of the desirable relation between theory and experiment, let me make some final comments on theory-building in relation to research in personology. Again, I will have to be brief and dogmatic. The field is too young, in relation to the complexity of its subject matter, to expect of it any highly sophisticated, rigorous, overall theory. It is not necessary to derive testable propositions from such a theory for models and experiments to stimulate and fructify each other; the much looser relationship that is possible in personology is still most useful. With Marquis (1948), I consider the times right for small-package theories dealing with a limited range of phenomena, though it seems desirable to frame those subtheories so that they fit into the general framework provided by some overarching theory.

But how should we arrive at variables to be quantified and woven into the fabric of theory? I have suggested above that we should exploit existing models and the suggestions of exploratory research, and also that we should go ahead and quantify whatever we can. What a mess! you may shudder; concepts of every stripe jostling each other without any perceptible order. I have been occupied for parts of 20 years with the problem of how some order can be introduced, or how a self-consistent set of concepts might be generated, but so far in vain. Using a uniform typographic format, or giving all concepts names with Greek roots, or other such phenotypic approaches will not do it, for the concepts under their identical uniforms may still be unable to come into contact with one another. I am not convinced that factor analysis will always do it, either, even though at times it is very useful, for the following reasons:

A. Factor analysis would perform a great service if it could come up with basic dimensions in psychology comparable to the centimeter-gram-second system in physics that makes possible dimensional analysis, since these dimensions are involved in all classical physical equations. But it has not yet done so.

B. Factor analysis can digest only sets of data that can be measured in comparable ways and correlated, thus must omit aspects of personality that are not yet so measureable. It cannot go beyond the limitations of the data that are fed it; if an aspect of personality is not implicit in the data you have thought to supply, it will not be found.

C. At best, factor analysis can provide only a set of variables; it can tell us nothing about the equations into which they are to be entered to make a model of functional dependencies in nature.

D. The concepts that result may be intuitively unintelligible, and thus unusable.

E. The relations among the resulting factors, whether orthogonal or oblique and correlated, are predetermined by the choice of factor-analytic method.

F. One of the strongest criticisms that can be leveled against factor analysis does not take issue with it on principle, but in terms of practice. With the advent of high-speed computers and factor-analytic programs for them, it has become too easy to toss any miscellaneous batch of data into this seductive hopper and subject them to the Procrustean program that happens to be available. This point amounts to little more than coming out against sin, since one of the seven deadly sins is Sloth—the lazy habit of using an easy analytic method instead of the one that is most appropriate to the problem and the data.

As an alternative, then, I propose experimental use and refinement of concepts. Put them to work! Let them prove themselves in suggesting new work and ordering new phenomena; and if the propositions they generate consistently fail to be verified, let them expire gracefully.

7

For the first few years after I came to New York University in 1953, I taught a graduate course on research methods in clinical psychology. A lecture course, it accompanied a practicum taught by George Klein, in which students developed their own problems and carried out studies, some to the point of publication. The latter was so obviously the better course that my more didactic presentation was abandoned. Most of what was of lasting value in my lecture notes went into the chapter I prepared for the Handbook of Clinical Psychology *(Wolman, 1965a), here reprinted with very few changes as Chapter 7, or into Chapter 8.*

Experimental Methods in Clinical Psychology

Even someone who has read all the standard works on experimental design and who has a good general grasp of experimental research methods is likely to experience some difficulty when he tries to apply these methods within the broad territory known as clinical psychology. The principal aim of this chapter, therefore, is to focus on the role of experimentation in clinical psychology, to consider the kinds of special problems encountered in clinicoexperimental research, and to suggest a number of ways of coping with these problems.

THE PLACE OF EXPERIMENT IN CLINICAL PSYCHOLOGY[1]

For the purposes of this chapter, the term "experiment" will be used in its broadest sense, following R. A. Fisher, to mean "only experience carefully planned in advance." "This simple phrase," comments Kaplan (1964), "already makes reference to the two most general and fundamental traits of

---

[1]This section is much indebted to secs. 17–19 of Kaplan (1964). In particular, the various types of experiment listed follow Kaplan's classification and definitions.

scientific inquiry—that [it] . . . is both empirical and rational. . . . Experiment is the consummation of the marriage of reason and experience, and though it is not in itself the [entire] life of the mind, it is the most passionate and fruitful expression of our intellectual life and loves."

This seductive phraseology ought to raise some doubts about the common assumption that experimentation is the pedantic and austere preoccupation of bloodless compulsives, an antithesis to the way of the clinician. There are more conflicts of outlook here than the above passage implies, even beyond the obvious personal and political ones, but the diversity that they express may as easily be complementary as competitive. Let us begin, then, by examining the differences in outlook connoted by the terms "clinical" and "experimental."

The clinical orientation grows out of the traditions of medicine, especially the medicine of the working physician at the bedside, who is directly involved in real problems about which he is obligated to do something and who must intervene as much as possible in the causal sequences he sees. The good clinician is a keen naturalistic observer, not afraid to rely on subjective—even intuitive—judgments and predictions; his approach is qualitative, holistic, molar, and personal. If he records his observations, it is a distinctly secondary activity of a participant-observer hoping to increase his future effectiveness by organizing his impressions and experience, usually as "recollected in tranquility."

By contrast, the experimental tradition grows out of the laboratory work of academic scientists, whose concern has always been with knowledge rather than action, with precise and objective measurement rather than sensitive and comprehensive looking, and thus with the precise handling of small, manageable segments of behavior rather than the struggle to do justice to the richness of a real-life encounter. The experimental researcher often relies on instruments and tests to help him record observations at once and with a minimum of bias. For the sake of objectivity, he strives to intervene as little as possible in what he sees. The experimentalist's ideal is to know what he knows as exactly as he can or with a known margin of error; the clinician's cognitive ideal is to know what it is *important* to know about a person. Moreover, the experimentalist worships truth monotheistically, while for the clinician truth is but part of a pantheon including service and social responsibility.

But clinical psychology is a science as well as a profession, and it needs to learn and use all it can that is of value from experimentation. The experimenter who hopes to learn something about personality and its disorders stands to gain a great deal from the clinical viewpoint, too. The trick is to keep the best of both worlds with a minimum of the faults of each. When he turns to the experimental method, the clinician should try to hold on to his sensitivity, his ability to see the relevance to important human issues, the breadth and richness of his outlook, his motivational orientation, and his flexibility. He should try to put aside his distaste for measurement and for objective methods of gathering data, his emotional reaction against the allegedly dry and dusty academic traditions of careful control, his resistance to analysis of such sacred confines as clinical judgment, and his nervousness about brass instruments.

The clinical psychologist will discover that his training and orientation provide him with a number of advantages when he tries his hand at controlled investigation. Even in a rigorously planned laboratory experiment, the clinician will notice that as long as the subjects are people, they have the capacity to understand communications on many levels simultaneously and to react in equally many-layered complexity. Since we are always being faced with the unexpected, it helps to be prepared for it. The "evenly hovering attention" of the therapist can be most useful in picking up incidental bits of laboratory behavior that may explain why a whole experiment went awry. His intuition, too, should not be left at the couch-side; the experimenter needs to have plenty of it and to be willing to *listen* to his intuition without being carried away by it. Ironically, physicists tend to respect intuition more than traditional experimental psychologists do! [Einstein wrote, for example: "To these elementary laws there leads no logical path, but only intuition, supported by being sympathetically in touch with experience" (quoted in Holton, 1973, p. 357).]

Hunches may tell us where or how to look, but looking alone is not research. Whether the clinical psychologist is primarily interested in pursuing a theoretically important topic or in trying to learn the answer to a practical problem in his clinical work, he must eventually pass from the initial phase of merely keeping his eyes and ears open, to the discipline of systematic research. The experimental method is essentially reality testing refined and systematized, and therefore it is neither intrinsically arcane nor difficult. It is largely a matter of focusing on answerable questions and of introducing enough controls so that it is possible to trust and understand the answers.

Let us turn from such very general characterizations of experiment and examine some of the types of investigation that merit this proud name. To begin with, "some experiments are *methodological* (so-called): they serve to develop or to improve some particular technique of inquiry" (Kaplan, 1964). For example, after Aserinsky and Kleitman (1955) first verified the hunch that rapid eye movements during sleep indicate dreaming, it was necessary for Dement and Kleitman (1957a,b) to conduct a series of experiments in order to develop efficient techniques of identifying the objective indicants of dreaming. When Shapiro, Goodenough, and Gryler (1963) studied the effects of different methods of awakening the S to obtain his dream report, their experiment was a methodological one. Tooling up of this kind can and should be experimental simply because there is no equally good way of getting empirical knowledge with a known margin of error. When a methodological experiment focuses on establishing the limits of variables to be studied more systematically in a later series of projects, Kaplan calls it a "pilot study." Before he could explore the ramifications of dream deprivation, Dement (1960) had to discover through a pilot study whether it was possible to keep awakening a sleeper as soon as REMs began and thus prevent an appreciable amount of dreaming while still retaining his cooperation, how many times a night this would be necessary and for how many nights before any effect could be demonstrated, and so forth.

Initial investigative forays at times have the aim of opening up possible new fields of research, proceeding from the hunch or the theoretically engendered guess that a certain kind of controlled observation and intervention might yield fruitful results. Lilly (1956) was embarked on such a *heuristic or exploratory experiment* when he decided to immerse himself in a tank of tepid water and minimize all sources of external sensory stimulation. He was guided by some theoretical notions concerning sleep, but in large part he was simply curious to know what would happen in such an unusual situation; the effect was to provide many leads that have been followed up by other investigators. Notice that although not all exploratory research is experimental, a heuristic investigation may follow the general experimental model in that a phenomenon is studied under controlled conditions and with some attempt to manipulate one or more variables.

The fact-finding kind of research is often not considered experimental at all, since, for example, surveying the mental health of a community does not in any obvious way constitute an intervention. Contrast, however, the precise and reliable findings of such surveys as those of Hollingshead and Redlich (1958) and of Srole, Langner, Michael, Opler, and Rennie (1962) with the unsystematic impressions of a literary observer who visited American cities and their insane asylums almost a century ago (Dickens, 1842), and it begins to be apparent why the careful procedure of a modern sample survey can be called "experimental." Controlled interviewing and testing, as opposed to unsystematic conversation, intervene in the communicative processes of the respondents in a way precisely analogous to the sequences of controlled stimuli introduced in, say, psychophysical experiments. To want to know what would happen if you asked a probability sample of a city's citizens "What do you understand by mental illness?" is not intrinsically different from wanting to know what would happen if you gave a sample of people a new drug; both are properly called "experiments," and many of the same principles and techniques of research apply to both and to the most classical laboratory test of a rigorously derived hypothesis. But *fact-finding experiments* include a good deal more than surveys. Systematic studies of the natural course of a clinical syndrome like hysteria—a too-much neglected type of psychopathological research—or of the typical stages of ego development are fact-finding experiments, too. Much of Piaget's developmental research is experimental in this sense, in contrast to Erikson's (e.g., 1963), which is essentially retrospective reflection on unsystematically obtained clinical experience.

In the *boundary experiment,* an attempt is made to discover the range of application of certain known laws or functional relations. When does anxiety function as a generalized drive in learning experiments, as K. W. Spence and his co-workers have painstakingly shown (Taylor & Spence, 1952), and when does it start to become disruptive or paralyzing panic? At what degree of impoverishment of a supraliminal stimulus does the paradoxical limiting effect of awareness described by D. Spence and Holland (1962) give way, and what are the other parameters of what seems to be a phase change in the cognitive reverberations of a stimulus? A great many boundary experiments are called for to establish the precise limits of such relationships.

When we set up an explicit model of some real-life situation and manipulate it, we are involved in a *simulation or analogue experiment.* This is the strategy of choice when we want to investigate conditions that are beyond our current reach in real life (e.g., perceptual isolation experiments as simulacra of space travel to enable us to study its cognitive effects) or matters that are closed to direct study for ethical reasons (compare the use of animals in the first clinical trials of potentially dangerous drugs—many experiments with animals as Ss may be considered simulations of the same thing with human beings). The well-known study by Keet (1948) compared miniature replicas of several psychotherapeutic techniques on their ability to uncover an experimentally induced repression, achieving thereby great economies and some advantages of control, as compared with an attempt to do the same experiment with real patients and real therapy. A different type of simulation with interesting possibilities for clinicians is the programming of high-speed computers to simulate personological processes such as free association (Tomkins & Messick, 1963; see especially chapter by Colby). Even though the behavior of no actual persons is observed, computer simulation makes possible the testing and clarification of theory in a way that should prove most salutary.

The ideal type of experiment, in the minds of many of us, is the specific one the Kaplan calls *nomological,* to which most of the written methodological discussions are directed: the experiment that tests some hypothesis or, more specifically, attempts to decide between a null hypothesis and one or more alternatives. This is the kind of experiment that makes it possible "to transform an empirical generalization into a law . . . that is, to identify what is both necessary and sufficient for the empirically given connection, by varying the experimental conditions" (Kaplan, 1964). Usually, it will take a series of interrelated experiments to establish a law in this way; very exceptionally, a single *crucial experiment* can settle a theoretical issue—at least temporarily—by decisively altering "the balance of probabilities," such as between alternative explanations for a phenomenon. Thus, Fiss, Goldberg, and Klein (1963) set up an experimental situation in which the "partial cues" theory of Goldiamond, Ericksen, and others yielded diametrically opposite predictions from the conception that stimuli may affect behavior without the involvement of conscious awareness, and they verified the latter. By the time these words are in print, yet another theory may have been found more comprehensive and better able to predict than either of these, but that is the way science grows.

Finally, there are *illustrative experiments*—replications motivated by didactic purposes, as in the training of researchers, or by the wish to see with one's own eyes a reported phenomenon or relationship that seems important, puzzling, or otherwise interesting. Replication is so important and so neglected in clinical psychology, as well as in other branches of behavioral science generally, that it is good to see it included in such an authoritative classification as Kaplan's. It not infrequently happens that failures to replicate originally reported results lead to important discoveries or at least suggest that the initial publication neglected to point out significant parametric limitations on its findings. See, for example, the various attempts to replicate the 1948 experiment of Keet (Grummion & Butler, 1953; Heim, 1951; Merrill, 1952), which failed through an inability to reproduce his experimental analogue of repression. These may result in redoubled investigative attention to this side issue in Keet's work, which is important in its own right [see Fredenthal, 1966].

A dozen types of experiment may be described without even touching on the issue of pure versus applied research, for essentially the same methods are used whether the question addressed to nature grew out of theory, out of simple curiosity about concrete clinical phenomena, or out of practical necessity. A great deal of clinical research seeks to explore the reality of human lives and may help us formulate relatively precise questions. Whenever a clear-cut question can be posed, however one has arrived at it, experimentation is the method of choice to provide precise and reliable answers. Therefore, it can and must play a growing role in clinical psychology.

SPECIAL PROBLEMS OF CLINICAL RESEARCH

As we shall see, many of the problems that seem to be unique to clinical psychology turn out to exist, in disguised or attenuated form, in *any* kind of experimental research. Yet there are at least enough quantitative differences to make the following more outstandingly problematical for the clinical experimentalist than for his nonclinical brother.[2]

Problems Arising from the Nature of the Subject Matter and Basic Orientation. For the purposes of this chapter, clinical psychology will be understood to differ from the rest of psychology in that it has a major commitment to understand and deal with the major "real-life" issues and problems of living,

---

[2]This listing owes a good deal to the survey of clinical research made by Hilgard, Gill, and Shakow for the Ford Foundation (unpublished).

striving, suffering human beings. Thus, general experimental psychology is concerned with perception; clinical psychology is interested in it too, but with an emphasis on the nature of the person who is perceiving and the role of his ways of contacting and testing reality in his pattern of adjustment or maladjustment. Both are concerned with learning, but the experimentalist wants to analyze learning processes in the laboratory, where he can control all the variables specified by theory, while the clinician wants to find out how the person learns his major motives, his styles of coping with challenge, and his mechanisms of defense and how he can unlearn maladaptive or self-destructive ways of behaving and replace them with ways that are more generally satisfactory to others and to himself. The social psychologist wants to learn how people in general respond to the manipulations of power in human relations, while the clinical psychologist more characteristically seeks to learn how and why individuals differ in their relations to authorities and what such styles are related to in other departments of personality.

As a practitioner, the clinician learns to look for the fox without getting too fascinated by each bit of fur; his practical experience forces him to develop the habit and techniques of keeping his eye on the main point, the fact that all the phenomena in front of him are part of a unique, valuable, and staggeringly complex human life. As a scientist, however, he is up against a basic paradox: most of the principles of scientific method seem predicated on gaining control over knowledge by limiting vision, whereas he is convinced that he will betray his first principles if he loses sight of the entire panorama. Here, then, is the first and most fundamental problem of experimental research in clinical psychology—how to discipline observation so that questions can be answered with some known degree of confidence without abandoning a commitment to ask humanly *important* questions (see Loevinger, 1963).

Problems of Value Judgments. Experimenters are understandably loath to rush into the area of good and bad, where only angels are at home. Yet clinical psychology is interested in personality and its pathology: the patterning of behavior viewed in the large and from the perspective of a life as a whole, with an emphasis on the difficulties and problems people encounter in living, the ways they function badly, and the types of intervention that can significantly affect major trends of behavior. This emphasis on pathology and dysfunction leads inevitably to a parallel concern with patterns of "normal," adaptive, and comfortable or creatively struggling life. One has to have some conception of normality to understand the abnormal, some grasp of health in order to know how to ameliorate disease. As Jahoda (1958) has argued—and I agree with her conclusion—the very concept of mental health is an unavoidably normative one, ultimately a statement of socially valued forms of behavior. The further one gets from the reduction screen of the laboratory, which narrows one's focus of observation down to a precise and isolated function, the more insistently questions of value raise themselves. Even the term "personality" itself, in common parlance, refers to a social ideal of attractiveness. [See also Chapter 10, below.]

Problems of Temporal Scope. As Murray *et al.* (1938) and White (1952) have defined it, personology is the study of lives, scientific biography. Freud's genetic emphasis has convinced the majority of psychopathologists that the disorders they are concerned with cannot be understood without the reconstruction of the person's past, preferably back to earliest childhood. Longitudinal studies of child development (see, for example, Kagan & Moss, 1962; MacFarlane, Allen, & Honzik, 1955) have been made in attempts to broaden observation to include a substantial segment of the life cycle. But it remains a heavy burden to be obliged to take into account the whole sweep of a subject's life, when the experimenter himself belongs to the same mortal species. Some means must be found to take account of the genetic dimension in cross-sectional, brief experiments.

Problems of Situational Embeddedness. Once we admit to an interest in who our subjects are and how they are doing, we cannot ignore such homely but troublesome matters as where they live, where they came from, what they do for a living and how, whom they interact with, and what kinds of opportunities, dangers, or predicaments these others present. In short, we have to face the fact that psychology must be supplemented by sociology, anthropology, economics, political science, linguistics, and history—i.e., with *all* the social and behavioral sciences. The kinds of variables they deal with affect human behavior, and thus they cannot be ignored by clinical research.

Problems Arising from the Personality's Relations with a Body. The only behavior we need to concern ourselves with in clinical psychology is indulged in by human organisms prominently characterized by bodies: organized, mobile, sensitive, space-occupying aggregations of matter. The more we learn about any one person, the less we can ignore the far-reaching interdigitation of his behavior with the biochemical, physiological, anatomical, biophysical, and neurological nature of his soma. Moreover, we learn to recognize that there are many bodily nonverbal channels of communication and expression, which often convey the message or betray the reaction for which the clinician is listening. Thus, the body is of concern as a source of both independent and dependent variables.

Problems of Objectivity about the Subjective. It was perfectly possible for Watson to decide to ignore and deny the importance of anything about the behaving subject that could not be externally and objectively observed. It is equally possible today to put a schizophrenic into a room where he has nothing to do but pull a lever and then to concentrate one's attention entirely on the quantitative data generated by this apparatus. By my definition, however, this is not clinical psychology, though I would not deny that it is as legitimate an object of scientific curiosity as any other specifiable aspect of nature. The clinician's commitment forces him to be as much interested in the delusions and hallucinations that occupy the patient's consciousness while he is or is not pulling the lever as in any easily quantifiable aspect of his functioning. Clinicians have preoccupied themselves with these mentalistic phenomena, not because of any allegiance to Wundt or Titchener, but because they have found empirically that patients do talk a good deal about dreams, fantasies, moods, and other subjective states when allowed to discuss whatever is on their minds and because they have discovered that these kinds of data are indispensable in the therapeutic enterprise. Yet the requirements of intersubjectivity in science are valid and cannot be ignored.

Practical and Ethical Problems of Privacy. It follows immediately from the above that the clinical researcher must have some means of gaining access to inner, subjective experiences of his subjects. This is not easy to do, for most people are reluctant to reveal their dreams, their daydreams, their longings and fears, and their private beliefs and values to a stranger. And serious ethical questions are raised: does a human being have the right, even in the name and for the cause of science, to require other persons to reveal to him the aspects of their personalities of which they are most ashamed and about which they feel most guilty? Even if the experimenter can spare his subjects the embarrassment of directly revealing such secrets by the use of projective and other indirect techniques, is it ethical for him to peek through their defenses in this way? What for example, is he to do if the subject reveals— wittingly or not—some antisocial acts, past or contemplated?

Problems of Nonconscious Determinants of Behavior. The one great lesson that clinical psychologists of all persuasions have learned from Freud is that behavior is determined, on the *psychological* level (quite in addition to the levels of determination just alluded to), by motives, defenses, and controls of which the subject is not fully aware at the time and which he thus cannot report on even if he wishes to. The problems posed by this state of affairs have the same dual practical and ethical nature as those just discussed.

Problems of the Interactional Nature of Clinical Data—"Countertransference." The subject is not the only fallible, driven, unconsciously motivated participant in an experiment; the experimenter is just as much a human being. This is true, incidentally, whether he is a clinician or not; his own hopes, anxieties, or prejudices may bias the data even when he is interested only in some isolated segment of objectively measurable behavior. But the clinician has learned that he has to look out for his own defenses and for the distorting influences of his current life problems and the residues of infantile experience alike, and so he is more likely to become aware that these sources of error exist in the laboratory too. There can be "acting out in the counter-transference" in an experiment, just as there can be in a clinical encounter. The data may be affected by the tendency of *both* parties in an experiment to react in terms of unconscious repetition of old patterns of response to significant people in their personal pasts. The experimenter's blind spots and patterns of systematic distortion may be particularly troublesome when he has to analyze ambiguous and subjective data of the kind so often generated in clinical experiments.

Problems of the Interpersonal Setting: The Lone Investigator versus Interdisciplinary Team Research. Most clinical research has always been done by single investigators, typically private practitioners of psychoanalysis or psychotherapy who used their clinical work as an opportunity to observe people and their problems and to form hypotheses about functional relationships. Although the research methods used in the typical clinical case study are not within the purview of this chapter [see Chapter 8], many of the same difficulties dog the steps of the lone investigator who is pursuing one of the kinds of experimentation listed above. He lacks the stimulation and correction of his ideas afforded by daily interchange with colleagues. Because of his involvement with his patients, he has the greatest difficulty in gathering data without biases and contamination; the problems of countertransference, blind spots, and the necessity to intervene for therapeutic reasons make systematic experimentation difficult indeed. So many of the phases of research require independent observation to establish the reliability (intersubjectivity) of judgments that the isolated experimenter's range of researchable problems is severely restricted.

Plainly, a consequence of many points already made is that much clinical research requires the cooperation of several experimenters with a variety of talents and training. Despite its advantages, such cooperative group research has several drawbacks. (1) It is expensive, not only in salaries, but also in the time and effort that investigators must put into administration. (2) As some wit pointed out, interdisciplinary research makes possible not only cross-fertilization of ideas but also cross-sterilization—a reduction of diverse contributions to their greatest common denominator, which may be disappointingly small. (3) Difficulties in communication are the primary source of trouble. People who have different contributions to make also use different jargons and approach things from subtly different points of view, which may require quite a lot of talking at cross-purposes to discover. Learning how members of other professions talk and think may be valuable educationally, but it does not directly contribute to getting research done. (4) It is difficult to plan an interdisciplinary experiment to the satisfaction of all concerned and to coordinate the work of many hands in carrying it out when different parts of a problem are divided among people with a variety of ways of working. (5) Finally, problems of interpersonal relations always obtrude themselves when people are dependent on one another in something as important as their work. It frequently happens in clinical research that the members of a team represent disciplines having different levels of prestige; thus, there are obvious barriers to maintaining equality in a group of psychologists and psychiatrists in a hospital setting, where the physician is the traditional authority. This kind of problem can be particularly severe when the person who is nominally in charge is actually less qualified to direct the total research enterprise than someone with less power.

Problems in the Analysis of Data. Clinical experiments often generate such data as verbal protocols, drawings or other graphic records of expressive movement, and qualitative notes from the observation of nonverbal behavior. Free associations and projective test responses are wonderfully rich and sensitive behavioral products; yet anyone who has ever struggled to reduce them to some manageable form so that they yield dependent variables that can be entered into a statistical formula knows that many of the headaches of clinical research are located precisely here. The main problem boils down to coping objectively with symbolic (meaningful) content.

The easy availability of tape recording has transformed the problem of analyzing qualitative data from a persistent nuisance to a crisis of glut in many clinics. Closets are filling to overflowing with reels not only of raw, untranscribed, primary data from psychotherapeutic interviews but also from projective testing, diagnostic interviews, and experimental sessions. Just to get such recordings transcribed is often a herculean task, to say nothing of subjecting them to a content analysis.

Some Suggested Solutions

It would be presumptuous to imply that there are many real solutions to the difficulties listed above. The following paragraphs are in a number of cases only orientations toward coping with the problems and tolerating the lack of clear guidelines.

Fortunately, with respect to the most *basic issues,* some reassurance can be given. There is no intrinsic reason why rigorous experimental research cannot be done on important human problems as well as on isolated, segmental functions. Psychoanalysts and academic personologists who have otherwise seemed poles apart have agreed on a pessimistic outlook in this respect, but the doubt that there can be scientific study of individuals grows out of an anachronistic methodological confusion (Holt, 1962b [Volume 1, Chapter 1]). Many other disciplines (e.g., astronomy, meteorology) apply the scientific method to the study of individuals, and it is indisputable that the subject matter of all science is in principle as infinitely complex as personality. Other biological sciences have succeeded in dealing analytically with the intricate interrelatedness of living organisms (which are surely *Gestalten*), so that it is possible in fact as well as in principle to abstract for experimental study single aspects of the most complexly organized totalities. There remains some danger that the experimenter may lose sight of the fact that pieces have to be put back together again and that the lawful relationships he discovers probably apply within narrow parametric limits; but the clinician ought to be less prey to this shortsightedness than other psychologists. His problem is more likely to be that his professional commitment to considering "the whole patient" and respecting the interactive nature of human transactions will make him react emotionally against the thought of trying to "reduce this human richness to a set of numbers." An almost equally unfortunate, but widespread, reaction occurs when working clinicians concentrate their research efforts entirely on "safe," simple problems and neglect the experimental approach to the sorts of problems that concern them professionally.

There are some specific research strategies for applying the experimental method and simultaneously keeping the characteristically clinical breadth of outlook. Murray and his co-workers at the Harvard Psychological Clinic (1938) pioneered in one such strategy that has been successfully applied by many other experimenters: the simultaneous clinical and experimental study of the same group of Ss by a team of investigators. Various specific functions are studied and hypotheses tested in controlled laboratory experiments; but the Ss' personalities are clinically assessed by means of tests and ratings based on qualitative data. The experimental findings may then be illuminated and their limitations understood in relation to the extraexperimental data. To some extent, this kind of understanding may be attained by scrutinizing life histories or clinical syntheses of case data on Ss who are extreme on experimental measures; by statistically relating experimental results (taken as measures of individual difference) to measures of personality; or by relating dependent variables from one experiment to those from another. The logic of this strategy is to try to achieve control of sources of variance that are not experimentally manipulated by learning their values for each S through independent measurement. For any given S, then, his assessed ego strength, authoritarianism, n Achievement, or paranoid tendency is a parameter for the degree of relation found between the experimental variables. [For an example of this kind of research, see Holt & Goldberger, 1959, 1961.]

The other principal strategy is to attempt to control experimentally as many of the important sources of variance as possible, in a multivariate design (see Cohen, 1964). Theoretically, many independently measurable and manipulable variables may be studied simultaneously in a factorial design, from which measures of main effects and interactions can be obtained. Practically, however, this strategy is more difficult to apply than the preceding, since as more variables are added, the computation becomes very laborious (if one does not have a high-speed computer available), the number of cells to be filled and thus the number of subjects required grows rapidly, and it becomes more and more difficult to maintain true experimental independence of measurement.

The demand for degrees of freedom is actually just as great in the first approach, but it is less obvious; the more measures one adds without increasing the number of Ss, the less confidence can be put in the obtained patterns of statistical relationship because of the cumulation of alpha errors (see Cohen, 1965)—if you are computing 500 correlation coefficients, you must expect to get five times as many apparently significant at the 5% level by chance alone as from 100 *r's,* and some of these randomly generated coefficients will be quite high. Likewise, as compared with multivariate factorial experimentation, it offers an only apparently easier approach to the problem of getting independent measures of independent variables, such as personality traits: measure them by whatever tests or ratings are the best available, and then control the inevitable redundancy by intercorrelating the measures and factor analyzing them. This solution, too, calls for many cases if the answers are to be trusted. And of course the objection to large numbers is not merely one of human laziness; it is extremely difficult to apply a complex experimental design or a set of multiform assessments—especially when clinical judgment is involved—in a uniform way so that the hundredth *S* actually receives the same treatment as the first.

There is no easy way out. The ultimate solution, however, is *replication.* A complex clinical experiment usually cannot hope to provide definitive answers, but it can provide valuable leads, which can then be followed up by more focused experiments with larger groups of *S*s, in which the experimenter manipulates only the independent variables that the exploratory study had suggested were probably crucial.

Value-laden areas are as subject to scientific study as any other, since the essence of science is its method rather than its subject matter. Another fallacy to guard against is the mistaken belief that science can *decide* questions of value [See Chapter 10, below]. The scientific method can, for example, be applied to the study of persons socially adjudged delinquent or creative, but a scientific study cannot in itself decide whether an act is positively or negatively valuable. Thus, clinical psychology as a science cannot hope to discover the intrinsic nature of mental health or mental illness, since these are ultimately value judgments external to the behavior that the scientist studies (see Szasz, 1961). Even if he chooses to study evaluative behavior, his research cannot uncover the truth about the values in question. In all other respects, however, valuing is as subject to scientific study—including experiment—as anything else.

The need to consider the *genetic roots* of behavior does not have to pose insuperable problems. A great deal of behavior is situationally determined, or at least its determinants have a substantial autonomy from infantile events. Consider, for example, a fact that Fisher (1954) has point out: that the voyeuristic implications of a tachistoscopic exposure are important to consider in understanding some *S*s' responses to this teasing partial glimpse. Yet one need not know any of the actual details of an *S*'s possible exposure to primal scenes in his early childhood in order to take this kind of thing into account adequately; a contemporary, cross-sectional assessment of his motives will tell all that we need to know about the strength of the wish to look, the degree of its involvement in conflict, and the nature of the *S*'s defenses against it.

For many problems, our need for a reconstruction of the S's personal history will be adequately met by having him write an autobiography, by interviewing him, or by administering a biographical inventory. These direct data, when supplemented by the judicious and cautious use of projective test responses, can often fill in the essential elements of the story to the necessary degree of approximation. When we pass from clinical studies of individuals, however, it is usually desirable to introduce some control over personal history by means of content analysis, which will enable us to abstract from many unique lives the aspects of general significance. Again, Murray *et al.* (1938) were the first to show how life histories could be analyzed in terms of such rated variables as amount of parental love (p Nur), degree of castration threat experienced by S, parental ego idealism, etc., and how these variables could be related to contemporary experimental findings.

To some extent, the same kind of approach can deal with the complexities of the S's *life situation* and its effect on his experimental behavior. The underlying principle remains: be aware that any dependent variable in an experiment can be determined in part by uncontrolled factors, and find ways of assessing such a variable so as to investigate its degree of statistical association with the behavior in question. The further step is always desirable in case a notable degree of association is found (not just a significant one): replicate the experiment either holding the situational variable in question constant or systematically varying it. Even such a peripheral function as differential threshold for brightness may be affected by a contemporary crisis of discrimination against the S because of the shade of his complexion; this variable could be controlled by *selecting* Ss, either so that all have the same attitudes toward skin color or so that there are two contrasting groups otherwise treated identically. Clinicians are at times too ready to assume that because a variable such as the S's contemporary living arrangements *can* affect behavior in the laboratory, it probably does and needs to be controlled. Fortunately, Murphy's law ("Anything that can happen to foul things up will happen") is not that universally valid. The shrewdness or intuition of a good experimenter is in part his gift for informally and even unconsciously assessing the need to control or take account of the many kinds of possible contaminants of experimental measures.

It still remains true that you are not likely to consider the possibility that such a situational variable as barometric pressure can affect your GSR results unless you have at least a minimal grasp of the relevant but tangential sciences (in this case, meteorology and biophysics). The example is based on an actual finding (P. D. Watson, DiMascio, Kanter, Suter, & Greenblatt, 1957): the psychophysiological data from repeated measurements taken over the course of some months of psychotherapy did not make sense until the significant effect of barometric pressure, temperature, etc., on sweating was partialed out—despite the fact that the experiment was conducted in an air-conditioned room! Therefore, the more you can know about the possible relevance of other sciences—behavorial and physical—to your data, the better chance you have of holding down your error variance. It may be too hard to get all the necessary knowledge within one head, in which case the interdisciplinary team approach will be necessary.

Logically, the problem of the behaving organism's *somatic involvement* is the same as its being part of an ecosphere or a social system. We should reflect that there would not be a separate science of psychology if there were not considerable autonomy, if behavior were not to a large extent and most of the time essentially independent from the intrusive effects of nonpsychological determinants. The need to consider biochemistry is much greater for someone who is working on motivational problems than for his colleague who is interested in psycholinguistics, just as the contemporary closeness of a nation to nuclear disaster may have more impact on the data of someone studying adult anxiety than on those of the student of social conditioning in infancy. In a certain sense, everything is ultimately related to everything else, but most conceivable sources of error remain below the threshold of detectability. When measurement in any realm has proceeded to a certain stage of precision, it becomes possible to consider seemingly unrelated phenomena with some hope of finding that they actually do have an effect. But granted the crudeness with which it is possible today to measure latent homosexuality, for example, it would probably be a waste of time to test even as plausible a hypothesis as that this covert motive is related to the balance of sex hormones in the blood. Yet the fact that many such physiological variables can be rather precisely and objectively measured encourages a good deal of psychosomatic research, in which the behavioral measures are so crude as to preclude the discovery of any but the grossest relationships. The greatest need of psychosomatic research is probably better measurement in the psychological realm.

It is indeed difficult to work with *subjective meanings* rather than objective movements or with implicit and hardly verbalizable private experiences like dreams or images rather than externally defined achievements. In principle, however, there are no fundamental methodological differences (Holt, 1961b [Chapter 3]). Though psychologists avoided such subjective "mentalistic" concepts as imagery, states of consciousness, and attention during the early decades of the behavioristic "American revolution" (Hebb, 1960), there are many signs of a revival of interest in these peculiarly psychological matters, even among psychologists (Holt, 1964b). What is needed to work with them is essentially a faith that they are real and worthy objects of study; the rest comes relatively easily. This is not to say that the experimenter sits back and introspects to get his prime data, in the style of the old structural psychology of consciousness. We still must be operational in our approach. In large part, this reduces simply to getting verbal, introspective reports from our *S*s and applying to them the same kinds of judgmental analyses that we use on other qualitative data.

The *ethical problems* alluded to have been adequately dealt with by the American Psychological Association's code of ethics (APA, 1973, 1975); it should go without saying that any clinical experimenter must be thoroughly familiar with the ethics of research. The practical barrier set up by the issue of the research S's privacy is not easily taken care of. One must anticipate the S's feelings of not wanting to reveal everything he knows about himself— and *what he does not know*—and make it amply clear to him that his confidences will be respected. Here is the great advantage of research in a clinical context. When the S is also a patient, the data usually serve a diagnostic or therapeutic purpose as well as research purpose, so that he is motivated by self-interest to cooperate as fully as his defenses will let him. If the S has no such opportunity to get help with his own conflicts and anxieties from participating in a project, the usual motivations that can be induced—the desire to help a friend or to contribute to science and the wish for monetary gain—may be insufficient to counterbalance the psychic pain, shame, and other negative affects the S will have to suffer in the process of directly confessing the aspects of his life he is least happy about. At times it is possible to supplement the conventional motivators (which may also include satisfying a course requirement) by offering to let the S know what you find out about him. Such a feedback session is a delicate matter, not to be undertaken by experimenters without clinical experience and skills; Ss can be severely disturbed by being told too much too bluntly or by getting false impressions about themselves. It is almost equally undesirable and unethical to frustrate the S by leading him to expect an enlightening self-confrontation and then telling him only a few overgeneral or completely bland items.

Because of these difficulties, it is usually helpful to the S, as well as necessary for the success of the experiment, not to demand too much direct self-revelation and to supplement direct with indirect approaches. When projective techniques are used for research purposes, Ss should not be deceived about the nature of the information desired, for example, by presenting such techniques as "tests of a kind of intelligence" or the like; it should be clearly understood that they are "personality tests." If the S has some guilty secrets that he fears he may give away, he can then refuse to proceed further with the experiment. Best of all, when the S is recruited for the research in the first place, he should have a general understanding of the nature of the investigation and the type of data needed, so that he comes in knowing that he is going to reveal himself and assenting to it.

The psychotherapist or psychoanalyst is truly a participant-observer, and he is often so much *involved emotionally* with the patient or with his clinical role that it is exceedingly difficult for him to achieve the disinterested and dispassionate distance that is necessary for carrying out research. It is generally advisable in any experiment, such as in research on psychotherapy, for the responsible experimenter to be a third party who has no relation to the patient other than an investigative one. This division of labor is often desirable for clinical reasons, too, to maintain an unambiguous role for the therapist without incurring any conflict of loyalties, real or fancied, to the goals of treatment and to the goals of research.

Even without any mixture of roles, the clinical experimenter is more likely than most other researchers to become intensely involved with his *S*s. To the extent that the data he elicits touch on affectively important aspects of his own life, he runs the danger of distorting the facts or his interpretations of them. The sovereign remedy offered the therapist for such countertransference difficulties is equally applicable here: self-knowledge and mastery of tendencies to act out in rigid, inappropriate ways, through a personal therapeutic experience. The clinician who tends to see castration anxiety everywhere can, after successful treatment, often turn such a proclivity to good account. Once he calibrates himself, so to speak, and does not project unconsciously, he can make use of his own special sensitivity to minimal indicators of castration complexes, or whatever, in his *S*s. Even without undergoing psychoanalysis, the well-trained clincian will often learn from supervision of his diagnostic and therapeutic work to know his characteristic patterns of relationship, something of his own stimulus value for others, and the kinds of blind spots he has. If he makes the effort to transfer this knowledge to the laboratory, he can be considerably ahead of the nonclinically trained investigator in his sensitivity to what is going on between the main parties in an experiment. For example, a physiologist without clinical training was conducting an experiment that involved keeping male *S*s in the laboratory all night and awakening them when there were EEG indications of dreaming. He was using the technique of entering the bedroom and shaking one very sound sleeper by the shoulder when to his astonishment and dismay, the *S* started to act as if a homosexual approach were being made to him. Fortunately, a clinician friend was able to show the physiologist the many elements of seductiveness there were in the situation and to point out to him some indicators in the *S*'s behavior outside the dream laboratory of strong latent homosexual wishes, so that this situation did not arise again.

The preceding incident also exemplifies one of the advantages of *team research*. The various members can not only supplement one another's skills but also help counteract the effects of blind spots, acting out in relation to *S*s, and other personal problems summed up under the heading "countertransference." The many levels of determination that enter into personality and its disorders have already led to the prescription of interdisciplinary cooperation.

In many ways, the ideal interdisciplinary team conference takes place within a single skull. Multidisciplinary training is one solution to the problems outlined earlier, albeit a heroic one. Even such a protean experimenter cannot provide several fresh perspectives on a problem, as separate persons can. And when the *S* has a variety of human beings with whom he must interact, a more complete sample of his behavioral repertory is elicited. For many kinds of research, the requirements of controls, sampling, respecting the complexity of data, getting reliability of judgments, and the like make it difficult to avoid the judgment that a group effort is necessary.

There are many virtues in solitude which should not be sacrificed on the altar of togetherness. Many investigators seem to be lone wolves by temperament. Working alone may foster originality and depth of penetration into a problem—the results of prolonged immersion and of thinking matters through—instead of large-scale but shallow coverage. Perhaps there is even a general relationship between being truly generative and being inner-directed. The task of the research administrator, then, is to create a kind of institutional structure within which people can get what they need from one another without constantly being in one another's hair. In such a setup, the person in authority will not necessarily have the most prestige, but he will be the one who has the requisite administrative and research skills. Truly democratic leadership is needed, not the authoritarian domination of a tyrant who will not let others develop their own ideas and thus contribute their best or the wishy-washy *laissez faire* of someone who is unwilling or unable to take responsibility and who refers everything back to the team for a group decision.

To a lesser degree, the headaches of interdisciplinary research come up in any collaborative intellectual enterprise. The authors of *Frustration and Aggression*—Dollard, Doob, Miller, Mowrer, and Sears (1938)—remarked that collaborative writing is intrinsically frustrating. Representatives of different schools of psychology may have as much trouble understanding one another as different kinds of scientists. There is always a need for a clearly understood structure of authority and responsibility in any working group, and it is desirable that there be clarity in advance about who gets what kind of credit in the published report. Collaboration demands a good deal of frankness between people, true respect for one another, and a willingness to compromise; it works best if there is a natural complementarity of skills and thus a congenial division of labor. In sum, the point is that tact, skill in human relations and plain decency play a surprisingly large role in the desirable equipment of an experimenter, though this fact is rarely stressed in books on research method.

But what about the plight of the experimenter faced with the opposite problems, those of isolation? What can he do? Fortunately, he can protect himself against his most serious danger—ignorance and self-deception—by knowing what the limitations of his work are. Just as long as the clinician is not unaware of the restrictions on the conclusions he can reach that are imposed by the conditions under which he must work, he can go ahead and learn a good deal. His first guide should be Freud's remark in regard to the many difficulties attending dream interpretation: it is always possible to make *some* progress. Perfectionism is the enemy of enterprise, just as it is the ultimate guardian against error. If you must work alone, by all means do not give up in despair, just because you cannot perform complex, crucial experiments. Go ahead and learn what you can, realizing that all knowledge is relative and probabilistic and that larger probable errors attach to your findings than to those of many other investigators. The psychotherapist has one great advantage that can do much to compensate for his problems with objectivity—close contact with the great issues of human life and extended, repeated opportunities to observe, which give him the chance to make important discoveries. He should learn as much as possible about experimental method, asking always how the principles of control can be applied to the kinds of study he wants to undertake and instituting as much system, order, and objectivity as possible into his gathering and analysis of data. Even if you must work from notes taken after interviews, record them in a uniform manner, file them carefully, and try to systematize them as much as you can so as to make your collection of data maximally pertinent to the objectives of your study.

Some therapists who know about a number of techniques of testing and recording that are available are nevertheless reluctant to use them because they fear that they may contaminate the therapeutic relationship. No doubt there are times during the treatment of some patients when the greatest pains have to be taken to maintain trust, allay suspicion, and refrain from antagonizing the patient or giving him excuses to quit. Many clinicians have found that their anxieties about tape recording were wholly unfounded, and successful psychotherapy and psychoanalysis have been carried out while the entire process was being recorded on a sound movie or while both patient and therapist were hooked up to psychophysiological measuring equipment! Another clinical catchphrase is the keynote here: "It's all grist for the mill."

Cohen (1964) has a number of suggestions about ways that Q-sorting (see below) and multivariate methods such as P-technique (Cattell & Luborsky, 1950) can be used by the lone investigator. Snyder (1959) gives a useful example of the extent to which a therapist can use systematic ratings made by himself and by the patient.

Finally, there is a good deal to be said about ways of coping with the kinds of *qualitative data* that are typically generated by clinical research. Note that qualitative data may include any kind of verbal report by the S (ranging from free association or the description of a mystical experience, to the answer "male" to a question about one's sex), a free drawing or copy of a presented design, a recording of the sounds made by the S or a movie of his expressive movements, or a verbal description of some aspect of his behavior, such as his nonverbal communications.

To consider a problem mentioned earlier, unanalyzed qualitative data may be less likely to pile up if the experimenter always makes sure that he has a clear idea of how he is going to analyze the responses he photographs or records before he begins doing so. A healthy respect for the frustrations and tediums of content analysis can do a lot to make a man think twice before he decides to "tape everything—we'll decide later what we are going to use out of it." That way lie enormous secretarial expenditures and usually interminable waits while typists struggle to reduce sounds on tape to words on paper (a process that takes at least three or four hours for every hour of recording). After he gets the typescript, the experimenter will frequently find that swallowed words and side remarks have been overlooked entirely, personal style and faults in speaking that point to such pathological indicators as anxiety and defensiveness have been automatically edited out, and "inside" references that are perfectly clear to him have been entirely misinterpreted by the brightest of typists because she was ignorant of petty details of the procedure. Then he must take more hours to listen to the tape and edit the typescript, kicking himself for not having made a decision earlier about just what it was he wanted to measure anyway. Often he ends up with ratings made less easily and validly than could have been done if he had had an observer on hand at the time the original data were produced. In many a routine structured interview, it is easy and quite adequate for the interviewer simply to jot down the substance of the S's replies, selecting at the moment the wheat from volumes of chaff, which would take a typist at least as long to transcribe from a recording as the few kernels that are wanted. Where a verbatim text is required, there is usually no substitute for modern electronic gadgets, but the experimenter must always remember that scientific observation is always and intrinsically selective and at times may advantageously be severely selective.

There are two basic methods of translating discursive or presentational symbols, as S. K. Langer (1951) calls them, into quantitative form: content analysis (measurement by counting) and rating (measurement by scaling). The essential operation of content analysis is assignment of a symbol (meaning) to a category. It is objective in that different persons can learn to perform this operation with satisfactory reliability, and it is systematic, orderly, and comprehensive. Various forms of content analysis have been used for decades in a number of disciplines, so that there is a substantial literature on it containing many helpful procedures and techniques.

Briefly, content analysis consists of the following six steps:[3]

1. Decide on the units into which to break the data (for example, the behavior observed in a given period of time, the sentence, the answer to a question, the word). This step may seem simple, but it is often extremely vexatious (see Guetzkow, 1950; Leary & Gill, 1959).

2. Decide on the aspects of these units to be categorized, which will usually be dictated by the objectives of the research. "Headings" (groups of categories) may be derived mainly from theory or mainly from observed regularities and recurrent themes in the data or from some combination of both.

---

[3][For further references on content analysis, see Chapter 8, p. 242.]

3. Build a scoring guide, code key, manual, or what D. P. Cartwright (1953) calls an "analysis outline" on the basis of a sample of the materials to be analyzed. The guide lists each heading and its categories with operational definitions. It may be necessary to give examples of scored and not-scored material for each category and a general set of rules to guide decisions.

4. Train coders or judges to do the scoring until a satisfactory level of agreement has been attained, preferably with another sample of the *kind* of data that will finally be used.

5. Have the judges score the critical data, maintaining a constant spot checking of reliability. The proportion of cases needing to be coded twice will depend on the level of reliability attained and needed and on the extent to which the judges tend to develop different interpretations of the categories ("drift").

6. For ease of quantitative analysis, the specified types or categories under each heading are numbered arbitrarily from 1 to k, and the judges enter only the numbers on large cross-ruled coding sheets set up so that the lines represent Ss and the columns the various headings. For example, suppose the data being analyzed are initial psychotherapeutic interviews: the first two columns on the coding sheet are for the identifying case number, and the third column might be assigned to such a heading as "Nature of Complaints Verbalized." The scoring manual would indicate that in column 3, the number 1 indicates somatic complaints, 2 indicates sexual difficulties; 3 indicates overt anxiety; etc. It would then list the next heading for the next column and would give the new specific meanings assigned to these numbers for this context. From such sheets, the rows of coded numbers are easily punched on cards for machine analysis, usually a separate card for each S (or row).

Rating is a notoriously fallible approach to quantification (Loevinger, 1965), and yet it remains an indispensable tool for the clinical experimenter. The essential operation of rating is a psychophysical type of judgment: more, equal, or less. Thus, operations as seemingly different as Q-sorting, ranking, quantitative scaling, and paired comparison are basically techniques of making ratings.

Ratings are subject to the same errors as other judgments, plus some of their own, all of which can be reduced to constant or systematic errors and random errors. Each kind calls for more or less specific countermeasures.

Contamination is the confounding of the judgment required of the rater by other cognitive contents. Note that there are two subtypes here: contamination by the intrusion of unwanted but true information (e.g., knowledge of the criterion when predictive ratings are being made) and contamination by intrusion of inaccurate information or other biasing cognitive content relative to the S in question. Since raters are not able to set up artificial information-tight compartments in their minds, various kinds of steps have to be taken to ensure that each rating is based only on the intended data. It is ideal when raters have no other information beyond what you furnish them, thus running no risk of recognizing Ss; when they cannot discern any systematic differences among Ss that might indicate what your independent variables are; and when they do not concern themselves with hypotheses about what the experiment is trying to prove. But it may be that the only available raters who have the requisite skills already know more than you want them to about at least some of the Ss. The problem is still not serious if this information is irrelevant to the kind of rating being made; any influence on their ratings will simply constitute random error. Likewise, if raters have no way of discriminating subgroups of Ss who are homogeneous with respect to an independent variable, no harm will be done by their notions of what hypotheses are being tested. But if raters believe that they see common elements of some independent variable in the data from a subgroup of Ss, all of whom do happen to have the same experimental treatment, then whether or not the raters *correctly* guess the common element, their ratings are likely to be contaminated.

Let us consider some concrete examples. In an attempt to predict performance as psychiatric residents of young physicians on the basis of personality assessments at the time of application, external circumstances made it necessary for test data to be analyzed by psychologists who had a certain amount of social and professional contact with the Ss after they entered the school of psychiatry (Holt & Luborsky, 1958). These contacts occasionally provided information directly relevant to the criterion of psychiatric performance, though more frequently the contact merely affected the psychologists' feelings of liking or disliking, or supplied information irrelevant to the criterion (e.g., eye color, wife's maiden name). The first of these three types of information would have directly contaminated predictive judgments; the second might have indirectly contaminated them (since liking would probably bias ratings in a positive direction), though it could have led to spurious error or to spurious success of prediction; and the third kind of information would probably contribute only a small amount of random variation to the ratings. Obviously, contamination had to be prevented or kept to a minimum. The first, most obvious step was to code all the data to be analyzed, replacing Ss' names by numbers and blotting out other possibly revealing data. This is not quite as simple as it sounds; it was a task which took a good deal of judgment and which could not safely be left to a secretary who might not realize that if there was only one resident from Alaska, all references to the far north had to be expunged from the test data. Second, the raters made a prolonged effort to keep to a minimum all their contacts with the Ss until after the predictive ratings had been completed so that any possible recognition would not have serious consequences. Finally, the raters were instructed to make a note as soon as any hypotheses about the identity of any S occurred to them. Such notes included the name of the possibly recognized S, the data suggesting the hypothesis, and all criterion-relevant information the rater had about him. The design involved making a series of ratings of personality traits and predictive ratings at each of several levels of information as the raters worked their way through a thick dossier on each *S*. Consequently, the later stages of analysis inevitably contained more recognitions and pseudorecognitions—as well as repudiations of earlier guesses about Ss' identities—and the earlier stages were more unambiguously uncontaminated. Outright certain recognitions were rare; but when they occurred, raters made the usual notes and then stopped any further analysis of the case in question.

This procedure made it possible to study the effects of contamination of various degrees on the ratings, principally by correlating predictions and criteria with and without contaminated cases. As it happened, the "information" that raters had about Ss they thought they recognized was as often misleading as helpful, so that adding the partly contaminated cases did not significantly affect the validity coefficients.

Halo—the biasing of ratings by an impression of liking-disliking or general positiveness-negativeness of reaction—is a second source of error in ratings. It is a sobering and instructive experience to intercorrelate a set of supposedly quite differentiated ratings of many separately defined aspects of personality or predictions about diverse sorts of behavior and then discover one enormous general factor that accounts for most of the variance. If the ratings have included any frankly evaluative traits or judgments (good-bad, attractive-unattractive, choose-reject as friend, etc.), they will usually be found at the center of this general halo factor. Since it seems to be a human necessity to express this type of basic emotional adience or abience with respect to another person, it is advisable to get such a rating as social desirability or "general goodness" along with the desired variables. If necessary, you can then partial it out afterward, or you can instruct raters to be quite aware of their feelings and to record them before going on to make additional and independent judgments about aspects of the person or his productions. But as Bingham (1939) pointed out, there is such a thing as "valid halo"; the aspects of the data that arouse the judges' admiration or antipathy may be the very ones that are most relevant to performance on some independent behavioral criterion. In the experiment on selecting psychiatric residents already referred to (Holt & Luborsky, 1958) *liking* was rated along with predictions about various types of psychiatric performance so as to make possible the elimination of its expected interference. To our surprise, however, the ratings of liking turned out to be consistently more highly correlated with the principal criteria of performance than any of the direct predictions (Holt, 1958a [Chapter 2])!

In many experimental contexts, however, halo is a nuisance that tends to swamp any other source of variation in the ratings. It can be controlled to some extent by the following measures:

1. Do not ask raters to make large numbers of independent judgments

of the same material. Even well-trained psychologists find it difficult, for example, to judge many separate aspects of a drawing or to predict many discrete forms of behavior on the basis of an interview. Specific rules cannot be dogmatically legislated, for a single brief TAT story may be said to contain a great many independently discriminable bits of information capable of supporting separate ratings (e.g., the hero's needs, press, his adequacy in attaining his goals, optimism of the outcome, degree to which the teller complied with instructions, literary quality, etc.). The more that such ratings are pinned to specific, easily identifiable informational units, the more one can include; see, for example, the carefully specified scoring criteria for *n* Achievement, *n* Affiliation, and a few other needs described by McClelland, Atkinson, Clark, and Lowell (1953), Atkinson (1958), and their collaborators. On the other hand, raters find it onerous to have to make more than half a dozen overall judgments that are based on an impression of the story as a whole.

2. Define all variables to be rated as concretely and clearly as possible. Provide examples of data that fit and do not fit *each rated point* on a continuum, with general rules or principles involved in the ratings, to the extent that you can without providing an excess of reading matter. Often it will help to clarify the theory underlying the choice of variables and of criteria for scoring. [See Holt (1977a) for an example of an attempt to apply this principle to the scoring of the primary process in Rorschach responses.] The Fels Scales of Parental Behavior (Baldwin, Kalhorn, & Breese, 1945) are excellent examples of highly reliable rating scales, each of them containing examples of concrete behavior illustrative of several orienting points along the continuum involved. It is particularly important to anchor high and low points of scales with concrete examples.

3. Keep all scales as unidimensional as possible. When a single aspect of the data has to be considered, the judgment to be made is a great deal easier than when a number of more or less correlated criteria must be mentally weighted and balanced. This principle is closely related to the next.

4. Require as few stages of inference as possible between the data and the ratings. Sometimes the objectives of a research project require the rating of constructs that are several inferential removes from the data (for example, mental health—see Luborsky, 1962a). As Schafer has pointed out (1949), clinical diagnosis typically involves essentially the same sort of chains of inference. We directly judge the degree of effort a patient seems to make in handling color and form simultaneously, infer from that the degree of emotional inappropriateness, and then put together a number of such primary inferences to enable us to make the secondary inferential step to schizophrenia. In research, we do well to follow his suggestion and require explicit rating at each such level. In using the Health-Sickness Rating Scale (Luborsky, 1962a), for example, raters first record their judgments on the specific criteria before casting a balance and inferring from these first-level ratings what the *S*'s overall degree of health may be.

5. Do not overload raters with data. Clinicians who are accustomed to working with as much information as can be obtained about a patient and who are dedicated to the study of the "whole man" are especially liable to strain raters' integrative capacities by giving them too many data to work with. It is all too possible to overload any data-processing system's channel capacity by an excessive informational input, in which case a variety of types of inefficiency result (Miller, 1960). It may seem harmless to furnish essentially irrelevant but orienting background information to set the stage for the sort of data that are most relevant to the judgments needed, but it has been found that even skilled clinicians become confused and perform less well when given information beyond a rather low optimal level (Bavelas, 1952; Kelly & Fiske, 1951). This kind of problem is particularly acute when raters have few specific guidelines, must make extensive inference, and do not have much experience in processing the particular types of data for the purpose in question. With too much to hold in mind at once and not enough knowledge to help one sift wheat from chaff, it is no wonder that many raters oversimplify, fall back on halo, or otherwise fail at their task.

6. Consider carefully the number of points to be rated on each scale. It is all too common a custom to make all rating scales of some standard length or degree of differentiation because of a local tradition or some other irrational basis of preference. A scale should not have more points than will ever conceivably be used, for that will tend to overload the judges, requiring them to make a wasteful number of discriminations, and it will greatly increase the size of the job of preparing the scale. (A research team can easily spend years of hard work producing a set of well-designed and "debugged" rating scales; see Baldwin *et al.*, 1945.) Obviously, if a scale's degree of differentiation requires judges to make finer discriminations than they are in fact capable of, ratings will be unreliable and subject to influence by irrelevant sources of variance.

On the other hand, if judges are capable of making fine discriminations and are accustomed to doing so, they may find it frustrating to be given too coarse an instrument—a pair of pliers with which to sort pearls. The shortest and simplest rating scale contains two points: present and absent, yes and no. At this point, quantitative analysis and qualitative, or categorical, analysis meet. Such a binary scale contains but a single bit of information and therefore may throw away much usable and even needed information that may be easily obtainable from the data. In general, it is desirable to err on the side of providing more differentiation in the rating scales than you think you may need. It is always possible later on to collapse a fine scale into a coarse one, with a gain in reliability (and often more reliability in the final rating than could have been attained if the raters had made only the smaller number of discriminations to begin with). Holt and Luborsky (1958) used a 51-point scale for predictive ratings, subsequently testing the effect of collapsing it to varying degrees; in the end, we reduced it to nine points, primarily to get each variable into a single column on IBM cards, although there was a demonstrable loss of information and of predictive power in the reduction. Since a ten-point scale can also be punched in one column, we might have saved a bit of this lost information by following Canfield (1951) in adopting "sten" scores, which are also easier to dichotomize. On the grounds of a mathematical and information-theoretical analysis, Tukey (1950) argues that if more than 10% of two judges' ratings agree exactly, the scale is *too coarse,* and usable discriminations are being sacrificed.

7. Get as good judges as possible to make the ratings. It is generally reported (Taft, 1955) that the good judge of personality is an intelligent, sensitive, and highly differentiated person who is motivated by an intrinsic interest in the subject matter and whose efforts will therefore be maintained at an even high level. Other things being equal, raters should be objective, mature people; but to list such vague criteria amounts to little more than the redundant advice to "get good judges." In the end, there is no certain way of predicting who will be best able to perform any specific task of rating, and when it is possible to validate ratings against an external, face-valid criterion, by far the best technique of selection is a trial at the actual job. [For further discussion of this issue, see Chapter 5, above.]

8. Train raters intensively in the task with materials of the kind they are ultimately to use. The sort of procedure described above for the training of coders applies here too, *mutatis mutandis.* By dint of intensive training and practice with two talented undergraduate students, Murray once obtained reliabilities above .9 in the rating of needs on six-point scales from TAT stories (Tomkins, 1947). In reporting such results, one should not give the impression that any reasonably intelligent person could attain a similar level of reliability by briefly studying a scoring system and applying it without any apprenticeship. The reported reliability attributed to many a rating scale is more properly a function of extended practice by raters who have worked together enough to learn to think alike. [On the other hand, Loevinger, Wessler, and Redmore (1970) have worked out a rating scale for projective test data embodied in a self-teaching manual, which otherwise untrained psychology students can learn to use with judge reliabilities in excess of .8.]

9. If ratings are stubbornly low in reliability despite the above measures, add more raters. As Ebel (1951) has demonstrated, the reliability of the *mean* rating produced by a group of judges goes up steeply as the number of individual ratings per S increases, even though none of the judges agrees with any other particularly well. Pine and Holt (1960) found, for example, that pairs of clinical raters could not easily be trained to agree with one another in ratings of the humorousness of titles supplied cartoons by Ss. We therefore used seven raters, and the reliability of their average judgment rose to the acceptable level of .865.

Response sets in raters are the third major source of systematic error in ratings. A rater's freedom to be sensitive to nuances of meanings and to extract the quantitative variations of genotypic constructs in the phenotypes of clinical data also permits him to express and record his own personal rating behavior. Such behavior may be a legitimate object of study, but when it obtrudes itself and becomes confounded with independent variations in the behavior of Ss, it is a major source of error.

Several types of response sets in rating behavior may be distinguished, some of them so widespread as to be considered typical (Allport, 1961). In a number of the early investigations of ratings, a cautious tendency to stay close to the mean and not spread ratings enough was noted; for example, when children's intelligence is rated, the IQs of the retarded are usually overestimated, and those of the gifted underestimated. The oft-given advice, after this discovery, that raters be bold and step up their sigmas leads to even more error, however. Cronbach and Gleser (1955) and Meehl and Rosen (1955) have demonstrated that the rating process in predictive and diagnostic investigations works best when judges are conservative and stick to *base rates*—that is, assume that each case is like the known central tendency in the population from which it is drawn—unless the information supplied gives positive indication that this one is different. As long as prediction is not perfect, *any* error will result in the underestimation of cases at the high extreme and overestimation at the low, as a brief reflection on the relation of regression to correlation will verify. It is a false inference, therefore, that most people have a mean-hugging response set that must be resisted. Clinicians particularly may be prone to infer spring from a single robin and to glory in their inability to explain an intuitive hunch that a man who looks ordinary enough to the uninitiated is actually about to sprout a florid psychosis. One does not earn a reputation as a diagnostic wizard by hewing to the base rates. When the boast of one's colleagues is, "When I make a mistake, it's a beaut," it takes a perverse kind of courage to persist in playing it safe with one's ratings. There are plenty of opportunities during the course of scientific research to vent one's intuitive flair and place the rent money on long shots; in the humble process of transforming qualitative data into quantitative ratings, however, it pays to play the favorite to show.

A common response set is overrating, giving the Ss the benefit of the doubt on any evaluatively tinged scale. Since most people abide by the law, are decent, and conform to culturally shared standards of good behavior, it is hard to resist the feeling that they should be rated not at the mean but above it on any facet of being a "good guy." Raters should be well aware of this tendency and of the emotional need to demonstrate their own benevolence by saying nice things about others. Notice that this point is closely related to the halo problem, with the focus now interindividual rather than intraindividual. Many of the same kinds of recommendations hold, therefore. It is helpful to keep the variables to be rated as free from connotations of value judgment as possible. A good deal of attention in psychometric circles has been given to the biasing effects of social desirability on test items, in recent years (A. L. Edwards, 1962; Messick & Ross, 1962; Block, 1965). Since the cognitive process involved in taking most personality tests is essentially the same judgmental one that is involved in quantitatively rating someone else, the experimenter who needs to use ratings can learn a good deal from the sophisticated stratagems of the psychometricians (see Loevinger, 1965).

These mischievous effects of response sets would not be troublesome if it were not for the fact that judges differ so with respect to them; otherwise, we could simply apply a correction factor. To some extent, judges can be calibrated and a constant subtracted, for example, from the ratings of someone who consistently and persistently overrates everyone. Even this procedure has a limited range of applicability, however; raters are disappointingly human in their proneness to such errors as the interaction of their response sets with individual differences in the Ss being rated. Since it has often been found that most of the variance in both the elevation and scatter in sets of ratings is contributed by the rating behavior (or response sets) of the judges, it is a logical enough step to the procrustean bed of the Q-sorter.

Stephenson's (1953) Q-sort procedure, for all its pretentions to being a "methodology," something uniquely "idiographic" (Beck, 1953; cf. Eysenck, 1954; Holt, 1962b [Volume 1, Chapter 1]), or otherwise special, is a technique of getting ratings. It contains a few valuable contributions—well stated by Block (1961)—notably, the fact that the ratings of every judge are forced into the same distribution and thus have identical means and standard deviations. The Q-sort is usually presented as a "package deal," however, in which you have to buy the so-called "ipsative scaling," the normal distribution, factor analysis, the physical sorting of cards into piles, and correlating persons, along with the device of eliminating raters' response sets. It is worth emphasizing, therefore, that each of these features may be detached and considered on its own merits for the piece of research in question. There is nothing sacred about normal distributions for ratings; a rectangular distribution gives even more spread and may be better suited to the nature of some kinds of problems. There is no intrinsic reason why one might not decide on an asymmetrical distribution, too.

Suppose, for example, that you want to assess the defenses of patients applying to a clinic for therapy as part of an attempt to predict who will remain in treatment and who will fail to return a single interview. As part of its regular procedure, the clinic has a diagnostic work-up, so that there are decided advantages to introducing a systematic evaluation of these data at the time the diagnosticians have them freshly in mind. This means considering each case one at a time, the sort of situation to which ipsative rating is well adapted. Instead of considering each trait individually and distributing the cases with respect to one another, you take a set of traits as the population to be distributed within the single case, giving highest ratings to the ones that are outstanding for this person. With a mixed bag of several dozen miscellaneous items, such as the California Q-set (Block, 1961), it works quite well to rate the population of traits on a normal curve for each S. Surprisingly, the resulting ratings on a given trait may be extracted from the total group of sorts and found to be reasonably well distributed across Ss and thus quite usable as an interindividual variate. In our particular example, however, the hypotheses under test deal with defenses and do not call for assessing all the other aspects of personality that are included in typical Q-sets, so that it would be wasteful of diagnostic effort to embed the defenses in a larger group of items that had to be rated too. It is in the nature of defenses, however, that they are rarely conspicuous by their absence; it is easy to identify the ones that a patient relies on most heavily, but it is not possible to say which defensive strategies are *least* used. Why not, therefore, present a comprehensive list of defenses to be evaluated for each patient, requiring the raters to select the two most outstanding (most heavily relied on by the S) defenses and from three to six second-line but still characteristic defenses and let the rest simply be called "not noteworthy"?

Long before Q-technique was proposed, Murray and his co-workers (1938) developed a similar technique of controlling response sets using normative rather than ipsative scales. The experimenters studied a group of a dozen or two Ss intensively, independently rating each on a large number of simple scales and attempting to use all points of each scale and to distribute them normally within the sample. Next, a series of diagnostic conferences were held on each S in which the independent ratings were pooled, differences were discussed, and an internally well-distributed set of consensual ratings was decided on. Finally, at another set of meetings, the resulting distributions of Ss were considered variable by variable, and the ratings on each trait were forced into a roughly normal distribution; in addition, when the samples were small enough, Ss were rank-ordered on each variable. Though this procedure consumed a great deal of time, it resulted in highly differentiated ratings, free from distortion by the response sets of any raters and ideally suited to being correlated with independent experimental results. Horn (1944) contributed one further step, which he called "syndrome analysis": rated variables of a given type (e.g., needs, defenses) were intercorrelated, and combined distributions were prepared for highly interrelated clusters of items. Such a simplified version of factor analysis can eliminate a good deal of the redundancy in a group of ratings and present the researcher with a reduced set of variables that cover the domain of personality, as the research group was able to perceive it, with a negligible sacrifice of information.

The method of paired comparison was developed in psychophysics as a way of systematizing judgment and has been used in social psychology (as in the construction of attitude scales) but as yet rather little in clinical research. Through the vigorous advocacy of Sargent (1956), it was adopted by the Menninger Foundation research project on psychotherapy (Wallerstein, Robbins, Sargent, & Luborsky, 1956) as a means of quantifying a number of aspects of clinical case folders. If a diagnostic tester has, for example, a battery of psychological tests given a patient before and after treatment, he can make a judgment "improved," "no change," or "worse," but it is difficult for him to quantify such a global concept on much more of a rating scale than that. But he can examine two such pairs of test batteries and make a simple comparative judgment—"this one shows more improvement, on the whole, than that"—or he can make the judgment in terms of such specific variables as anxiety level, severity of symptoms, insight, and ego strength. In the Menninger project, systematically extracted and condensed clinical assessment data from a whole team's evaluation were used and entered onto research forms as the basis of the clinical judgments.

> In Sargent's form of the paired comparisons procedure, the name of each patient was paired with every other in a batch of only 12 patients. The 42 cases [in the total project] had been broken down by random sorting into overlapping batches of 12 patients each. . . . The clinician had only to decide for each pair "Which of these two patients has more (of the variable)?" The clinician was not expected to make a new assessment of the patient but rather to refer constantly to the forms compiled by the research team. . . . Clinicians find themselves quite comfortable in making these choices, much more so than when they are asked for ratings of the variables (Luborsky, 1962b, p. 118).

Yet the pairings can rapidly be consolidated to produce "a scale that is more than ordinal but less than equal interval." (On the question of ordinal and equal-interval scales, see Cohen, 1965.) Reliabilities of two judges doing this task independently were consistently over .85 (Luborsky, 1962b). This is a method of considerable power that deserves to be tried more widely.

When all is said and done, ratings remain at best a crude, laborious method of quantifying data, always prone to the intrusion of many sources of error and never any better than the clinical skill of the available raters. Wherever possible, they should be replaced by better methods of measurement. For the immediate future, however, it is difficult to see how clinical research can do without them. When the techniques outlined above are followed with care and understanding, rating makes possible the quantitative treatment of data thus far intractable to any other kind of measurement. Moreover, even in areas that have been industriously worked over by psychometricians, ratings often turn out to have more construct validity, better correlations with independent criteria, and more predictive efficiency than competing objective tests. [See, for example, Volume 1, Chapter 11.]

STAGES IN EXPERIMENTAL RESEARCH

In the remainder of this chapter, I shall briefly run through the main stages of research as they are usually or ideally described. In practice, seasoned experimenters rarely plan as meticulously as will be implied here, so that it is tempting to push aside all such prescriptions as smelling more of the lamp than the laboratory. But the situation is like that of most other highly skilled endeavors: the master is allowed to break rules that an apprentice does well to obey until he learns and understands them thoroughly. It is fatal for the novice to flout the laws of perspective or harmony until he can see from the inside how the logic of his work of art requires them. So it is in experimentation. When the investigator is so experienced that he no longer needs to consult checklists such as the following, he can afford to settle into a personal style of investigation that may be quite different from the sequence recommended here.

To help concretize things a bit, the discussion will make frequent reference to a specific (though hypothetical) clinical experiment: the comparison of two forms of treatment. Just to make things difficult enough for ourselves, let us suppose that a form of psychotherapy and a psychoactive drug are to be evaluated.

By choosing a practical, applied problem, I do not wish to minimize in any way the importance or the problematical nature of experimental research that is concerned with theoretical issues. As Ackoff (1953) has argued, almost any research problem can be viewed as an attempt to decide which of two or more means is the most efficient way of attaining some specific end. Most of the problems of clinical experimentation will come up in this, one of the most difficult types of research.

Defining the Problem

Research begins with a problem; a problem well stated is a research partly completed. How can one learn to ask good questions?

A good way to start is to *clarify objectives*. Try to find out what the "real problem" is, why the issue as first posed came up, and why anyone is interested in it. Usually, in applied or operations research, whoever is paying for the research is the one whose ultimate interests need to be inquired into in the process of clarifying what the research is to be focused on. Suppose a psychologist in a hospital has been presented, by the hospital administrator, with the task of therapeutic evaluation alluded to above. On making discreet inquiries, he may learn that the main objective in the administrator's mind is to get some research going as a way of sprucing up the staff and making the various disciplines work together more closely. This information may in turn lead to the discovery that interprofessional rivalries have grown administratively bothersome, which actually may indicate that any experiment requiring the coordinated effort of the several staffs runs the danger of being greatly delayed or even sabotaged. Another possibility is that a drug company has offered a grant to support evaluative research. The administrator is attracted by the prospect of drug therapy that will be cheap and easy, but the professional staff is so committed to psychotherapy that he believes they will not cooperate properly unless the comparison is included. A third possibility is that there has been a series of troublesome minor episodes of acting out on the part of patients in psychotherapy, and an administrator who much prefers sedately sedated patients wants to show that a tranquilizer will produce better results.

In the first of these hypothetical instances, more direct action to improve morale and interprofessional relations will be a better means of attaining the true objective than carrying out any research at all. In the other two, the project as originally proposed may be carried out, but with different emphases and different problems of control. In the second situation, there will be special problems of equating the attitudes and enthusiasm of the staff for the different treatment modalities being compared; moreover, in light of the prevailing preference for psychotherapy, it will probably be necessary to show that the drug is significantly *better* than psychotherapy to convince the staff, even though the administrator would be content to switch to the drug if it could be shown to be not significantly worse (see Cohen, 1965, for implications in terms of setting alpha and beta values). In the third hypothetical case, the designer of the research will have to keep in mind that the administrator's objective will call for a short-term criterion emphasizing ease of ward administration, whereas the ultimate good of the patients might better be served by a criterion based on a longer-run follow-up and emphasizing personal adjustment rather than administrative convenience.

These are only a few of the more obvious possibilities that can be uncovered by the attempt to clarify objectives. Often, the result will be that the original statement of the problem will be significantly altered, to the greater ultimate satisfaction of all concerned. Ackoff (1953) has described how to go about asking questions so as to find out what the real underlying need of the "research consumer" is.

Finding a Problem. To digress a bit from the topic, suppose that the underlying need is to *find* a problem of theoretical importance to work on. Examples of psychologists who may feel this way are a graduate student looking for a dissertation topic and a clinical psychologist who has managed to clear some time from clinical responsibilities because he feels a general urge to "get back into research" but who does not have a specifically formulated target.

The first advice to be given such a person is to concentrate on areas of greatest interest to him, personally. It is all very well to consider the needs of psychology generally, but the fact is that any research involves work, and it is likely to turn into pure drudgery unless one finds it intrinsically interesting. To choose a problem because it seems to be convenient or expedient or possible to complete with a minimum of time and effort is to ask for trouble. Any problem has its knotty aspects; research usually takes longer than one most liberally estimates, and you have to *believe* in, and care about, a problem to get over the rough spots.

[Confronted with a list of major problems facing mankind like the ones assembled by Platt (1969), a clinician may feel at once guilty at the thought of not trying to help prevent one of the many disasters facing us and powerless to do so. However awesome the dangers and puny the individual may seem in comparison, the choice is not between grandiosity and despair. If we can just think through some of the implications of any great social issue for individuals, we can begin to see ways to make small contributions that may cumulate to constitute something of real social value. Consider overpopulation and the corresponding need to limit family size. The more we know about the motivation of those who resist contraception or who want many children, and the more we understand about the unconscious fears involved in their decisions, the better job can eventually be done to plan means of controlling fertility. Looked at in this way, what is literally a global problem can be approached helpfully by even a solo investigator with his usual psychotherapeutic case load as a sample of subjects.]

As our hypothetical instances suggested, *too much* commitment to a hypothesis is a serious difficulty for the researcher. It not infrequently happens that after his clinical and academic education and some years of clinical experience, a man develops strong convictions and then wishes to undertake research in order to develop objective data to coerce others into sharing his beliefs. In our example, the persons who design and carry out the research may themselves be committed to a faith in the efficacy of the particular form of psychotherapy under study, and so deeply committed that it is extremely difficult to avoid motivated errors. Let us assume that they have planned as controlled a study as possible, in which patients are randomly assigned to the drug or to psychotherapy and then, after a period of treatment, are interviewed and tested by a team of clinicians who do not know which therapy has been used. In practice, it is exceedingly difficult to accomplish what can be so simply stated. Physicians in charge of the wards will argue that clinical responsibility to the patient has an overriding importance, and who can deny that ultimately they are right? The trouble is that a controlled experiment to find out how well therapies work *must* involve some predictable therapeutic failures (if existing clinical lore has any predictive validity at all). If the responsible physicians are allowed to intervene at all on the grounds that "this patient is special" and really must or must not have the randomly assigned treatment, a critically important feature of the experiment is lost. Note that unless assignment to treatments is truly random (determined by rigid adherence to some unbiased method decided on in advance, preferably the use of a table of random numbers), judgment will creep in, and unconscious bias will have a chance to foul up the works. Another type of error to which the described design is vulnerable is the accidental discovery of a patient's treatment at the time he is being evaluated. The interviewers may start out uncontaminated (though it is difficult for them to, if they work at the same hospital), and the patients may know that they are not supposed to reveal what kind of therapy they have received, but it is easy for the patient to let a hint drop which neither party to the discussion takes explicit note of; yet the harm will be done, and the criterion judgment of improvement will be contaminated.

It is so hard for ordinary mortals to overcome the biasing influence of their emotional convictions that it is better not to undertake a piece of research if you cannot honestly contemplate without disturbance the prospect of having the results come out either way. When you feel tempted to use a one-tailed test because an equally large effect in the opposite direction seems inconceivable, that is a warning signal to stop and ask yourself whether you are honestly able to *let* it happen that way. Suppose your study proved that psychoanalytic psychotherapy made a sample of patients *worse* off than they were before treatment—could you publish that and still face your colleagues? Would you examine your data with an equally fishy eye, looking for sources of error and reasons to doubt the findings no matter what the results? Of course not; and I do not want to argue that only completely isolated, compulsive-schizoid personalities without any sense of clinical identity should do research. Just remember that it is in the end self-defeating to invest the time and labor that research demands if you are in danger of biasing your results. The truth wins out, ultimately. We know today that administering limewater and pulling out all a patient's teeth are irrational and ineffective therapies for schizophrenia. Yet many earnest and hopeful investigators managed to produce and publish remarkable series of "cures" by these means. Advances in experimental method make such fiascoes somewhat less likely today, but only somewhat. Choosing a research topic can still be a steering between Scylla and Charybdis, between the stony aridity of uninteresting topics and the whirlpool of too great emotional involvement. For most of us, the passage is fortunately wide enough, and there is plenty to study with enthusiasm but not fanaticism.

The second requisite of any researchable problem is that it be within the powers of the investigator to carry out the research to completion. If it will take too much time, too much money, special skills you do not have, collaborators you cannot line up—and sew up!—ahead of time, or equipment that cannot be made available to you, then it is best eschewed.

Completed research in clinical psychology seldom resembles the original germinative idea very exactly. When closely examined, the initial formulation of the problem is frequently too sweepingly grandiose or too trivial to be worth carrying out. Neither state of affairs means that it should be abandoned forthwith. If the interest is there, mulling over a problem, reading about it, and discussing it with friends will usually result in a practicable and worthwhile approach if you keep at it long enough. For someone who has not had a great deal of experience in research, the first job is usually to narrow down the scope of an interest into something researchable. This can be done in several ways: in terms of the particular focus of your interest, in terms of what is feasible for your resources, and in terms of other intersecting theoretical problems.

Originality in research, as in any kind of thinking, is largely a matter of synthesis: putting together familiar elements in new combinations. Wide reading, plus acquaintance with a range of issues and problems in psychological theory and research, can interact with more specifically clinical studies and experience to yield a new approach.

The besetting antagonist of originality is rigidity, stubborn clinging to one way of organizing experience when many others are potentially possible. The trouble is that we so often are unaware of what our assumptions are and thus cannot see how they blind us to a host of possible fresh questions to ask of nature. For about two thousand years, the Empedoclean-Hippocratic doctrine of the four humors and four corresponding temperaments so completely shaped the educated man's conception of personality that there was a virtual inability to see any other form of diversity in people. Every now and then, however, someone suggests a way of asking questions that can be extended to open up many researchable topics. Thus, in the late 1930s and during the 1940s, several people hit on the idea of taking seriously the error term in most standard psychological experiments as representing valid variance due to individual differences. W. Langer (1938), for example, showed that the individual differences in all the usual measures generated in rote-learning experiments could be treated as indications of various types of personality organization and could be meaningfully related to independent assessments of personality. This kind of insight played an important role in the whole "new look" movement in perceptual research, and it still has a good deal of research applicability. The fruitful concept and research area of cognitive style (Gardner, Holzman, Klein, Linton, & Spence, 1959) is essentially based on this idea, married to the concept of ego structure as developed by Rapaport (Rapaport, Gill, & Schafer, 1945–1946).

Klein and his co-workers have shown how the ego-structural viewpoint can give rise to a great number of theoretically meaningful experiments. The central point Rapaport stressed clinically was that the same dynamic conflict could lead to very different behavioral outcomes (e.g., symptom-pictures) in patients with different types of favored defenses and adaptive controls. In research terms, this outlook can lead to asking what the structural differences are between people for whom a given clinical proposition holds and those for whom it does not. Klein (1954) found such differences between persons whose perceptual judgment was "autistically" influenced by the aroused drive-state of thirst and those who were not so influenced. Alper (1946) similarly found ego-structural differences between subjects who remembered their failures and those who forgot them. Probably most testable psychoanalytic propositions will turn out to be valid under certain conditions and for persons of specific structural characteristics; at least a generation of researchers can be kept busy discovering the parametric limits of psychoanalytic theories (see also Sarnoff, 1962).

Another good set-breaking generative principle for research is to take any apparently established experimental or clinical fact and retranslate its theoretical statement into concrete terms with a different set of operational definitions from the usual ones. When a new technique of measuring an important construct is introduced, it tends to be taken up and widely adopted by a generation of researchers, most of whom assume that it solves the problem of operational definition for the construct in question and who generalize freely in terms of that construct. Consider, for example, the amount of research on anxiety that used the Taylor scale of so-called "manifest anxiety" before a few skeptical souls started asking what some of the results would look like if a different set of operations were used, perhaps closer to clinical reality. It is usually healthy in psychology to be cautious in assuming that any one set of operations provides a sufficient measure of a construct. A great deal of useful research can be generated by the attempt to replace a standard measure by looking at the concept in question as naively as possible, asking yourself what would be the most direct and ideally face-valid way of getting at it.

Ideally, research should grow out of an interest in the phenomena under observation themselves and should also be relevant to theory. In practice, researchers tend to be more interested in one side or the other of this dichotomy, either becoming fascinated by some empirical problem and pursuing it as long as they can find new questions to ask about it or trying to test only propositions that have direct bearing on theoretical issues. Though the latter style has more scientific prestige in many quarters, both can lead to excellent research. What matters is to find one's own style and make the most of it.

There are many published sources of specific research topics. Unsolved problems, often already formulated in experimentable form, abound in reviews of literature such as are found regularly in the *Psychological Bulletin,* the *Annual Reviews of Psychology, Progress in Neurology and Psychiatry, Progress in Clinical Psychology,* the *Annual Survey of Psychoanalysis,* the annual surveys in the *American Journal of Psychiatry,* and the *Journal of Clinical Psychology,* or in works such as Wolman's *Handbook of Clinical Psychology* or Eysenck's *Handbook of Abnormal Psychology.* Yet it rarely works well simply to comb through such a source and pick a nice, manageable-looking problem. The choice has to be guided by preexisting, genuine interest in a problem area.

Reviewing the Literature

Reading is an activity that should never cease for the researcher. Fairly early in his pursuit of a specific project, however, there should be a phase of redoubled activity in the library, for several reasons. Reading what has been done and thought by others in your area will help specify the hypotheses and questions that define your problem sharply. You may even find that what you are thinking of doing has already been carried to publication by others or has been tried and found impractical. Just because a piece of research has been carried out once is no reason not to do it again; on the contrary, one of the greatest needs in psychological research is more replication of experiments (see below). Why worry, then, and why bother to find out whether someone has anticipated you? It is always poor scientific manners to barge into an area and write as if you were the first one ever to think about it, but far more than politeness is involved; if psychology is to make progress as a science, we must build on one another's work. Science is one of the largest and most complicated human enterprises ever to go on for so many years and in so many places without some kind of central control, but it would be a complete anarchy without its main mechanism of social control, its literature. This mechanism does not work unless people use it, which means prompt reporting of all potentially useful parts of one's own work—including negative findings!—and a conscientious effort to keep up with the work of others, at least in areas of immediate interest. Without constant efforts at scientific communication, researchers duplicate one another's work unnecessarily, with unplanned and unintelligible variations in technique and instrumentation, so that an ultimate synthesis becomes impossible. Two apparently similar studies with different findings turn out to have many seemingly arbitrary differences in design and execution, so that the variables that are actually responsible for the difference are too confounded to be discerned.

If, however, you have a good grasp of where research stands in your field of interest, what its major unsolved problems are, what the standard techniques of experimentation have been, and what the usual methods of varying and measuring independent and dependent variables are, then you can design an experiment which will be rationally related to an existing body of work and which will make a useful contribution to it. One of the most valuable types of research is a complete replication of an outstanding study with one crucial variation; this is J. S. Mill's method of difference in pure form. No one is compelled to follow in the footsteps of predecessors, and there may be good reasons why your investigation uses different methods to get a new type of data on unusual types of subjects, but such a foray is a gamble. If it yields good results, it may set a new style of experimentation, but if not, it may open up only a private blind alley.

Our hypothetical example touches on one enormous literature, that of experimental pharmacotherapy, and a smaller but rapidly growing one in psychotherapeutic research. The clinical psychologist who is accustomed to leaning on the *Psychological Abstracts* will be surprised to find, if he looks conscientiously, that much of both types of research (but especially the work on drugs) is not covered at all in this source. For the years 1956–1971, there is an excellent guide to the important books in this field in the *Mental Health Book Review Index*. A couple of bibliographic journals in medicine, the *Index Medicus* and the *Current List of Medical Literature*, provide good entries into the literature of psychopharmacology and various forms of therapy. A good entry into the other literature is provided by two handbooks (Bergin & Garfield, 1971; Meltzoff & Kornreich, 1970). The principal way to go at it is to look up the references cited in the papers or books you do know and note down relevant-sounding titles from their reference lists. In this way, you quickly find out which are the most frequently cited reports, which you can read first, extending the same process. Thereby you also learn the names of journals in which the kind of paper that interests you is published; to find the current literature, scan the most recent volumes (usually there is a lag of at least a year before papers are cited in bibliographic journals, and sometimes the *Psychological Abstracts* runs as many as five years behind). Other journals can be found by consulting a librarian in a good psychological, psychiatric, or medical library. [A computer-generated bibliography may be helpful, but is no easy substitute for scholarship.]

A lazier but occasionally effective technique is to write to a prominent center of the kind of research in question and ask if a ready-made bibliography is available. Drug manufacturers are usually happy to send you lists of publications dealing with their products, though you may have to write to quite a few in order to find all the work on any widely manufactured drug, such as many of the ataractics. Books and journals devoted to reviews and surveys are other obvious sources. Buros's *Mental Measurements Yearbooks* contain cumulative bibliographies on all psychological tests, and a number of (non-APA) journals, such as the *American Journal of Psychotherapy*, abstract or list current references likely to be of interest to their readers.

If you get interested in collecting a complete bibliography and in reading in an area that has not recently been reviewed, you can do the field a great service by preparing an article that collects, organizes, and critically evaluates a specifiable segment of literature. With the growing realization that science is in danger of being choked by its own output, we are all becoming increasingly dependent on such reviews, and they are becoming recognized as important contributions.

Problems of Designing Research

Experimental design has become a highly technical subdiscipline in itself, on which a number of books and articles are readily available; perhaps the best brief guide to it is the paper by Campbell (1957; see also 1969 and Campbell & Stanley, 1966). [Other useful discussions may be found in Boring (1954), Cronbach (1948), and the references on experimental design cited in Chapter 8, p. 221.] This section will therefore deal with just a few miscellaneous points that bear stressing.

A useful procedure, recommended by Ackoff (1953), is to begin a research project by drawing up an idealized research design. From your initial formulation of the problem in terms of the underlying objectives there will follow indications for the types of data needed to attain each objective. The review of previous research (plus correspondence, visits, or other communication with others who are active in similar work) will suggest specific procedures and instruments as well as needed improvements, such as controls of previously ignored possible sources of error. Putting all this together with your knowledge of experimental design, plan a study which would be proof against all criticism and which would provide definitive results, regardless of expense or feasibility. Then make your compromises; scale it down to what your resources allow, and you will be aware of your project's actual limitations to a much greater extent than if you had never gone through the exercise of making an idealized design. The latter may show the need for a series of studies, each going at a piece of the total job to be done; it may even persuade you that you cannot get any unequivocal results at all. This last outcome is melancholy, but a far better one than to invest time, money, and effort in actually going through with something that will be unusable in the end.

An important minor part of designing research is to define your terms. All too often, this step is omitted until the writing up of the final report, when it may be too late. The process of definition should be twofold: all major terms should have both theoretical (conceptual) and operational definitions—the specification of data-gathering methods—which need to be carefully coordinated. It sometimes happens, for example, that an experiment gives an excellent treatment of the concept of anxiety in theory and then adopts a conventional, available measure like GSR without making any linkage between the two types of definition, which leaves it an open question whether his work has any relevance to theory or not. For it is at this critical juncture that the bearing of empirical work on conceptual models and propositions derived from them is established. It is a serious but common error to think that the problems of definition are solved simply by the declaration that a specified measure is the operational definition of a term from some theory, which the experimenter then proceeds to bandy about, taking advantage of all its surplus meaning in the theory and in common usage, little of which may have any relation to the operation in question.

In designing research, the hardest thing to make oneself do and the most necessary is to be sufficiently specific and concrete. In a way, this is the central point of operationalism; but even the most objective and operationally minded experimenters at times settle for a too *general* description of operations to be used. Consider our hypothetical project. If two types of treatment are to be compared, it will be necessary to measure the effectiveness of each in modifying outcome; in other words, a criterion measure will be needed. It may sound operational to say that "expert ratings of outcome will be the criterion," but such a statement is a long way from being concrete enough to give any idea of how to proceed. Who will rate what, how, when, and on the basis of what information? A review of publications on experimental therapeutics in clinical psychology and psychiatry will show that the obvious and easy ways of getting such criterion measures have many serious drawbacks. Indeed, the lesson of much predictive research is that the heart of the matter is getting a good criterion and that a great deal of the initial research effort ought to go into developing adequate criterion measures (Holt & Luborsky, 1958; Horst *et al.*, 1941; Kelly & Fiske, 1951). Facing this issue squarely will frequently result in a considerable scaling down of the original scope of the project. In our example, it might result in a decision to concentrate on studying the comparative merits of the drug and the psychotherapy at issue in bringing about reduction of acting out in character disorders as assessed after six months and at discharge. It will not be easy to define acting out objectively enough so that nurses, psychiatric aides, psychiatrists, psychologists, and social workers can agree in rating the same behavior the same way, but the effort to sharpen the definition will be instructive and may yield a contribution in itself.

A final word of warning about research design. Investigators who know about research primarily from reading books like this one or from having taken courses in experimental design rather than from actual experience not infrequently lose sight of the fact that design is a means and not an end in itself, and they plan highly complex experiments using multivariate models or analysis of variance. When they try to carry them through, they find that such designs are extremely demanding of precision and meticulous adherence to plan, allowing for little serendipity and no spontaneity in execution. The more complex the design, the easier it is to get confused about just what treatment to apply to each *S*, and the more costly each such error is. Moreover, a design in which very few *S*s get the same treatment will confound some of the independent variables that a clinical experimenter is likely to want to investigate; he will not be able to measure the personalities of his *S*s and correlate the resulting variates with experimental findings in the way advocated above. Unless there are compelling reasons, therefore, it is generally wise to err on the side of simplicity of design and not try to investigate many aspects of a problem at once.

Sampling

No part of research planning is more often slighted and more important than the drawing of samples. For *sampling is the key determinant of how findings can be generalized*. Since Brunswik's (1956) important expositions of representative design, it has become evident that the selection of subjects is only half of sampling, which must concern itself with the selection of the other determinants of the behavior under study—situations, objects, experimental stimuli, persons. If our criterion behavior were to be acting out, it would become necessary to define the situations in the patients' lives in which this kind of behavior typically takes place and the kinds of persons and provocations involved so that we could make sure to obtain meaningful measures. Suppose, for example, that we decided to use only ratings of observed behavior in the ward and in the OT shop (assuming a population of hospitalized subjects). We might arrange to have professional personnel observe a great deal of behavior directly, which would be in a number of ways a good basis for a criterion and which might yield interpretable results. Yet there are few hospitals in which patients never have *any* unobserved moments, and those are the very times when certain forms of acting out take place almost exclusively, such as drinking and sexual behavior. Thus, it would be necessary either to sample situations more representatively or to restrict generalization to ward behavior.

In the therapy, also, considerations of representative design (sampling of objects) are important. A single project is not likely to be able to compare more than one form of psychotherapy and one drug. It would be tempting, if the results were clear-cut and in line with our preexisting prejudices, to publish conclusions that "drugs are inferior [or superior] to psychotherapy in controlling acting out in psychiatric wards." It is a little more obvious that a single ataractic cannot stand for all drugs, but it is easily overlooked that the psychotherapy practiced in a given hospital by a certain group of staff members has just as little claim to represent the probable achievements of all other therapists elsewhere. The range of techniques covered by the one term "psychotherapy" is staggering; moreover, one cannot simply accept the word of the therapist that he used "classical *x* technique." Empirical studies of the behavior of psychotherapists who claim adherence to the same schools have shown great diversity (Strupp, 1960). Then, too, researchers in psychotherapy are increasingly recognizing that the personality of the specific practitioner who applies a technique is a major determinant of the effectiveness of therapy (see, for example, Holt & Luborsky, 1958; Betz & Whitehorn, 1956). To be able to make valid statements about client-centered therapy, for example, one would have to study a representative sample of all the therapists who are currently using this technique. To return to the pharmacological side of the problem for a moment, considerations of dosage are as important as the nature of the specific ataractic and again set limits on what claims can be made for the results.

The principle that the nature of his samples limits the generalizations an experimenter can make extends to the sample of personological items contained in a Q-sort. Writers who cite Fiedler's (1950) well-known study showing more similarity among expert therapists of different schools than among experts and tyros within the same point of view usually neglect to mention the marked limitations imposed by the items in the Q-sort used, which all referred to a few aspects of the psychotherapeutic relationship. Many of the critical points of technique that usually come to mind when one thinks about therapy of the kinds Fiedler studied were not touched on at all in the Q-set. Block (1961) has argued that if two Q-sets both include a heterogeneity of items covering many aspects of personality, findings with both will be similar, and he performed a little study that supported his point. Nevertheless, it is logically inescapable that the concept of "similar personalities" is meaningless without reference to the specific points of identity or near-identity (Cronbach & Gleser, 1953). In Block's demonstration study, the Q-set that a secretary made up by a commonsense selection of adjectives describing people contained no items dealing with specific mechanisms of defense; even though descriptions of people with this set acted statistically very much like descriptions in terms of the California Q-set, which does contain defenses, the former might be seriously misleading if used in a problem for which just this aspect of personality happened to be crucial. Moreover, since there is no rational way of getting a complete inventory of all items describing personality, there can be no sure way of sampling them in a representative way.[4]

Until the advent of sample surveys, experimental psychologists were mostly blithely unconcerned with sampling subjects. The old tradition used the E himself, his wife, plus a few lab cronies and on this basis solemnly concluded general laws about all mankind. More recently, psychologists have begun to be aware that getting a large enough sample is a problem, but even today the size of the n is usually the only question that is considered (for that, see Cohen, 1969). Experimenters who work with clinical groups of Ss must perforce be aware of more sampling variables than n and availability, but we still lack a firm tradition of responsibility in this connection.

The essential point about sampling is that we study a few persons and wish to find out about the many, so that the sample must *represent* the target population in relevant ways. Thus, in a sample survey to predict an election, the relevant sampling variables are those that are known to determine voting behavior: party affiliation, income, age, sex, ethnic-group membership, and education. These are not the only determinants, but they account for most of the variance, and information about them is obtainable for the target population and the sample. Therefore, one can draw a sample in such a way as to create a miniature replica of the population in these respects. The validity of generalization is a function of the adequacy with which the determinants of the behavior in question have been identified, the accuracy with which one knows their distribution in the target population (that is, the group whose behavior is to be predicted), and the fidelity or representativeness with which the sample duplicates the population in these respects. Note that n, the size of the sample, enters only as a determinant of the power of the statistical tests

[4] I am aware of Hilden's (1954) efforts to provide such representative Q-sets by randomly sampling Allport and Odbert's (1936) listing of all personologically descriptive terms from an unabridged dictionary, but for a number of reasons, I do not consider the listing an adequate parent population of personality descriptions.

one can make and thus of the size of the random error of measurement; it has in itself nothing to do with how representative or "valid" a sample is.

The example may be misleading, since in most psychological research we are not trying to predict concretely what a specific population will do but are looking for general laws of behavior. It is vital to realize, however, that the logic of sampling still holds in the same way. A psychological law amounts to a prediction that, given conditions c, people will react with behavior b—but not just any people. The laws of verbal learning, for example, despite the virtually universal neglect of this issue in the experimental literature, are tacitly assumed to hold for persons with roughly normal sensory and motor capacities, normal intelligence, and normal familiarity with English and the ability to read and speak it. It may very well be that to a much larger extent than is generally recognized, they also hold only within certain limits of other parameters, such as capacity to get interested in abstract intellectual problems, education, and social class. These limitations (which are only suppositions, or hypotheses, at this point, because the issues are largely uninvestigated) result from the *de facto* restriction of the population sampled in most academic experiments and are not a result of an intention to sample in this way. The burden of proof is therefore on anyone who generalizes unrestrictedly to demonstrate that the actual limitations of his sample are irrelevant to the behavior he is studying.

In the days when psychology was the science of the average adult human mind, the target population was always normal, mature mankind, visualized (if considered at all) as well-educated, white, male, and American or Western European. There was thus a special psychology of women, one of children, one of members of off-brand ethnic groups ("ethno-psychology"), and one of hospitalized people ("abnormal psychology"). As psychology comes of age, it will become less ambitious, seeking to generalize about the behavior of more restricted groups, and also more ambitious, seeking to unify all these special psychologies into one science of behavior in which laws will have sampling parameters attached to them but will be otherwise general.[5] For many of its laws, sex, ethnic-group membership, eye color, and

---

[5][Cronbach (1975) has since written even more pessimistically about the prospect of general laws in psychology. To find them, we must discover the appropriate systemic level on which to work. Compare Weiss (1973, pp. 19, 20) on the lack of lawfulness at too molecular a level in other sciences: "We have recognized the states and changes of such [*i.e.*, living] systems as being conservatively invariant over a given period, and hence predictable, without a correspondingly invariant micromosaic of the component processes. We have to conclude, therefore, that the patterned structure of the dynamics of the system as a whole coordinates the activities of the constituents. . . . If physics has had the sense of realism to divorce itself from microdeterminism on the molecular level, there seems to be no reason why the life sciences, faced with the fundamental similitude between arguments for the renunciation of molecular microdeterminacy in both thermodynamics and system dynamics, should not follow suit and adopt macrodeterminacy regardless of whether or not the behavior of the system as a whole is reducible to a stereotyped performance by a fixed array of pre-programmed micro-robots."]

many other characteristics of the subjects will be irrelevant, and the fact that they were first studied in United States college sophomores will turn out not to be restrictive. But just as comparative psychology has to broaden its purview beyond the cage of the white rat (Beach, 1950), human psychology must sooner or later find out the parameters that limit its generalizations, too.

There are essentially two ways of getting representative samples: probability sampling and stratified sampling. If you know the population values of the important variables to control, you can look for specifiable people who will create your miniature, that is, a form of quota or stratified sampling. In psychology, however, for the most part we do not know what are the appropriate constraints to put on our samples, and we have no way of finding out their distribution in the populations about which we wish to generalize. Logically, therefore, we should turn to the other technique, random or probability sampling. Such a sample can attain representativeness, not because efforts are made to include certain sorts of people, but because efforts are made *not* to *exclude* anyone in the population. When everyone in the parent population (the one from which a sample is drawn) has an equal chance of being included, a probability sample results. Randomness is an essential part of the technology involved, since considerable pains have to be taken not to proceed in an unconsciously biased and selective way. To pick people at random sounds extremely easy but is actually quite difficult. Buttonholing people in a park, for example, will get you a sample of mostly unemployed people who are not actively involved in community activities, who have few hobbies and other interests, who have smaller families than average, and who probably would turn out to have a restricted range of personality structures. Active, involved, busy people do not have an equal opportunity to be included, so the method is a biased one.

The simplest random way of selecting a sample is to give every member of the parent population a number and then enter a table of random numbers until you have as many as you need, using the people corresponding to the resulting set of numbers. This technique is practicable only with relatively small, captive populations that are already listed, such as students in a school or patients in a hospital. Even so, as far as institutions are concerned, you have a sample of only one, so that a randomly drawn sample of schizophrenics in a state hospital in Blackfoot, Idaho, may be a poor basis for generalizing about the people carrying a similar diagnosis at Chestnut Lodge or Manhattan Veterans Administration Hospital. And we typically want to be able to reach conclusions about relationships between variables x and y in schizophrenics, generally, or at least in adult Americans so diagnosed by a competent clinician and declared relatively free of other types of disorder. Nevertheless, it is usually helpful to introduce randomness whenever possible in drawing samples (Cochran, Mosteller, & Tukey, 1953).

What ways out of this dilemma are at hand? Ignoring it, while traditional, accomplishes nothing except to reduce anxiety, and it perpetuates one of the prime sources of the recurrent nuisance in psychology: that different experimenters get different results. More than a nuisance is involved, for this phenomenon means that we have not begun to locate some of the most important sources of variance in the behavior we study. First of all, we should describe our samples as completely as possible with respect to possibly relevant variables. In a study of catecholamine secretion in relation to mood fluctuation, the texture of the Ss' hair and their clerical aptitudes can safely be neglected, but not their cultural backgrounds or diagnoses. Diagnosis, in turn, should be given in terms of a standard nosology and a specified set of criteria (such as those published by the American Psychiatric Association, 1968). One of the reasons for the widespread (and, in my view, unjustified) rejection of diagnostic classification of patients is the tendency to develop local idiosyncrasies of category and criteria, so that you have to know that 90% of the patients at a certain hospital are diagnosed schizophrenic and only half that proportion at another one, which draws on an apparently similar population, before you can interpret disparate findings from the two institutions. In addition to the bald label "schizophrenia," one needs to know the type, whether acute or chronic, and the history of previous hospitalizations and remissions and of previous therapy, not to mention the current therapeutic regimen, its type and duration. Age; sex; number of years of education; religion; geographic, ethnic, and cultural origin; occupation; and marital status are other easily obtained facts that should routinely be included in the published descriptions of samples and of subsamples. Experimental and control groups need to be matched on every such sampling parameter that might affect the dependent variable.

This may seem a tedious amount of detail, though it can usually be rather compactly stated; but without it, we shall continue to flounder in ignorance of how far our results are a function of unknown sampling parameters. This is another way in which we can make sure that our results will add up with those of others and be of some ultimate scientific value.

As far as the actual selection of Ss is concerned, we should first of all become aware of the nature and implications of the sampling problem and know what we are doing. To a large extent, any experimenter is limited by the necessity to use available Ss, though often less so than he realizes. If you are not studying clinical groups and are working in an academic setting, do not settle for the easily obtainable students every time. The surrounding community contains sources that are hardly more difficult to exploit: clubwomen of many kinds, firemen, prisoners, recuperating patients in general hospitals, people in homes and day centers for the aged, and many others. Whatever the population you are drawing on, try to sample them in as unbiased a way as possible; if you have to use every volunteer you can get, make it clear in your paper that the sample *was* self-selected, and do not imply that it was random. A number of studies have shown that volunteers differ strikingly from nonvolunteers (e.g., Lasagna & von Felsinger, 1954). Just this device of using a variety of samples, each carefully described, will help psychology expand its horizons.

The maximum benefit will be obtained, however, if you *replicate every experiment with a different sample of Ss before attempting to generalize* from its results. The more divergent the samples, the more safely can you assume that cross-validated results are generally true or are limited only by the few features both samples have in common. Any replication is better than none, and if you have any reason to doubt that a result was more than a fluke in the first place, you should cross-validate it as exactly as possible, including a sample drawn in the same way. Otherwise, however, replication with the same type of Ss does *not* make it more legitimate to generalize beyond the descriptive characteristics of those Ss' parent population. When Bach and Klein (1957) found essentially the same influence of a subliminally presented word on descriptions of a pictured face as G. J. Smith, Spence, and Klein (1959) had, they gambled by changing the experimental technique while simultaneously going from male VA schizophrenics to female summer students of education; if the results had been negative, it would not have been possible to tell what was responsible. As it was, however, they increased the generalizability of their results quite markedly. When Goldberger and I (1961) replicated an earlier study (Holt & Goldberger, 1959) of personological correlates of reactions to perceptual isolation, we changed from first-year undergraduates in the NYU School of Education to unemployed members of Actors' Equity. There had been a striking correlation of an adaptive pattern of reaction with measures of femininity in the earlier sample; among the actors, the relationship reversed completely, the adaptive pattern now correlating with masculinity. At the same time, measures of ego strength continued to show significant positive correlation with the adaptive pattern. This example illustrates both the futility of relying on results at the .01 level when going outside the bounds of the original sample and the way that the strategy of replication advocated here can fractionate the stable from the unstable findings, so that the later study illuminates the earlier one.

Planning Qualitative and Quantitative Analysis of the Data

The conventionally given advice in this area is so often and so unfortunately ignored as to make it worth repeating: plan ahead *specifically*, in advance of collecting your final data, just how you are going to analyze them—all of them. This step will pay for itself in labor saved gathering unnecessary data alone. The time to get expert statistical consultation is before the results are in, not after. The same advice applies when performing a content analysis of qualitative data.

Except in the simplest experiments, it is virtually impossible to foresee all relevant and useful analyses of the data. Discoveries are made only by those who keep their eyes open. The experimenter who compulsively follows his original plan to the letter and stops there will rarely learn anything new, though he will turn out better work than the freewheeling impressionist who cannot be bothered to gather and analyze his data in a uniform manner. The best style is a mixture of discipline and freedom, responsibly sticking to what is essential in a design but flexibly taking advantage of the unexpected opportunity for exploration.

The Pilot Study

Whenever possible, it is usually helpful to have a dry run of an experiment with a few Ss as comparable as possible to the ones who will actually be used, going through as many parts of the total research process as you can before finally crystallizing the design and procedures. In this way, by trying out several versions you can work out exact instructions to Ss, collect sample data on which to develop a coding system for a content analysis, train your raters, check reliabilities, etc., without sacrificing any of your final data. In our exemplary project, a pilot study might help work out dosages of the drug and alert us to any side effects.

A pretest of this kind is particularly important in any large-scale study in which many Ss are to be used over quite some period of time or, in general, whenever a major investment will be made in an investigation. Once the gathering of the final data has begun, it may be too late to turn back and start again, so that all procedures need to be checked out before they are fixed. Under these circumstances, it is tempting to make a change in some instruction or what not after having analyzed the pretest data and then go ahead and use it, overlooking the fact that it is still untried and may have just as many unanticipated "bugs" as the original, discarded one. Pretesting then should ideally continue until every part has been tried out in its final version and the decision has been made that nothing more needs changing.

Last Steps

Collecting the crucial data, analyzing them, performing the statistical analyses, writing up the findings for publication—these are of course the critical steps of experiment; yet if planning has proceeded adequately, they usually may be run through relatively uneventfully. If not, there is little by way of general advice that can be given other than such homiletic stereotypes as to keep your head, note down everything untoward that happens, be accurate, try to understand the deviant cases as well as the ones that behave in predicted fashion, and have the courage to write up and publish negative findings. What, then, is the final step, the end point? An argument could be

Table 7.1   Checklist of Questions to Be Asked About a Research Proposal

---

 1. What is the problem?
    a. Is it clearly stated?
    b. Is it focused enough to facilitate efficient work (*i.e.,* are hypotheses directly testable)?
 2. What are the underlying objectives?
    a. Is the problem clearly related to the objectives?
 3. What is the significance of the proposed research?
    a. How does it tie in with theory?
    b. What are its implications for application?
 4. Has the relevant literature been adequately surveyed?
    a. Is the research related to other people's work on the same or similar topics?
 5. Are the concepts and variables adequately defined (theoretically and operationally)?
 6. Is the design adequate?
    a. Does it meet formal standards for consistency, power, and efficiency?
    b. Is it appropriate to the problem and the objectives?
    c. Will negative results be meaningful?
    d. Are possibly misleading and confounding variables controlled?
    e. How are the independent and dependent variables measured or specified?
 7. What instruments or techniques will be used to gather data?
    a. Are the reliabilities and validities of these techniques well established?
 8. Is the sampling of subjects adequately planned for?
    a. Is the population (to which generalizations are to be aimed) specified?
    b. Is there a specific and acceptable method of drawing a sample from this population?
 9. Is the sampling of objects (or situations) adequately planned for?
    a. To what population of objects (situations) will generalizations be aimed?
    b. Is there a specific and acceptable method of drawing a sample from this population?
10. What is the setting in which data will be gathered?
    a. Is it feasible and practical to carry out the research plan in this setting?
    b. Is the cooperation of the necessary persons obtainable?
11. How are the data to be analyzed?
    a. What techniques of "data reduction" are contemplated?
    b. Are methods specified for analyzing data qualitatively?
    c. Are methods specified for analyzing data quantitatively?
12. In the light of available resources, how feasible is the design?
    a. What compromises must be made in translating an idealized research design into a
       practical research design?
    b. What limitations on generalizations will result?
    c. What will be needed in terms of time, money, personnel, and facilities?
[13. Is there provision for finding out from the subjects what the experience of the research
    meant to them and for making sure that it had no untoward effects on them?]

---

made that it should be a replication of the entire experiment or the publication of the written report. The fact is that there is no logical stopping place in experimentation; since science does not know any final truths, any study points inevitably to further problems that need to be investigated. That is one reason why research can be such an endlessly fascinating pursuit.

8

About five years after the first publication of the preceding chapter, I was approached by another editor to do another piece on clinical research methods. Not wishing to repeat what I had just written, I decided to concentrate on nonexperimental methods, chiefly exploratory clinical research, on which there was a relative dearth of easily accessible literature. Hence, the title used here for Chapter 8 indicates its contents somewhat better than the original one (Holt, 1973a). To some extent, Chapter 8 plows ground traversed in Chapter 7, but in more depth (for example, ethical issues in research), or it introduces further material with as little repetition as possible. Taken together, these two chapters constitute a brief general treatise on how to do investigative work in clinical psychology and related fields.

Nonexperimental Methods of Research in Clinical Psychology

Any text on clinical or abnormal psychology presents many facts or apparent assertions of fact about people with unusual and distressing patterns of behavior and about ways of trying to help them. Such a book also usually contains a diversity of theories, attempting to advance our understanding about the origins and amelioration of such abnormalities, their inner nature and connections with the rest of personality. Where do these kinds of information come from? The following pages present an overview of the principal methods that have been used in the past and others that show promise for the future.

FACTS VERSUS THEORIES

It might be supposed that the field could be subdivided into factual and theoretical research. There is an immediate difficulty, however: the line between facts and theories is not always easy to draw. Indeed, people who

187

distrust theories and wish to avoid them usually do not realize how difficult it is to make a statement of fact without some implicit commitment to a theoretical point of view. Suppose we try to ask some simple, factual questions in the realm of abnormal psychology or clinical psychology (two terms that will be used interchangably here). "How many kinds of mental disease are there? How many people suffer from the most common kinds?" This way of wording the issues immediately commits us to the position that clinical psychology is concerned with mental diseases, which are implicitly assumed to be clearly distinguishable and thus objectively countable conditions.

For many years, it was not at all obvious that this set of silent assumptions constituted a theory, for the field was dominated by the medical tradition of psychiatry. Anything that caused people such distress that they had to seek help, it was taken for granted, must be a disease comparable to pneumonia or at least to an affliction like a broken arm or a club foot. In recent years, however—particularly since the work of Szasz (1961)—psychologists have increasingly begun to notice that these *were* assumptions and to question their appropriateness. For to classify any human function that is both unusual and in some way undesirable as an illness is to adopt a concept from medicine and to generalize it quite broadly. If a person who feels compelled to spend most of his time washing his hands is the victim of a disease (usually called "compulsion neurosis"), then how about a person who feels compelled to drink alcoholic beverages to excess? Oh yes, "Alcoholism is a disease like any other," we are constantly assured. Then what if the uncontrollable behavior is stealing? Is that a disease called "kleptomania," or is it a moral failing called delinquency or crime? No difference, many psychiatrists will assert; so-called criminals are really sick people, who should not be punished but cured. And if the unusual and undesirable behavior is an inability to get interested in work or to perform successfully on a job? Is that another moral failing called laziness, or is it a socioeconomic condition called unemployability, or is it too a disease—a form of "character disorder" ("inadequate personality," or perhaps "sociopathic personality disturbance")? It seems that there is some kind of medical term for almost any form of behavior that most people do not like, so that this one can indeed be classified as a disease. Yet it is quite evident that the same behavior can as easily be viewed from any of several alternative points of view, which also constitute theories (formal or informal).

It may begin to be apparent that the way we conceptualize our subject matter will subtly but pervasively affect the way we investigate it. If we want to study unemployability, then it will seem natural to direct our attention to the person's situation rather than to internal processes in him. We will be led to ask what jobs he has had, how he lost them, what opportunities for work and what barriers to his getting employment exist. If the problem is presented as one of laziness, the first inclination of most people seems to be not to study it at all, but to condemn it and exhort the person to change his behavior—which implies that he could be different if he saw sufficient reason to get to work. If we undertook any research on "shiftless" people, then, it might be a study of which arguments were most effective in getting a lazybones to see the error of his ways. Notice how diametrically opposite is the assumption of the medical conceptualization: The nonworking person is seen as unable to decide to get a job or unable to make himself work at it because he has a mental illness of some kind. Therefore, an inquiry into his problem will be directed along lines traditional to medicine: we will study the history of the illness, looking for predisposing factors (e.g., genetic or hereditary) and precipitating factors (e.g., special stresses or other recent pathogenic influences on the person). We will tend to classify any other unusual behavior, thoughts, or feelings as additional symptoms, probably signs of other illnesses from which he may be suffering concurrently.

Because of this close intermeshing, the distinction between facts and theories is not a useful way to subdivide the job of examining the kinds of research methods used in abnormal psychology. Instead, let us split it up into three areas implied by these general questions:

1. What are the phenomena studied in clinical psychology? (Descriptive research)

2. What are the causes of these phenomena? (Dynamic research)

3. What can be done to alter these phenomena? (Therapeutic research)

A medically trained person will say, "Aha, you mean nosology, etiology, and therapy." By now, we should be wary enough to answer, "Yes, in the terms of your theoretical frame of reference, that is what these three areas would be called." Obviously, a great deal of the work that has been done in abnormal psychology is put in precisely these terms, and this frame of reference has shown its usefulness in organizing much research and in directing it toward answerable questions. But we do not want to put on the blinders of the illness theory—or of any other theory—more than provisionally and temporarily, for it is both a strength and a weakness of any theory that it narrows our field of vision. Thereby we are helped to concentrate and by focusing our gaze to see more sharply with less confusion and distraction; but we also necessarily fail to see a good deal of what is there and is visible via the alternative refraction of a different pair of theoretical spectacles.

DESCRIPTIVE RESEARCH IN ABNORMAL PSYCHOLOGY

Before we can make much headway on the first of these topics, we shall have to take care of a number of general issues. Fortunately, we do not need to get into the tricky matter of defining what is abnormal; we can accept the field of clinical and abnormal psychology as it has defined itself. We shall do well to consider what the subject matter of this field is, and then to examine a number of basic methodological principles, before we take up some of the main types of descriptive clinical research.

The Subject Matter of Clinical Psychology

First, it will avoid confusion to adopt an explicit definition of the ambiguous term "phenomena." It is used here in its most general sense, referring to everything of interest to scientists and professionals in clinical psychology and the other "mental health disciplines." More concretely, it denotes the behavior of people who are socially defined as actual or potential mental patients (largely by the act of their seeking or being brought to the help of a clinical psychologist, psychoanalyst, psychiatric social worker, psychiatrist, or psychotherapist); and not just behavior in the restricted sense of action or conduct, but also verbal and expressive behavior and the inner states thereby reported—thoughts, feelings, emotions, fantasies, moods, impulses, wishes, and the like. Moreover, the clinician is interested not only in such phenomena as he can observe directly but also in reports of past behavior and inner states, as well as future-pointing fears, longings, plans, and expectations. Since every person is part of many social institutions and systems, his behavior is inextricably linked to that of other people. It is therefore critically important to view it in a *transactional* or interpersonal way—as part of a pattern of give-and-take with other persons, whose relationships with the person of primary interest must be understood. Finally, the clinician's interest in behavior extends to the settings in which it typically takes place and all the potential harms, benefits, threats, and opportunities they offer. The complex realm of phenomena just described will be called *disordered behavior* when a brief phrase is needed.

In adopting this definition I have taken a stand on a highly controversial issue, one that pervades all of psychology. In the field of clinical psychology, it comes to sharpest focus in the division of therapists into those who, like psychoanalysts and existential psychotherapists, believe that the subjective world of experience is of the greatest importance, and the various proponents of behavior therapy who stress externally observable behavior and who generally minimize the role of inner states even when they deal with them. These differences in emphasis may be traced back to fundamentally different stances on what are essentially philosophical issues—philosophical, because they are matters of assumption and basic scientific method rather than matters of fact capable of being settled by an appeal to any conceivable data. I like to think of the conflict as one between a mechanistic and a humanistic conception of man (Holt, 1972a). The most vigorous and successful proponents of the mechanistic image in psychology have been the heirs of behaviorism, the best-known theorist among whom today is B. F. Skinner.

The behaviorists (including behavior therapists) tend to take a more or less open and explicit position that the only realities are those of the physico-chemical world; hence, they do not like to use subjective meanings as part of an explanatory system, but only as dependent variables to be explained in other terms—i.e., as effects but not as causes (which are often called "independent variables" in an experimental design). The fact that people claim to act because of wishes, fears, intentions, and the like is not to be taken seriously, Skinner (1971) argues; that is only an illusion. Behavior is actually determined by external rewards and punishments ("schedules of reinforcement") and by inner physiological, biochemical, and other nonpsychological determinants, the mechanists believe. This is, then, a reductionistic position, what Boring (1942) called the psychology of "nothing but," instead of a psychology of "something more," which characterizes the humanists.

Though psychoanalysis contains important elements of mechanism (particularly in its abstract theory, metapsychology; see Holt, 1972a), it and most other schools of psychotherapy are basically humanistic in their approach. In these conceptual systems, the world of subjective experience and meanings is as much a part of reality as the world of physical measurements and exact observations of behavioral acts, and it cannot be reduced to the latter. Moreover, for the humanists the most important data are verbal and emotional *meanings* and interpersonal *relationships,* to understand which the researcher must be capable of empathy in addition to the more narrowly intellectual skills and capacities demanded of any other scientist.

To some extent, the conflict between these two viewpoints can be resolved in the following way. The person is an organismic unity; when he gets angry about being overcharged in a store, this event may be analyzed in terms of the overt, publicly observable behavior (e.g., loud verbal complaints), in terms of the activity of the person's autonomic nervous system and the ductless glands, in terms of the subjective experience of outrage and indignation, and in terms of unconscious fantasies and memories of being exploited or treated unjustly in childhood which are stirred up and may come to light subsequently in dreams. So far, the event may be seen to have behavioral aspects, biological aspects, phenomenological aspects, and psychoanalytic aspects; but it can also be viewed in social-psychological terms as a transaction between two people, in economic terms as a part of monetary and marketing processes, sociologically in terms of the role relationships of customer and storekeeper, and anthropologically in terms of the values and other culture traits expressed. Each of the many disciplines that may be interested in the event (the above list is by no means exhaustive) isolates for special study a small number of special aspects of what is a complex unity, and no one of them should claim that only his level of analysis is valid or real.

Some Basic Methodological Principles

Murray and Kluckhohn (1949) once sagely remarked that each person is like *every* other person in some ways, like *some* other persons in some ways, and like *no* other person in some ways. This seemingly simple, self-evident proposition—let us call it the *principle of human diversity*—contains a good deal that we can profitably dwell on. First, however, notice that the middle category may be almost endlessly subdivided: everyone is like very many others in some ways, like many . . . , like a few . . . , like a small handful of others in some ways.

To begin with, the principle acknowledges that people are unique to some degree, but not totally. This fact makes a science of personality possible. If individuality were absolute or nearly so, as a few theorists— notably Allport (1937, 1961)—have argued, it would be impossible to use general concepts or indeed any intelligible language to describe personalities [see Volume 1, Chapter 1]. The prejudice that the scientific study of personality is impossible dies hard, surfacing from time to time as part of a mystical or otherwise anti-intellectual ideology. Nevertheless, the principle of human diversity is enough to show how little foundation there is for such objections.

If a person is like a fair number of other people in *several* respects, we are tempted to call that group of similar persons a *type*. But if all personality traits were uncorrelated and independent of one another, it would still be possible to find a sizable number of people who were, let us say, at once meticulous, stubborn, and parsimonious. That constellation of traits (known as the anal personality) might occur in a few people just coincidentally, even if knowing that a person likes to save money told you nothing about the likelihood that he would be orderly or rigid. Typological conceptions grow out of informal observations that such correlations do exist. They depend, therefore, on the existence of determinants that influence the development of more than one trait or characteristic of personality. We might call this the *principle of divergent causality*, which is well established in many theories of personality and psychopathology: A single cause has many effects. Perhaps the most elegant demonstrations of it have been provided by geneticists, who have proved that single genes determine several phenotypic characteristics. Examples of other such divergent causes are early learning experiences, cultural traits, and environmental influences, any one of which may have many consequences for personality development.

Another property of these determinants of human traits is also noteworthy: the fact that they themselves are patterned rather than varying randomly. Genes are linked in strands of DNA; culture traits are linked into patterns; and environments have stably interrelated features that enable us to categorize them into types of habitat. Such patterned influences exert correlated effects, so that we could speak of a third *principle of convergent causality*, which is partly responsible for the persistence and usefulness of typological concepts: several nonindependent causes work together to bring about one effect (or group of effects). For example, successful intellectualization as an adult trait may be brought about by good genetic endowment of verbal intelligence, parents who themselves are intellectuals, and attendance at schools that stress intellectual achievement. It is easy to see that these three determinants are by no means independent: successful intellectual parents probably have superior genetic endowment to transmit and also the money and motivation to send their children to the kinds of schools in question.

The notion of personality types and of types of disordered behavior is nevertheless a controversial one. Many psychologists never tire of reminding us that the correlations among personality traits are less than perfect, so that knowing the presence of one component trait of a typological pattern makes it only somewhat probable that we will find the other expected traits. The proper retort should be that *all* scientific knowledge is probabilistic and that there is no point in vainly hoping for complete certainty; we must instead accept the challenge of finding out empirically what the probabilities are. There is no a priori way of knowing just how far the natural clustering of traits goes—much less, what causes it—so we must do research to find out. Less abstractly put, the upshot of the argument for the anal personality type is as follows. If you observe that a person is particularly neat and clean, you are likely to be right if you predict that he will resist attempts to change him, and that he will tend to save and hold on to his possessions—both to a more than average degree. The original observations by Freud (1908b) and Abraham (1921) on this personality type have been replicated by many other clinical researchers (see Fenichel, 1945), and the typological concept *anal character* has won considerable acceptance by nonpsychoanalysts as well. Note, however, how approximate the knowledge yielded by this type of qualitative observation is: it gives us no way to estimate just what the probabilities involved are.

Descriptive research must move on to a quantitative phase in which two kinds of measurement are used. First, some way has to be found to replace imprecise qualitative terms like "frugal" (just how much must a person be concerned with saving to be called frugal?) by numerical measures of some kind. And second, after the investigator has scaled (given a quantitative rating to) each of the traits in the anal personality syndrome on a group of subjects, he must interrelate them quantitatively by correlations and other statistics such as regression equations. Only then will he have a sound factual basis for this important kind of empirical inference: predicting the strength of one trait from assessing the others. Multiple regression provides numerical measures of the confidence with which he can make such predictions and an elegant way of doing so.

The Individual Case Study. The first principle, that of human diversity, has further important implications for clinical research. Consider a popular research method among clinicians of all kinds, the individual case study. People are undeniably interesting and worthwhile in themselves, and when you have spent a long time studying one personality intensively and have described him in detail, you feel you have made a valuable contribution to knowledge. The principle reminds us, however, that no matter how thoroughly we know one man, we have no way of telling whether any particular trait or characteristic observed or measured is universal to all mankind, unique to this individual, or somewhere in between. There is simply *no way* to know how far we can generalize safely or accurately from what we observe in a single case. And that is true no matter how many observations we make, over no matter how long a time and in a design of whatever sophistication. The only possible valid conclusion from a case study is: here is one possible way that human beings can be. That is not as small a contribution as it may at first appear to be, but it is still only the beginning of useful knowledge. (For a different viewpoint, see Davidson and Costello, 1969).

Generalization and the Parametric Principle. How many cases do we need, therefore, in order to conclude that what we observe is universally valid? Logically, it follows from the principle of human diversity that the only way to know for certain that something is true of an entire population is to observe every member of that population. What a discouraging conclusion! Is there no way around it? Of course; by abandoning the ambition to know "for certain." Common sense tells us, with justification, that if you observe something to be true again and again, and again indefinitely (that is, for a "very large" number of observations), it is increasingly likely to be universally valid. But a child growing up in many American communities will observe that all the people he sees have two arms and two legs, that their skins are more or less white, and that they speak English. He is almost sure to conclude, unless otherwise taught, that each of these is a universal characteristic of human beings. We teach him otherwise, of course, by introducing contrary cases: this person has all the other expected human characteristics but his skin is black, or he speaks Norwegian. Here, then, is a way of getting certain knowledge: with a single case, you can disprove any universal proposition. More formally, it is the principle of the *null hypothesis*. If you turn your proposition upside down and state it in the form of a universal negative, you can then plan your observations to prove that this negative statement (null hypothesis) is wrong (see below, p. 220). Instead of trying to prove that hope makes a difference in psychotherapy, for example, you plan your study instead to disprove the negative statement that treatment is equally successful whether the therapist is hopeful or not.

Disproving the null hypothesis is more useful in dynamic than in descriptive research, however. True, you can disprove that obstinacy is unrelated to orderliness, but if you want to go on to find a quantitative measure of the relationship between them, the problem of how to generalize comes up again. For the hypothetical example of the child's inference that all people are white and speak English shows that traits may be strongly linked in a given population without there being any intrinsic relationship among them. Correspondingly, it could very well be that the clinically observed relationships known as the anal character hold true only in certain localities, or at a given time, or in a particular culture. Freud and Abraham explained the intercorrelation of the personality traits in question as being the results of a common cause: unusually strong anal erotism, in turn largely a result of severe toilet training. If these hypotheses are correct, the correlations ought to break down in a culture that did not put any particular stress on early and prompt learning to use the toilet.

Incidentally, it is interesting to notice that Freud did not limit his generalizations to specific societies or times in this way. He was trained in the natural sciences, in which it seems intuitively obvious that the phenomena are quite general. Once Newton had found that a prism could split light into a spectrum of colors, it occurred to no one that the effect might occur only in Britain in the seventeenth century. A single experiment seemed capable of discovering a universal, absolute truth. That was the ideal Freud attempted to carry over into psychology. When, in Freud's middle years, physicists began to discover that there were in fact limitations on Newton's truths (the celebrated laws of motion holding, for example, only at velocities well below the speed of light), it did not immediately become obvious that this *parametric principle* holds true in psychology also, except that a different set of parameters[1] are involved.

The parametric principle implies that no matter how general a finding may appear to be, it probably holds true only for a certain population defined by a set of parameters (e.g., for many of the findings of experimental psychology, the Wistar strain of the mutant white Norway rat; or white, middle-class, male college students in the United States of our historical era). This principle is very widely ignored, because investigators like to think that they are discovering universal truths. (For more discussion of this point, see pp. 199–200, 243–251 below.)

If, however, we take the parametric principle seriously, we will pay a good deal of attention to the nature of the population we are actually sampling when we decide to do psychological research of any kind, for the population parameters and the techniques of sampling used sharply limit the inferences we can validly draw from our findings.

Let us take a concrete example, the commonly quoted descriptive statement that every other hospital bed in the United States is occupied by a

---

[1] A parameter is a fixed value of a determinant, a specified condition that must obtain for a given relationship between variables to hold true. Thus, for Newton's laws, the relevant parameters are that such determinants as velocity, gravitation, mass, etc., should vary (approximately) within the range observable on earth in our general era. For Freud's findings, the relevant parameters are more cultural and social, and time can be neglected as such if we realize that in any one locality culture may change drastically in historical time.

"mental patient." In order to have complete confidence in a statement like that, you would have to make a complete enumeration of all hospital beds, dividing them into the two categories, with psychiatric and nonpsychiatric occupants. Usually, it is possible to do so by compiling published statistics from the various hospitals, which takes a good deal less time and effort than going to each institution in person and counting. Ultimately, however, someone has to gather the basic data, and a descriptive statistic is no better than the original observations it summarizes.

Relatively little of the information in books on clinical and abnormal psychology comes from such complete enumerations, however confident and factual the tone in which assertions are made. For one thing, the advent of modern sampling techniques makes it possible for a person to acquire much descriptive information of satisfactory accuracy by studying only a relatively small part of the entire population he wishes to describe, whether that is people, hospitals, or whatnot. More basically, however, the reason that not much research of this kind goes on is that descriptive statements, however precise, have little scientific value in psychology. For purposes of public policy, it is important to know how many people in a country are addicted to heroin or cocaine or alcohol, or how many psychiatric symptoms are complained of by a specifiable population (e.g., citizens of a certain state who are over 60 years of age). Yet it is hard to see what difference it would make to any *theory* whether the answer to either of the preceding questions were 100,000 or 10,000,000. In the physical sciences, by contrast, certain descriptive facts may have great theoretical significance, because theory is much further advanced. It can be argued that most of the important advances in astronomy, for example, have come from increased precision of observation and measurement. Even the crude instruments of the pretelescopic era gave good enough measurements of the planets' movements to make trouble for Ptolemy's theory that they moved in circular orbits around the earth; and today astronomers go to enormous pains to measure the orbit of Mercury because perturbations in it have important implications for predictions from relativity theory.

Notice that in both of the examples just given, description is not an end in itself, but that precise description (which usually means measurement) is useful for its *theoretical implications.* All sciences started out with simple description, but they began to make real progress when they contributed to our understanding of nature by putting the observations into coherent patterns. Gradually, what first appears to be a bold theoretical leap—like the Copernican model of the solar system—comes to seem a rather simple description which itself demands explanation in terms of a more embracing theory. In the example just cited, notice that certain kinds of descriptive research are much more useful than others. No one knows precisely how many bodies are in orbit around the sun, and it is questionable that there would be any particular value to this piece of information. A census of asteroids, or (switching to biology) of the number of insect species, or (in meteorology) the exact number of ordinary cyclonic systems during any given period of time—such counting of what exists has some value, but descriptive research of this enumerative character rarely gets high priority for scientific budgets, nor do the results of such work make scientific headlines. Yet increased precision in the measurement of the speed of light or in the description of the biochemical events during the passage of an impulse from a neuron to a muscle cell is important enough to win a Nobel prize. The first of these descriptive findings was important because the velocity of light is a key variable in the central structure of physical theory; thus, knowing its value to extra decimal places aids in the precise determination of many other quantities, which can help settle theoretical issues. The second descriptive finding is important because it opens up the understanding of most processes of biological communication and control within organisms.

Explanation, Inference, and Understanding. Most of the time, then, descriptive research is a means to some other end—either to provide information for some practical action, or to provide information on the basis of which inferences may be made. These words are being written at a time when there is a resurgence of interest in phenomenology in clinical psychology, an affirmation that it is worthwhile just to look long and carefully at the natural events that form clinical psychology's subject matter. Undeniably, people are fascinating, and it *is* interesting to find out in detail the life stories of people who are having one or another neurotic or psychotic problem. Interest in description here, however, imperceptibly passes over into the desire to understand—to know how someone got that way. And as soon as we venture into the realm of understanding, we begin making *causal inferences.* Psychologists do not wholly agree that it always takes inference to discern causation; Michotte (1946) and Heider (1944) have experimentally demonstrated that causality can be directly seen, as when we see momentum imparted to one billiard ball by another, and that a person's motivation may be perceived like any other attribute. The scope of such direct perception of causes is limited, however, and most explanation in psychology is the result of inferential thinking.

It may be because of the wish of many psychologists to play down the role of judgment that these matters are usually discussed in terms of explanation and prediction instead of understanding and inference. It is easy to show, however, that prediction is of relatively minor scientific interest if it is not the result (and proof) of understanding. Prediction without understanding is the simplest form of inference, little different from description, for it is describing what will be rather than what is. It requires that you notice a repeatable sequence of events in which (at least most of the time) if *A* occurs or is made to happen, *B* will reliably follow.

Thus, von Meduna noticed that schizophrenic patients who underwent convulsions seemed to improve, and so he tried to make them happen by giving a convulsion-inducing drug (Metrazol), thus inaugurating an era of convulsive and shock therapy. Patients of many kinds did apparently improve, whether the shock was pharmacological or electric, convulsive or subconvulsive. Other psychiatrists began noticing, however, that patients who were discharged after shock-induced remission of psychosis (seeming recovery) were showing up again in admissions wards of hospitals a few months later, so that this form of treatment has fallen into disfavor except for certain kinds of depression. Yet despite this accumulation of experience, which enables us to predict pretty well what usually happen if an acute schizophrenic is given shock therapy (improvement, but only for a little while), we understand virtually nothing about how and why it has its effects. Though over 50 theories exist, "No explanation or theory of shock therapies has gained general or even wide approval" (Wolman, 1965b, p. 1017). If we did understand how the limited effects occur, we might be able to design a modification of shock therapy that would work better, and who can say what wider ramifications it might have?

Explanation and understanding are intimately linked with theory and the construction of theoretical models. A theory is an attempt to extract from the concrete particulars of scientific observation certain abstract features or *concepts*, and to construct an orderly, logically consistent structure of concepts. Such a structure must faithfully follow the main outlines of the original observations, and make it possible to go beyond them, to predict what will happen in exactly specifiable circumstances not yet encountered. Thus, the true test of an explanation is not just the inner sense of satisfaction—"now I understand"—but its capacity to generate testable predictions, which are validated (i.e., found to be true).

Selecting Samples for Research. As already noted, an extremely useful and important aspect of descriptive research is sampling: selecting a segment from a population in such a way as to enable us to draw statistical inferences about the probable properties of the whole population. But how do we go about selecting such a representative sample? One obvious answer is that, other things being equal, large samples are better than small ones. Yet even very large samples are misleading to the point of worthlessness if they are biased. We call a sampling method biased if it tends to give one kind of person a greater likelihood of being chosen than others. Suppose, in terms of our hospital bed problem, you decided to get a sample of 100 hospitals and to make it easy for yourself, started by visiting hospitals in the biggest cities in the country. Clearly, since hospitals in rural and nonmetropolitan areas would have no chance of getting into the sample, you could have no confidence whatever that the results from your big-city sample could be extended (or *generalized*) to them, even if you did not limit yourself to a sample of 100 but took every metropolitan hospital.

A good or representative sample is obtained by a *random* sampling method, one that in fact gives every member of the population about which you want to generalize an equal chance of being selected. There is something deceptively simple-sounding about random sampling. Just take people at random, right? Wrong, because of the "just"—it is actually quite difficult to take people in a truly unbiased way. If you do not set up a careful system and follow it rigidly, you end up taking people who are easy to get, and they are systematically different from people who are hard to get. You can get away with it sometimes, because the ways they are different may not be relevant to the problem you are studying, but you can never be sure.

The hospital example is unusual, in that complete lists of all hospitals in the United States do exist. Once you have such a list, you need only give each hospital a number (in any order—no need to alphabetize them), and then select as many as you need with the help of a table of random numbers. With a sample of this size (100) and such a truly random sampling method, you can treat the data you gather by means of all the standard statistical methods with assurance that you are meeting the most important assumption underlying the statistics. Therefore, you can know just how confident to be about the accuracy of your generalizations; precise methods exist for determining the probable error of all estimates made from a random sample.

Notice that the logic of random sampling remains the same, whether the research in question is descriptive, dynamic, or therapeutic. Indeed, whenever we want to generalize from a set of particulars, throughout psychology and all of science, the same principles hold true. Generalizations are perilous if there is any bias in the sample of data on which they are based, and there is no way to be sure you have guarded against bias without random sampling. Unfortunately, the tradition of researchers in most branches of psychology has been to ignore this point. Unaware that they are sampling in obviously restrictive and biased ways, experimenters continue to take any subjects they can get and assume that their results are quite generally true. Small wonder that psychological findings are so notoriously hard to replicate! Even when another experimenter selects subjects in much the same way, so that many biases are similar, he can get a systematically different group of subjects who give surprising findings. Suppose, for example, experimenter #1 studies the relation between verbal intelligence and the number of neurotic symptoms reported on a questionnaire, and finds no relationship in his sample of male students of introductory psychology. Experimenter #2, also using his captive audience of the male Psych. 1 students in another college, finds a positive relationship. Such results are perfectly possible if the first college is a small, expensive one with very high academic standards and the second is a large state institution with open enrollment; in the former the range of intelligence would be so much smaller that even if a substantial correlation existed in the population at large, it could not be detected from such a sample.

It is hard enough to do research in psychology without being crippled by the requirement of having to draw a random sample of humankind every time. The answer is not for the researcher to shut up shop nor for the student to become completely disenchanted with the scientific status of psychological knowledge. What we need is not cynicism but appropriate skepticism, not despair but modesty in making generalizations. Remember the principle of human diversity. Since every person is in some ways like every other person, when the phenomena we are studying happen to be universal any available sample will do. And though we usually do not know the exact nature of the sector of mankind for which a finding holds, the chances are good that it is generally enough valid to be useful here and now if it has been reported by several independent workers in different places. This consideration is one reason psychologists should spend a good deal more of their research time attempting to replicate important findings.

In clinical and abnormal psychology, particularly, there is no tradition of random sampling. Rather than defining some population about which we wish to generalize and then drawing a sample from it, we usually proceed the other way around. A group of persons comes to our attention, usually because they seek out our clinical services, and we take advantage of the opportunity to study them. For example, a psychotherapist might happen to treat a fetishist successfully, after which he might get several referrals of other patients with fetishes. Since fetishism is a rare condition, he would decide to make a special study of these patients in the hope of learning more about them. In such a situation, a clinician usually assumes that he can generalize about the population in question (here, all fetishists), though he actually knows nothing about how representative his sample may be or how biased. In this respect, he follows an old medical tradition of writing up series of cases of unusual diseases, or even single cases if the condition in question is rare enough.

The Use of Control Groups. Surely, this seems a natural way to go about any descriptive research: take a group of people who seem to constitute an interesting type and then try to find out what they have in common. That is indeed an extremely common kind of descriptive research design in clinical psychology and psychiatry, despite the fact that it is obviously subject to a major objection. All you can conclude from such a design is that the characteristics observed were common to the persons studied. Thus, you are one step ahead of the single-case study, in that you know at least that none of the common features of your group are unique individual traits; but you have no way of telling whether any given trait in your list of findings is universal, true only of the type studied, or true of some larger, undefined group of people.

Suppose you were working in a large urban hospital in the late 1960s and noticed the following similarities in a dozen newly admitted people: they are between the ages of 15 and 30; they are relatively unkempt and unconventional in appearance; they seem to be in a daze, a dreamy state, or some kind of withdrawal that makes it difficult to communicate with them; they show similar oddities of speech, for example addressing anyone they are talking to, regardless of sex, as "man"; they are not violent, making little resistance to police or other persons who pick them up and bring them in, but often speaking about "peace" and "love"; they seem to have no visible means of support other than begging, lack ambition, and show little concern about how they are going to make a living. In spite of these many similarities, they are heterogeneous in several ways. Some are male, some female; they come from various ethnic and class backgrounds, etc. The obviously abnormal states of consciousness they experience turn out, on examination, to be a result of various drugs, self-administered and illegally obtained.

What could you conclude from studying such a group more intensively, or a larger sample with the same defining characteristics? You would probably find that they reject many of the norms, values, and institutions of the contemporary "establishment," but enjoy rock music; a majority of them might profess belief in one or another mystical religion or ideology, and reject any but organically grown foods. It would probably not occur to you to note the fact that all are bilaterally symmetrical, however, for you know that they share this characteristic not only with all mankind but with many other animal species; and if you found on testing them that all correctly identified the emotion expressed by a picture of a laughing person, you might guess that this achievement did not distinguish them from any other group of people with nondefective intelligence. In short, the common sense that silently guided your choice of what to notice and report would actually consist of implicitly *comparing the common elements in this group with common elements to be expected of people of other types.* This process of comparison is vital to all inquiry, and what distinguishes science from common sense is the methods scientists have developed to control errors and allow the drawing of conclusions with specifiable degrees of probable truth, by making careful comparisons.

The above example illustrates some of the dangers of not being explicit about the comparisons you make and not learning the parameters that limit your generalizations. Before the "hippie" pattern became well-known, it would have been easy for the hypothetical researcher to conclude that most of the ways in which his subjects resembled each other and differed from himself and his associates were part of an internally consistent pattern. Then, when he found someone else looking and talking the same way and hanging around rock musicians, he would infer that this new member of the type was also a chronic drug-taker and dropout. As we know, very often he would be wrong; the most deviant hippies who are least able to take care of themselves share many but not all of their salient characteristics with a much larger group of people. The widely shared traits make up what we often call the counterculture or new life-style. Yet this same error of inference was very common among older citizens of our society: if a young man wore his hair long and opposed the Indochinese war they inferred drug addiction, sexual deviation, and other violations of legal and moral codes that characterized only a minority of contemporary exponents of the counterculture.

It is necessary, therefore, in any research to have a control group which is studied in the same way as the "experimental" or critical group. Moreover, it matters a great deal how you choose these control subjects, for your method determines what conclusions you can reach. As a foil for the above-described hippies, you might decide to select a group of subjects who fit the middle-class Rotarian's notion of what the silent majority of (nonhospitalized) young people is like, matching for sex, age distribution, socioeconomic class, and ethnic group. Many of the subsequently observed differences between your two groups would be characteristics of the culturally radical minority as a whole. The fact that your two groups differed strikingly on the hip versus square dimension might well overshadow the consequences of their differing in general social competence. But suppose that you recruited your group of control subjects by offering "easy bread" to long-haired patrons emerging from a rock concert, matching on the same parameters—now the experimental-control differences might arise in large part because of the critical group's hospitalization, and your findings would highlight the disturbance and social incompetence of the troubled hippie rather than his counterculture membership. Many different possible control groups could be chosen for any study, each of which would control different possible determinants of the dependent variables, and the conclusions might vary greatly depending on which was used.

Diagnostic Research

Because of the historical accident that clinical psychology had major roots in psychiatry, almost all of the early descriptive research was conceptualized in medical terms. Even to this day, we lack nonmedical concepts to refer to many phenomena of clinical interest. And a century ago, before books on abnormal psychology were being written and when psychiatry was a relatively young discipline, it was dominated by not only a medical but an *organic* bias. It was assumed that the sorts of behavior that brought people to psychiatrists' attention were caused by hereditary defect, injury to the nervous system, or some physicochemical agent that affected the structure or functioning of the brain. Hysteria was a highly controversial topic at the time, for some psychiatrists (notably Charcot) saw it as a disease of the central nervous system and thus as a legitimate object of research, while others dismissed it as "mere malingering," a form of naughtiness or disagreeable misbehavior which was the proper province of the moralist or disciplinarian rather than the scientist. Psychiatry was already distinguished from neurology, however, for the latter field dealt with the untoward consequences of demonstrable lesions of some part of the nervous system, leaving it to the psychiatrist to concern himself with people who behaved so strangely or inappropriately that they could not lead normal lives. The field of psychiatry and abnormal psychology has always been defined in part socially; its subject matter was people who were so aberrant that they could not make a living or otherwise perform satisfactorily in their major social roles. And in part it was defined residually—in terms of what is left over after a specified group has been excluded; its subject matter was presumed disease resulting from as yet undiscovered disorders of the brain. In practical terms, this division of labor meant that the neurologists dealt with "ambulatory" patients whose almost entirely bodily symptoms did not incapacitate them, or with persons who had to be hospitalized because of severe paralysis, for example, but who still were not "crazy."

The madmen and lunatics were left to the psychiatrist, along with anyone else who could not make a go of it outside the supposedly protective walls of the asylum. The prevalent organic theories implied nothing specific by way of therapy, just good physical maintenance and general nursing care; so psychiatry was a largely descriptive discipline, a branch of what in medicine is usually called *nosology*, the taxonomy of illness. During the last quarter of the nineteenth century, an astonishing variety of diagnostic (nosological) terms were in use, varying from one country and one institution to another. Gradually, over a period of many decades, the number of such presumed diseases shrank, and consensus on a good many of the main distinctions developed. The nosology that survived and emerged from this winnowing process differed in one main way from the ones that sank out of sight: it classified people according to patterns or *syndromes* of symptoms instead of by single symptoms.[2]

This phase of descriptive psychiatry has often been called one of natural history, because the researchers looked for diseases in the same way that naturalists look for species: by observing individuals carefully and systematically, with an eye to similarities and differences. Distinctive similarities, characterizing some but not all patients, made it possible to group them. But on what basis *should* they be grouped? That question was not usually raised in any explicit way. The obvious way to group patients was in terms of what made them patients: the symptoms of which they complained, or the ones that caused relatives to bring them to the asylum. Medical diagnosis had begun with single symptoms, like fever, and had progressed to the discovery that certain symptoms tended to cluster together into recurrent patterns. So psychiatric researchers tried to follow this model. A diagnosis like the now-defunct "hallucinosis" groups together everyone who persistently seems to have experiences in the absence of adequate stimulus conditions (hallucinations), regardless of the context of other symptoms. To be useful, however, a

---

[2]For convenience, in most of this discussion I neglect the distinction in medicine between signs and symptoms, using symptoms to mean both.

diagnosis not only puts together people who have *many* similarities (which should not be the consequence of some other nonpathological cause, like a common ethnic background, or membership in some subculture); it also groups according to *common causes*. But it is extremely difficult to find such common causal elements in terms of which to group psychopathological conditions. Until we can do so, the field of psychological diagnosis will no doubt continue to be vulnerable to the criticism it encounters today on almost all sides.

Much of the diagnostic research of such an important psychiatric pioneer as Kraepelin was not particularly systematic. Kraepelin did take notes on what he observed, but his main instruments were his own eyes and ears as he made his regular rounds in the hospital in Heidelberg where he worked for many years. He interviewed patients and their relatives when they entered the hospital, trying to find out as much as he could about how the "illness" started, what symptoms (subjective complaints) but particularly what signs (objectively observable indications of malfunction) appeared in what order and under what circumstances. He kept records on patients, adding to them as he or other members of the hospital staff reported what they thought were interesting developments. To some extent he used such formal diagnostic methods as the neurological examination (testing reflexes with rubber hammers, testing the strength of limbs, looking for asymmetries of function, etc.). And he was able to follow for years what physicians call the course of the illness—its presumably intrinsic pattern of change when nothing special is done except to hospitalize the sufferer.

A disease, we should keep in mind, is a process, not a static condition. The principal symptoms of scarlet fever are sore throat, vomiting, fever, and rash; but measles too is marked by fever, rash, and a harsh cough. The two diseases may be distinguished by the presence of other symptoms and by qualitative features of these, but an obvious difference is that measles has a slow, gradual onset while scarlet fever strikes suddenly and hard. Some of the acute infections have long incubation periods between exposure and the outbreak of noticeable symptoms, and some are marked by lingering, slow convalescence. Therefore Kraepelin and others like him paid particular attention to the suddenness of onset, the length of the acute and chronic stages (if any), and the outcome, which might range from recovery to deterioration. Indeed, it was largely because he concentrated his attention on the course of the illness that Kraepelin was able to see the common threads that gave unitary significance to many diverse symptom pictures. When others were classifying patients according to whether their delusions concerned themselves or others, and similar hairsplitting distinctions, Kraepelin looked for the long-term changes in what he considered fundamental signs of disease. A large group of psychotic patients, he found, had this in common: Their disturbance began in youth or early adulthood, and followed a generally downhill or *deteriorative* course; hence the name dementia praecox, which be borrowed in 1896 from Morel (who in 1860 had coined it for a smaller group of patients)—*praecox* to indicate early onset, and *dementia* to indicate the process of mental deterioration which he thought the essential feature beneath all the bewildering variety of delusions, hallucinations, mannerisms, peculiarities of speech and conduct, etc. (Havens, 1965). Thus he was able to group together the previously described syndromes of catatonia, hebephrenia, and deteriorative paranoid psychoses, and to distinguish them from the often superficially similar manic-depressive psychosis, with its later onset and cyclical course marked by many periods of normality.

It is easy to get the impression that the era of natural history in clinical psychology is over, and that nothing much remains to be done by way of descriptive research. Far from it! There is every reason to expect that new diagnostic entities will continue to be discovered. As times and institutions change, shaping personalities in new ways and putting new kinds of strains on them, new configurations of symptoms will appear, suggesting new typologies to help us see order in the diversity of suffering individuals. Erikson (1950) hypothesized that the study of ego identity is as crucial for our time as the study of sexuality was in Freud's, for his wide clinical experience led him to notice that many people, particularly adolescents and those in their twenties, seemed to be struggling above all to find meaning in their lives through understanding who they were and how they could fit into the world. A large part of Erikson's contribution has been dynamic—his explanatory formulations and hypotheses about the role that identity plays in the causal network of personality and its disorders—but he has also given us the useful diagnostic concepts of *negative identity, identity confusion,* and *identity crisis* (Erikson, 1964, 1968).[3] It is important for every psychological or psychiatric diagnostician to be familiar with his work, for he has shown how a young person in the throes of a severe crisis of identity confusion can appear to be schizophrenic, whereas the prognosis with appropriate psychotherapy is markedly better than that of the classical psychotic.

Another example of recent progress in clinical research within the framework of the traditional illness model of psychopathology is D. Shapiro's description of *neurotic styles* (1965). This investigator was able to look afresh at the most ordinary kinds of patients whom he encountered in the everyday process of his work as a clinical psychologist and to see new features of traditional syndromes—for example, impressionistic thinking in hysteria and narrowly focused attention in compulsive neurosis—because his vision was renewed by the structural outlook of Rapaport, Gill, and Schafer (1945–

---

[3]Negative identity: an identity "perversely based on all those identifications and roles which, at critical states of development, had been presented to [a person] as most undesirable or dangerous and yet also as most real" (Erikson, 1968, p. 174). Identity confusion: "The inability of young people in the late teens and early twenties to establish their station and vocation in life, and the tendency of some to develop apparently malignant symptoms and regressions" (Erikson, 1964, p. 64). Identity crisis: a period when a person suffers loss or interruption of "a sense of personal sameness and historical continuity" (Erikson, 1968, p. 17).

1946), the concept of cognitive style (Klein, 1958), and the viewpoints of other recent psychoanalytic thinkers (e.g., Kaiser, 1965; W. Reich, 1933).

A more far-reaching change in theory is under way, as we have seen—the abandonment of the concept of mental illness—which may be expected to reopen many seemingly settled issues of descriptive research. One of the earliest indications that the old model was unsatisfactory was widespread dissatisfaction among clinical psychologists with diagnosis as a mere classification or pigeonholing. It is evident to everyone who works in this field that the vast majority of people who come to the psychiatrist or clinical psychologist are not suffering from neatly distinguishable, clear-cut syndromes, which the disease theory of "mental illness" presupposes. It is a typology, but people do not completely fit into any set of types. Each patient has a unique configuration of complaints and observable characteristics (signs and symptoms), and though similarities are recurrent it is much more difficult to make internally homogeneous groupings of patients on psychiatric wards than on the medical wards of a general hospital. At best, the so-called diagnostic entities (syndromes like acute paranoid schizophrenia) are useful not as categories within which to classify people, but as reference points or ideal types toward which actual patients tend to converge.

The growing use of diagnostic psychological tests helped bring into being a conception of diagnosis as the systematic (and, so far as possible, the quantitative) description of personality, its malfunctioning, and its remaining areas of strength. Initially, diagnostic research with tests accepted the illness model and concentrated on putting new content into the accepted syndromes. Rapaport and his colleagues (1945–1946), for example, first used psychiatric observational criteria to group their subjects into internally homogeneous diagnostic categories and then attempted to find quantifiable features of test responses that distinguished these groups of patients. In the attempt, it became evident that the data lent themselves more naturally to a different treatment, in which scores or qualitative signs were correlated with single descriptive characteristics of personality or of psychopathology. Schafer (1954) pointed out that the tester can properly infer from, let us say, a profusion of CF responses (that is, responses mainly to the color of the ink blots, form being used in a vague nondefinitive way) only that the subject controls his desires and emotions loosely, so that his experience is likely to be frequently flooded by vivid feelings and impulses. Depending on other aspects of the test, this characteristic may be part of an hysterical *or* a schizophrenic (or some other, less common) pattern; therefore, the tester must not jump inferentially from a test score to a diagnosis.

The consequence for research is clear: there is little to be gained from attempts to find pure cases of depressive neurosis or simple schizophrenia or whatnot in the hope of discovering unique patterns of test scores for each diagnosis. Rather, it seems much more likely that we shall make progress in *test validation* research by refining clinical observation, developing techniques like rating scales for measuring symptoms and other significant aspects of disordered behavior, and then correlating independent indices from tests with these features of behavior which either cause them or share with them the status of being effects of common causes. [On the problems and possibilities of rating scales in clinical research, see Chapter 7.]

One alternative to a theory of types is a theory of *components*, which leads to a different kind of research method. According to this view, the phenomena of clinical psychology should, as just described, be quantitatively scaled or measured. Then the researcher should study the patterns of their interrelation by statistical methods, using correlation to measure the degree of association of each phenomenon measured to each other one, and component (factor) analysis to find underlying unities in recurrent clusters of the phenomena. There has been a fair amount of this kind of research, but we need a good deal more. Interestingly enough, some of the earliest studies (Wittenborn & Holzberg, 1951; Lorr, Klett, & McNair, 1963) that factor-analyzed ratings of mixed groups of patients on many miscellaneous symptoms found factors that are highly reminiscent of diagnoses long ago formulated by Kraepelin.

Research on components of disturbed behavior needs to be extended to samples from many more kinds of populations. Going beyond the samples of hospitalized neurotics and psychotics so far studied would enable us to discover whether the same components characterize troubled persons who are still functioning in their communities, and people from a variety of cultures and subcultures. For example, in what respects are the components so far discovered specific to developed western culture, and in what respects are they universal? It would also be extremely useful to widen the range of variables measured: first, to make sure that all kinds of disordered behavior, thought, affect, and motives are included; second, to add measures of normal personality traits, intellectual factors, and the like, in order to make it possible to study the interrelations of the components of disturbed behavior with already established factors of personality and intellect; third, to include situational measures—important aspects of the settings in which the subjects live, or the press (Murray *et al.*, 1938) to which they respond. The last step would make it possible to view disordered behavior in a more transactional way, contributing to the emerging discipline of environmental psychology by finding components of situations and relating them to intrapersonal dimensions.

DYNAMIC RESEARCH IN CLINICAL PSYCHOLOGY

As soon as we start to go beyond the description of phenomena and become curious about how or why people got to be the way they are, we get into the realm of what is usually called psychodynamics. This area has been very largely dominated by exploratory clinical research. The term "psycho-dynamics" does have the connotation of psychoanalysis and other schools of intensive, interpretative psychotherapy; many behavior therapists dislike the term and do not use it for their own hypotheses about the causes of symptoms. It is used here in the most general sense, however, intended to include *all* hypotheses in clinical and abnormal psychology that deal with psychological causes, whether in terms of unconscious motives and defenses, existential anxiety, schedules of reinforcement, or whatnot. For the most part, we shall disregard such important classes of causes as injuries to the brain, disorganization of the person's social milieu, and faults in the operation of his genic mechanisms, since they fall outside clinical psychology (in the narrow sense) and have not been discovered and studied by exploratory clinical research.

Exploratory Clinical Research

A distinction is commonly drawn between exploratory or hypothesis-finding research and verifying or hypothesis-testing research. The former is frequently presented as the preliminary, natural-history phase of science, in which investigators make discoveries and get hunches about causal relationships, which must then be laboriously and rigorously tested in a different kind of research, the experiment. As a first approximation, this dual conception has its uses; but in the actual work of scientists no such clear-cut phases exist. As we shall see, the line between exploration and verification is particularly blurry in the field of clinical psychology and psychiatry, but there is a strong tradition of (essentially exploratory) clinical research.

It is generally agreed that this type of research has been the most fruitful source of explanatory hypotheses in clinical psychology. Curiously enough, however, it has rarely been subjected to much systematic examination in a critical but sympathetic attempt to learn just what it consists of, what its strong and weak points are, what needs to be improved about it, and how it could be done better. This section will therefore emphasize such a consideration of the means by which psychodynamic hypotheses are generated. [Table 8.1 presents in summary form a number of the most troublesome difficulties in conducting research and some suggestions about ways to cope with these sources of error.]

First, a definition (and some abbreviations). I will use the phrase *exploratory clinical research* hereafter to refer to work with the following characteristics: (a) it is typically done by lone investigators, though occasionally by pairs or small 'groups of collaborators; (b) the subjects (Ss) are patients or clients who are being diagnosed, cared for (custodially), or treated by the experimenters (Es) or researchers—most typically, via psychoanalysis or some

Table 8.1.   Some Sources of Error and Difficulty in Clinical Research, with
Suggested Countermeasures

Intrinsic difficulties	*Possible remedies*
1. The necessity of dealing with subjective inner states	Rely on intersubjectivity (e.g., test judge reliability); self-analysis; introduce objectivity wherever possible; supplement therapy data by tests or ratings
2. Necessity to work with value-laden concepts	State one's relevant values and consciously try to look for ways they interfere and try to be as objective as possible
3. Inaccessibility of crucial data: Ss may be unconscious of, or unwilling to reveal, important facts and feelings	Increase S's motivation to cooperate and lower his resistances by good therapeutic technique; use projective techniques; avoid unnecessary resistance by using a clear contract, get informed consent
4. Necessity to work with verbal and presentational meanings, thus, need to use inference and judgment	Train judges, achieve reliability in categorizing content and formal properties of data. Be systematic and orderly in gathering and processing data
4a. Danger of reading a hypothesis into data: qualitative data typically can be plausibly interpreted in more than one way (often many ways; in principle, in an infinity of ways, though of course not all with equal plausibility). Thus, plausibility ("it makes sense" in commonsense or theoretical terms) is a fallible criterion for the correctness of interpretations. The Chapmans' specific form of this: "illusory correlation."	Can't control by gathering *more* data of same kind. Look for *other* implications of the hypothesis, test them
5. Retrospective error, in use of therapy (or other anamnestic) data to reconstruct childhood events; e.g., adultomorphic constructions, projections backward of later fantasy	Direct observation of children; look for independent confirmation of constructed events in nonleading interviews with parents *et al.*
Problems within the investigator 6. Emotional attitudes interfering with collection of complete and valid data: fear of personal exposure, often attributed to the patient; emotional commitment to a method or theory, which guides and distorts observations and judgments; projection (complementary or supplementary) of own tendencies onto the patient, seeing one's problems everywhere	Training analysis (for many of the problems in this group); have outside, independent observers, or more generally research collaborators, who ideally do not have the biases in question; double blind designs
7. Emotional involvement with the patient (countertransference) producing bias and contamination because of involvement of *E* in the data; *E*'s reaction to patient provides feedback shaping future material	Same as above (also, supervision of the treatment); in general, in research using data of therapy, it's important to objectify data-gathering process, and separate roles of *E* and therapist

(continued)

Table 8.1.   (*continued*)

Intrinsic difficulties	*Possible remedies*
8. When the data are provided by *E*'s notes, distortions may arise from *E*'s cognitive style, esp. in interaction with patient's from lack of ability (poor memory), and from selectivity of memory (motivated bias)	Use tape recording; or systematize and objectify data-gathering process as much as possible (training, comparing notes with tape; have secretary on-line taking short-hand, or *O*'s behind one-way mirror)
9. Limitations of the lone *E*'s knowledge, skills, or other abilities	Learn own limitations, try to supplement by special training, use of consultants, collaborators (even by mail, if need be)
10. Bias in the selection of data (e.g., overconcern with pathology; overattention to intrapsychic matters; neglect of, or overconcern with, sex, early childhood, reinforcements, etc.)	Learn own biases and consciously strive to counteract them: deliberately look for strengths and adaptive features, or the contributions of culture, everyday life situation, biochemical status, etc.
10a. Misplaced precision: overattention to getting highly accurate measures of easily quantifiable data (e.g., physiological variables) which are to be related to other, grossly measured data (e,g., life events and patient's reactions to them)	Change emphasis to improving quantification of the worst-measured variables, so the level is approximately the same on side of independent and dependent variables alike
11. Difficulties in trusting cumulative clinical experience as a research method: systematic errors may cumulate, traditions may be taken as observed facts, feedback from results is slow and tends to be replaced by invalid feedback of various kinds	Use your clinical experience mainly as a source of hypotheses and as a guide in the interpretation of systematic findings: don't imitate Freud!

Some miscellaneous problems of research in psychotherapy

12. When patients are *S*s, it is at times necessary to abandon research design (usually, controls of some kind) for therapeutic reasons: patient's welfare takes precedence over investigative nicety	Observe and record just what happens, what deviations from plan were necessary and what the response to them seems to have been. Data don't have to be ideal to be usable, at least in part
13. Paradox of recorded psychotherapy: there is a plethora of data, but a narrow data base (limited to what patient says and does in "the hour"), a very limited situation in which to observe behavior and probably not representative	Various techniques of selecting (sampling) and reducing data; use multiform assessment (or at least some additional methods of gathering data) as a supplement, especially in areas where patient can be expected to select and distort in his reporting
14. Difficulty of building up adequate sample size for many analyses	Use cooperative teams of independent therapists, or of people working in same setting; conscious effort at *replications*
15. Patients don't constitute a random sample of any definable population: obvious (e.g., mainly affluent whites) or subtle	Describe patients as carefully as possible in report on research; get control groups whenever possible, introduce as much ran-

Table 8.1. (*continued*)

Intrinsic difficulties	Possible remedies
sampling biases (e.g., patients seek out therapists who provide what they need or want)	domness as possible in sampling or assignment to groups
16. In outcome research, difficulty of finding an appropriate control group. Untreated controls (for example, those put on waiting lists) often look for help elsewhere, and one should not try to stop them.	Compare outcome of the form of psychotherapy in which you are interested with some other form of treatment (e.g., drug, milieu). It accomplishes little to show that something is better than nothing; and the practical question is usually, "Does the proposed treatment do more than what is available (if it is more expensive), or do as well (if it is less expensive)?"

other intensive psychotherapy;[4] (c) the data are primarily those generated by the processes of diagnosis and treatment (to a smaller extent, by administrative or educational conferences), rather than data planned for and gathered expressly for the needs of research; (d) the purposes of the research are always secondary to clinical purposes. Occasionally, a patient may be given tests his treatment does not require, or the E may inquire into some areas more for investigative than for therapeutic reasons, but even in these instances the exception is quickly abandoned if the clinical consequences seem to run counter to the S's best interests.

It follows from the above definition that exploratory clinical research must be carried out mainly by *participant observation* (a term borrowed by H. S. Sullivan from cultural anthropology). That is, the E directly interacts with the S, and that fact inevitably affects the nature and quantity of data she elicits. More is at stake here than the kind of situation familiar in physics as indeterminacy—which means that the process of measuring one attribute makes it impossible to get an unbiased measure of others—for E and S are in addition linked by intense, largely unconscious emotional bonds, usually referred to as transference and countertransference. The difficulties that E has in maintaining objectivity and getting data that are not subtly distorted are fairly obvious. Nevertheless, these questionable data are at the same time invaluable because it is almost impossible to get access to many of the most important facts about a person outside a clinical (helping) situation; only when he is motivated enough by personal distress to define himself as a

---

[4]In the hope of making it clearer who is doing what to whom while retaining the economy of pronouns, I shall adopt the convention of assuming a male patient and a female therapist or clinical researcher hereafter.

patient seeking help will a person ordinarily reveal a great many of the most important facts of his past and present, his inner thoughts, longings and aspirations, fantasies, dreams, fears and resentments. As Freud pointed out, much of this mass of objective and subjective data is not usually accessible because shame, guilt, embarrassment, and similar feelings prevent a person from acknowledging them to anyone else, and much more is not easily accessible even to himself. Only in a prolonged therapeutic process, with the aid of the positive emotional bond with the therapist, key interventions by her (such as interpretations and constructions[5]), and with sustained effort to follow up associative leads can the S overcome enough of his own resistances to become aware of much about himself and then to acknowledge it.

The word "important" was used in the preceding paragraph to imply that the kinds of data specified have a particular value for personality theory or psychopathology. That is, of course, a value judgment, which grows out of a mainly psychoanalytic viewpoint.

Let us return to the task of specifying what exploratory clinical research is, by examining it in terms of the methods used. The clinician exposes herself to the data generated by her clinical practice, and from her encounters with her patients generates propositions of various kinds. How does she do so? The answer to this question cannot be given with any confidence; indeed, right there is a currently active and controversial area of research. Nevertheless, I will offer my own observations and hypotheses, some of which might conceivably be testable in future investigations.

The field we are considering is that of clinical intuition, clinical judgment, clinical prediction, the study of the way clinicians work with their data and reach conclusions from them. In Polanyi's (1958) terms, these processes are subclasses of the general class of expert judgments, which that author persuasively argues have extensive tacit components. That is to say, when a highly trained and experienced professional makes a judgment in an area of her expertise, she draws on an extensive body of past information, theory, evaluative standards, and the like; exercises observational (including empathic) and inferential processes that are shaped by her professional past in ways she could not recall even if asked to; and integrates all of these components into propositions. She cannot be expected to be able to be aware of all these multitudinous and subtle influences on her judgments; indeed, for the judgmental process to function adequately her attention must be directed outward, toward the object of her interest. As soon as she introspects, asking herself, "How do I know that?" or "What makes me think so?"

---

[5]An *interpretation* is a formulation of the underlying meaning or significance of a patient's production; a *construction* is an account of some critical sequence of formative events synthesized by the therapist from direct and indirect bits of evidence provided by the patient. "'Interpretation' applies to something that one does to some single element of the material, such as an association. . . . But it is a 'construction' when one lays before the subject of the analysis a piece of his early history that he has forgotten . . ." (Freud, 1937d, p. 261).

or "Where did that notion come from?" she will be in the same pickle as the self-conscious centipede after having been asked "How do you know which foot to move when?" If the centipede can do it without knowing *how* he does it—which I believe almost anyone would allow—the clinician can, too.

Because of this tacit component in clinical judgments, they are often viewed as mysterious (which they are) and therefore mystical (which does not follow logically at all). There seems to be no reason, in principle, why intuition cannot be analyzed and eventually understood. It is by now a cliché (though one that people often rediscover with a great show of having solved a marvelous mystery) that the thought processes in intuition are the same as those that occur in introspectively available types of cognition except that they take place without awareness. That still remains a hypothesis, however; if Polanyi is correct, some components of intuition are not directly knowable by the clinician herself—though they may also operate in apparently simpler and more transparent types of thought.

In another paper (Holt, 1961b [Chapter 3]), I have analyzed the processes of clinical inference and judgment of verbal texts into a dozen kinds of operations. First, six kinds of internal analyses may be performed on a single text itself: (1) Summary—getting rid of redundancy and irrelevancy by abstracting and selecting the "essentials." (2) Collation—examining a verbal message for internal consistency, locating inconsistencies for special attention. (3) Interpretation of content—translating sentences in the patient's language into another, technical language, which conceptualizes it. (4) Structural analysis—conceptualizing formal or structural properties of the data. Note that both (3) and (4) may be done either by *coding* (assigning an aspect of form *or* of content to a category, i.e., conceptualizing), or by *rating* (essentially the same task, only replacing the two-point scale of present versus absent by a more differentiated scale on which the quality is judged as more or less present). (5) Recipathy—analyzing a communication by reacting to it and observing your own reaction. (6) Perception or inference of causes—discerning causal relations, or generating hypotheses that *A* causes *B*.

The other half-dozen kinds of analyses are called external because they draw much more on data outside the verbal text in question: (7) Selection—choosing the sample of text, either by random sampling or (more usually) by use of various criteria of relevance to an explicit or implicit theory. (Actually, this is the first step of all.) (8) Genetic analysis—reconstructing the historical chain of events that brought about the text or the events it refers to. (9) Comparison—noting similarities and differences between the text and others that are partly identical with it, noticing the presence of the unexpected and the absence of the expected. (10) Contrast—essentially the same operations as the preceding, but carried out in relation to other types of data. Thus, for the interpreter of a TAT story, comparison means looking for elements it shares with TAT stories told by other subjects; contrast means looking for elements it shares and does not share with responses given by the same subject in interview, Rorschach, etc. (11) Evaluation—considering a text in relation to a set of external, normative standards (pragmatic, esthetic, ethical, etc.). (12) Synthesis—bringing the pieces of analysis together into a coherent verbal formulation; often it involves making further, secondary inferences on the basis of the primary inferential analyses [see Volume 1, Chapter 2].

Though the preceding analysis is confined to clinical operations on verbal texts, the operations listed need to be supplemented only by empathy (an identification-mediated perceiving of inner states in another person; see Schafer, 1959b, and Holt, 1971c) to encompass all processes used in exploratory clinical research regardless of the type of data. Moreover, these are the operations used in all sciences and indeed in all kinds of disciplined human inquiry in forming hypotheses and in reflecting on the meaning of one's findings. Therefore, the processes of exploratory clinical research are neither to be specially venerated as mystically wondrous nor to be sneered at as beyond the pale of normal scientific methods.

Parenthetically, I want to point out one way in which the preceding analysis is potentially quite misleading—something it shares with a great deal of writing on methodological issues. It makes the process of clinical work sound too simple, too clear-cut, too orderly, indeed too cut-and-dried. In actuality, clinicians sometimes sweat and strain, plunge enthusiastically ahead only to bang against seemingly insuperable obstacles, stew and fume until a new insight shows the way, or simply try out a great many possibilities until something seems to work. They are often passionately involved in their work, and not at all conscious of or deliberate about carrying out the various operations described. When the processes that must go on are spelled out, they look unnaturally tidy; operations that are logically early may nevertheless take place at any time. By no means should you leave with the impression that the sequence indicated has any necessary relation to the order in which things happen.

If these are the basic operations used by the clinical researcher in making discoveries, how does she actually proceed? Most typically, she simply sees her patients—on ward rounds, in case conferences, in diagnostic interviews and testing sessions, and above all in therapeutic encounters. As she keeps her eyes and ears open, much of what she perceives fits into existing patterns or schemata in her head—she recognizes again and again many syndromes about which she has read and which were demonstrated to her during her training; she verifies causal sequences she has similarly been taught to expect; and she finds instances of many phenomena and processes that are described in the existing literature. If she is a routine and uncreative worker, she never goes much beyond these acts of recognition, even though her experience will quickly begin to show her patterns that do not quite fit the ones she was taught. The varieties of people are infinite. Many—perhaps most—of the variations are slight changes rung on familiar tunes, always interesting and important for a good clinician to note if she is to treat each patient as a real and thus unique individual, not just an instance of a standard pattern. None of this variability is to be dismissed as "random error," nor should the researcher ever fall into the traps set by certain outmoded positions in the philosophy of science, which teach that individuality is beyond the purview of science. Useful generalizations can often be found by attempts to understand the unique nature of single cases, attempts which of necessity make use of general concepts. (For further discussion of this issue, and a refutation of the fallacious distinction between the nomothetic versus the idiographic approach to personality, see Holt, 1962b [Volume 1, Chapter 1].)

There are no rules to guide the complex act of judgment that leads the creative mind to decide that certain failures of fit between the expected and the actual are "interesting"—that is, of potentially wider applicability. All we can say is that in principle this is how discoveries are made, and that not every surprise is of general enough significance to constitute a discovery. Yet this much enables us to make a few general statements about the preconditions for discovery. The clinician must have a good stock of schemata against which to check new observations for fit; in short, the wider her experience and the more extensive her knowledge of her field's literature, the better prepared she is to discover the truly new. There is a paradox here: the larger her store of schemata, the more chances that any new observation will fit one of them; thus, in principle, she should be surprised less often. In fact there is a real danger in oversophistication. The person who feels that she has seen it all already is not likely to make *any* discoveries. At the other extreme, a curious but ignorant visitor to a mental hospital may be surprised at every turn, so that in the end his head is spinning with confusion, and he cannot give a coherent account of his "discoveries" to anyone. The somewhat better prepared graduate student or psychiatric resident knows enough of what to expect so that soon he is not dazzled by sheer novelty. He is well enough oriented to make real discoveries, such as the fact that it is surprisingly possible to communicate with psychotic patients, who do not all seem to have "cut their ties with reality" nor to have "retreated into inaccessible private worlds." And yet there is some truth in these clichés, too: for some patients most of the time, for most of the hospitalized at least some of the time or in some ways, they are applicable. All of which is so familiar to the jaded old clinician that she fails to notice the unsolved problem in the discrepancy between prevailing conceptualizations and reality. Her mistake is to confuse familiarity with understanding.

The physicist Bridgman once remarked that an explanation is a description that proceeds to the point where curiosity rests. The definition is not wholly satisfactory, but it contains the insight that curiosity logically need never rest, and indeed must not do so if we are to make progress. Yet it tends to do so when surprises are repeated, for they are like jokes that do not bear repetition. The excitement of seeing a discrepancy between an existing theoretical formulation and a clinical reality is easily lost when the gap becomes a familiar part of the landscape. This is one reason that teaching can be an impetus to discovery, for the amazement of the new student can reopen the instructor's eyes to the fact that a well-known mystery is still unsolved (see also below, pp. 244–245).

Just as experience can dull the necessary sense of wonder or puzzlement about what is familiar but not understood, so is it possible to be too deeply involved in theory. The most obvious danger is that the devoted student of theory will become a dogmatist. That is, what is supposed to be a collection of cool scientific propositions will become an article of faith, an ideology attracting her emotional adherence, and it will be impossible for her to use it as a vehicle of discovery—which is as a means to its own eventual disproof. Often, to be sure, the problem is not so much that the clinician studies the relevant theoretical literature too intensively, but that she is taught it in a way that encourages fidelity to a school's way of thinking rather than skeptical independence of mind. This tendency is notoriously (though not universally) true of psychoanalytic institutes, but graduate schools are not free of it either. All graduate and postgraduate centers for the training of clinicians must make a conscious effort to encourage students to question theories, clinical traditions, and established ways of doing things if there is to be more progress.

Even when a clinician is relatively free from the feeling that she must be loyal to a theory or that she must not betray her teachers (especially her own psychotherapist or analyst), and is without other hindrances to her freedom to question and to reject any existing theoretical proposition, she may become so accustomed to looking at reality from the perspective provided by a given point of view that she is unable to think in any other way. Such a person cannot be expected to make any major reorganization of a cognitive field, and there will be severe limits on the scope of any discoveries she can make.[6]

An even more serious interference comes from the relative lack of empirical referents of some theoretical terms, and the general difficulty of confronting theoretical assertions with empirical tests. If a person gets accustomed to thinking in such terms as those of classical psychoanalytic metapsychology, in which the linkages between concepts like psychic energies or structures and observations are remote at best and in which there are so many degrees of theoretical freedom that any observation whatever can

[6][As Einstein (1916) put it: "Concepts which have proved useful for ordering things easily assume so great an authority over us, that we forget their terrestrial origin and accept them as unalterable facts. They then become labelled as 'conceptual necessities,' 'a priori situations,' etc. The road of scientific progress is frequently blocked for long periods by such errors." Quoted by Holton (1973, p. 5).]

be accounted for but virtually none predicted, she often finds it difficult to define researchable problems. In a way, there seem to be no unsolved mysteries crying out to be explained, because the theory seems to explain everything without actually explaining much at all (Rubinstein, 1967). In addition, of course, there is the well-known fact that *any* theory helps us see some facets of reality by blinding us to others. The remedy is again not to become too exclusively immersed in one theoretical school, but (ideally) to be familiar with the full range of available concepts.

So much for the perils of theory; let us now go back to an attempt to examine the procedure followed by the clinical researcher. The experience of surprise does not always occur simply and directly in the act of observation itself. It may develop only slowly, as for example when a therapeutic impasse forces her to review what she knows of her patient and what has been going on in treatment. Then she may begin to be aware that, for instance, an assumption underlying some part of her conception of how symptoms arise does not really hold. A classic instance is Freud's growing awareness during the middle 1890s that the facts of his clinical observation did not really demand his earlier formulation that neuroses were caused by incestuous seduction in early childhood.

This example helps us see the next essential step, after the experience of surprise or mismatch between schema and observation: The novelty must be *formulated.* That is, it has to be stated in something more than a negative form (that the alleged seductions of neurotics-to-be did not occur). This means restating it, at least implicitly, in the form of a hypothesis—such-and-such *is* the case, either generally or (preferably) under specified parametric[7] conditions. The formulation of any scientific discovery (not just in clinical psychology) ideally encompasses both the expectation and the conditions that violated it. On rare occasions, a discrepant observation may even over-turn fundamental assumptions underlying a whole theory, in which case we say (following Kuhn, 1962) that a scientific revolution has occurred. In a small way, Freud felt that he was in the midst of such a revolution when he began to realize that his patients' stories of early seduction were not to be taken at face value. Quoting Nietzsche in a letter to his friend Fliess, he spoke of it as a "collapse of all values," even though he felt a sense of triumph over being able at last to admit his error. At first, he had nothing to put in place of the overturned formulation. In fact, it was only after several years that he was able to offer a new formulation, which could explain the earlier observations (giving rise to expectations) as well as the later ones (violation of those expectations); the seductions existed for his patients, all right, but usually in the form of oedipal *fantasies,* not real traumas. Nothing less than a reorientation of his understanding of neurosis—and of human nature more generally—was at issue.

[7]See definition above, note 1, p. 195.

Discoveries are rarely so dramatic and far-reaching, of course. And formulations do not need to embody wholly new concepts, much less new models. I stress the issue of formulation because it is the beginning of generalization or abstraction from the particular of an observation on one patient. Being in the form of a "wild surmise" that the little bay glimpsed may be part of a vast ocean, it encourages the researcher to look further. The next step, then, is checking the new formulation on fresh data, usually from other patients. In this respect, the border between exploratory and hypothesis-testing research begins to break down. The distinction thus comes down largely to the degree of formality, precision, and objectivity with which the whole process of stating and testing hypotheses is carried out. It is easy to sympathize with the clinician who treats repeatedly checked findings as firm, scientific conclusions rather than as hypotheses.

To be sure, clinical researchers all too often publish discoveries without checking them, in the conviction that a well-formulated new phenomenon or a new type of causal linkage is worthy of being shared with colleagues, who may be in a better position to test it independently on their own cases. For the lone clinician—for example, the clinical psychologist in the private practice of behavior therapy or psychoanalysis—often sees so few patients at one time, and with such a slow turnover, that he might have to wait years to find the necessary conditions to verify a discovery.

Almost any person, if closely enough studied, will prove to have had interesting kinds of fantasies—interesting, that is, in the casual sense, because unusual. But when are they of scientific interest? There has been a tradition that any phenomenon becomes interesting to science if it occurs often enough, and that it is trivial if it does not recur. The brute fact of frequency itself is *not* what creates scientific relevance, however: a *single* failure of any well-established scientific law, such as Newton's laws of motion, would be of extraordinary scientific interest, for the exception proves (i.e., severely tests) the rule.[8] To be sure, such an exception remains a mystery, a challenge which is scientifically sterile and thus often overlooked until it can be met by a new formulation. Thus, it was known for a long time that Newton's laws of motion did not satisfactorily predict certain aspects of Mercury's orbit around the sun, but until Einstein's alternative and more beautifully comprehensive formulation was available this failure of fit was not taken seriously as a challenge to Newton's otherwise overwhelmingly successful theory. A new formulation accounts for the exception as well as

[8]The usual misunderstanding of this wise old saying is an interesting instance of the return of irrationality. The adage states in brief form what was argued above: that an assertion of a universal kind (a rule) can be falsified by a single contrary case (exception). Yet, aided by the fact that "proof" has come to connote "verification" rather than "test" in common usage, the saying is cited as if an exception in some mysterious way established the truth of what it negates; cf. *credo quia absurdum est* (I believe because it is absurd). It is a clear example of primary process, the bland acceptance of logical contradiction.

the old rule, thus enabling us—at least in principle—to set up the special conditions that produced the exceptional observation and thereby to repeat it at will. By this token, an unusual fantasy would be scientifically interesting if it seemed to constitute an exception to some established psychological law but could be formulated in a way that would permit it to be successfully predicted in another person. Unfortunately, psychology has few if any laws with the generality and precision of Newton's, certainly not in the realm of fantasy, so for the time being it is highly unlikely that an unusual fantasy will constitute a scientific discovery.

Incidentally, one of the main reasons that "psychic" or *psi*-phenomena have attracted so little scientific interest is not that they offend scientists by seeming to violate fundamental laws, but that they have so far not been well formulated. They are precisely in the class of unexplained mysteries alluded to above, so long as they are stated in terms of hypothetical (but essentially tautologous) functions such as ESP, psychokinesis, or the like. To say that some subjects are able to predict far beyond chance the fall of not-yet-dealt cards because they possess clairvoyance is not a formulation in the sense used here; it merely names an unexplained phenomenon, and does nothing to explain why it occurs only some of the time in some people.

Similarly, Freud's attempt to explain the baffling distortions of the dream, and the dream-work mechanisms he postulated to account for them, in terms of a hypothesized "free mobility of psychic energy" is also only apparently a formulation. The tautologous concept of psychic energy could never be measured directly, nor assessed in any terms other than those of the phenomena it was invoked to explain; hence, it has proved to be a scientific cul-de-sac, whatever value psychoanalysts may feel it has in ordering their thinking (Holt, 1967e). It was a valid discovery, however, that dreams could be interpreted on the hypothesis that they were disguised fulfillments of wishes. Freud formulated this discovery so well that others were able to do what he had done with their own patients, and thereby to understand and treat them more effectively.

Consider another kind of discovery, that of a new phenomenon. Freud reported, on the basis of what his female patients told him, that there were two types of orgasms in women, clitoral and vaginal. That was an apparently well-formulated discovery, for other analysts were able to verify it with their patients. Now Masters and Johnson (1966) report, from detailed direct observation, that they are unable to find any such differentiation: all feminine orgasms follow the same course and are physiologically indistinguishable, they say, whether attained by stimulation of the clitoris or of the vagina, or even without any genital stimulation at all.

It is the difference in formulation that is critical here. Masters and Johnson seem to have refuted Freud's claim until you notice that they are formulating the complex organismic and experiential phenomenon of an orgasm in purely objective (anatomical, physiological, and behavioral) terms.

There is still a possibility that women whose orgasms are indistinguishable on this level may have *psychologically* different experiences. To clear up the question, someone must produce a better psychological formulation of the difference, beginning with a codification of the subjective characteristics of clitoral and vaginal orgasms, based on psychoanalytic writings. Next, these reported differentiations should be verified or corrected and extended, if possible, by phenomenological studies with women who claim to have both types, in which consensual core definitions will be sought. If then the investigator is able to find reliably determinable characteristics of women who have vaginal orgasms, distinguishing them from those who have only clitoral orgasms, or can establish reliable differences in the circumstances under which the two kinds occur, and can cross-validate the findings by a successful predictive study, he or she will have made a legitimate new discovery.

Methods of Verifying Hypotheses

This last example brings us to the context of justification, as Reichenbach (1938) called it, or to research methods in the narrow sense in which that phrase is often understood. Obviously, "verify" means to test the truth of an assertion (hypothesis)—to gather new data and see whether the alleged fact, observed phenomenon, or theoretically predicted relationship can be produced at will. Two main methods of doing so are traditionally distinguished, though as usual this distinction too breaks down in practice in transitional cases: experiment, the generally preferred method, and observational-statistical study. As Kaplan (1964) has pointed out, psychologists often construe the term experiment in an unnecessarily narrow way; he describes no less than a dozen types of experiment in addition to the classical form in which the investigator sets up two conditions, one in which he predicts that an effect will occur, and one in which he predicts that it will not, and then "manipulates the independent variable" or makes these two occurrences happen, measuring "the dependent variable" (the effect) in both.

The logic of verification is rather straightforward. Since (as we saw above) it is logically impossible to establish the truth of a positive assertion, you restate it in negative form as a *null hypothesis:* not that A is related to B, but that there is no relationship between A and B, or there is no difference between group X and group Y who have been subjected to different treatments. Powerful statistics exist that enable us to specify the confidence with which we can reject such null hypotheses, with randomly drawn samples of known sizes. As I have already noted, the requirement of random sampling is rarely given the attention it deserves, and in most experiments the custom is to use available persons without much regard to the larger population of which they are a sample, trusting that systematic errors will not conceal or distort the results. If there is bias in the assignment of subjects to differently treated experimental groups, we have a serious source of systematic error called *confounding*. That is, if a difference appears under such circumstances you have no way of telling whether it is attributable to the different ways you treated the two groups or to the fact that they were different kinds of people to start with. It is therefore important to use a carefully random method of assigning subjects to the various experimental treatments; only then can you trust the probability values given by your statistical tests: how frequently a given finding—for example, that two variables were substantially correlated—would occur in random samples drawn from a population in which the overall difference (correlation, etc.) was actually zero. The main point, however, is that when properly applied, the experimental method makes it possible to establish a fact with a known degree of confidence.

Standard texts on research methods (e.g., Cochran & Cox, 1957; A. L. Edwards, 1972; Lindzey & Aronson, 1968; Selltiz, Wrightsman, & Cook, 1976; Winer, 1971) give excellent coverage of the ins and outs of experimental designs and technique, so there is no need to go into much detail about them here; the writings of Campbell (e.g., 1957, 1969; Campbell & Stanley, 1966) are especially recommended for their critical exposition and evaluation of types of experimental and quasi-experimental design. The special problems of experimenting in the field of clinical and abnormal psychology are discussed in two easily accessible sources (Group for the Advancement of Psychiatry, 1959, and Holt, 1965b [Chapter 7]); for another discussion of both experimental and nonexperimental methods of research in psychopathology, see Millon and Diesenhaus (1972).

The prestige of the experiment is such that many psychologists disparage any instance of what I am calling the observational-statistical method of verification as "just a correlation study." In both of these methods, the investigator uses statistics to evaluate his findings and establish his points, and so of course he must measure his dependent variables ("effects") as precisely and reliably as possible. The main difference is that in the typical experiment the investigator acts in such a way as to vary the independent ("causal") variable; hence we say that he manipulates it. Whereas in the observational-statistical study he accepts the "naturally" occurring variation in the independent variable and measures it as best he can, correlating these values with changes in the dependent variables (Cronbach, 1957).

Let us consider the relative advantages and disadvantages of the two approaches, and their differences from exploratory clinical research, using a specific problem. Silverman (1972) has formulated the hypothesis that when aggressive feelings and/or fantasies are aroused in a person who is not in a position to act on them or let himself experience them fully, various maladaptive consequences ensue: he may be less able to function effectively in cognitive tasks of various kinds, and he may show a temporary exacerbation of such symptoms as stuttering. Before considering a possible observational-statistical approach to this hypothesis, let us look briefly at a clinical observation and two different experiments that have produced relevant data.

Though Silverman does not cite it, the very first instance in which a neurotic symptom was "analyzed" might well be considered a relevant bit of clinical evidence. The patient was the famous "Anna O." who, with Breuer's help, discovered for herself the "chimneysweeping" or "talking cure," a nightly recounting of her troubling fantasies, usually with the aid of hypnosis (Breuer & Freud, 1895). On one of his regular daily visits to this severely disturbed and incapacitated young woman, during a period of six weeks in the summer when she was wholly unable to drink from a glass, Breuer hypnotized her as usual and she began to speak about her dislike of a "lady-companion." Anna

> went on to describe, with every sign of disgust, how she had once gone into that lady's room and how her little dog—horrid creature!—had drunk out of a glass there. The patient had said nothing, as she had wanted to be polite. After giving further energetic expression to the anger she had held back, she asked for something to drink, drank a large quantity of water without any difficulty and woke from her hypnosis with the glass at her lips; and thereupon the disturbance vanished, never to return [Breuer & Freud, 1895, pp. 34–35].

Both Breuer and Freud, to whom he related this episode, were so struck by the therapeutic implications of her recovery after "abreacting" the previously "strangulated affect" that they did not take special note of the fact that the specific affect involved was suppressed anger.

Horwitz (1963) reports a complicated experiment by one of his students, Goldman, which I shall summarize very sketchily. Undergraduates were randomly assigned to one of several experimental groups (only two of them need concern us); all subjects were taught how to fold paper to make various objects, by a specially trained confederate who at a certain point insulted and berated his pupils. Some had been instructed to verbalize their feelings on rating sheets that were handed out from time to time, while to one group it was strongly suggested that it would be wrong of them even to experience any hostile thoughts about their instructor, and that they should vigorously put out of their minds as unworthy any anger, resentment, or the like. After they had experienced the provocative vituperation of their instructor, both groups went on to try to make the paper designs they had been taught, and also took some brief tests of intellectual functions. Those who were asked to suppress any hostile thoughts or feelings performed significantly worse than those who had been encouraged to experience and express their affective states in writing.

When we compare Breuer's case report with this experiment, the former seems a more convincing kind of data in some ways: it deals with real life, with an actual provocation more genuine than the one in the experiment, and with much more striking reactions or behavioral effects. Moreover, the reversibility of the effect makes the attribution of causality quite compelling.

To anyone who is thoroughly familiar with this well-known case, however, there are grounds for skepticism. To begin with, Anna O.'s condition was notoriously labile, and she continued to have sudden remissions and exacerbations long after Dr. Breuer had done his best to help her ventilate all her inhibited affects. When the pre-existing likelihood for the appearance and subsidence of the kind of symptoms described above (often referred to as "base rate") is so high, it is more difficult to be confident that any one is attributable to unexpressed anger. Moreover, Breuer and Freud may have been right not to single out anger as the relevant affect: Anna O. verbalized disgust as well as anger during her brief bit of self-initiated psychotherapy. From a single episode of this kind it is risky to accept the hypothesis that is suggested, for the only data we have are the reconstructed experiences verbalized by an unstable, hysterical person, trying to please a physician to whom she was attached by emotional bonds of which neither was yet fully aware, and hysterics have long been accused of "romancing" or "confabulating"—in short, embroidering the truth if not actually lying. It is quite possible that Anna herself was not aware of all the important aspects of the minor trauma that she recounted; nor can we be certain that she actually suppressed her feelings instead of venting them. She could, for example, have kicked the dog and then have been overcome with guilt, none of which she revealed. Finally, even if this episode were backed up by numerous others of the same structure, there would be no guarantee that the loss of function after suppressing anger would hold true in anyone else, or in anyone but similarly disturbed hysterical women of the 1890s.

For such reasons, the experimental evidence has special value. The subjects were all ordinary college students not known to have any hysterical or other neurotic symptoms, so we can be reassured that the general effect is not limited in the ways suggested at the end of the last paragraph. It does not seem likely that the effectiveness of their cognitive functions had been fluctuating spontaneously as much as it did in the experiment, though this is a possibility that was not explored. On the other hand, the subjects of this experiment (and most others) remain anonymous and are known only in very limited ways for a short time, whereas Breuer had the advantage of observing his patient over a considerable period of time and recorded many aspects of her behavior in an attempt to come to an understanding. The presence of the control group does a great deal to reassure us, however, that the variation in performance was in fact caused by the suppressed anger, since the two sets of subjects and their experiences were alike in all respects except the critical difference in the independent variable (the instructions about expressing their feelings). Another advantage is that the subjects were observed for the entire period of time from the provocation until the performance measures (dependent variables) were obtained, so no doubts need arise about the accuracy of their reporting—the data are not dependent on the subjects' accounts of what happened.

As to the greater genuineness of the provocation in the clinical instance, that makes the positive findings of the experiment all the more impressive. If any subjects suspected that the gratuitous sneers of the teacher were phony, they might be expected to be *less* affected by them, which would weaken the predicted effect. They might, however, have become angry and disgusted at the whole experiment because of the effort to deceive them, which could have undermined their motivation to do well in the cognitive and motor tasks at the end. There is a real question, as well, about the ethics of this kind of lying to people who have put their trust in you, manipulating them without their informed consent, and arousing feelings which the experiment itself shows had deleterious effects upon them. (Ethical issues will be discussed in more detail in the final section, below.) Again, it could be argued that there is no particular reason to believe that subjects who were told to suppress their anger would be more suspicious or discerning than subjects who were encouraged to express it. This argument does suggest, however, that it is important to interview subjects in a study of this kind afterwards and try to get them to report as fully and frankly as possible what they thought and felt during the experiment. Such sessions are usually held in this type of experiment to inform the subjects of the deception and give them an opportunity to express their feelings fully, and that was the case in the Goldman experiment.

The approach worked out by Silverman (1965) has the advantage that there is no deception or manipulation, and the arousal of aggression is managed without the subjects' conscious awareness. He uses a tachistoscope to present threatening or benign pictures so briefly and dimly that the subject reports having seen only a vague flicker or flash with no discriminable content (something that is later verified by psychophysical procedures that determine the thresholds at which the different pictures can be distinguished). Immediately afterward, Silverman obtains his dependent variable: some measure of cognitive function. The procedure also makes it possible to test subjects repeatedly, so that each can be his own control; measures of cognitive abilities are obtained before any tachistoscopic flashes, after the benign picture, and after the aggressive one, and the order is counterbalanced to cancel out any practice or sequential effects. Though Silverman (1972) does report that in a number of such experiments patients' characteristic symptoms were exacerbated—for example, schizophrenics showed more thought disorder—and performance declined on various kinds of intellectual tests, the effects were relatively slight and transitory, and the subjects showed no sign of being either harmed or benefited by their participation.

An important variant of Silverman's experimental design is to include a condition in which the pictures are shown at long enough exposures to be clearly perceived and reported. In this supraliminal condition, the independent variable (the difference in meaning between the experimental pictures) had no effect! As long as the subject was fully aware of what he was shown and could fantasy about it, no deleterious effects whatever could be observed. Hence, Silverman's formulation that the aggressive material stirred up by such pictures as a tiger attacking a monkey or a snarling man brandishing a big knife has a pathogenic effect only if the subject is not allowed to experience it fully.

But how does Silverman know that the relevant dimension of his pictures is aggression? Could it not be that any picture that aroused strong feelings would be equally effective? Another advantage of the experimental approach is that it allows one to answer such questions quite readily. It was not difficult to repeat the experiment, using a picture of two men in a homosexual embrace as the subliminal stimulus; no clear-cut arousal of symptoms or interference with cognitive functions occurred.

Here, then, is another strength of the experimental method: not only is it the most direct way to test hypotheses, but with it you can carry out many kinds of explorations. You can systematically try out a series of variations on every aspect of a study that has yielded a promisingly significant finding to discover its limits—the conditions under which a relationship shows up most strikingly and those under which it disappears.

In clinical psychology, however, a great many of the topics we want to investigate can be studied to only a limited extent by the experimental method. When we are concerned with the causes of psychopathology, for example, ethical considerations restrain us from trying to bring about anything more than the most temporary, reversible, and mild forms of symptoms, and we have no assurance that all the relationships involved are simple and linear, an assurance that is necessary if we are to extrapolate from our experiments to clinically important conditions. For that matter, exploratory clinical research has its limitations, too: the behavior the therapist observes directly and what the patient chooses to report to her is only a part of the patient's total repertory, and usually the most disturbed and maladaptive part. When a psychoanalyst gets the unusual opportunity to observe (more usually, to hear about) the everyday behavior of a patient, it is not uncommon for her to be surprised at how well he functions.

These considerations bring us to what I am calling observational-statistical studies as a second major type of hypothesis-verifying research. As in the experiment, the investigator seeks to find a relationship between one set of variables and another; but instead of deliberately and more or less artificially bringing about variation in one or more independent variable(s) so as to measure the concomitant changes in the dependent variable(s), he counts on the vagaries of life to make the former ones vary and simply measures the simultaneous values of all variables in a sample of subjects, interrelating them statistically.

To be concrete in terms of the problem we have been considering, let us consider a hypothetical study since I do not know of any actual ones. We have to begin by asking ourselves under what real-life circumstances do people predictably become incited to anger or hostile fantasies that they cannot express or fully experience, circumstances in which it would be both possible and realistically plausible to obtain measures of their cognitive functioning. We do not want the very process of measurement to make the situation artificial. Taking the last consideration first, an obvious setting within which to get such measures unobtrusively is an educational institution. Moreover, it does happen that in some schools and colleges there are teachers whose usual style of behavior tends to infuriate students; we could then seek the cooperation of such a natural instigator in some "research on cognitive function." If his students could be given our measures of dependent variables at the very beginning of a semester before the teacher has had a chance to anger them, and then again some time later after he has been observed administering a characteristic tongue-lashing to the class, that would be a rather close approximation to an experiment. Such a study is usually called an "experiment in nature." True, the proposed design does not fully test Silverman's hypothesis, because it provides no way to control the issue of whether subjects consciously experience anger or hostile fantasies. So, we could simply ask them: we could include an interview or questionnaire inquiry into what their thoughts and feelings were during the class, and correlate the degree to which subjects admit to aggressive content with the degree to which their test performance is impaired, predicting that the more freely they admit hating the teacher, daydreaming about telling him off, etc., the better their cognitive test scores. An alternative would be to approach the same issue indirectly, with a projective test like the TAT, scored for the story characters' absence of anger and hostile reactions in imagined or depicted situations where they might normally be expected.

Aside from the fact that this imaginary experiment in nature uses a real provocateur rather than a staged one, its critical difference from the Horwitz-Goldman experiment is that we have not attempted to manipulate the inhibition or expression of anger, but to control it statistically: we let it vary as it will, but measure the degree of the subjects' inability to experience hostility when it is called for and then statistically determine whether or not that inability is related to a deficit in cognitive function. A closely related kind of hybrid design is the experiment in which you systematically vary A and study B, but are unable to match your groups with respect to some third variable, C, which you proceed to measure. By analysis of covariance, you then statistically remove C's contribution to variation in B before studying the effect of A.

The design sketched above has a serious defect, which can be removed by a different approach. Why did we test each subject twice? Because if we simply took performance on the critical occasion we would have no way of being sure that those who did badly were performing any worse than was usual for them; to an unknown extent, variance in the dependent variable might be caused by determinants quite different from the ones in which we were interested. An obvious but not always good solution is to pretest all subjects, thus treating subjects as their own controls. Not always good, because even under the best of circumstances people tested twice rarely get identical scores, particularly those who are at the extremes. Anyone who does particularly badly may have had a rough day or a sleepless night before the test; anyone who performs outstandingly well may correspondingly have been in unusually fine fettle. Since such special circumstances rarely repeat themselves, retesting always produces a certain amount of *regression toward the mean:* the worst performers move up, the best ones move down toward the mean of the whole group. In a test-retest correlational design, there is no way to distinguish such "regressive" changes from effects of the experimental manipulation.[9]

There is another way to find out what to expect of a person, however: Give him an ability test. With generations of effort, psychologists have produced tests of aptitude for college that generally are correlated fairly highly with college grades, and we are familiar with the terms *underachievers* for those who do worse than predicted (whose grades are not up to their presumed potential) and *overachievers* for those who do better than predicted. Since most colleges and universities have on file students' scores on scholastic aptitude tests as well as their grades, which may be viewed as measures of their cognitive efficiency, a simple method of testing Silverman's hypothesis suggests itself: if we could get access to these scores, we might select groups of extreme underachievers and overachievers, and then approach them for their cooperation in a "study of personality." Making the plausible assumption that college life entails plenty of frustrations and other provocations to anger for all students, we could simply assess all subjects' capacity to experience anger and to entertain hostile fantasies, predicting that these assessed capacities would be better in overachievers than in underachievers. The persons who do the testing and interviewing (for it would be prudent not to put all our eggs into one basket but use several simultaneous assessment approaches from different angles) and those who analyze these data should not know either the hypothesis being tested or which group the students belonged to, to prevent contamination. Quite without intending to do so, a person who has such knowledge about a subject may act toward him in subtle ways that tend to elicit the "right kind" of

[9][In addition, Campbell (1957, 1969) has pointed out other disadvantages of the test-retest design; principally, many tests lose validity or are influenced in unknown ways by the loss of novelty on a second administration; and a first administration may alert subjects to the intent of the experiment, changing their responsiveness to the intended manipulation.]

responses; and when judges are carrying out a content analysis of qualitative data like interviews or TAT stories, their wishes and expectations can bias the scores they give.

This design is a good example of observational-statistical research. It studies real-life behavior of an important kind, using the normal vicissitudes of life instead of trumped-up and never wholly credible experimental manipulations to incite anger, and counts on the usual variability of personalities to spread the subjects out on the variable of inhibitory overcontrol. Its main weakness is that it does not attempt to measure in any way the provocations experienced by the subjects, but simply assumes that such unhappy experiences will be randomly distributed across subjects. It does seem safe to assume that during the course of a college semester most students will encounter threats, frustrations, insults, and the like; but the study will be seriously compromised if there is any reason to expect that overachievers and underachievers will differ systematically in this respect. Indeed, may it not be that one reason a student ends up in our underachieving group is that precisely when he was trying to study for exams his roommates formed a rock group, or he found that several key books were missing from the college library? In these examples, incitements to rage unfortunately coincide with (are confounded with) real obstacles to achievement. Underachieving may tend to perpetuate itself, too, because the knowledge of past failure to live up to expectations may make a student particularly anxious and irritable as examination time comes around.

It certainly would be desirable to supplement the proposed design by assessments of provocation to anger, therefore. But you have only to think about it to realize that it would not be easy. We simply do not have as many readily available techniques for assessing the anger-producing potentiality of situations as we do for measuring inhibitory controls, and there has not been much systematic spade-work in this area, despite the wealth of anecdotal information about the tribulations of college life. Many years ago, Murray *et al.* (1938) proposed the twin concepts of *need* and *press;* the former, an inner motivational variable, caught on far more readily than the latter, the dynamically relevant aspects of situations. Nevertheless, it would be worthwhile to try an approach like the following. By informal interviewing, make up a list of the main types of provocations to anger frequently experienced by students; then in the interview with all subjects already planned for, review a standard period like two weeks just before the exam, inquiring whether any provocations occurred *and* what the subject's response to each was. The content analysis of the interview would then provide a separate measure of the frequency and intensity of instigations to anger as well as one or more measures of the subject's reactions.

In observational, real-life studies of the type just sketched, the most appropriate kind of statistic is correlation of some kind, usually multiple. A prime characteristic of the clinical researcher is that she tends to be interested in many aspects of people, and thus wants to study the simultaneous and interactive effects of many variables. By contrast, classical experimental designs are framed in terms of a single independent variable, which is manipulated while everything else is held constant, and its impact on a single dependent variable is measured. The clinical experience of the psychotherapist presents her constantly with events in which there seem to be many causes and many effects; small wonder that clinicians so often are scornful of traditional experimental research, claiming that it so oversimplifies the tangled web of reality as to distort it hopelessly.

With the advent of computers to do the difficult arithmetic, it became possible to design and carry out complex experimental designs using factorial analyses of variance with several simultaneous classifications of subjects corresponding to several independent variables. Such designs are exceedingly complex to carry out, however, especially if an effort is made to do more with each independent variable than dichotomize it, dividing subjects into "highs" and "lows." And in the end, the experimenter is told which relationships are significant, but not how strongly the variables are related.

As Cohen (1968) has demonstrated, multiple regression analysis has many advantages as an alternative way of analyzing the data from a multivariate study. First, the unjustly derogated correlation coefficient not only provides a measure of how significantly different from zero a relationship is, it also gives a direct and intelligible indication of that relationship's strength—free, additional, and useful information. Moreover, it uses all the information you have in your measurement, thus extracting more ability to test hypotheses from discriminations *within* the "high" and "low" groups of analyses of variance. [For other advantages, and for tricks of adapting the method to the study of interactions between variables, etc., see Cohen and Cohen, 1975. For a sophisticated discussion of ways to use correlational methods to assess cause, see Blalock, 1972.]

Strictly speaking, even multiple (and multiple partial) correlations are not multivariate statistics, a term that implies more than one predictor and more than one criterion (or variable being predicted)—i.e., plural independent and dependent variables. Psychologists are beginning to become acquainted with such multivariate techniques as canonical correlation, which is an elegant way of expressing the pattern of relationships between two sets of variables. At first, they seem to offer the answer to the clinician's dream of a way to deal with the full reality of the clinical encounter, or at least a defensible approximation to it. Unfortunately, however, they involve many restrictive assumptions which cannot be violated with impunity, they require very large samples of subjects, and they are difficult to interpret. So the millenium has not yet arrived for the clinical researcher who yearns after the twin but so far irreconcilable goals of quantitative rigor and fidelity to the bewildering complexity of the intrapersonal-interpersonal-situational transaction.

It should be evident by now that our proposed observational-statistical study is not the kind of research that can be easily carried out by a lone wolf, whether he be a graduate student or a seasoned and sophisticated therapist. That may be one reason so little research of this kind is done. Hypothesis-testing research in clinical and abnormal psychology grows more expensive and requires the cooperation of larger teams the further we get away from the classical but usually oversimple two-variable experiment. The only alternative to technological sophistication is ingenuity. With the right intuitive flair for picking important topics where effects are large (that is, having a good nose for the major determinants of a kind of behavior) a solo investigator can still carry out scientifically impressive tests of hypotheses.

RESEARCH ON THERAPY

Do psychological and psychiatric therapies really help people? If so, which forms of treatment help what kinds of patients with what problems, and how? What actually goes on in psychotherapy, and which of its ingredients have what kinds of effects? Answers to questions such as these have made up increasingly large segments of books on clinical and abnormal psychology, and the answers have been changing in their substance and in the methods used to provide them.

The first emphasis in the above questions characterizes one of the main streams in research on therapy, which is known as *outcome research*. It focuses on studying the effects of various forms of treatment. Originally, the questions asked were simple, even naive, being framed in terms of cure, or success and failure. As this kind of research has grown more sophisticated and more differentiated questions have been asked, it has tended to converge with the second stream, *process research*, in which an attempt is made to describe and understand what goes on in the psychotherapeutic transaction.

Until around 1960, the great preponderance of what was written on both kinds of topics was based on exploratory clinical research. Particularly in the various psychotherapies, people who had had experience in a given form of treatment simply wrote about their unsystematically accumulated impressions, or at best kept rough tallies of successes and failures as judged by themselves. Early descriptions of process are vulnerable to the criticism that a therapist has less control of her actual behavior in the heat of the therapeutic interaction than she believes, so that her most important interventions may be other than what she intends and reports. Also, her theory may lead her to consider some things she does as not even worth mentioning. Granted that knowledge in this area has to begin in such a fashion, there are many glaringly evident sources of bias in it, particularly on the issue of outcome. Both therapist and patient have great financial and emotional investments in believing that the work they have done together was worthwhile, for example. They are not disinterested enough to be sufficient sources of evidence on outcome, therefore, but they are uniquely qualified to know many vitally important facts and cannot simply be disregarded. Because of these problems with objectivity in exploratory clinical research, something approximating the hypothesis-testing experiment has come to be the major research method in outcome research.

Outcome Research

From the standpoint of experimental design, there are many similarities among outcome studies whether the therapies are psychological or somatic. There has been a long tradition of outcome research in medicine, particularly studies of the effectiveness of drugs in treating somatic disease, and so it was natural for psychiatrists to adopt the established methods and assumptions of pharmacological research in testing the effectiveness of not only drugs but treatments using various types of shock (principally electric), brain operations, and other typically medical modalities.

Because of these medical origins, outcome research tended for a long time to be set up in terms of the medical model of diseases. It was implicitly assumed that there were mental illnesses that could be cured, just as was true in somatic medicine. Likewise, everyone assumed that the therapeutic agents in psychotherapy were essentially similar to the agents used in the treatment of bodily illness: specific forms of therapy existed which were relatively independent of the person administering them, and which could be taught, learned, and carried out by any member of the profession who had reasonably good basic training. It was to take many years and a great many misunderstandings to free psychotherapy research from the effects of these assumptions.

It has long been known that patients suffering from a variety of maladies often respond quite favorably to medication, no matter what it is just as long as it is not actively harmful. "Pink pills" made of harmless sugar became the mainstay of many professional as well as make-believe physicians, and are known as placebos (A. K. Shapiro, 1971). If you invent and try out a new drug, therefore, the first thing you have to be able to do is to demonstrate that it has more of an effect than a placebo. So, you randomly assign patients with the same diagnosis to the new drug or to placebo, making sure that none of them knows what he is getting. Research physicians found that more control was needed: the person administering the pill should be "blind," too, because the difference in expectations and hope subtly transmitted to the patient when the agent was "only a placebo" and when it was "a promising new discovery" proved sufficient to bring about substantial differences in effects. The history of medicine is full of apparent breakthroughs—wonderfully effective initial results, which got steadily less good as time went on—until the *double-blind* design was perfected.

The double-blind procedure ensures that no one who is in a position to affect the results in any way has any *criterion contamination:* knowledge of the status of the subjects on the independent variable, in this instance, whether they are getting the new drug or a placebo. The researcher cannot usually be involved in the care of the patients or in evaluating effects, therefore; he arranges for all patients to be told the same thing (e.g., "This is the medication your doctor has prescribed") by nurses who ideally do not even know that an experiment is going on, and for their symptoms and other indices of possible effect to be systematically noted by equally blind nurses and physicians.

An important variation of the double-blind design compares a new drug with the established form of therapy for the disease in question. Such an experiment directly answers a practical question: Is there any evidence that we should give up our usual, established way of doing things? It is clearly more helpful to know the answer to this question than merely whether the drug is more effective than a placebo. There is also the advantage that the subjects who are not getting the new treatment are getting something, so the "blind" is less likely to be pierced by either the patient or those who attend him, and the ethical problems involved in deliberately withholding treatment do not arise in as troublesome a form as they do in the standard double-blind design with placebo. (There, the counterargument, briefly, is that the greatest good of the greatest number is served in the long run only by efforts to do a better job of therapy, which must be evaluated by well-designed research, and that placebos are not to be despised, having shown remarkable effectiveness against an amazing variety of maladies. Moreover, if the drug-treated patients show significant improvement over the placebo-treated, the latter are switched to the drug as soon as the experiment is over.)

In psychopharmacological research, the double-blind experimental design has worked reasonably well. For one thing, drugs were initially used mainly with hospitalized, psychotic persons who are easily regarded as patients suffering from mental illnesses. Their symptoms and their incapacitation are obvious enough so that "the problem of the criterion" (that is, what is to be regarded as an appropriate measure of success or effectiveness) does not usually arise in troublesome form.

As soon as we consider psychotherapy, however, the difficulties mount thick and fast. A drug like chlorpromazine has a known chemical constitution, so the purity and strength of any dose of it can be precisely stated, and the presumably nonessential aspects of the pills (size, color, etc.) can also be satisfactorily equated to those of the placebo or other competitor. In no sense can psychotherapy be considered a comparable entity, not even psychotherapy of a given brand. We cannot even be completely certain which of its aspects are essential and which are not. Even a presumably standardized technique like psychoanalysis is not only multidimensional, it varies tremendously from one analyst to another in many known dimensions, not to mention the unknown ones. Patients accepted by psychoanalysts range from those so incapacitated that they have to be hospitalized, all the way to persons who are considered by most of their associates to be highly effective and successful in almost every way. Correspondingly, the appropriate criteria for improvement would have to be entirely different for analysands at different points on this hypothetical spectrum. In behavior therapy, where the therapist's objective is usually to remove symptoms, not to reconstruct personalities in any far-reaching way, the criterion is a relatively simple matter, and outcome research is greatly facilitated.

Finally, what procedure could be the functional equivalent of a placebo? It would have to be an apparent attempt to treat his complaints that would be accepted by the patient but would lack most of the presumably effective ingredients of the form of psychotherapy under scrutiny. So far, no one has compared such a procedure with psychoanalysis in a double-blind design. Indeed, in a recent survey Luborsky and Spence (1971) found only a single small (four patients, four therapists) controlled attempt to compare psychoanalysis with another form of treatment, in this instance client-centered. (No differences were found; R. Cartwright, 1966.).

Instead, outcome research in psychoanalysis has been almost entirely uncontrolled. Reports of analysts' own judgments of the degree of improvement of their patients are summed across all kinds of patients and reported as an overall percentage of success. Along came Eysenck (1952, 1966), who compared what he presented as the average percentage of improvement in five outcome studies of psychoanalysis and 19 studies of eclectic psychotherapy with some data from what he described as studies of the proportions of neurotic patients who "spontaneously" improved. In 1952 he claimed that the rate of spontaneous remission (or improvement without psychotherapy) was 72%, the improvement rate for psychoanalysis 44%, and that for eclectic (miscellaneous) psychotherapies 64%; 14 years later, he added a half dozen more studies, in only one of which (considered by him to be methodologically inadequate) were there any positive findings of therapeutic efficacy.

Since Eysenck's conclusions have been widely reprinted and quoted by himself and others, I cannot pass them over without a few comments. The most that can be said for Eysenck's work is that it has stimulated a great deal of research, which has rather decisively refuted his pessimistic conclusions. Other investigators (Bergin, 1971; Meltzoff & Kornreich, 1970) have carefully scrutinized the research summarized by Eysenck and have found his survey riddled with errors, biases, and prejudicial inconsistencies. Bergin's re-evaluation of the *same* data reported in Eysenck's 1952 paper yields almost the same figure for eclectic psychotherapy (65% improved) but 83% for psychoanalysis instead of Eysenck's alleged 44%. (Eysenck obtained this last percentage mostly by classifying psychoanalysts' ratings of patients as "improved" under "unimproved," and by counting those who prematurely withdrew from treatment also as "unimproved.") Numerous critics (e.g.,

Luborsky, 1954) have pointed out many inadequacies in the two studies from which Eysenck drew his data on the rate of spontaneous remission, but the most effective rejoinder has been Bergin's (1971). He found 14 other methodologically more satisfactory reports on the rate of improvement of untreated neurotics, ranging from zero to about 50%, with a median at 30%! Both Bergin (1971) and Meltzoff and Kornreich (1970) report, at sharp variance with Eysenck, that as studies have become better controlled there is a slight tendency for the results to look *more* favorable to the effectiveness of psychotherapy. Moreover, better results are correlated with more experience on the part of therapists and with longer terms of treatment.

What are some of these improvements in types of control? One is the use of criteria other than the subjective evaluations of the therapist herself. In the Menninger Foundation Psychotherapy Research Project (Wallerstein, Robbins, Sargent, & Luborsky, 1956; Sargent, Horwitz, Wallerstein, & Appelbaum, 1968; Kernberg, Burstein, Coyne, Appelbaum, Horwitz, & Voth, 1972) each patient was evaluated at or just before the beginning of treatment, at its termination, and three years after termination, by interdisciplinary teams which did not include the therapist, though she as well as the patient was interviewed. At each of these times, independent evaluations of the patient were made from a battery of psychological tests alone, and by psychiatrists and/or social workers who relied mainly on interview and external facts such as employment and marital status. All evaluators were trained in the reliable use of a "Health-Sickness Rating Scale" (Luborsky, 1962b), which gave rules for combining various kinds of data into a single dimension with scores ranging from zero to 100.

Some controls that have become more generally used seem to be mainly the systematic application of common sense. Patients are more carefully described, as are therapists; important changes in life circumstances external to the therapy are noted; the techniques and circumstances of the therapy itself are described with some thoroughness, as well as its duration.

A good deal of controversy surrounds the use of control groups, however. Granted that a measure of the post-therapy status of a group of patients needs to be compared with something more than the same people's pretreatment status, what constitutes an appropriate control? Some studies (e.g., Rogers & Dymond, 1954) have attempted to compare treatment with no treatment, but this can help answer only the minimal question, Is therapy any good at all? And it turns out to be more difficult than one might think to make even this comparison. Ideally, after an intake procedure and the decision that psychotherapy is appropriate and needed, patients should be randomly assigned to two groups, of which one gets treatment at once and the other does not. Since many clinics have waiting lists and realistically cannot treat all comers when they want help, such a procedure can be carried out ethically and plausibly; so "waiting list controls" have been used in a number of outcome investigations. What you cannot do ethically, however, is to *prevent* people on a waiting list from seeking some other form of help. Bergin (1971) presents persuasive evidence not only that most people with problems of living of the sort we call neurotic do find nonprofessional help (or help from professionals not usually thought of as psychotherapists, such as lawyers and ministers), but that most of what is usually described as "spontaneous remission" is attributable to such help.

One can look at the issue of professional versus nonprofessional therapy in at least two ways—from a professional and from a scientific point of view. The profession has a legitimate concern to discover whether on the average people derive more aid from psychologists, psychiatrists, or other trained psychotherapists, *or* from friends, relatives, or other informal confidants. From the scientific standpoint, however, the issue is different: we are interested in finding out what kinds of interactions help people change in what kinds of ways, and it makes no difference in principle if those interactions are with one kind of person or another, for pay or for friendship. Unless, of course, it makes a difference in fact, as many psychoanalysts have claimed, citing the old maxim that advice is worth what you pay for it.

Another kind of control represents an attempt to emulate the pharmacologist's placebo. Patients are assigned either to the form of therapy being studied or to regular but brief contact with a therapist who tries to refrain from any specific technical interventions (like interpretations) and is merely a benign, supportive presence (Frank, 1961). One problem is that such contacts probably differ little from what is called psychotherapy in other contexts, and they often prove to be actually helpful to many patients. Notice that in this design a more interesting kind of question is asked than in simple outcome research: not "Does psychotherapy help?" but "Which ingredients in psychotherapy help the most?"

Now that the basic point has been well established that on the average psychotherapy does help neurotically suffering people, the leading researchers in the field agree that little is to be learned from more outcome research of the simple type. Instead, we need to move on to ask more specific and scientifically interesting questions, of this kind: how can we help different kinds of people to change in particular ways?

Let us focus for a moment on the last part of that question. Notice that it does not ask about cure, or improvement, or success, but about specific changes in behavior (construed, as usual here, to include reported feelings like anxiety and happiness). There are two great advantages to the newer approach. First, if we are getting more specific on the side of the independent variable (what we do to people—specific ingredients of therapy), it makes good sense to look for specific effects, and we can legitimately expect to find something more like lawful regularities. Even when a therapist tries to say as precisely as possible what she considers improvement to mean, which is unusual, there is no way to know precisely what happened from her statement that a given patient improved "very much" or to the extent of four on a five-point scale. Second, specifying changes instead of merely evaluating overall effectiveness gets around the knotty problem of values in the criterion of outcome.

Let me say more simply what is meant by that last abstract assertion. A psychotherapist does not ordinarily *measure* outcome, she *evaluates* it. That is, she compares the patient as she knows him at termination (or, preferably, after some follow-up period) with a standard or ideal, the embodiment of a system of values. Almost everyone agrees that it is better to be well than to be sick, and as long as the concrete signs of sickness are fevers, coughs, and the like—or even blatant psychotic symptoms such as delusions and hallucinations—it is clear enough what improvement or even cure means, and there is little questioning of the value premises involved. In Freud's day, patients came to psychoanalysts and other psychotherapists complaining of distressing and incapacitating symptoms like phobias, senseless compulsive acts, tormenting obsessional thoughts, and paralyses or anesthesias without organic cause. At first, he was quite content to declare a patient cured if these classical neurotic symptoms could be banished. As time went on, however, Freud began to notice what he called "transference cures"—the original symptoms disappeared soon after the beginning of treatment but long before their underlying causes had been dealt with; indeed, Freud thought, precisely *because* he was starting to get at these causes. Such a "flight into health" rarely lasted, he reported, and he developed techniques for keeping patients at the work of treatment even when it began to be unpleasant and seemingly unnecessary.

If Freud or his followers had been able to establish conclusively that such quick, superficial abolition of symptoms was only an illusion of cure, and that neurotic difficulties were bound to recur if pathogenic conflicts were not psychoanalytically resolved, the discovery of transference cures would not have led to such difficulties. The issue remains controversial; many psychoanalysts are convinced that their accumulated clinical experience has established Freud's belief in the evanescence of such symptomatic relief conclusively, but nonanalytic therapists—particularly behavior therapists (e.g., Yates, 1958)—stoutly maintain that solid data are lacking to prove the Freudian case, while they cite many cases of apparently permanent removal of symptoms without the substitution of others.

Meanwhile, people were bringing a wider variety of miseries to psychoanalysts and psychotherapists of all kinds—troubles that could less easily be regarded as symptoms. Moreover, it often happened that the patient himself confessed or realized shortly after beginning treatment that the complaint with which he began was not the problem he most wanted help with. In thinking about this issue, we must also keep in mind the fact that, in a large proportion of cases, therapy does not follow the ideal course of being terminated by mutual agreement when the presenting problem is solved. Treatment is often interrupted or ended for other reasons, some of them practical (money runs short) or adventitious (therapist moves away), and the patient decides that he has been helped "enough," even though some complaints remain. I vividly recall one such ambiguous termination. I tested the patient, a phobic young woman, at the beginning and at the end of several years of psychotherapy with a gifted colleague. She became engaged to an apparently suitable young man and was feeling well enough to leave the city to marry him. Her test responses showed a striking transformation of a flighty, anxious, dependent, self-centered girl into a thoughtful, vivacious, but well-controlled woman. Yet her phobic fears remained, not so intense but still strong enough to limit her activities! Clearly, in such a case, you could consider the treatment highly successful (the major advance in ego development: maturity, or what the analysts call "structural change") or a failure (persistence of the symptom that brought her into therapy)— depending on your values.

The novel *A Clockwork Orange* (A. Burgess, 1963), which has been made into a controversial but popular movie, poses another such difficult problem in evaluating the effects of therapy. A sadistic psychopath gets himself treated by a form of behavior modification (aversive conditioning); the outcome is that whenever he feels the impulse to rape or fight, he is overcome by an overwhelming feeling of sickness that prevents him from acting on these desires. But he is incapacitated in protecting himself from violence of others, and (worst of all, in the evaluation of other characters) lacks the freedom of choice to act on his own impulses, which apparently persist undiminished. A popular outcry is raised that he has been deprived of his essential humanity by the treatment, which is then reversed. The person is of course not real, so it is not possible to demonstrate that before treatment he was no more free to restrain his violent impulses than he was to act on them after the first course of therapy. That issue aside, however, there is obviously a conflict of values here: which is worse, for a man to be a sadistic criminal or for him to be in the "reconditioned" state in which his behavior therapy left him? From his own subjective standpoint, there was clearly no problem; he preferred his original state. Psychopaths (and character-disordered persons generally) by definition cause others more suffering than they are able to experience themselves, so the values of society must play a role in any overall evaluation of their treatment.

A number of authorities (e.g., Jahoda, 1958; M. B. Smith, 1961) agree that what started out as apparently a medical issue—how to define "mental health"—ends up as a problem of ethics or axiology, the branch of philosophy concerned with values. In any event, to define the criteria by which psychotherapy should be evaluated is clearly not a scientific problem. There is a simple way out, however. We merely shift our focus from "success" or "improvement" and start dealing with particular aspects of behavior, leaving it to others to make their own value judgments.

Again, notice how the attempt to go beyond the medical model of mental disease and therapy creates a set of new problems for us. In particular, note that if we give up the notion of diseases, defined in terms of specific symptoms and signs the removal of which constitutes cure, we find ourselves in need of a good deal of advance in personality assessment (to replace medical diagnosis). We need better ways of classifying types of people in therapy-relevant terms, types of problems or disorders or difficulties in living, types of therapy, and types of therapists. Hold on. Isn't the very conception of types in this context a holdover from the medical tradition? True, it lent itself well to the categorical classification of subjects called for in experimental designs for analysis of variance. Fortunately, as theoretical considerations persuade us that we should replace typologies by quantitative measurements of the relevant dimensions of subject, treatment, and therapist, correlational designs (especially multiple regression analysis) which make efficient use of just such data have become more generally known. Still, in many ways, research in therapy is limited by the level of attainment in personality assessment, which must provide the instruments and techniques of measurement, and this field is currently out of favor and attracting insufficient research interest.

An important issue in drug research, neglected in the brief section above on such work, is that of side effects—undesirable consequences of taking the drug, which may be anything from drowsiness to fatal circulatory collapse. The lesson is that any potent agent for good may be an agent for evil also, and that an evaluation must weigh benefit against harm. The same thing is clearly true for psychotherapy. We believe that sustained communicative relationships (in the family) cause many psychological problems, despite good intentions, so there is every reason in principle to assume that the putatively therapeutic relationship can have deleterious consequences as well as helpful ones. (Again, what one person considers good in what a psychotherapist achieves another may deplore—for example, the capacity to experience anxiety or grief.) And, as research in psychotherapy has moved from overall evaluations toward specific behavioral measures, not surprisingly evidence has accumulated that there are not only "side effects" in many cases but main effects in some, results that are considered undesirable in almost any value system (see Bergin, 1971, for a review).

The initially distressing discovery that professional efforts to help can do harm was nevertheless instrumental in starting a fruitful line of research on the qualities of therapists and of the therapeutic relationship that have proved most beneficial when present and hurtful when absent (Truax & Carkhuff, 1967). Interestingly, this is an instance of a program of research that began in the usual way, with unsystematic clinical observation and reflection (or, if you will, wisdom) set down by a psychotherapist with many years' experience in treating and training others (Rogers, 1957). His hypotheses about the relevant interpersonal skills were taken up by colleagues who painstakingly translated them into empirical techniques of measurement and experimental designs. A considerable body of research (recently summarized by Truax & Mitchell, 1971) has verified that "good" therapists—those who bring about favorable changes in their patients—are *genuine* rather than phony, nonpossessively *warm* rather than either cold or smothering, and *empathic* rather than inaccurate or deficient in their understanding of the patient.

It would certainly be premature to assert that we now know why some therapists get good results and others poor. For example, one study (Holt & Luborsky, 1958, Vol. 2, pp. 392 ff.) reported that a consensus of experienced psychoanalytic teachers, on the one hand, and empirical findings from a predictive study of psychiatric residents, on the other, agreed on the relevance of ten personality variables, which overlap Truax and Mitchell's list only on empathy. But it has been established well enough that genuineness, warmth, and empathy are important determinants of what goes on in therapy for any investigator to have to control these variables in future outcome research.

When one considers the great variety of plausibly important variables in psychotherapy, it is too easy to get discouraged. If we are going to have to view outcome in terms of relatively specific forms of behavior, if many attributes of the therapist seem to be possibly important determinants, if therapy itself proves on examination to be multidimensional, if many properties of the patient (aspects of his illness or problems in living, his personal assets and liabilities for the kind of therapy in question, demographic and miscellaneous variables) may affect the outcome, and if there are numerous other circumstances in the patient's life outside of therapy that can affect the dependent variables, is this not a multivariate problem requiring impossibly great numbers of cases for the necessary statistics to be applied? (For an excellent brief discussion of these classes of relevant variables, see Fiske, Hunt, Luborsky, Orne, Parloff, Reiser, and Tuma, 1970.) No. Fortunately, it is not necessary to work with perfect designs to make some progress. As the studies that verified Rogers' hypotheses testify, if you get hold of an important independent variable—one that determines a substantial part of the variance in your dependent variable—you can get replicable results even with relatively simple designs. In research on psychotherapy, as in any psychological investigation,

> the objective should not be the impossible one of providing controls for every conceivably relevant factor, but rather to design a study that can reasonably be expected to tell the field something not now known (Fiske *et al.*, 1970, p. 728).

Process Research

As outcome researchers begin to investigate specific effects of therapy, and as they become more sophisticated about the many possible causes of these behavioral changes, they have naturally begun to look at any given form of treatment as a cluster of separately measurable variables. In doing so, they enter the realm known as process research, an originally separate preoccupation of investigators who became fascinated by the nature of psychotherapy itself. What a remarkable, even unique, form of interpersonal transaction it is that can have such profound impact on some people, many psychotherapists reflected, and how worthy of study in its own right, regardless of the exact extent of its benefits!

Freud's discovery and formulation of transference and countertransference, and of the transference neurosis in psychoanalysis—these are typical examples of the early fruits of exploratory clinical research with a process orientation. Valuable as Freud's concepts and observations have proved to generations of therapists of virtually all schools, they are only quick sketches where we would like to have the equivalent of microphotography. Process research could hardly go beyond that level, however, until the invention of electronic sound recording. Even after it became technically possible to record every word spoken throughout a complete course of therapy, process research was held up by the doubts and anxieties of therapists. Though such resistances were often expressed as legitimate concern for the patient and the need to protect his rights and respect his confidences, the major obstacle has usually proved to be the therapist's own fear of exposure. Patients generally agree quite readily to recording, and it is not difficult to devise means of protecting them; neurotic resistances do at times center on the fact of recording, but they can be dealt with like any other such reality-based resistance (such as the kind that focuses on payment). Once therapists take the plunge, they usually find that being recorded is not so terrible, and the measurement device soon ceases to have important effects on what is being measured.

From its beginning, the nondirective or client-centered school of psychotherapy made it an almost routine practice to record therapy sessions, using the tapes in training as well as research. As a result, the largest single body of process research is probably the work of Rogers (e.g., 1959) and his many associates and students, especially Gendlin (1969), Truax and Carkhuff (1967), Kiesler (1966), and Snyder (1963). His co-workers have taken up several of his suggestions and have developed methods for measuring such process variables as experiencing and focusing, which have proved useful for research.

Researchers have had two legitimate but opposite kinds of hesitation about sound recording of therapy. On the one hand, some say, it is too little; on the other, it is too much. Too little, because there is obviously a great deal of nonverbal communication, especially in face-to-face psychotherapy, and analysts have argued that much of what is important to the process of therapy is not even communicated—it goes on inside the head of the therapist. Perhaps the most conscientious attempt to apply the inclusive approach to psychotherapy research was the treatment of a patient at the National Institute of Mental Health in Bethesda by the late Paul Bergman. The entire treatment was recorded on movie film, with stereophonic sound, the concealed camera being placed so as to photograph every expression and gesture of both therapist and patient. After each hour Dr. Bergman dictated as much as he could remember of what had passed through his mind, and he had frequent supervisory sessions with another senior psychoanalyst, which were also tape recorded. The result was an enormous accumulation of raw data, which have proved difficult to work with (Shakow, 1960; Bergman, 1966).

The main difficulty is the quantitative one. Even when the only data obtained from a psychotherapy are tape recordings, the number of reels to be stored mounts rapidly if the therapy goes on for more than a few sessions. Unless the quality of recording is excellent, the task of transcribing is difficult as well as enormous, and even when that hurdle is surmounted, the typescript is huge and very hard to find one's way about in. Think how these difficulties are multiplied if the researcher is interested in psychoanalysis, which may go on for hundreds, even thousands, of hours per case! Nevertheless, the task is by no means impossible, and a major effort to collect a library of recorded psychoanalyses is well under way, under the direction of Dahl (1972). Using a procedure that was worked out by Gill (see Gill, Simon, Fink, Endicott, & Paul, 1968), in which the analyst dictates hourly summaries, Dahl has devised a system of indexing the major themes and technically interesting events of each hour. The texts of both the summaries and the analytic hours are fed into a computer for long-term magnetic storage (e.g., on disc memories). Dahl (unpublished) and Spence (1969, 1971) have written programs for content analysis by computer which make it possible to find all hours containing a given topic quickly, and then to process either the summary or the raw data in many ways. The great capacity of the computer to accept and process gigantic quantities of data quickly may prove to hold one major answer to the problem of "too much." (Luborsky and Spence, 1971, describe this and several related programs of process research in psychoanalysis.)

Content analysis, whether computer-assisted or not, has always been the principal tool of process research. It is a set of systematic methods for identifying, scaling, and/or categorizing specified types of meanings, usually (but not necessarily) in verbal texts. A content analysis of something like the transcript or the videotape of a therapy session generally begins with a decision about units and a set of rules for dividing the material into them. With written texts, the unit is often the sentence; but it may be as short as the word or as long as the "speech"—the interval between successive remarks of one person in a conversation during which the other speaks. Scaling is assigning numerical ratings to a unit on a given scale, like the degree of emotional intensity. Categorizing is classifying a unit according to a preset list of qualitatively different categories; for example, therapists' remarks may be categorized as questions, reflections, interpretations, clarifications, and directives. The content-analytic scheme (embodied in a coding key) is generally made up expressly for each study and is no more elaborate than required by the research objectives; comprehensive, all-purpose schemes (see, for example, Leary & Gill, 1959) have proved to be too cumbersome for practical use (see, however, Gottschalk's method of measuring anxiety and hostility in interview texts: Gottschalk and Gleser, 1969). In any event, content analysis deals directly with the meanings that are the main interest of many psychotherapists, and converts them into quantitative form (in the case of categorizing, the numbers are frequencies) for statistical processing.

The computer has difficulty in carrying out content analysis when the unit is longer than the word, but it is surprising what a lot can be learned with that microscopic a focus. It is quite compatible with a psycholinguistic approach, which has characterized the work of such productive researchers as Dittman and Llewellyn (e.g., 1967) and Laffal (e.g., 1965). Computer programs have also made possible the automatic vocal transaction analysis of Cassotta, Feldstein, and Jaffe (1964), which converts the electric signal from a microphone directly into information about the patterns of speech and silence in the therapist-patient dyad. Matarazzo and his colleagues, who began a long program of research on dyadic interaction in a highly structured interview much earlier (see Matarazzo, Saslow, & Matarazzo, 1956) have recently turned to a computer-assisted method (Wiens, Matarazzo, & Saslow, 1965) which yields data somewhat similar to those generated by Cassotta's device. While this approach deals with the problem of "too much" by disregarding semantic content almost entirely, it shows some promise of yielding a measure of something like identification, because both teams (as well as Lennard & Bernstein, 1960) found that certain therapist-client pairs show a converging pattern: as time goes on, they adopt similar formal patterns of communicative interaction.

Content analysis is one of the most powerful and flexible investigative tools in the behavioral sciences. I cannot go into more detail here about how it is done, but several standard reference works are available (Berelson, 1952; Holsti, 1968, 1969; Pool, 1959). Gottschalk and Auerbach (1966) have edited a useful collection of papers presenting several kinds of content analysis as applied to psychotherapy; and Auld and Murray (1955) and Marsden (1971) have made valuable surveys of process research using content analysis. A major recent trend in content analysis is its automation by computer programs for processing verbal texts; see, for the most influential example, Stone, Dunphy, Smith, and Ogilvie (1966).

Luborsky (1967) has developed an ingenious application of content analysis called the symptom-context method; it can be used in many kinds of process studies. Ideally, the researcher works from complete recordings of therapy, but Luborsky has shown that detailed notes on each hour such as many therapists keep may also be used. After settling on the phenomenon he wishes to study (e.g., the report of a symptom, the phenomenon of temporarily forgetting what one was about to say, or the spontaneous occurrence of a vivid mental image), the researcher systematically combs the raw data for all instances, excerpting a standard segment of the text just preceding and just following each. He then selects by a random method an equal number of pages of the transcript that do not contain the phenomenon, and excerpts equally long passages from them as controls. Then, using either some standard content analysis or one that is built on the basis of a small sample of experimental and control passages, he intermingles and codes all of the passages so that their nature cannot be recognized and has them content-analyzed. Themes that are significantly associated with the phenomenon in question can then be interpreted as causally related to it.

Still another way to cut down the size of the job is to concentrate on the remarks of the member of the dyad who is usually less verbose—the therapist. Examples of research programs that have made good use of this stratagem are those of E. S. Howe (e.g., 1964), who used Osgood's method of the semantic differential to study therapists' remarks, Pope & Siegman (e.g., 1968), who have studied such aspects of the therapist's behavior as his productivity, specificity, and warmth, and Strupp (e.g., 1960), whose multidimensional analysis of the therapist's activity has been particularly influential.

Now that the major resistances to tape recording are being overcome among psychotherapists of all schools, it is becoming possible to build up libraries of the raw data of therapy, making available to the scientific community what was for generations the special preserve of the individual therapist. Such files of data can be analyzed as often and by as many new approaches as desired. As their size and representativeness grow, process research in psychotherapy will inevitably make much more rapid strides forward.

GOING BEYOND THE INFORMATION GIVEN

This title, deliberately borrowed from a stimulating paper by Bruner (1957), is intended to highlight the essential nature of what it is we do when we get around to writing the last section of a scientific report: the interpretation of findings. Interpreting results is the final, and a very necessary, step in research of *any* kind. "Just let the data speak for itself" is not only ungrammatical, it is bad advice which is very rarely taken. Just as deplorable and far more prevalent is wild overgeneralization. Even Skinner, the outstanding contemporary spokesman for a psychology devoted to objectivity in every respect, went far beyond the information at hand, which was based primarily on observations of white rats, when he titled his first major book *The Behavior of Organisms*. The impulse behind such wild overgeneralization is understandable and human—indeed, the propensity to go beyond the information given, to generalize, abstract, draw remote implications from evidence, and attempt to predict the future, may be a uniquely human trait. It is surely one of the great strengths of man that he has the gift to lift his nose from the concrete, the particular, and the immediate, and get a glimpse of something beyond. What wonder, then, that the impulse to generalize gets out of hand? Most scientific papers deal with intrinsically trivial matters, of little interest except as they have broader implications. The ability to go beyond the data but to do so in a controlled and responsible way is one important difference between a great and a merely competent scientist.

In a case study in scientific discovery, the sociologists Barber and Fox (1958) show in detail how "nature favors the prepared mind" and how differing interests and preconceptions can cause two people, starting from the same phenomenon, to go beyond their initial data in divergent directions and make quite different discoveries. At about the same time but for different reasons, two experimental biologists, Thomas and Kellner, had occasion to inject the enzyme papain into rabbits and noticed that their ears collapsed. Though the phenomenon was unexpected, completely reproducible, and amusingly spectacular—imagine the foolish appearance of a bunny with floppy, spaniel-like ears—neither of them published anything about it because they had no idea how to go beyond this datum and see its broader implications. Their initial searches for a reason were frustrated. Sections of the limp ears showed no change in muscular, vascular, or connective tissue! Neither saw any way to formulate the finding that made acceptable biological sense. But the fact that such a visually dramatic and bizarre effect could be produced reliably and easily without any microscopically visible accompanying change caused Thomas to use it several years later in teaching experimental pathology. To demonstrate to his students how the scientific method should be applied, for the first time he prepared sections of the ears of experimental and control animals, and to his great surprise now discovered why the ears collapsed: a marked effect of papain on the cartilage. Thomas thereupon published the discovery and went on to pursue this hitherto unknown effect of the enzyme on cartilage, which turned out to be quite general.

Because Kellner was primarily interested in muscle, Thomas in the circulatory system, and both shared the common conception that cartilage is an inert, uninteresting tissue, both researchers had failed to see what later seemed embarrassingly obvious cartilaginous changes. Kellner paid no further attention to the ears, for three reasons, probably: (1) The very fact that the rabbits looked so ridiculous made him consider the phenomenon not a scientifically interesting one; (2) he "took care of it" by using it as a handy way of checking the potency of papain solutions; and (3) he discovered in the same rabbits that papain produced equally unexpected, specific lesions in certain muscles, including those of the heart. Muscle was his specialty, so he was the one to discover and publish this last, potentially important bit of cardiac pathology. As to Thomas, three hypotheses seem plausible in helping us understand why he discovered the cause of the original observation only after some years' delay: (1) in his teaching role, he followed the complete experimental method in a way scientists often shortcut in daily practice; (2) when he made the discovery, he happened to have on hand for the first time an ample supply of rabbits that were not needed for other research; (3) he was temporarily stymied in his other lines of investigation, and so had the time, interest, and animals to devote to an intensive follow-up of the effect of papain on cartilage.

This case history highlights the fact that any phenomenon is likely to be much more complex than it at first appears. Different interests will cause two people to select from it and formulate quite diverse facts. In doing so, each necessarily goes beyond the information immediately at hand. If Thomas had not extrapolated from what he actually observed, he would not have discovered the effect of papain on cartilage in the joints; and if Kellner had not (with even less rational justification) looked for an effect on other muscles after not finding any in the ears, he would not have made his discovery. As a general rule, in interpreting scientific results you must go beyond the particular facts initially yielded by an investigation, whether incidentally or as its major findings, if you are to make significant contributions to knowledge. Yet there is no easier way of being absurd or irresponsible than by an unwise and overzealous interpretation of findings that may be perfectly sound in themselves.

Since inspired interpretation is *par excellence* a creative act, there can be no set of rules that will lead you to it. Nevertheless, a couple of obvious points can be made. A fact can always be seen as an instance of a larger class of similar facts, or as the particularization of a theoretical concept or law. Evidently, then, the more you know of relevant facts and theories, and the more you try to find overarching unities, the better your chance of seeing useful implications in the data at hand. That means seeing your finding as an instance of a larger generalization, whether that be empirical or theoretical. The genius of a man like Linus Pauling is partly his ability to see common elements or similarities in findings from many diverse areas of science, which enables him to produce surprising and fruitful new conceptual unifications of scattered data.

The basic process in interpretation, I believe, is generalizing: taking a fact as an instance of a larger class. But that is the logical reverse of sampling, which is the technique of choosing from a large class instances that represent the whole; so the theory and practice of drawing samples may help us in drawing conclusions. The point is obvious enough, but it is not usually made, and it is common for the most reputable and scientifically sophisticated psychologists to ignore sampling considerations when they come to the section headed Conclusions.

Since the term "sample" in psychology almost always refers to the group of persons studied, sampling considerations are most obviously relevant to the population of organisms about whom we generalize. Scientists are characteristically ambitious people (if they are not so motivated, they often do not achieve much), and ambition makes you "think big." Therefore, the natural tendency is to generalize broadly: not, "The Sexual Behavior of White Middle-Class Men of Indiana" (which is what Kinsey *et al.* mainly studied), but "The Sexual Behavior of the Human Male." Freud once expressed the underlying feelings well in a letter to Jung: "I feel a fundamental aversion towards your suggestion that my conclusions [about the sexual etiology of neurosis] are correct, but only for certain cases. . . . That is not very well possible. Entirely or not at all. They are concerned with such fundamental matters that they could not be valid for one set of cases only" (Jones, 1955, p. 439). And again, Freud wrote: "It is as if I were obliged to compare everything I hear about other people with myself; as if my personal complexes were put on the alert whenever another person is brought to my notice. This cannot possibly be an individual peculiarity of my own: it must rather contain an indication of the way in which we understand 'something other than ourself' in general" (1901b, p. 24). In this last passage, he wanted to generalize to all mankind on the basis of a sample of one—himself! As was noted in the section above on sampling (pp. 23ff.), if you have the good luck to be focusing on one of those ways in which each person is like every other person, the size and makeup of your sample will fortunately be irrelevant. Not just good luck is responsible, perhaps, but also intuition (Polanyi, 1958), an important component of which (in psychology) may be the accumulated residue of many informal as well as formal observations of human beings.

Humanistically oriented psychologists often criticize their laboratory-dwelling colleagues for generalizing about "behavior" and implicitly being primarily concerned about human behavior while spending most if not all their time working with samples of rats or pigeons. Biologists estimate that there are about a million known species of animals living today (not to mention millions more that are unknown to science, or extinct). As Beach (1950) pointed out, even comparative psychologists have studied the behavior of only a paltry few dozen species, most of them mammals. How arrogant to claim that we are discovering the laws of behavior without further qualification! This at least is one danger into which researchers in clinical and abnormal psychology rarely fall.

More to the point, are they justified in generalizing about schizophrenics after having studied a few disturbed members of affluent contemporary American families, or even a few hundred persons labeled schizophrenic who happen to be available in an accessible state hospital or two? In the strictest logical sense, no; but practically, perhaps so. To carry the logic of sampling to its bitter end is as rigidly unrealistic and counter to the true spirit of science as the attempt to set up and follow to the letter any other set of rules for scientific behavior. We must not forget that research is the creative work of fallible human beings. It is logically impossible to sample all past and future schizophrenics in the present, and our practical interest is almost always in precisely that unknowable region, the future. So, is science futile and knowledge impossible? Of course not. The point is to be sensible, and to temper audacity with humility when we generalize about any class of persons. A little acquaintance with the pitfalls of generalizing from nonrandom samples can teach a good deal of humility, or at least caution.[10]

A helpful antidote to overgeneralization is not to take significance levels at face value, not even those that seem "safely" beyond the mystical .01 level, and to be particularly cautious about generalizing from results that have not been replicated. The obvious function of replication is to protect us against taking seriously a finding that turns out to have been a fluke, a freak of random sampling or an artifact of experimental method like inadvertent contamination by knowledge of the criterion. But there is an important further advantage to withholding any extensive interpretation of a study until it has been replicated. What is particular to any given sample tends to fall away and the limits of the appropriate generalization show up more clearly. You can often tell the scientific greenhorn from the old hand by the former's tendency to take every specific turn of his data as revealed truth, while the latter discerns the main trend and properly emphasizes only that. Partly, he does so because of an incommunicable "know-how" that comes from much experience in sequential research—the kind that follows up the leads from one study to another, thus providing corrective feedback for attempted extrapolations and other predictions. The researcher who constantly hops from topic to topic is less likely to develop this kind of feeling for what is meaningful in his findings. And in part, the skilled interpreter manages to sift grain from chaff in his findings by an integrative effort, implicitly matching the different aspects of his data with findings in allied and even remote fields of research, and with expectations from a variety of theories, until he hits on the way of looking at the results that best formulates them.

Thanks to Brunswik (1956), it is possible to see that the logic of sampling subjects applies sweepingly to all aspects of any empirical investigation. There are few enough psychologists who show any awareness of the necessity of paying attention to the population of persons about whom they can properly generalize after studying their subjects; Brunswick was the first to

[10][Another reason for caution and prudence in writing the final, interpretive section of a research report is the fact that it is the one part of a scientific paper most likely to be read by nonscientists. Persons who are not trained in the evaluation of research method and who do not know the conventions of a scientific "linguistic community" are likely to take rash generalizations more literally than they are meant; and we cannot shrug this problem aside by saying that we write only for our colleagues when we are not deliberately "popularizing." If anything, all of us should try to make our technical writings accessible to a more general audience in order to meet our responsibilities to the society that is paying us to do our work.]

point out that even these few almost never realize that any experiment contains a sample of "objects," too, and usually a very small sample selected without any consideration of its representativeness. Students of perception, he declared, typically present their subjects with meaningless bits of colored paper and then proceed to generalize about the visual world of real life, where people respond to colors primarily as attributes of three-dimensional objects seen at a great variety of distances and in all kinds of lighting, contexts, etc. Until we study people perceiving color in their actual life settings, he asked, how can we be sure that the "laws" discovered in the laboratory are not peculiar to it and the flat, moderately near, monochromatic objects it contains?

In clinical psychology, this kind of error is made constantly. An investigator gets the idea that male and female patients may respond to the Rorschach differently when it is administered by a man and by a woman; so she looks for and interprets differences, using *one* male and *one* female tester! Essentially the same error is being committed when an investigator wants to (and does) generalize about a concept like creativity or the achievement motive or field-dependence after presenting subjects with a single test of that concept. The Embedded Figures Test, for example, is an interesting instrument, in which the subject's task is to extract simple geometrical figures from their camouflage in complex, colored (but abstract, two-dimensional) designs. But it is hardly worth all the effort that has gone into studies using it unless it can be interpreted as a direct and sufficient measure of field dependence or psychological differentiation—which it is not. Either of these closely related concepts applies sweepingly to a great range of human behavior, which is by no stretch of the imagination validly sampled by a single test of a single function. Witkin and his colleagues (1962) wisely recommend the use of their whole battery of perceptual tests, just as Guilford (1967) recommends that anyone wishing to get a measure of one of the many factors into which he has analyzed the monolithic notion of intelligence should use at least three high-loading tests of that factor. Any one test's score measures not only the factor or concept in which we are interested (true score), but an often unknown number of others, some of which are test-specific (error variance). Therefore, when you combine scores of several tests you tend to cancel out the influence of errors and irrelevant test-specific abilities, so that what comes through is a measure of what they have in common—the factor. Though the point is here expressed in the jargon of factor analysis and test theory, it is essentially Brunswik's insight about the need to sample "objects." The rationale is the same as that for replicating whole studies. Until you have repeated what you believe to be essential while letting unimportant particulars vary, you cannot be certain of how to interpret your findings.

To go back to Silverman's research on aggression for a concrete example: on the grounds of not asking for trouble, he might have decided, after an initial verification of his prediction, not to change the subliminally presented aggressive picture. If that had been the tiger leaping after the monkey, the results would have remained moot. Conceivably, the poorer performance on story recall (or other cognitive tests) that followed could have been attributed to regressive fantasies stirred up by an aspect of the picture considered unimportant by the experimenter, its quality of being an illustration from a child's book. By demonstrating that a photograph of a man brandishing a knife had the same effect, at one stroke he erased from consideration all of the aspects of the two pictures that they did not share in common. In other, similar studies using subliminal presentations cited by Silverman (1972), short verbal messages were shown to have the same effect as the same meanings represented pictorially. Again, broadening the sampling of experimental "objects" greatly strengthened the certainty with which Silverman was able to put his finger on their effective property. Notice, however, that as long as he kept the aggressive meaning constant while varying nonessential features (like the nature of the actors, type of aggression, pictorial versus verbal presentation, etc.) he succeeded only in eliminating irrelevancies; but he did not touch the question of what it was about the aggressive theme that produced the effects. The following are almost equally plausible: the arousal of an aggressive drive (Silverman's original interpretation); the arousal of affects (anger or fear) connected with the theme of attack; the arousal of fantasies—subconscious but affectively intense ideation; the arousal of defenses against threatening aspects of the experimental "stimulus." Notice that the latter two interpretations say nothing about aggression or related concepts (e.g., anger). They recognize the possibility that part or all of the effects may be caused by aggressive themes not as such, but as instances of strong motives, which in turn might interfere with cognitive performance because of the allegedly disruptive properties of the emotions connected with strong motives or because of the effects of defensive processes stirred up by such motives.

The lesson is plain. Any investigation can be interpreted in more than one plausible way, often in many ways. The researcher who is too eager to be convinced that his original idea was right will be blind to alternative hypotheses and may thereby miss opportunities to follow up an experiment (or other study) with others that can more precisely define the nature of the appropriate generalizations. An experienced and gifted investigator may happen to be right in his interpretation of findings, but there is no substitute for further research to test and verify it.

Consider another example, this time of interpretation that extends across a number of studies and attempts to integrate all their findings. Meehl (1954) and Sawyer (1966) both surveyed several dozen investigations, from various behavioral sciences, which had in common the fact that in each, two somewhat differently arrived-at predictions were empirically tested. Both Meehl and Sawyer chose the same level and type of generalization about their somewhat differing collections of highly miscellaneous studies: they were comparisons of clinical and statistical prediction. (Notice that once again, the very titles of their respective publications assert this level of generalization and constitute much more of an interpretive assertion than either author probably realized.) But when we look closely at the particular researches collected and reviewed in these influential surveys, we soon find that what is being called clinical prediction only exceptionally has anything to do with diagnosis or treatment of abnormal persons; and in only a minority of the studies were the predictions made by persons who considered themselves clinicians (Holt, 1970a [Chapter 4]). Rather, the predictions called clinical had in common the property of *not* having been made according to a statistical formula or mechanical rule. All of them involved judgment; a prediction made by a clinician about a patient involves judgment (and rarely the use of any statistical or actuarial rule); therefore, they were clinical predictions. A perfect instance of predicative reasoning![11] And notice how the same kind of "paleologic," which is often cited as characteristic of schizophrenic thought disorder (Arieti, 1975; von Domarus, 1944), is used by that very large segment of psychologists who conclude that the diagnostic activities of clinicians have been proved worthless: "clinical prediction" is (in the studies surveyed) no better than statistical prediction; psychodiagnosis involves some clinical prediction; therefore, psychodiagnosis is a waste of the psychologist's time and the money of those who pay for his work.

To be sure, whenever we go beyond the information given, we may use some degree of predicative reasoning. Perhaps *conclusions* might be differentiated from *implications* by the tightness of the logic involved. Let us say that when the careful investigator surveys the subjects and objects used in his study and induces their common properties on the *lowest* (most conservative) applicable level of generalization, he is drawing conclusions. That is, he is stating what he found in a form that is somewhat generalized, but he does not consider as established any proposition that ventures above the level that just characterizes all of his experimental subjects and objects. If his subjects are male undergraduates in a large American university, and if he is studying the relationship between authoritarianism and cultural alienation, he will probably be less tempted to generalize on the level of "the behavior of organisms" than he would if he had studied the effects of a schedule of reinforcement on learning lists of words. When he extends his generalizations to classes of subjects or objects that do include those of his study but a good many others, let us call that drawing implications. In this sense, implications always imply predicative reasoning: I know A to be true of B; B has property X in common with Q, and X may be the psychologically salient property of B that is responsible for the finding; therefore, A may be true of

---

[11]Predicative reasoning is the (usually implicit) use of false syllogisms, in which the existence of a common predicate is taken as sufficient basis for asserting the identity of two disparate entities.

Q. Notice the difference in the wording of this near-syllogism and the ones of the previous paragraph, however. To say that something *may be* true is far different from asserting that it *is* true.

Declaration is a manner of speech appropriate for conclusions but not for implications. The failure of criminologists and prison physicians to predict which prisoners will violate parole after an unsystematic analysis of an interview *may* imply that all predictions in which human judgment plays a large role are equally fallible; and when the fact on which the implication is based is supplemented by similar failures of sports writers to predict the outcome of football games and of engaged couples to predict how many children they will have had after 20 years, the larger generalization may seem more plausible. In each case, predictions *were* judgmentally made. But before any valid inference can be made, it is necessary to examine the studies in which judgmental prediction failed to surpass or equal statistical prediction, in order to see whether they have any other properties in common that might be responsible for the findings. As I have demonstrated elsewhere (Holt, 1970a [Chapter 4]), there is such a property—the successful predictions are cross-validations, involving prior study of the relationship between predictive and criterion data, and the unsuccessful ones are not. This hypothesis accounts not only for the differences between many "clinical" and many statistical predictions, but also for the fact that some judgmental predictions are more successful than others; therefore, it seems more likely to be true than the usually accepted interpretation that all clinical prediction is inferior to statistical prediction. Notice, also, that my inference is on a somewhat lower level of generalization than that of Meehl, Sawyer, *et al.*, and is therefore less speculative.

In the end, the issue of predicative (or, perhaps more kindly, speculative) reasoning and that of sampling turn out to be the same. Science cannot advance without taking any risks; implications as well as conclusions are useful, though for different purposes. Conclusions tell us where we are, while implications point out possibly interesting, even useful directions to try next. All kinds of mischief may be done when the two are not properly distinguished, particularly when something that is only a possibility (implication) is taken as a demonstrated actuality (conclusion). Then the scientific process is short-circuited, and sometimes it takes years of blundering around in the dark to find the source of the trouble.

THE ETHICAL AND SOCIAL RESPONSIBILITIES OF PSYCHOLOGICAL RESEARCHERS

Research in clinical psychology is not and can never be an ethically neutral undertaking. Psychology has officially recognized this fact through its adoption of an ethical code containing a whole section of principles dealing with research, which has recently been revised and published separately (APA Ad Hoc Committee, 1973). Anyone who is seriously interested in psychological research, either because of actual or planned involvement in doing it, or because of a need to evaluate it, should study the APA code of ethics, both the older, general code and the specialized "Ethical Principles in the Conduct of Research with Human Participants," both of which contain not only principles but brief accounts of real ethical dilemmas and recommended solutions.

Rather than attempt to summarize what is available elsewhere (which does not lend itself well to summarizing anyway), I want to dwell on some of the less obvious ethical implications of research in clinical psychology and the closely related issue of responsibility. I am writing in the first person because this section is inevitably a statement of personal conviction, and one of my convictions is that all of us in psychology need to accept personal responsibility for our work, despite the existence of strong, subtle, pervasive pressures against doing so.

Let us begin with a practical question: where does the money come from? Research is an expensive undertaking, especially in its more developed, hypothesis-testing phase. Ultimately, it is paid for by the society that we live in. That in itself is a sufficient reason for researchers to be aware of the wider impact of their work on society. In addition, however, the basic premise of our ethical code is that psychology is a science *and* a means of promoting human welfare. Even in our most purely scientific role of producing empirical and theoretical knowledge, we are not discharging our ethical obligations if we evaluate our work only in terms of scientific criteria. Indeed, the very attempt to do just that is responsible for some of the ethical abuses of science that have led some writers (e.g., Roszak, 1969) to overreact and attack the whole enterprise.

There has been a strong tradition in science, which has affected even such a relatively applied branch as clinical psychology, that overstresses its abstract and objective nature to the point of building and maintaining a myth that the scientist is actuated only by pure curiosity and need be responsible only to the pursuit of truth, regardless of its consequences. In this view, basic research—the pursuit of intellectual problems for their own sake, irrespective of any possible application—is the most important activity of a scientist, worthy of the greatest respect and prestige, and demanding unquestioning support by society on the argument that in the long run it is the shortest route to useful knowledge and social benefits. This ideology of science presents it as an objective endeavor in the sense that it is uncontaminated by values (other than the value of truth), and that it uses exact and machinelike methods which do not require human judgment or feelings and hence are unmarred by human fallibility.

To anyone who has worked in a laboratory, or even to those who have read such frank accounts of how scientific work is actually done as J. D.

Watson's (1969) story of how he and his colleagues solved the mystery of DNA's structure, the above ideal is obviously mythical. Scientists are as human as anyone else; values and irrational considerations of many kinds pervade their actual choice of problems and methods of working on them. [Einstein once wrote: "science as something coming into being, as aim, is just as subjective and psychologically conditioned as any other of man's efforts" (quoted in Holton, 1973, p. 17.] And as Polanyi (1958) has shown, the notion of complete objectivity is not only a fiction, it is a false, unattainable, and in fact mischievous ideal. It is one with which clinical psychologists and psychoanalysts are familiar, for Freud long ago described its psychopathological form: the vain attempt of the obsessive-compulsive neurotic to get control over his anxiety and impulses by living a life of pure rationality and intellect. Distrusting emotion, he isolates thought from affect and attempts to replace judgment by the amassing of information. Since choices have to be made ultimately in terms of values and the human needs that underlie them, the obsessional quest must fail, and paradoxically no one is more irrational than the isolated hyperintellectualizer. In his overevaluation of thinking, he opens the back door to magical thought and ritualistic practices, which may in the end completely cripple his capacity to act effectively.

The analogy between obsessive-compulsive neurosis and certain abuses of science is far from accidental, for scientific work is most congenial to people with obsessive-compulsive personality structures and in many ways it tends to encouarge such defenses. Fortunately, the intellectualizing, obsessive-compulsive way of dealing with reality can be stabilized in a highly efficient form which still permits its possessor to be fully human. Yet it remains a constant occupational hazard of the scientist that these same strategies may degenerate (or decompensate) into their neurotic forms. At one extreme, the result may be personal paralysis; at another, the Nazi "scientist," cold-bloodedly carrying out grisly experiments on Jews and gypsies. [For further discussion of these issues, see Chapter 10, below.]

I am not arguing that any scientist who wants to devote himself to the ideal of pure, basic research has started down a path that leads inevitably to either the concentration camp laboratory or incapacitating obsessive-compulsive neurosis. The argument for basic research is good enough so that I believe we should always have people doing it, as we will in a free society. If scientists have the liberty to choose the kind of work that appeals to them, and if they are fully aware of the direct and indirect consequences and implications of their work, I have faith that relatively few will choose work that has *no* discernible relevance to practical problems, and that the others will be able to avoid the worst of the subtler dangers. To these ends, every researcher has an ethical as well as practical obligation not to live in the mythical world of hyperobjectivity, but to be aware of certain important realities and probabilities.

As Platt (1969) has persuasively demonstrated, mankind is on a collision course with a terrifying multiplicity of dangers to the quality of life and perhaps to life itself. We may have only a few decades in which to bring about the massive redirection of research that will be necessary to help provide the answers to overpopulation, famine, environmental degradation, and suicidal wars—to name only the most obvious of these threats. If there is even a small chance that this seemingly apocalyptic view is correct, it would violate the most fundamental ethical obligations of psychologists not to point out the probable consequences of "research as usual." The education and special skills of researchers give them a peculiarly strategic position in modern society, making them a privileged elite whether they wish to be or not; for they are in a position to decide where to direct the movement of science, to determine whether it will be used wisely to promote human survival, or short-sightedly to pursue the illusory goals of profit, prestige, and power. Knowing that, we cannot disregard the direct and indirect impact of our investigative work on the overridingly important crises of the society that supports our work.

By direct impact, I mean the relevance of research to the solution of problems relatively high on Platt's ranking of "crisis problems." At first glance, the disciplines of abnormal psychology may not seem to be very applicable to any problems other than those of mental health, which are low in the list. To relieve human suffering is and always will be intrinsically important, though it would not accomplish much to empty the state hospitals if their former inmates found themselves unemployed and embroiled in a race war, for example. But the work of the psychiatrist Lifton (e.g., 1961, 1968) and that of the clinical psychologist Keniston (1965, 1968) show ways in which the special research skills and training of this field can be brought to bear on issues of great relevance to the crises of our time. Consider also the fact that even problems like air pollution, solutions to which seem to be entirely in the province of the physical sciences, demand social action, which is ultimately a matter of public opinion, information, values, and political behavior. From this perspective, the behavioral sciences have a critical role. Unless we can learn how to help people help themselves, all the efforts of the physical and biological scientists will be in vain. And surely issues like changing behavior and values, particularly the self-defeating behavior of people who refuse to help themselves, are central to the fields of clinical and abnormal psychology.

In considering the indirect impact of the researcher's work on threatened human values, let me go back to the apparently trivial and tangential matter of writing in the first person. The APA Publication Manual discourages it, many editors carefully undo it in scientific writing, and students soon learn that it is taboo. If research gets done, individual people do it, but the prevailing tradition is to pretend that the whole process proceeded automatically, untouched by the grimy humanity of anyone's personal hands. Thus, "Ss were told . . ."; never: "I told the Ss. . . ." The passive voice is approved and becomes standard in spite of the protests of a few quirky lovers of good English prose who point out how it grays, levels, and deadens scientific writing. It is hard to resist the conclusion that this dull monotone is specifically wanted, and that it serves the function of perpetuating what Roszak (1969) calls "the myth of objective consciousness," which is part of the hyperobjective caricature of science as an abstract, impersonal process. Of course, if it were actually that sterilized and automated, the words we use would not make it any the less so. Notice, further, that many of the greatest figures in all branches of science write in a simple, personal style, not obtruding themselves in a narcissistic way but using the first person naturally and directly. They do not have to pretend or perpetuate any myths. Perhaps we don't have to either, really—none of us.

The heart of the matter is to recognize the proper role of objectivity in science, to respect and work for the ideal of minimizing self-deception and maximizing fidelity to reality, but not to make a cult of it. When objectivity becomes (or seems to become) an end in itself, when we find ourselves *pretending* to be more impersonal than we actually are, or acting the role of a scientific robot rather than being ourselves, then we should begin to realize that the pursuit of objectivity is getting ritualistic and irrational. That kind of pseudo objectivity serves no real function; it does not promote fidelity to the truth, and may in fact get in its way. Surely pretense is ultimately self-defeating.

As clinical psychologists we have learned that behavior is multiply determined, serving functions of which people are often not aware. The flat, boring, jargon-filled prose of science seems to serve the function of making it readable only by insiders—certainly not by intelligent laymen whose lives may be touched by it. It reassures the scientist that his work is part of a vast, impersonal machine, remorselessly and automatically proceeding its value-free way toward objective truth. That fiction may be seen as part of a larger "myth of the machine" (Mumford, 1970) which silently pervades many aspects of our culture. This mechanistic ethos is linked to a hierarchical, authoritarian, power-centered social structure, Mumford argues persuasively, one that has long seduced intellectuals by making them part of a powerful elite, rewarded with money and prestige. Along with several others (e.g., Revel, 1971) he claims to see evidence that this hierarchical model of society is breaking down,[12] for it is inherently irrational in many respects— paradoxically, in its very pursuit of rationality. Devotion to rationality becomes self-defeating when it leads the scientist to assume implicitly that people are or should be moved by considerations of efficiency alone, so that he overlooks or underestimates the degree to which esthetic, religious,

[12][Marxist critics have of course been making similar predictions for a good many years. In the retrospect of only a few years, the evidence adduced by the authors mentioned does not seem impressive, and the conclusion of an imminent collapse of hierarchical and exploitative social systems appears more wishful than realistic.]

security-seeking, and impulse-gratifying motives and needs to avoid anxiety determine behavior—including social policy.

I believe that we have a profound responsibility to try to understand these indirect consequences of our behavior as scientists (including the ways we do our research and the ways we write about it), and to act in such a way as to promote our most precious values. Reverence for life and respect for human individuality and freedom are as important to scientists as the pursuit of truth. And the most immediate danger of the hyperobjective outlook is to the researcher himself, because it tends to dehumanize him at a time in history when it is of the greatest importance that humanistic values be fostered in their losing competition with the onrush of technology as an end in itself. The environmental pollution of which people generally have become suddenly conscious came about largely because of this imbalance in values, the human costs of production being ignored or considered second- ary·to economic and technological efficiency.

I suggest, therefore, that we adopt the following variant of the ethical "golden rule": *Design, carry out, and report research in such a way as to make it, as much as possible, a growth-enhancing experience for everyone concerned.* "Growth- enhancing" is shorthand for "an experience that helps the experimenter, subjects, and audience advance to as high a level of ego development (in Loevinger's sense; see her 1966 paper and 1976 book) as they are capable of, or at least does not demand or encourage behavior at low levels of ego development." Fidelity to the spirit of this rule does not require that we assess the developmental level of everyone affected, nor that we accept Loevinger's theoretical position. I have used it because it has the virtue of incorporating many of the relevant values into an empirical scheme, in which ideals of science and democracy are concretized in behavior patterns found on the highest developmental levels (the Autonomous and Integrated): empathic identification with others, control of behavior by internalized value systems, the cherishing of individuality, and the free and responsible choice of one's course of action.

Conversely, the view of the world as a zero-sum game, a power struggle in which the aim is to be the dominant winner who can get his gratifications at the expense of the inferior majority—this characterizes a relatively low level of ego development, which Loevinger calls the Self-Protective. Yet precisely this world-view underlies a good many of the most irrational and objectionable aspects of science. Take the issue of free will: the traditional scientific stance has been to deny its existence. Thus, the individual scientist feels justified in treating people as if they did not have freedom of choice anyway, while he tacitly reserves such freedom for himself. In his behavior, when he designs research, teaches, and communicates with his peers, he acts as if he believed that he could choose and is choosing and expects his students and colleagues to choose to do what is rational, not what a past history of reinforcements would necessitate. In denying this capacity to his subjects and to people in general, he implicitly conceives of them as less fully human than himself.

Moreover, the basic theoretical models of behaviorism and Freudian psychoanalysis (Holt, 1972a) incorporate the assumption that people are passive pawns of their drives or of external stimulus control, or both. What could be more natural or appropriate, therefore, than a model of research in which the subject's role is entirely passive? The ideal subject is docile, credulous, without idiosyncratic desires, purposes, viewpoints, or interpretations; he shows up on time, accepts everything he is told, and responds only by the "response channel" the E has chosen, thus giving purely quantitative, easily processed data. He is recognizably the same subhuman being who is the ideal docile servant of the machine and of the authoritarian state, also— the submissive subject of a royal master, the robot-worker who fits smoothly into an organizational machine and performs as reliably as a well-tooled cog. A psychology whose model of man is this mythical creature is, wittingly and willingly or not, exerting a pressure on people to conform to such expectations, rather than helping them to grow into mature, individually responsible human beings, capable of autonomy, freedom, and creativity.[13]

Here is a dilemma for anyone who is convinced of the intrinsic validity of the passive S-R model of man, but who does not like its social consequences. He may deny that there are any such consequences, or point out the fact that the implications I have asserted are at best plausible hypotheses, not backed up by empirical proof. In this respect, he is much like the scientists who reject the proposition that smoking causes lung cancer and other diseases on the grounds that it has not been conclusively proved by experimental evidence. Both positions are logically tenable; but scientific proof is never absolute anyway, and the *probable* consequences of a position must be weighted by the social and vital importance of those consequences. At the least, the advocate of one of these passive "images of man" (see Chein, 1972) owes it to his subjects to take particular pains not to infantilize them, and to act *as if* he believed in their right to be respected as responsible, active agents.

It is characteristic of the hyperobjectivists to proclaim their adherence to the truth above all else, yet paradoxically many of them seem to feel thereby freed to lie to subjects, to deceive them systematically in order to manipulate the independent variables of their experiments. Here is an ethical dilemma about which there is considerable controversy (Kelman, 1968). The position of the APA Code of Ethics is that deception should be kept to an absolute minimum and used only when there is no acceptable alternative way of studying a problem. Moreover, it must always be followed up by an adequate explanation (or "debriefing"), in which subjects are given a true account of

---

[13][Argyris (1968) persuasively develops the additional argument that the data an investigator gets in the social system that arises when one follows traditional notions of rigorous research are likely to be less valid than data from research structured so as to make the subject a respected and willing partner.]

the nature of the experiment and deleterious consequences are undone to the best of the experimenter's ability.

In practice, those rules have not worked well. Experimenters are more willing to lie than to admit the fact to their subjects, so that all too often the explanation of what the experiment was really about consists in a further set of untruths, intended to be mollifying or reparative. I cannot recall having read an experiment of this kind in which there was adequate follow-up to find out whether the subjects did in fact accept the cover story and were unharmed by the total experience, although it seems perfectly evident that anyone who undertakes to make subjects angry, anxious, or guilty or who attacks their self-esteem has thereby shouldered the profoundest responsibility toward them. Simply to explain that "It was all a harmless hoax, ha-ha, so you don't need to feel bad," is *not* enough. Even when this typical ploy succeeds in abolishing the deleterious feelings that were originally aroused— which it often does not—the experimenter usually overlooks the fact that he has left the subject with an experience of passive victimization. Even that would not be so bad were it not for the fact that modern life buffets all of us with countless, more or less traumatic experiences of being exploited. The feeling of helplessness and the impotent rage it tends to evoke are pathogenic influences which are virtually endemic. That fact makes an otherwise relatively innocuous entrapment by a psychologist a possibly traumatic experience. It tends to confirm cynicism and suspicion, teaching the participants that psychologists are not to be trusted—surely not the lesson most of us have in mind when we assure students that they will learn something about psychology by serving as research subjects!

The challenge to the experimenter, therefore, is to find ways of making it not only nontraumatic to people but growth-enhancing to aid the process of research. Since I cannot think of any way to convert an experiment that uses deception into a positive experience, I believe that the ethical code should be more stringent and should put the burden of proof on the experimenter that he has managed this bit of psychological alchemy. Anyone who looks back over the history of deceit in psychological research would be hard pressed to demonstrate that it has resulted in solid advances in science, the ultimate utility of which is great enough to counterbalance the moral and psychological damage it has probably caused.

Another facet of the generally exploitative orientation of much research is the issue of the invasion of privacy and the respecting of confidences. These matters were extensively aired in Congressional hearings, which focused particularly on the use of such instruments as the MMPI for personnel selection (see the May 1967 issue of *American Psychologist*). That kind of misuse of clinical psychological tests is not strictly within the purview of this essay, but it does highlight some implications of research with tests and with data from psychotherapy.

When is privacy invaded? First, when an investigator asks directly about matters that the subject considers private and sensitive; and second, when he persuades the subject to provide seemingly neutral data from which he makes inferences about such private matters. "Private" here alludes to facts of which a person is ashamed, and to anything from events in his past to his secret fantasies that could cause him guilt, embarrassment, or anxiety if known to other people. It must also include, however, anything that could cause others to threaten or harm him in any way, as by bringing a suit against him, reporting him to the FBI, etc. Private data of this kind are unfortunately the life-blood of clinical psychology. We have a heavy obligation, therefore, to remain alert to the dangers of violating our subjects' confidences.

Obviously, being responsible in this way means not gossiping about subjects, not passing along psychologically interesting tidbits revealed by them even to colleagues without taking pains to conceal identities or protect the subjects in other ways. It means carefully planning a system of gathering and storing data with enough controls to make sure that they cannot fall into the hands of persons who might misuse them to the subjects' detriment, even if inadvertently. And of course it means being extremely circumspect about what is published. There is little problem in the traditional experimental report, which presents only quantitative data on groups in which no individual is named. Even when these are supplemented by direct quotations of subjects' remarks, so long as the latter are not intrinsically identifying and no names are used, no problems arise. But whenever there is the least chance that someone may recognize the subject of a case history, no matter how brief or disguised, the best practice is not to publish without first showing it to the subject and asking his permission.

Lovell (1967) presents an excellent approach to the use of psychological tests for research, which can be generalized to other kinds of data as well. The essence of it is to offer the subject a contract, which frankly states what is wanted of him and why, the use that the experimenter means to make of the data, and the measures he will take to protect the confidences he is inviting. In its direct frankness, lack of deviousness, and evident respect for the subject's feelings and individuality, it is an excellent example of the principle suggested above. For extending to another person a mature and responsible relationship is one of the best ways we know to encourage his personal growth.

AFTERWORD: ON THE SOCIOLOGY OF RESEARCH

In these pages, I have tried to press for high standards of investigative work while maintaining a realistic perspective. Perfectionism is often destructive, since it degrades the possible by contrasting it with the ideal. Without ideals, however, we cannot steer our way out of complacency and the status quo. Therefore, both pragmatism and idealism are parts of the scientific temper.

One aspect of realism is recognizing some of the reasons for persisting discrepancies between what is known to be good practice and what people keep on doing. Methodologists and other critics often make the point— about all the sciences, not just about clinical psychology—that the literature is filled with uninspired, mediocre work. One of the worst aspects of much that meets conventional standards of publishability is that it lacks a critical characteristic of good scientific work: cumulativeness. (Fiske *et al.*, 1970, point out some of the ways researchers can help insure that their work will cumulate—that is, add to the work of others so that a *field* advances, not just one man's career.) Researchers do not spend as much time in the library as they should, finding out what is known and has already been done on a topic before plunging in with a set of idiosyncratic measures of common concepts, or even with concepts that cut the pie of fact in trivially unique ways.

I put the criticism in that way deliberately to bring out the often unquestioned assumption that it is good to be original. Our culture as a whole, and surely the culture of science, does place a very high value on originality. Couple that with the competitiveness that is so endemic in America (and perhaps in "modern" culture generally), and you get a pressure on the person who wants to do research, a push in the direction of being different. Replicate someone else's research, when you might be making a name for yourself by staking out your own investigative claim? Use *A*'s concepts, or *B*'s definitions, or *C*'s technique? Maybe, if it will speed things up and help get out another publication, but it will be at the cost of (apparent) originality.

Perhaps even more conspicuous than the qualitative kind of competitiveness in our scientific culture is the quantitative. Otherwise put, it is the "publish or perish" phenomenon. To get ahead in any academic or scientific field, do more research or at least make your bibliography grow. Obedience to this maxim has been suggested many times as the probable cause of the triviality of so much of the scholarly literature.

If a person is interested in a topic—let us say achievement motivation— and if there exists or can be easily produced a quick and easy index of it, he knows that he can complete a study and get out a precious research publication in the time it would take him to get barely started on developing a truly valid measure. I do not wish to derogate the impressive research program of McClelland, Atkinson, and their co-workers, nor to suggest that the n Ach measure and others like it were quick and easy to develop; quite the contrary. Now that they are available, however, there seems to be little interest in developing better measures, even though it is evident that McClelland's thematic test score is more to be regarded as a predictor (or correlate) of achievement motivation than as a direct measure of it.

Here is my idealistic complaint, then: with all too few exceptions, psychologists use *available* measures of the constructs they are interested in studying (and, when several are available, prefer measures that are quick, easy, and cheap even if of doubtful validity), rather than asking what is the most direct and meaningful way to find out about the phenomena in question. It would be difficult, slow, and expensive to get to know each of your subjects well enough to find out how hard he really works; how much he is elated by actual successes and how much discouraged by meaningful failures (or indeed what the precise quality of his reactions to these experiences may be); how seriously he wants to attain high standards in his work, in his avocations, and in other major aspects of his life; and how distant are the goals for which he strives. To study achievement motivation in that way would not get you quick promotions in most departments of psychology; the probable outcome would be a long monograph, which would be hard to get published. Even if it did appear, it might not be widely reviewed, and if it did not come up with a technique others could adopt in the service of quick publications for themselves, it would not be likely to make you a big reputation.

And yet, when a major contribution to science is made, it does get recognized. A person does not win a Distinguished Scientific Contribution award from the American Psychological Association by the mere length of his publication list nor by the cumulative total of pages he has written—not even by the frequency with which his name is cited in the publications of his peers, though that does help. Such awards are made for cumulative, nontrivial work in which important problems are studied in appropriate (i.e., valid) ways.

My point is not just to exhort the young to cleave to high ideals and beware the bitch goddess, cheap success. I hope, rather, that it may be possible to make some moves toward modifying the aspects of our culture that seem to work against good quality of scientific work. The APA awards just alluded to were a useful social invention of a kind we need to encourage. The more we can do to reward scientists who take the hard, slow road, working persistently on problems of true scientific or social importance in ways that yield repeatable, theoretically or humanly useful knowledge, the better it will be for everyone. Hypotheses about the sociology of research can thereby be used in the service of actively changing conditions of our work which so far we have been observing passively, however much we may deplore them. As David Rapaport once remarked about the characteristic of being able to convert passively suffering something into actively coping with it, "That is the human miracle."

9

With a gulp, I recently realized that I have been refereeing articles for publications for 30 years. During much of that time, I have been put into or have assumed a variety of other roles that required that I evaluate research at various points: serving on study sections of the National Institute of Mental Health and private foundations that gave grants and research training fellowships; sponsoring and reading masters' and doctors' dissertations; reading manuscripts of books and monographs for publishers; serving on program committees for scientific meetings (sometimes chairing them), university committees charged with the financing of faculty research; reviewing published books for journals and book clubs; preparing integrative surveys of research literature; serving as an outside (and thus presumably disinterested) evaluator of faculty members up for promotion or tenure at other universities, as well as similar assessment of my colleagues, each such request being accompanied by a sheaf of reprints; and teaching the design and execution of research to graduate students of clinical psychology. All along the way, I have done a lot of consultation on research at different stages of its planning, sometimes in my role as Director of the Research Center for Mental Health (for almost 20 years), sometimes as a formally hired consultant, more often as a favor to friends and colleagues. In addition, a few times I have served on such committees as the American Psychological Association's Communications Board, charged with thinking about the association's policy concerning its publications, what kinds of new outlets are needed now and in the future, and how manuscripts are to be processed (see Holt, Chotlos, & Scheerer, 1953; Holt, 1971b). I have had the good fortune to work closely with a truly expert technical copy editor (Sue Annin, long in charge of working over manuscripts for Psychological Issues *and* Psychoanalysis and Contemporary Science*), and with a deep student of bibliographic problems in the behavioral sciences, the late Dr. Ilse Bry. I learned a great deal from both of them, as well as from other editors under whom I have worked over these decades, enough to have a lot of respect for the difficulty of doing a job that is at once fair to the struggling researcher and faithful to high scientific standards.*

I have not learned any neat formulas to be transmitted, no happy shortcuts or other insider's tricks of the trade that make a hard job easy. I have come to distrust profoundly the present trend toward increased mechanization of the task of storing and retrieving scientific information, and the mistaken belief of some that computers will be able to evaluate the literature also (Weizenbaum, 1976). The very fact that so many are giving up reliance on human judgment in face of the information explosion makes me feel that it is urgent to give the judge all the help we can. I feel an obligation, therefore, to try to communicate what I have learned, to help the many who must evaluate research despite the paucity of published guidance and despite the Zeitgeist of derogat-

ing value judgments in science (see Chapter 10) instead of accepting the challenge of improving them.

That was one reason for my decision a couple of years ago to offer a graduate course on the design and evaluation of clinical research. A second reason was the work I had done, largely inspired by Larry Kubie (see for examples his papers of 1954, 1964, and 1967), on planning for a new mental health profession centered on psychotherapeutic practice (Holt, 1963b, 1965e, 1969b, 1971d). If clinical psychologists are to continue to be trained to be research producers (as I have always advocated), the new profession of practitioners needs a new and different kind of emphasis in their graduate education. They need to become expert and sophisticated consumers of research, critical readers who learn to evaluate investigative work without having to undergo the long apprenticeship in its production that a Ph.D. should require. Paul Meehl (1971) proposed such a course, and I thought I ought to try my hand at teaching one to students who by and large were not planning to do more research than was required of them.

After having taught the course two years, I have learned a good deal more by trying to formulate the task of evaluating research and to communicate it, though I am not at all satisfied that I have found the best way of running such a class. I began by asking my graduate students to help me prepare a checklist of criteria for the practical guidance of someone who wants to appraise research of any kind in clinical psychology, psychiatry, or psychoanalysis. Then I assembled and integrated their separate lists, supplementing and expanding them but using as a framework the unusually complete and well-organized outline submitted by Judith Malamud, and fed it back to them. The second year, the students again worked over that product, applying it to the scrutiny of a number of published papers; with their help, I expanded and clarified the criteria. I want to acknowledge the work of Helen Levine and Irene Kaus, on whose thoughtful essays I have drawn for some of the introductory sections of the following paper.

No doubt it is somewhat premature to try to publish the checklist that follows. A few more years of trial by fire in the course would surely improve it. Several colleagues have assured me, however, that it serves a need even in this rather skeletal form. I invite feedback from you, the reader, and hope to continue this unfinished task, which perhaps can never be definitely completed.

Criteria for Evaluating Research in Psychology and Psychiatry

There is a sizable literature on how to do research in clinical psychology, but little on how to evaluate it. Surprisingly little, in light of the many occasions on which judgments have to be made about research projects and reports, from their inception to their publication and considerably thereafter. When an investigator gets an idea about a piece of work he would like to do, he relatively rarely is in a position simply to go ahead, plan it effectively, and put his plans into action. Almost universally now, he must at the least obtain the permission or approval of a committee in charge of protecting the rights of human subjects. If he is working in an institution, there are usually other clearances and concurrences to be arranged which entail judgments about the importance of the problem, the adequacy of the design, its feasibility under local circumstances, and the like—even if money is no problem. How seldom the latter is the case! Typically, the would-be investigator has to raise money to pay the costs of research by writing an application for a grant, contract, or other subvention, and such proposals need to be given careful evaluation, particularly in the current era of scanty funds in support of research.

Once enough money is in hand and he or she has obtained the necessary clearances and permissions—here let me take notice that it may have to come from a faculty committee overseeing the work of a student for an advanced degree—the investigator generally has a respite from evaluative scrutiny, sometimes even enough to get the work done. But when it is time to write it up, he/she must again begin to run an evaluative gauntlet. Most of us do well to get the help of a supervisor or colleague to read over our first drafts, appraising the project and its presentation once again. If the project is being carried out as a dissertation, the sponsor and the committee of readers have the responsibility to evaluate the work at various stages of near-completion, often in writing as well as in an oral examination. Sponsored research is very often evaluated by means of progress reports or site visits while it is being carried on (especially if the work goes on for more than one year), and further depends on the value judgments that are made.

If completed research is to be of much scientific value, it has to get into the mainstream of scientific communication, orally or in writing. Papers to be presented at scientific meetings have to pass the scrutiny of an evaluative committee. And of course, nothing gets published in whatever scientific medium without editorial scrutiny, which sometimes includes multiple refereeing.

When research is published, it begins a new series of evaluations. An academic's reprints may be critically read by colleagues and superiors when he is considered for employment, advancement, or tenure, or when he applies for a fellowship—even sometimes for further grants—and flaws in published research may hold him back, despite its quantity. Large projects are often published as books, which are evaluated by one's peers in professional and technical journals, some of which are exclusively devoted to book reviews. Not all published research gets into the major abstracting journals and similar keys to the literature, for many of them are more or less evaluative. But there are numerous more openly and thoroughly evaluative resource books and journals, which someone who wants to find the literature on a given topic is likely to use—for example, the critical surveys of research on a given topic in the *Psychological Bulletin,* or the *Annual Review* volumes, or the *Annual Survey of Psychoanalysis,* or various *Progress in . . .* annuals, or in one of the many available handbooks.

Anyone who has achieved even a modest degree of visibility as a contributor is likely to find himself suddenly put into the role of judge, called on to criticize, make recommendations about, or otherwise vote up or down the work of others. Some journals send referees brief guidelines, suggesting that they consider scientific importance, timeliness, appropriateness for the journal's audience, scientific merit, and clarity of writing. Sometimes there are more specific criteria, but by and large the referee is given little if any guidance. Moreover, she or he is likely to discover that nothing in the scientific training offered at graduate school bore directly on the task. It is generally assumed that if you have had courses in experimental design and statistics, and have published research yourself, you know what you need to know to do the job.

Conventional training covers only part of what the research evaluator needs, however. Many people who do good work themselves take too conservative a viewpoint when put in the position to judge others. They may become very perfectionistic, rejecting or otherwise disapproving of any study that does not seem flawless; or they may give excellent evaluations in their own speciality and particularly in the *kind* of research they themselves do, but look with disfavor on other designs, approaches, or problem areas. It not infrequently happens, for example, that members of study sections evaluating grant proposals and referees for journals are good laboratory experimenters who are at home with proposals or reports of research using classical experimental designs, but turn thumbs down on exploratory research, statistical investigations, or field studies that may be important, innovative, and worthwhile even though not up to the standards of rigor that prevail in more traditional areas.

But evaluating research is by no means the exclusive responsibility of professors, active investigators, some elite of "older, wiser heads," or a combination of these. Everyone in a science or profession has to be able to do it, if she or he is to be a self-respecting, growing person. Books and journals are written to be read by all of us. How can you consider yourself part of a discipline if you do not make some effort to keep up with what is happening—and in a disciplined, that is, critical, way? An educated reader is not credulous, which means that he or she evaluates constantly while reading. Even a practitioner who never plans to publish a thing should learn how to tell how much credence to put in the research she or he reads about.

PRELIMINARY ORIENTATION

Evaluation should be balanced. When you are called on to judge someone's work, that does not mean that you are to accentuate either the positive or the negative. "Don't knock if you can't boost" is perhaps a nice slogan for some kinds of conventional interpersonal relations, but it has no place here. Nor should you succumb to the common temptation to assume that being critical means looking only for weaknesses and deficiencies you can criticize. Try at all times to notice and weigh both assets and liabilities, balancing them out in terms of their relative importance, and arriving at an overall judgment. The criteria in the accompanying checklist are, perhaps unfortunately, cast largely in terms of possible flaws, but consider the countervailing merits and strengths in each case.

Control your hostility. No matter how bad the proposed or completed research, do not criticize *ad hominem,* or with unnecessary sarcasm, insults, or other forms of anger which will probably be so wounding or infuriating as to be counterproductive. Criticism can and should be productive, not destructive.

When possible, be constructive. Frequently, when research is being evaluated in its early stages, it can still be influenced for the better. If your role does not explicitly rule it out, do not confine yourself to critique, but also make realistic suggestions for the improvement of the research, within the framework of the investigator's intentions, resources, and limitations. Conceivably, a given researcher should not try to work on a specific problem with the limitations under which (s)he must work, so the kindest and most helpful thing you can do in the long run is to persuade him/her to turn to something more appropriate and manageable. Usually, however, it is better to give people the benefit of the doubt and help them find a way to improve a study rather than to abandon it. Do not call for additional controls or neglected niceties that might have improved a study but were not necessary (certainly not for aspects of design that are actually *irrelevant* to the nature of the study).

Stick to the task. Do not speculate about researchers' intentions or motives for what they propose or did and how. Do not seize the opportunity to show off your own knowledge, refer unnecessarily to your own work, or otherwise blow your own horn instead of getting the job done. If the time for constructive suggestions is past, an evaluation is ordinarily an inappropriate place to set forth an elaborate alternative design.

Keep your eye on the main chance. In the end, many evaluations must come down to a final Yes or No decision. Should this person get the grant? Should the paper or book be published or not? Here is where judiciousness and a sense of perspective are particularly needed. The work, proposed or completed, has to be considered within a frame of practical and realistic considerations. For example, a struggling journal is under external pressure to fill its covers and meet its deadlines, even if that means accepting work of a lower quality than should ideally be published. A ground-breaking, stimulating project in a neglected area can be worthwhile despite many faults. The amount of money to be awarded in grants, fellowships, contracts or the like may vary greatly, so that selection ratios may go from high to low. Even if we see again golden days like those of the 1950s and early 1960s, when Congress pressed money on the National Institutes of Health faster than they could find researchers to give it to, it will probably never be socially constructive to approve some proposals, for research can be so badly planned that it is sure to yield misleading results. It may happen when a university committee is considering the use of small amounts of money for faculty research that a relatively weak project should be funded over a strong one, because the former is the first effort of a young person struggling to get started and the latter has been submitted by an established and generally well-funded investigator, to whom rejection will mean little. In any event, when coming to your final decision, pay special attention to the relative seriousness or importance of the various criteria, for they differ greatly in the extent to which they concern crucial or merely desirable features. Remember that some historically important research has had serious deficiencies, which did not matter as much as the fact that something new was discovered, or a path was opened up through which others could subsequently go much further. No research project can attain the ideal; and no single study should be expected to settle all questions. Beware of perfectionism and sloppy standards alike!

Watch out for values. In general, be vigilant about the intrusion of values into research and its reporting at every point, from the conception of the study through its execution to its publication. In most cases, the values concerned will be commonly accepted ones in science, but only by the careful scrutiny of the research at all stages is it possible to note the insidious intrusion of less-than-laudable values and their effects on the research, on those involved, or on its application. Watch out for your own values, too; remember, for example, that an author's interpretation is not invalidated by the fact you do not like it and can think of other (obviously, better!) interpretations. At the extreme, if you feel you cannot control your own value-reactions enough to evaluate the research fairly, you should refrain from doing so at all. (See also Chapter 10.)

Some special considerations in particular evaluative contexts. The doctoral dissertation: Be mindful of the special limitations on what a single, beginning investigator can accomplish in such a difficult area as ours. But insist that the student do as good a job as possible within those limits. In the long run, being held to high standards may be more important to the development of a good professional than being able to get through quickly and land a particular job or the like.

The research proposal: Naturally, the decisive role will be played by criteria grouped under the checklist's first eight headings and the last, for it was designed primarily to guide the assessment of completed (published) research. Do not be over-impressed with meticulous thoroughness in planning if the investigator does not seem to have a sure grasp of the practical realities of research. In particular, beware of the grandiose proposal-writer who seems to have thought of all sources of error and to have set up elaborate plans to cope with them—will he really be able to follow through? A highly complex and sophisticated design is fine if there are experienced and flexible people available to carry it out, but may even be a liability if those who are to put it into effect have no relevant experience and do not know what they are getting into.

The unpublished journal article or monograph: Originality, timeliness, and suitability to the outlet's mission and audience will all bear on a manuscript's acceptability. A referee is not ordinarily expected to give much weight to matters of format (e.g., are the references done in the journal's style? are there illustrations or charts of a kind the journal cannot easily include? Is the organization congruent with the journal's policies and preferences?) but editors are and must be influenced by them. And it should not be necessary to add, but perhaps is, that basic standards of clear and correct writing, of logic, and of common sense should be met in a research report— as in any other scientific publication.

The published paper: Remember that published research has been subjected to a given editor's standards and the exigencies of a given medium, which may have forced the omission of many details you wish you knew. Journals are generally hard-pressed for space, and editors often require the deletion of parts of a paper that are well done and desirable in themselves though not vital, such as a thorough review of preceding work. How ironically unfair to an author it would seem if you downrated him because his paper left out something he had pleaded with an editor to let him keep! When you are surveying an area of research, be careful not to discard without further consideration reports of research with serious flaws in design, analysis, or reporting; even though you might justifiably have rejected such work if you had been refereeing it for publication, it may still contain valid and usable findings which take on particular value in the context of other people's data. The author may be quite wrong in reaching his preferred conclusion because of having omitted some crucial control, yet his data may be read a different way and make an unintended contribution.

Finally, in evaluating research keep in mind human frailty, the probabilistic nature of all findings, the restrictions imposed by limited resources of time, money, and personnel, and the fact that even when a study has been so badly designed that its results are completely moot and uninterpretable, it may still be worth the paper to publish it because it asks a new question, opening up a fresh area of investigation, or dares to risk errors which others may learn from it how to avoid. The important thing, in the long run, is whether a study makes some contribution to the scientific process. If it can infect others with enthusiasm and curiosity, if it encourages an open-minded and innovative approach to ideas and experience, if it helps readers get on with their own independent, creative thinking and work, it has more value than many a competent but utterly humdrum, safe application of standard methods to well-worn problems.

CHECKLIST OF CRITERIA FOR EVALUATING PSYCHOLOGICAL RESEARCH

I. The objectives of the research; the problem or question.
   A. It is *Desirable* to know the underlying objectives of the researcher(s) and those who funded the work, as well as the immediate purpose behind it. They should be stated clearly, succinctly, and early in the report. (Often all this is left implicit, and it can hardly be made a major criterion. Note that researchers often tend to be much clearer about the specific question they are asking than about why they chose this research strategy.)
   B. Importance of the problem (*Essential* that good research be important in one of these senses).
      1. It is relevant to major human problems? (versus focused on minor, trivial issues. For an attempt to scale the importance of problems, see Platt, 1969.)
      2. Does it have any foreseeable applicability? (If so, it may be socially useful, even if not relevant to the crises of our time.)
      3. Is it relevant to a theory of some present or potential importance (regardless of one's personal agreement with the theory)?
         The issue of importance is especially relevant when you are reviewing research proposals for financial support or a completed report for publication, or an author's output in an evaluation of him for hiring, promotion, membership in a professional organization, honors, etc.
   C. Originality of the research. The work should ordinarily have some element of novelty or ingenuity—in the problem, the design or approach, the methods used, etc. (*Desirable*). Nevertheless, there is a great need for competently performed attempts to replicate important investigations, the findings of which are not securely established.
   D. Formulation of the research question—the specific focus or topic. (The following are all *Highly Desirable.*) The question should be:
      1. Clearly stated (as opposed to being implicit, vaguely or confusingly formulated).

2. Relevant to and following logically from the general problem and objectives.

3. Testable (if the research is empirical), and formulated in such a way that efforts to answer it could provide a maximum of useful information.

4. Ideally, it should take into account the multivariate, interactive, systemic nature of behavior in real life. Thus, the researcher should be aware of the possible relevance of variables on many levels of analysis, including the somatic-physiological, interpersonal, unconscious, conscious, institutional, historical, cultural, social, and physical-environmental, and should realize the diversity of individuals in most of these respects. Is the research directed at the appropriate systemic level, where order may be expected, or at too analytical (microscopic, molecular) a level, where effects will probably be weak at best (Weiss, 1973)?

II. Theoretical issues.

A. If there is relevant theory, ideally it should be explicitly discussed—all of it. (Conversely, irrelevant theory should not be discussed.) Note, however, that a problem may be essentially applied or practical and not much theory may be clearly relevant. *(Desirable)*

B. In a review of theoretical background, the coverage of theorists should be as complete as possible, taking into account the historical development of any theorist's thought, faithful to the spirit of the original, and respecting its embeddedness in the work of others and in a general intellectual milieu. *(Desirable)*

C. All important theoretical issues generally assumed to be involved in the topic should be given adequate review and discussion; or else the reader should be referred to an acceptable treatment of the issues in another published source. *(Highly Desirable)*

D. Sometimes, despite extensive discussion of theory (and often, when theory is neglected), an author leaves important theoretical assumptions quite implicit. The evaluator should always be on the lookout for hidden assumptions, therefore, especially when they slant or limit the discussion or conclusions. Just the stating of an assumption is often insufficient to bring out its impact on the study, something authors generally find it difficult to think through.

(Do not, however, be particularly concerned with "average expectable" assumptions, like the limitation of the study to contemporary United States culture, or the assumption that subjects tell the truth.)

E. Terms and definitions: All terms should be defined *except* when it can be assumed that the target audience understands them and shares the author's meaning. Where possible, terms should have both theoretical and operational definitions. *(Desirable)*

   (Some authors err in the direction of tedious, needless detail in defining the obvious and conventional. A special burden is on an author who proposes a *new* definition of a common term, to show that there are good reasons for it and to be consistent.)

F. Theoretical orientation of authors and of others involved in the research should be given when relevant, or not obvious. *(Desirable)*

G. Where the problem or the evidence generated have a bearing on philosophical, ethical/moral, religious, or social policy issues, these may be discussed, but should be clearly and sharply separated from empirical issues. Authors should be especially careful about the logic of inference if they believe that their data have implications for such heavily value-laden matters. *(Highly Desirable)*

III. Bibliographic issues: the review of literature.

A. A review of previous work on the topic should be included, unless there is good reason not to. *(Highly Desirable)*

   (Ordinarily, the only good reason is lack of any such work; but editorial policy, especially for brief reports, may severely restrict it.)

B. The first major criterion of a good review is that it should be appropriate in size *(Desirable)*, taking into account

   1. The focus of the study (primarily bibliographic, or theoretical, or empirical). If bibliographic, the way the search was conducted should be described *(Highly Desirable)*.

   2. The limitations of the publication medium (from book to one-page note).

   3. The size of the existing literature and the number of years it goes back (which may militate against comprehensiveness).

   4. The author's resources.

C. The second criterion is that the review should stake out a clearly delimited area *(Desirable)* and cover it comprehensively but selectively and faithfully *(Essential)*.

   (Almost any topic can ramify endlessly, and needlessly. And there is no value to including merely for completeness work that is so clearly inferior in quality that nothing can be learned from it. Selectivity should be in terms of scientific merit or some other kind of usefulness, not the author's preferences. Particular works may have irrelevant aspects which should be omitted.)

D.   The third criterion is that the review should be *analytic and critical,* evaluating previous work as well as collecting and reporting it. *(Highly Desirable)*

E.   Finally, the review should be *synthetic:* it should not merely report separate studies, but add them up, bring out their mutual implications, relate theory to empirical findings, and point up unresolved issues, gaps in knowledge, need for reformulation of issues, etc. It should be carefully organized and structured in a logical (not necessarily chronological) sequence, so that it builds and develops instead of merely plodding from one abstract to another. *(Highly Desirable)*

F.   If the review is a preliminary to empirical research, it should be *integrated* with the rest of the study: the immediate problem should be related to previous work, and usually there should be some reference back to the results of the review in the discussion of the findings. *(Highly Desirable)*

G.   In general, reviews may use secondary sources, but mainly as a way of finding primary sources, which should be the main focus. *(Desirable)*

H.   Allusions (explicit or implicit) to the work of others should ordinarily be accompanied by full referencing following such a standard format as that of the APA Publication Manual. Allegations of fact, where not documented by the research being presented, should be specifically attributed to an accessible public source. *(Desirable)*

IV.   Hypotheses or predictions (if any; there is no need for every research to try to test prior propositions).

A.   Hypotheses should follow logically from the issues and problems as stated. *(Essential)*

B.   Ideally, they should be clearly derived from a specific theory. *(Desirable)*

Note, however, that given the nature of most theories in psychology today, really rigorous hypothetic-deductive method is impossible. Nevertheless, hypotheses can be related to theories relatively clearly and directly *(Highly Desirable)* or only vaguely and loosely, or take off from empirical generalizations presented as theory. Such propositions might better be consistently called predictions when not tightly derived from theory.

C.   Since (according to the above-suggested usage) hypotheses are stated in terms of general constructs, they need to be translated into specific predictions stated in terms of the measurements that operationally define those constructs in the study—especially if there are multiple measures (e.g., several test scores as dependent variables). *(Desirable)*

D.   If not theoretically derived, the basis for predictions should be stated explicitly. *(Highly Desirable)*

(E.g., previous research findings, clinical tradition, case studies, informal observations, social needs.)

It is often desirable for a prediction to be followed by an explicit *rationale*, which may be theoretical, empirical, or both.

E.   Sometimes it is desirable for the sake of clarity that hypotheses or predictions be stated in null and alternative forms.

(E.g., H_0—There is no relationship between A and B; H_1—There is a positive correlation between A and B; H_2—There is a negative correlation between A and B.)

F.   Hypotheses or predictions should be tightly related to the design so that the latter provides tests of each such proposition. *(Essential)* (See V.C below.)

V.   Design. Note that almost any empirical research can be considered from the standpoint of its design—the way it is organized to yield new knowledge—not just experiments of classical types.

A.   Any research should have some planned, structured set of methods and procedures to provide data and ways of analyzing them so as to yield definite and trustworthy conclusions. Some discussion of design in this sense is *Highly Desirable*, even though it is often omitted in exploratory clinical research.

Ideally, the design (including all details of procedure, situation, subjects, measuring instruments, etc.) should be explicit and detailed enough to allow the study to be replicated by someone else.

B.   The design should be appropriate to the nature of the problem, the status of investigation in the area concerned (amount and sophistication of knowledge and method), the type of subjects, etc. *(Essential)*

C.   The design should be logically related to the problem as stated, providing data that will answer the investigator's questions. *(Essential)* (See IV.B and F above.)

1.   It should be clear in case of each control against what threat to validity it is directed. *(Desirable; need not usually be explicit)*

A common error is to attempt to control certain conventional demographic factors like age and sex, *whether or not* they are relevant to the problem or the variable being assessed. Another is to choose a control group or treatment group by what is convenient, not what is relevant to the problem. Thus, it accomplishes little to show that a diagnostic instrument differentiates schizophrenics from normals— not usually the differential diagnostic issue!

2. A touchstone for the adequacy of a design is to ask: would negative findings have been meaningful (interpretable)?

D. Control, and the issue of guarding against spurious or artifactual results. Controls are safeguards against threats to internal and external validity. Campbell (1957, 1969; Campbell & Stanley, 1966) has listed and described about a score of experimental and quasi-experimental designs; it is a pretty comprehensive job and will not be repeated here. The evaluator should be thoroughly familiar with these standard designs, their strengths and weaknesses, to be on the lookout for errors against which a design does not guard.

1. Above all, control is not an all or none issue! Some progress toward control can always be made, even in exploratory research, clinical case studies, field research, social reforms as experiments, etc. Judge by the appropriateness of the effort to the realistic difficulties of the problem.

E. Some common sources of error[1] (spurious or misleading results, preventing which is at least *Desirable* unless otherwise specified):

1. Biasing values of the researcher ("Rosenthal effect"); it takes a double-blind design to control it (often *Desirable* but *not* always).

2. Criterion contamination: influence of knowledge of the independent variable (outcome), or something correlated with it, on analyses of the data. (Preventing it is *Essential.*)

3. Confounding of variables: lack of independence between groups or measurements when the design calls for it, or where statistics assume it. (Preventing it is *Essential.*)

Various kinds of experimental designs, like crossover or Latin-square designs, aim at preventing confounding of treatments with sequences, when subjects are their own controls—more than one treatment per subject.

4. In descriptive research, failure to sample subjects or objects randomly; in experimental research, failure to assign subjects to treatments randomly. The nature of the random method should also be specified (e.g., by use of a table of random numbers).

5. Inadequate sampling of situations or objects ("stimuli"; measures of independent and dependent variables); failure to provide adequate information about them; use of conditions assumed to be different without independent demonstration that they are, or that the independent variables have been manipulated in an experimental design. (Preventing these is *Highly Desirable.*)

[1]See also Table 8.1, above.

6. Look out for overcontrol as well as undercontrol of spurious effects. Too zealous an attempt at control, ending in the isolating of a single "cause" and "effect," may bring about the loss of the appropriate systemic level and generalizability.

   Note: An ideal way to proceed in planning, and a possible way in evaluating research, is to draw up an idealized research design first, sufficient to answer your questions as well as possible, and then modify it or note deviations from it step by step, in light of practicalities; see Ackoff (1953).

7. Failure to recognize statistical regression to the mean, or to control for it.

8. Negative findings sometimes occur because the design (e.g., the manipulation or variation of independent variables) does not give the expected effect or phenomenon an adequate opportunity to develop.

9. Matching instead of random assignment of subjects to groups.

10. Inadequate power to detect effects of the size to be expected.

11. Failure to communicate a uniform *understanding* of what one means to subjects, who approach a research project from different backgrounds, with different structural characteristics, and otherwise are different in their capacity to experience the situation and its components in the uniform or systematically different ways the researcher intends. For example, using the same *words* with different people may yield different understandings. (See also X.D.2, below.)

F. If threats to validity are not experimentally controlled, they can be more or less effectively controlled statistically (e.g., partial correlation, analysis of covariance, MRA); at least, they should be described and their effects estimated if not measured. (*Highly Desirable*)

VI. Methods of gathering data: instruments and measurement issues (see also IX, below).

A. Where possible and appropriate, variables should be measured; but in many kinds of clinical research the principal data are qualitative meanings—verbal, presentational, graphic, or behavioral. Quantitative measurement should be used no more and no less than is appropriate. Nevertheless, qualitative judgments can and should be tested for intersubjective agreement or judge reliability. (*Highly Desirable*)

1. Qualitative data should be gathered in as objective and repeatable a manner as possible. The way such data as clinical observations, anamneses, life histories, dreams, or fantasies were gathered should be specified, and the methods should be such as to capture and preserve the subjects' words, drawings, gestures, etc., accurately and independently from other data (see V.E.3, above). *(Essential)*

2. Data of whatever kind should be as adequate as possible for assessing the constructs of interest *(Essential)*. This implies that methods of gathering data should ideally be of demonstrated validity, and the sample of behavior on which assessments are based should be large enough and representative enough (see B.2.a, below).

B. Issues in quantitative measurement.

1. Some variables (e.g., sex) are best treated as dichotomies, others as continuous quantitative variables, others as typologies or developmental stages (e.g., "milestones" of intellectual, moral, or ego development). In general, the kind of measurement should be chosen that best respects the nature of the data and preserves as much of the information in the data as possible. *(Highly Desirable)*

2. Variables should be measured with appropriate degrees of precision *(Highly Desirable)*, neither too grossly (as is often the case with rating scales) nor over precisely, nor (worst) with pseudoprecision. An important determinant of the appropriate degree of precision is the nature of other measurements in the same study; ordinarily, if one variable cannot be measured precisely, it matters little to expend great effort in attaining great precision on one to be related to it.

   a. The most important determinant of the precision of measurement is the number of indicants of the construct in question. The validity of measurement in most areas of psychology is so approximate that it is dangerous to use a single test to measure a given construct—in factor-analytic terms, there is usually too much item-specific variance and not enough saturation with the factor you want to measure. The unwanted, specific variances tend to cancel out when you add together the scores from several tests, leaving the emphasis on what they have in common (presumably the construct being measured).

   b. A common error is the attempt to measure change by means of instruments (e.g., some scales of the MMPI) that are insensitive to change, or by means of intrinsically unstable, unreliable indicators that are oversensitive to change (e.g., GSR deflections as a measure of anxiety).

3. For each measuring instrument used in a study, the following information should be provided:

   a. What is its origin? How can someone else who wants to use it get hold of it? *(Desirable)*

   b. What is the validity of each score actually used? What evidence is there that a score measures what it purports to? *(Highly Desirable)*

   c. For each score actually used, what is its reliability, in terms of internal consistency, stability over time, and the ability of different users to get the same results? *(Highly Desirable)*

      Reliability is a multifaceted matter, and there are many measures in use, some more appropriate for a given study than others. The particular measures used must be specified. A common failing is to report reliability of an unspecified kind for a score not used in the research at hand. Inclusion of the significance (p-value) of reliability coefficients suggests a failure to grasp the nature of reliability.

   d. What is its age? When was it last standardized? Cultural meanings change, and the content of many kinds of tests (semantic or pictorial) gets out of date rapidly; or the level of the relevant construct in the target population may change. *(Desirable)*

   e. What are the known problems in using this particular instrument (or the general type to which it belongs), and are they taken into account? *(Desirable)*

   f. It should be adequately described so that the reader has a clear idea of what the variables mean. *(Essential)*

4. Whether or not all the above information is given, a study may be defective if the *best available* instruments have not been used. *(Highly Desirable)*

5. Where observers are used to gather data according to the investigator's specifications, or where judges (including subjects themselves) provide quantitative data in the form of ratings, they should be generally qualified and specifically *trained* to a satisfactory level of interjudge agreement. *(Highly Desirable)* If the full details of the observational or rating scheme cannot be given, it should be possible for the

interested reader to get them in some specified way. The degree of inference or judgment required should be made clear. *(Desirable)*

6. Investigators too often uncritically accept and use popular or easily available tests and measures, without considering whether their own problems may not call for a new approach. Do the measures used go after the constructs at issue—the appropriate aspects of clinical reality—as directly as possible? *(Highly Desirable)*

7. A related point: psychologists in particular have a tendency to be overimpressed by measuring methods that are subtle, complicated, indirect, or nonobvious. Yet a good deal of research shows that it often works best to ask a person quite directly what you want to know. Be wary of findings based on indirect methods alone, as well as those that naively trust subjects as ultimate authorities about themselves.

C. Instruments should be used in the standard, intended ways, so that results are comparable with those of other experiments and are representative of what the instrument is supposed to do. *(Highly Desirable)*

VII. Subjects

A. Number of subjects. It should be sufficient so that the investigator can detect effects of a size appropriate to the nature of the problem. *(Highly Desirable)* (E.g., there is too severe a risk of a Type II error in a study of the effects of subliminal stimuli, which are likely to be small, with a sample large enough to detect only large effects.) A rational basis for deciding how large samples need to be is given by Cohen (1969). *(Highly Desirable)*

B. Sampling method

1. In a descriptive study, where it is important to generalize to a given target population, a satisfactorily random method must be used, and described in the report, as must the target population. *(Highly Desirable)*

2. Generalizability of findings in *any* kind of research depends on sampling considerations, and though a random sample of a specifiable population is theoretically always desirable, it is unreasonable to require it most of the time. The method by which subjects were selected, from how large a group and of what kind, should be given, however. *(Highly Desirable)* It is usually *Desirable* to specify the judge reliability of the selection process, which often involves clinical judgments.

C. Description of subjects used. Especially important when criterion B.1., above, has not been met.

1. Generally useful demographic data on subjects (including ethnicity) should ordinarily be supplied. (At least *Desirable*)

2. Other descriptive characteristics that might have a bearing on the results should also be given, for the sample as a whole and for different treatment groups. *(Highly Desirable)* In research with clinical groups, it is especially important—and often neglected—to give diagnostic information about subjects, according to some specified scheme.

3. Samples and subsamples should be described by appropriate measures of central tendency and dispersion (e.g., mean, variance, and range). *(Highly Desirable)*

VIII. Sampling of "objects": all other realms of persons, things, situations, etc., to which the investigator wants to generalize.

   A. Ideally, each such realm should be sampled as in VII.B, above. In practice, however, so few researchers are aware of Brunswik's (1956) point that one cannot be harsh in applying this criterion. Doing research this way is also very hard! *(Desirable)*

   1. In a study of psychotherapy outcome, for example, there may be not only patients to be sampled but therapists, therapeutic techniques, supervisors, treatment settings, types of behavior relevant to outcome, and criterion judges. It is *Highly Desirable* that they be carefully described—ideally, systematically sampled also—because one wants to generalize about them.

   B. All "objects" should be fully described in relevant ways, as in VII.C. *(Desirable)*

   C. Limitations on the generalizability of data obtained with inadequate sampling of objects should be stated. *(Desirable)*

IX. Analysis of data.

   A. Qualitative. In addition to the applicable aspects of VI.A, above:

   1. Research often involves many judgmental decisions about data that are made with no realization that they might be done differently, or that they might introduce bias. It is easy to overlook such deficiencies if the investigator does a good job of checking the reliability of other, more obvious kinds of judgments. (E.g., Rorschach research rarely gives any data on who divided protocols into responses or how reliably the task was done. There is lots of room for disagreement there!) In any event, the reader should be given a clear conception of how the qualitative analysis was done. *(Essential)*

   2. Judges or coders should be trained to a satisfactory level of agreement (interjudge reliability) on comparable materials, before they begin work on critical data. *(Highly Desirable)*

   3. Where large bodies of data are subjected to content analysis, using either categorical coding or rating scales, measures must be taken (and described) to keep constant check on

judge reliability and to maintain it at a satisfactory level, to guard against "drift," for example—systematic changes over time in judgmental standards. *(Desirable)*

4. When judgments are not very highly reliable, it is important that judges be guarded not only against criterion contamination *(Essential)* but against influence by the researcher's hypotheses or hopes (see X.D.1), as by a "double-blind" design. *(Desirable)*

B. Quantitative (statistics).[2]

1. Methods of reducing quantitative data as well as statistically processing them should be described (e.g., how are indices formed from raw scores?). *(Desirable)*

2. Statistical methods should be the most appropriate ones available *(Highly Desirable)*, in terms of
   a. Nature of the data, precision of measurement balanced against power of statistics to extract information.
   b. Size of sample (power).
   c. Assumptions made by various statistics and their robustness to assumptive failure (Cohen, 1965).
   Tests of these assumptions are *Highly Desirable*.

3. Nonlinear effects, when plausible, should be explored. *(Desirable)*

4. Interactions among variables should be considered and measured as far as possible, even when not called for explicitly by the design. *(Desirable)*

5. Researchers should be alert to possibility that subgroups of a sample (e.g., by sex) may react differently and should be analyzed separately. *(Desirable)*

6. Researchers should state their decision rules (e.g., alpha level; *Desirable*) and stick to them, appropriately balancing Type I and Type II errors. Nonfindings by these rules should *not* be discussed. *(Highly Desirable)*

   (If the author uses one-tailed tests, it is *Highly Desirable* for him to be explicit about it, but even better if he explicitly adopts a lower-than-conventional alpha level, instead. In general, there is no need to state that one is using the .05 level with two-tailed tests. It is a common fault to be more concerned about Type I errors—falsely rejecting the null hypotheses—than Type II errors—falsely concluding that an effect does not exist.)

7. Ideally, data should be given in enough detail so that the reader can try alternate statistical methods on them *(Desira-*

[2]This section is not comprehensive; see any good statistics text.

ble but rarely possible in practice except in dissertations or monographs).

8. Results should be given with an emphasis on (or at least a clear characterization of) *effect size*. It is generally agreed by statisticians to be much more important than "significance," the probability of a nonnull finding. Means and standard deviations of principal scores for all groups, for example, are essential for the full understanding of what the experimenter found and for further analysis of his data by others; just knowing that a difference or a relationship was significant says little.

X. Execution of the design

A. Was the research carried out accurately in accord with its own plan and stated principles? *(Essential)* For example:
   1. Accurate assignment to groups.
   2. Accuracy in reducing and combining data.
   3. Accurate use of statistics.

B. When it was not possible to execute the design with complete fidelity, were mishaps handled skillfully? *(Highly Desirable)*
   1. Were they recorded and reported?
   2. Were spoiled data discarded or used in appropriate ways? (When subjects drop out early, foul up only some parts of a study, or the like, it is generally *Desirable* to use the parts of their data that are available and valid.)
   3. What is the impact of mishaps on overall validity of findings?
   4. Where it was not possible to equate all groups on measurable aspects of the way they were treated (or in any other way they were supposed to be the same), an effort should be made after the fact to analyze the data for possible artifacts *before* the main effects are tested. Partial confounding (or contamination) of results should be explicitly pointed out and the reader should be warned what dangers of misinterpretation to guard against.

C. Were fortunate chance occurrences (serendipity) taken advantage of? *(Desirable)*
   1. Researchers should be flexible in switching to different methods of analyzing data from those originally planned, when that makes possible capitalizing on unexpected opportunities to observe interesting phenomena.
   2. Surprising occurrences may be used to generate new hypotheses.

D. Was an attempt made to find out (in case of an experiment, particularly) what the subjects believed was going on, what they thought the hypotheses were, how far the manipulation of independent variables succeeded, etc.? (always *Desirable;* sometimes *Essential*)

    1. Where the design does not guard against "experimenter effects," "demand characteristics," or "the Rosenthal phenomenon," there should be an effort to show that no such spurious effects occurred.

    2. In any event, most research that uses any "manipulation" or presents subjects with objects in Brunswik's sense makes the assumption that subjects understand these stimuli or press in a uniform way essentially as the investigator does. Research on cognitive syles and on the cultural relativity of meanings should warn us that people perceive and conceive the same objective situation or presentation in subtly and heterogenously variegated ways. Unless a researcher verifies that the meanings he *thinks* he conveyed to his subjects were actually received, his findings are moot (see V.E.11, above).

XI.   Results

    A. They should be clearly and comprehensively stated, but without unnecessary detail. *(Highly Desirable)*

    B. Where tables or graphs are used, the text should not restate the figures but discuss and explain them or translate them into words. *(Desirable)*

    C. Quantitative findings should not be presented with more apparent precision than size of sample and nature of measurement allow. (E.g., when N is under 1000, the third decimal place of a correlation coefficient is negligible, and it is *never* psychologically meaningful.) *(Desirable)*

    D. If hypotheses have been made, they must be tested and a decision to accept or reject clearly made according to decision rules that have been adopted. *(Highly Desirable)*

    E. The statistics used should be appropriate to the nature of the data, the number of cases, the kinds of hypotheses to be tested, and the level of statistical sophistication of the audience. If the otherwise requisite statistic is not generally known, it should be explained clearly enough to make the findings intelligible. *(Highly Desirable)*

XII. Interpretation (generalizations, conclusions, implications)

    A. Conclusions should be distinguished from implications according to the degree of inference involved (*Desirable,* though one cannot expect exactly that terminology to be used; see Holt, 1973a [Chapter 22]).

    B. Conclusions and other interpretations should be explicitly limited by sampling constraints on subjects and objects, or should be more generally restrained. *(Highly Desirable)*

(E.g., note difference between "Women surpass men in empathy" and "The female subjects surpassed the males on the experimental measure of empathy used here.")

C. Results when discussed should not be distorted, positive findings overemphasized and negative findings underplayed or ignored. *(Essential)*

D. Discussion should serve a synthetic function, referring back to opening summaries of literature and the state of the field, and to specific hypotheses, if any, also relating findings to those of other investigators. *(Highly Desirable)*

   1. Specifically, it should attempt to provide a logical and meaningful explanation for both expected and unexpected findings, positive and negative alike.

   2. More generally, it should place the findings in a larger interpretive context, often bringing in findings and principles from other areas or even other disciplines and pointing to implications of findings for theory, for future research, and for practical application.

E. It is *Desirable* that alternative explanations of findings[3] be considered and weighed as objectively as possible, and, if it is likely that readers will make misinterpretations, they should be explicitly considered and their falseness demonstrated.

This last point implies that a researcher has a duty to give careful consideration to views opposed to his own, and to be aware of controversies and emotionally involving issues to which his work may be seen as relevant, keeping in mind the fact that the judgment of the most intelligent people is clouded by strong affect, and thus guarding against the misuse of his findings. *(Highly Desirable)*

F. It is *Highly Desirable* to make a clear separation between hypotheses, data, and interpretations, which are typically best presented in that order to preserve such segregation in the reader's mind. Authors should avoid mixing together conclusions, new data, speculations or recommendations (especially those involving policies), and further analyses or adduction of new arguments and evidence.

G. Some miscellaneous interpretive caveats *(Highly Desirable)*:

   1. Authors should not be overcautious, refusing to generalize at all.

   2. Correlation should not be confused with cause.

   3. Systemic, interactive interpretations are to be preferred to

---

[3]Also, alternative interpretations of such other aspects of the research as the effects of attempts to manipulate the independent variables, or the meaning to subjects of the various measures used.

simple, mechanistic ones implying summation of independent effects. (Controversial, but I believe it *Desirable*)

4. Statistical significance should not be confused with substantive significance.

   a. A common error is to overinterpret slight trends in the data, losing sight of the fact that only major effects tend to survive cross-validation in psychology, and even then they may disappear or even reverse themselves. Beware of exaggerated claims for findings that are actually small even when reliable.

5. Deficiencies of the design and thus the possible effect of unwanted variables should be explicitly referred to in the discussion, taking account of threats to external validity.

6. Beware of logical errors (e.g., non sequiturs) in going from an actual finding to its generalized formulation. *(Essential)*

XIII. Some *Desirable* considerations of format, style, etc.

A. The title should be informative, giving the central topic or point of the work succinctly and accurately, *not* suggesting a much broader area or relevance than the work possesses.

B. Authorship. If more than one person participated, all who made any but routine paid contributions of a subprofessional sort should be, at the least, named and thanked or their contribution explicitly acknowledged. It is hard to lay down rules about authorship, but by and large the senior author among more than one should be the person who did most of the work or the one whose *intellectual* (*not* his administrative) contribution was most important.

C. The abstract should accurately summarize the salient points of the work, and the tone of the conclusions.

D. The writing in the report should be clear, comprehensive, logical, not too laden with jargon or too elliptical (assuming the reader knows more than can be expected.)

1. The style should be straightforward, neither pretentious and pompous nor inappropriately colloquial, slangy, jocular, or folksy. The nature of the intended audience or readership determines the appropriate tone and level of technicality, but remember that simplicity and readability are always desirable. The hallmark of good writing is that it never obtrudes itself: scientific prose should be an invisible medium of communication through which information flows readily and with a minimum of noise.

2. Wherever possible, the mood should be active rather than passive, so the reader can easily tell who did what to whom, who made the decisions, gathered and processed data, etc.

3. There should be just enough redundancy for easy communication and *no more.*
4. Figurative language (e.g., metaphor) should be used sparingly, and avoided as much as possible in theoretical exposition where it all too easily conceals unclarity of thought and inexactness of reference.

E. The total procedure should be well enough described to make it possible for a reader to replicate the study in all essential respects.

XIV. Ethical considerations

A. Throughout, the evaluator needs to be alert to any evidences of intellectual dishonesty or any infractions of the APA Code of Ethics. If the basic honesty and credibility of the investigator cannot be assumed, the work is worthless. If the work will involve or has involved evident violations of ethical standards, it should not be supported or published. *(Essential)*

B. Specifically, watch for the following common problems:

1. Failure to accept personal responsibility, and failure to share credit fairly and equitably with all who deserve it. *(Desirable)*
2. Failure to meet ethical standards in treatment of subjects *(Essential):*
   a. Failure to obtain informed consent.
   b. Lying to subjects; deceit.
   c. Failure to protect confidentiality (e.g., giving possibly identifying details about specific persons).
   d. Subjecting subjects to harm or trauma (watch out especially for psychological damage); e.g., failure to protect subjects against negative effects of research on therapy.
   e. Failure to give subjects full information about the research afterwards, or assumption that routine "debriefing" is sufficient to undo any possible damage from deception, insults, etc.

C. Ideally, participation in research should be a growth-enhancing experience for all persons involved. *(Desirable)*

AFTERWORD

One of the main difficulties with the approach to evaluation presented here is that it leaves a huge job of synthesis to the evaluator of a body research literature. He or she must consider so many facets of each study, using a distressingly large number of criteria in terms of which a given research may vary all over the lot, come out with a final judgment about each, and then try to synthesize this complex information across many varied researches. On the level of the individual study it is often enough to make a two-valued, go versus no-go, decision. When one is preparing a review or summary of a field of endeavor, the task is to find and preserve what is of value despite the fact that no one study is ever wholly satisfactory.[4]

In such a situation, I am happy to take note of a promising new development called meta-analysis of research. In his presidential address to the 1976 Annual Meeting of the American Educational Research Association in April 1976, Gene V. Glass, the distinguished expert on evaluation research (that is, systematic attempts to assess and appraise such human enterprises as social interventions, education, and psychotherapy; see Struening & Guttentag, 1975; Guttentag & Struening, 1975), outlines "a rigorous alternative to the casual, narrative discussions of research studies which typify our attempts to make sense of the rapidly expanding research literature." It is *not* suited for the evaluation of single studies, especially not for proposals or research at any stage before the compilation of findings. But it offers a new and much-needed supplement to the cognitive judgmental digestion of completed researches on a single topic when they begin to cumulate in large enough numbers to be processed quantitatively. Any classical or important topic is likely to have attracted the labors of large numbers of investigators, and it gets increasingly difficult to put together the confusingly varied findings that a little bibliographic diligence yields.

First, Glass notes that it is difficult but necessary to locate the relevant research. That means setting boundaries in terms of defining the problem, precisely enough so that only comparable studies will be compared, but not so narrowly as to exclude relevant evidence. And it means using a great deal of persistence and ingenuity in tracking down research, especially such unpublished work as dissertations, and not simply relying on one standard bibliographic tool like the *Psychological Abstracts*.

Then, each study is described—measured, if possible—in terms of such characteristics as relevant features of the independent variable (e.g., in studies of psychotherapy outcome, which Glass analyzed, type and duration of therapy, individual or group, therapist's years of experience, clients' ages, diagnoses [neurotic or psychotic], and IQs, therapists' discipline, social and ethnic similarity of therapists and clients, etc.), features of the dependent variable (in the above example, magnitude of effect, type of outcome measure, number of months after therapy when taken, fakeability of the measure), judgment of the internal validity of the research design, and the date

---

[4]It is a pleasure to be able to call attention to an excellent sample of an unusual genre: an evaluation of an evaluative summary of a research literature. In her long and careful review of *The Psychology of Sex Differences,* by Maccoby and Jacklin (1974), Jeanne Block (1976) not only gives a judicious appraisal of an influential book, but goes back to the literature it surveys and re-evaluates it in an exemplary way.

and form of publication. Notice that some of those are quantitative, others are categorical.

Glass proposes a simple and effective way of putting diverse studies on one continuum of the magnitude of effect: the mean difference between experimental and control subjects divided by the standard deviation of the control group. Since a study might present data from several measures of psychotherapy outcome, he was able to measure 830 effect sizes from 375 studies. This emphasis on size of effect is in refreshing contrast to the usual overemphasis on *significance* of findings, an issue that becomes relatively trivial when many studies' results are being cumulated. I believe that it would be useful, however, to add in as an important descriptor of studies in many areas the number of subjects—especially when a literature contains reports of research on samples ranging in size from 1 to 3000 (see Chapter 19, above).

Then, granted a large enough collection of studies, the data can be processed by various statistical means, for example, multiple regression analysis with effect size as the criterion being predicted. I was surprised to find that Glass's data support his contention that it is less important than one might think to throw out or give less weight to poorly designed research: internal validity (1 = high, 3 = low) was correlated only −.09 with size of effect. This relationship is significant, but surely small, as was that of date of publication and number of months after termination when the follow-up data were gathered.

The results of Glass's survey and integration of research on the outcome of psychotherapy are not easy to summarize, but they do dispel several myths: on the average, psychotherapy has been conclusively shown to be effective, and the superiority of behavioral over psychodynamic therapies is limited to objective outcome measures and quick follow-ups. In terms of major, long-term outcome measures such as achievement in school and work, the nonbehavioral therapies have larger effects.

It still seems unlikely to me, however, that any comparable approach will make it possible to speed up or make more objective the difficult, judgmental task of arriving at an overall synthesis of the assets and liabilities of individual research reports. At least for the foreseeable future, we must strive to cultivate our technical knowledge, our nose for true significance, our sense of what is fair and just, and our wisdom.

10

In my second year of graduate work, I was introduced to Max Weber's thoughtful analysis of the time-worn problem of values in science in a course with Talcott Parsons. At the same time, S. S. Stevens was trying to enlist all of us graduate students under the banner of logical positivism, another approach to the position that science was value-free by its nature and must remain so.

At that time I became acquainted with some of the ways in which science is distinguished from other kinds of human enterprises by its stance with respect to values. Weber showed to my satisfaction how vain was the hope of some earnest persons that scientific methods could settle value problems, or could choose for us what system of values a person or a society should adopt: every such apparent demonstration turns out, on close examination, to have silently postulated pre-existing agreement on the very question at issue—some basic value premise. For example, as long as you and I agree that human survival is such an ultimate desideratum that we don't even think to mention it, and as long as we both also implicitly agree on the rules of the discussion— accepting, for example, the assumption that it is better to be logical and factual than to threaten, cajole, or appeal to authority—then it can appear that scientific data force the acceptance of certain less ultimate value positions, for example the desirability of social control of population and pollution. But without such prior, question-begging agreements neither logic no science can prove that factual arguments are better—in some absolute *sense—than emotional appeals, nor that life is ultimately better than death.*

In the 30-odd years since I ceased being a graduate student, I have re-encountered the problem of values in many contexts and guises, enough to give me a healthy respect for the complexity of the issues, and to make me realize that there are no final answers. Periodically, I believe, it helps all of us to re-examine the problem of values in science and to ponder its relevance to our own work.

The Problem of Values in Science

Let me begin by stating briefly what strike me as the main problematic aspects of the relation between science and values. On the side of the traditional view that science is and should be "value-free," which I believe is dominant in psychology today, there can hardly be any argument with the general proposition that there are many dangers to the proper conduct of the scientific enterprise from the intrusion of the scientist's personal values. And I think we are familiar with a goodly body of empirical evidence that values, especially when strongly held, can bias and distort perception, memory, logical reasoning, and other cognitive processes that are central to scientific work.

I think we are familiar, too, with some of the abuses, the inappropriate mixing of values and science that have occurred. Let me remind you of the relatively rare but recurrent problem of faking results, which apparently occurs when the wish for certain outcomes overrides considerations of scientific control; the occasional spectacle of a scientist speaking out publicly as if he were an expert on matters in which he has no technical competence, thus taking unfair advantage of the public; the self-deception of a generation of astronomers who described linear "canal" systems on Mars, of which close-up photographs show no trace, apparently because of the wish to find evidence of intelligent life there. The last example is worth our pausing over, for it exemplifies the difficulty of setting the limits of the concept of value. What I spoke about was the *wish* to find life. It should remind us that value is a concept with one foot in cognitive, the other in motivational psychology, and that cognitive psychologists usually attribute the mischief to motivation, often fallaciously conceptualized as a "force" that can distort, or a homunculus that can capture and dominate a train of thought. Even though those are misleading metaphors, they do point to certain well-documented phenomena: for better or for worse, cognition is not an isolated, autonomous part-process, but a way of looking at the functioning of total and very humanly fallible organisms.

The simple reaction against the dangers is that we need all the help we can get to protect science against the human fallibilities of scientists, hence we must pursue objectivity as rigorously as possible. And that would mean— or so many scientists contend—banishing values from science, conceptualizing it as a separate realm into which, ideally, human wishes, goals, ideologies, and other manifestations of motive and value never intrude.

Since the dangers of uncontrolled subjectivity are so grossly evident, it is understandable that the reaction should be so strong. Laws are not necessary where there is no temptation, nor defenses where there are no threats. The trouble is that you *can* get too much of a good thing, and any virtue can be turned into a vice when pursued with unrelenting excess. Surely that is the case with objectivity when made a summum bonum of scientific method; for brevity, let me refer to it as "superobjectivity."[1] The eminent nutritionist Jean

[1]An important source of this position is the tradition of scientific materialism, so well described by Whitehead: " . . . the fixed scientific cosmology which presupposes the ultimate fact of an irreducible brute matter, or material, spread throughout space in a flux of configurations. In itself such a material is senseless, valueless, purposeless. It just does what it does do, following a fixed routine imposed by external relations which do not spring from the nature of its being. It is this assumption that I call 'scientific materialism'" (1925, p. 18).

Mayer (1972) began a thoughtful little paper on the problem of when a scientist should speak out on public issues as a scientist, by the following sentence from Rabelais: "Science without conscience is but ruination of the soul." One danger of overdoing objectivity and the value-free concept is that scientists may act without conscience, with enormous destructiveness to society: think only of the horrors of modern technological "advance" in antipersonnel weapons, or of the grisly experiments of Nazi scientists on human beings. No wonder one strand of the counterculture has been a rejection of science for what Roszak (1969) calls its "myth of objective consciousness." I don't agree with his hasty analysis and overgeneralized rejection of scientific method, but I can sympathize with it because of the grave abuses committed by scientists who have carefully shed their consciences before donning laboratory jackets. The sad irony is that the doctrine that science must be value-free enabled them to feel righteous and justified in attempting to function as nonevaluative machines.

In Table 10.1 I have listed the dangers of value-judgments at each of a dozen points in the processes of producing scientific knowledge and putting it to work, classifying them under two headings: the deleterious effects of too much, and those of too little involvement of values. Most of what our familiar devices of experimental and statistical control are aimed at turn up under the former of these columns. But the kind of thing that shows up under the dangers of too little is worth special attention. Suppose that we were in fact the kind of impassive, white-coated robots implicitly assumed by the advocates of superobjectivity. Without motives, passions, and values, we might indeed not make many kinds of errors, but we would also be incapable of wanting to work, of curiosity, of perseverance in the face of frustration, or of caring about maintaining good standards. Perhaps an automaton could be programmed to keep going until its switch was turned off and to do things only in prescribed ways; but it would be incapable of creativity, initiative, intuition, and judgment.

In this connection, I am reminded of Freud's wisdom concerning the role of emotion in thought. In 1900, he clearly recognized what the "New Look" of the 1950s proved, that strong wishes and affects could distort thought, bending it away from the lineaments of reality. Even when he described the ideal type of the secondary process, however, he said: "thinking must aim at freeing itself more and more from *exclusive* regulation by the pleasure-unpleasure principle and at restricting the development of affect in thought-activity to the minimum *required* for acting as a signal" (1900a, p. 602; emphasis added). The central process in judgment is *evaluation*, deciding which alternative is better, something that in the end must be felt, not coldly thought. Hence, without commitment to a specifiable set of values, a scientist could not function at all.

Elsewhere, in discussing obsessional thinking, Freud (1926d) pointed out how the obsessive's fear of his own impulses causes him to isolate his

Table 10.1. Deleterious Effects of Value Considerations on Psychological Science

Aspect of scientific work	Dangers of too much value	Dangers of too little
Choosing problems to work on (for self; guiding work of others in consultation, fund granting)	Being influenced by such values as personal gain, prestige, power, revenge; neglect of basic science because of overzealous pursuit of applied goals	Inability to decide (lack of affect signals), lack of motivation; indifference to value-implications of one's work, neglecting greatly needed problems, working on socially noxious ones
Choosing methods (planning and designing research)	Being too much influenced by fads and modes, prestige of models, dogma; failure to control where needed because of wish or fear; deliberately or inadvertently stacking the cards *for* one's hypothesis by choice of method or design, including choices contaminated by knowledge of results	Failure to maintain good standards by virtue of not caring (N.B.: this point applies at *every* step in the process)
Carrying out the work of research		
a. Getting started, keeping going	Irrational perseverance; reluctance to begin or to quit when appropriate	Dilatoriness from lack of interest; giving up too easily
b. Making observations	Misperception (observational errors) because of over-strong motivations or defense; too selective: overlooking, scotomatizing, or suppressing evidence. Faking observations	Failure to notice what is there because of a lack of priming ("set" effect); not being selective enough
c. Following plans	Opportunistic violation of research plan or design; deliberate (cheating) or inadvertent deviation from planned controls because of too-great motivation for results	Failure to seize opportunities to learn something more significant than original plan permitted
d. Interaction with Ss	Influencing Ss and being influenced by them via sexual attraction, prejudice, fear, hatred, or common group membership; "experimenter effects"	Callousness to Ss, failure to empathize and thus to treat them humanely
e. Handling of data	Motivated errors of content analysis, ratings, computation, etc. (experimenter effects); confusing own personal values with Ss' (e.g., projective distortion in dream interpretation)	Too restrictive a conception of what constitutes data, eschewing any analysis of values or any other meanings
Writing up the report	Overgeneralization or too speculative extension of implica-	Dull, boring, lifeless writing; giving everything equal

(continued)

Table 10.1. (*continued*)

Aspect of scientific work	Dangers of too much value	Dangers of too little
	tions from wish for more significance than is found or is logically permissible; distortion by emphasis, to minimize undesired findings, overemphasize desired ones; motivated errors in logic or reasoning about findings or about theory	emphasis; concealing personal responsibility by use of passive voice and other devices; overcautious refusal to generalize or draw implications for value-laden issues
Evaluating research (for publication, prizes and honors, in hiring, etc.)	Rejecting good work because of dislike of the findings, author, method, etc., or rewarding poor work because of similar but positive personal values	Inability to judge because of too much fear or avoidance of making value judgments
Conceptualizing issues (forming and manipulating constructs and theories)	Introducing value-laden terms that beg questions; theorizing guided by need to reach predetermined outcome	Refusal to deal conceptually with issues of human values
Applying scientific knowledge	Misusing it for personal gain, power, revenge, etc., or for socially destructive ends (e.g., exploitation of the weak, aggressive or inhumane modes of warfare, means of torture, controlling others against their will)	Indifference or resistance to any application, overemphasis on the ideal of withdrawal into the ivory tower; indifference to the use or abuse of one's work by others
Speaking out in public on the implications of one's work	Exploiting prestige of science or of one's competence in one area to take public position of advocacy outside that realm or deviating from truth (e.g., by exaggeration, confusing fact with extrapolation or inference)	Failure to speak up when one does have expertise relevant to important social problems

thoughts entirely from the influence of emotion, with the result that his judgment is seriously impaired. For small, "signal" amounts of adult emotions are necessary to let us know when we are on the right track, when we have succeeded or failed; without them, we do not know where we stand. Excessive isolation is a prime occupational hazard of all the intellectual professions. I am reminded of a cartoon of a critic knitting his brows before a painting, while in the background one friend whispers to another, "He knows everything about art, but he doesn't know what he likes." It is not for nothing that an acceptable synonym for *to judge* is *to feel*. Cut off from affect signals, the intellectualizer turns to the amassing of fact as a way of finding the answers that elude him. Indeed, Rapaport found that obsessive-compulsive persons could be recognized by their relatively large stock of information and weakness of commonsense judgment (Rapaport, Gill, & Schafer, 1968). Here is the secret of the stupidity often shown by brilliant people—they know a tremendous amount but lack the inner compass of emotion that helps the ordinary person find his way to sensible decisions and wise choices.

By reference to vividly recounted episodes in the history of science, Polanyi (1958) shows how the scientist makes a tacit and passionate contribution to every phase of his own work, and demonstrates the impossibility of scientific knowledge without the activities of appraisal and commitment. I strongly recommend his book, *Personal Knowledge,* to anyone who wants to see a devastating examination of the cult of superobjectivity.

Even more to be recommended for anyone concerned with its topic is a short, lovely book, *Science and Human Values,* by Jacob Bronowski (1965). This extraordinary polymath and poet, with solid attainments in biology, literary criticism, the history of ideas, and the philosophy of science, saw as clearly as Polanyi that the task of science is not to keep itself value-free, but to cleave to the special value system of science, the existence of which we can easily overlook because we share it. What is more, he made explicit for us this set of values to which scientists are committed.

Bronowski begins by asserting that science is a social enterprise; hence, a philosophy of its values must acknowledge both the need for social life and the need for individual freedom. Science thus presupposes the values of *trust* in others, and of reliability or *trustworthiness.* Science is impossible without these virtues, and of course "the habit of *truth,*" the very cement that holds society together. Verification is impossible outside a social nexus; it implies a "social axiom: *We* OUGHT *to act in such a way that what* IS *true can be verified* to be so" (p. 58, his emphases).

The progress of science moreover depends on a community of scientists "which is free, uninhibited and communicative." This "company of scholars . . . has been more lasting than any modern state, yet . . . has changed and evolved as no Church has. What power holds them together?" he asks (p. 58f.), answering: the power of virtue. Expounding it in terms that state an ideal rather than a factual description of scientists at large, Bronowski says: " . . . they do not make wild claims, they do not cheat, they do not try to persuade at any cost, they appeal neither to prejudice nor to authority, they are often frank about their ignorance, their disputes are fairly decorous, they do not confuse what is being argued with race, politics, sex or age, they listen patiently to the young and to the old who both know everything" (p. 59). Scientists are "trained to avoid and organized to resist every form of persuasion but the fact."

And where do these ideals of virtue come from? "The values of science derive neither from the [individual] virtues of its members, nor from the finger-wagging codes of conduct by which every profession reminds itself to be good. They have grown out of the practice of science, because they are the inescapable conditions for its practice" (p. 60).

Freedom and dissent are necessary, for science must protect its independence by standards of "free inquiry, free thought, free speech, tolerance" (p. 62). Moreover, "The society of scientists . . . can keep alive and grow only by a constant tension between dissent and respect; between independence from the views of others, and tolerance for them" (p. 63), a tolerance which in turn is based on respect. "Respect as a personal value implies, in any society, the public acknowledgments of *justice* and of due *honor*" (p. 63). And finally (are you listening, Dr. Skinner?), Bronowski argues that the scientist who strives persistently and plays the game right earns the respect of his colleagues regardless of whether he proves right or wrong, for "Science at last respects the scientist more than his discoveries." And "The sense of human dignity . . . is the cement of a society of equal men; for it expresses their knowledge that respect for others must be founded on self-respect" (p. 64).[2]

Notwithstanding the indignation of critics like Roszak, the values of science, thus brought into the open, are quite evidently "not at odds with the values by which alone mankind can survive. On the contrary, like the other creative activities which grew from the Renaissance, science has humanized our values. Men have asked for freedom, justice, and respect precisely as the scientific spirit has spread among them. The dilemma of today is not that the human values cannot control a mechanical science. It is the other way about: the scientific spirit is more human than the machinery of governments" (p. 70).

I recognize that you may not agree that every one of these values is a required part of science, or you may feel as I do that such a list might well include a few others which Bronowski did not specifically mention (see Table 10.2). Certainly it should not be taken as a complete system, adequate for all of us in our lives generally, for Bronowski says explicitly that it is not. But I defy any reasonable person to come away from his book unconvinced that the problem of values in science is not to escape them but to make certain that we hold to the right ones, which will exclude both the dangers of hyperemotional excess and those of superobjective dearth.

Perhaps I can make the problems more vivid by describing a couple of contrasting types of scientists I have observed, whom I will call "hots" and "colds." Hot seems an appropriate metaphor for the first group, because they seem to burn with zeal and indignation. They care deeply about the subject matter of their work, whether it be the physics of pollution, the chemistry of food additives, the psychology of women, or the sociology of intergroup conflict, and do not conceal their strong feelings about the human problems they hope to alleviate by means of their research. Indeed,

[2]Much as I like and tend to be swept away by this sequence of ideas, I must admit, in sober retrospect, that it contains gaps. The steps are not tightly organized; they do not follow by demonstrable logical necessity. At times, they depend on factual assertions, unbolstered by any empirical evidence.

Table 10.2.   The Value System of Science (Based on J. Bronowski, *Science and Human Values*)

Truth (in the sense of what is empirically verifiable and public)	vs.	Truth as revealed by dogma, private inspiration, mystical or magical divination
Freedom of inquiry, thought, speech, and communication generally		Deference to authority, tradition, or alleged need to put other values first
Dissent: the right not to join a consensus		Conformity, misplaced application of the majority-rule principle to ideas
Originality, creativity		Stereotypy, conventionality
Trust and trustworthiness		Suspicion and betrayal of trust
Integrity, honesty, genuineness		Pretense, phoniness, hypocrisy, faking
Fidelity to the nature of things, openness		Dogmatic preconceptions, closed-mindedness, prejudice
Respect for others, tolerance, egalitarianism		Prejudice, narcissistic self-aggrandizement, elitism
Justice, fairness		Indifference to such moral considerations
Rationality, clarity of thought, intelligible communication		Obscurantism, mysticism, murkiness, disregard for logic
Objectivity, replicability		Uncontrolled subjectivity, self-deception
Workmanship, pursuit of excellence, high quality of tools and work		Getting by, sloppiness, compromises with quality, concern only for quantity
Efficiency, control, orderliness, cleanliness (compulsive virtues)		Disorder, dirt, chaos, abandon
Integration: organization of data and concepts into structures and systems		Disorganization, fragmentation
Elegance, beauty, economy in theories		Awkwardness, redundancy
Concern for the future		Hedonistic immediacy
Perseverance despite failure, obstacles, difficulties; active effort		Giving up, quitting prematurely; passive adaptation
Responsibility		Irresponsibility
Honor, dignity		Antihumanism; misplaced determinism or egalitarianism
(Concern for human life, survival)		(Other-worldliness; callousness)

In general, values on the left grow out of and are intrinsic to the processes of scientific work, and are necessary for its effectiveness, while those on the right undermine the scientific enterprise. Parentheses at the bottom indicate some doubts that these are intrinsic to science in the same way as the others.

many hots are public advocates of causes; they use their status as scientists and the institutions with which they are affiliated (including their scientific societies) as means of drawing attention to their public stands on controversial issues. If questioned about the legitimacy of mixing science and politics, or of allowing their values to intrude upon their work, they will often argue vehemently that it is their moral duty to act as they are acting, and express strong conviction that their advocacy is necessary for the pursuit of truth or that advocacy at least facilitates it. In fact, however, they do make motivated errors, at times finding what they are convinced they must find, in part because of failure to use adequate controls or to consider a wide enough range of alternatives to the null hypothesis. Many are social activists whose indignation about injustice leads them to disrupt scientific meetings, shout down their opponents, and in other ways to flout the established rules of scientific decorum. No doubt all of us have become acquainted with some of them during the decade of the 1960s.

Their opposite numbers, the "colds," have been around and highly visible in science for even longer. Colds lay great emphasis on the importance of scientific method in general and objectivity in particular. Valuing method so highly, they tend to be the authors of texts on scientific method. Many of them are apolitical, not interested in social issues or apparently anything much outside of the boundaries of their own disciplines; but some do take value positions, even public ones, always carefully making it clear that when they do so they speak as citizens, not as scientists. All their convictions and value judgments, they believe, are rigidly segregated from their lives as scientists, kept as it were in separate hermetically sealed compartments, or doffed at the doors of their laboratories. Some members of this subgroup, for example, are devout adherents to traditional religions—on Sundays or high holy days only. It is fundamental to scientific work, they stoutly maintain, that it be carried out with cool detachment, with no prior stake in any particular result, and without concern for what is done with their findings. Indeed, they may argue passionately that passion has no place in the mind of a scientist. They pride themselves on their indifference to application and their concern only with scientific issues; many of them speak of their work as basic research or as pure science. This very detachment makes it possible for them to accept financial support from any source. For some, the indifference to application paradoxically allows them to work on applied problems so long as their designs are clean and their methods beyond reproach; their test tubes are for hire, so to speak, and they don't want to learn about the ultimate purposes of those who provide the financial support for their work.[3]

---

[3]A recent discussion of problems of scientific responsibility makes a distinction quite similar to mine between hot and cold scientists in pointing out two "partly opposed meanings" of *scientific responsibility*. Similar to my "colds" are those who believe that the primary responsibility of scientists is to the scientific community: "not to demean the community or to diminish the standing of colleagues, by acting in ways dissonant with the traditions of science or its popular

I don't intend to ridicule either type, but to call your attention to the strengths *and* weaknesses of both hots and colds, and to suggest that it is possible to find a synthesis that retains the best of both antithetical patterns. At first I wrote "find a middle way," but then I realized that I was slipping into a common concretistic misunderstanding of what synthesis is. It means transcending the ground rules in terms of which you must choose one of only two paths, and thus getting to a level at which antinomies and seemingly necessary dichotomies disappear. Synthesis is *not* evading resolution of a conflict by trying to steer through its middle. The obsessional attempt at evenhandedness—a little of this, a little of that—does not help much.

What we need for a synthesis is to find a way of retaining both passion and prudence, concern both for the uses to which knowledge is put and for the conditions necessary to the integrity of the truth-seeking process. In homely terms, scientific method was invented to help protect people from fooling themselves. No matter how admirable a person's values, no matter how socially constructive his intentions, if he is self-deceived, if he con-sciously or unconsciously guides the tools of science so as to predetermine the outcome, in the long run he defeats his own purpose. The apparent immediate victory will prove Pyrrhic, and when the truth ultimately emerges the incautious hot scientist will have discredited both himself and his cause. Meanwhile, in his attempts to define away his need to come to terms with value problems, the cold scientist may find that he has been acting as if he was trying to promote socially destructive values, while in his attempt to preserve science from any intrusion of value considerations he excludes the value system without which science must perish.

I am reminded of two other but somewhat similar types, whom Lester Luborsky and I encountered in our research on the selection and training of psychiatric residents (Holt & Luborsky, 1958). In trying to put together a criterion measure of our subjects' functioning in the Menninger School of Psychiatry, we had a good many talks with supervisors in which we encour-aged them to talk about concrete incidents of good and bad performance as a resident. Again and again, they referred to what they called "overidentifica-tion"—the resident would become concerned with the welfare of a patient, begin to care intensely about helping him, and then would start to behave in a complicated way. On the one hand, he would devote himself to his charge, be in very close touch with the latter's suffering and other emotional states, and sometimes get an excellent grasp of his problems; but on the other hand,

---

image." The opposing view (compare my "hots") defines the concept "primarily as a responsibil-ity to society rather than to the scientific community. . . . It accepts as inevitable that scientists involved in public debate will have to go beyond discussing what is scientifically known for certain. . . . the narrow view implicitly discourages involvement by scientists in public debate, while the broad view instructs them that such participation is their 'social responsibility.'" (All quotations are from an unsigned article on p. 1 of the December 1976 issue [Vol. 29, No. 10] of the *F.A.S. Public Interest Report*, a publication of the Federation of American Scientists.)

the young psychiatrist would show in a number of other ways that he was too close to the patient—he might become inpatient with rules and customary procedures and try to get special consideration for his patient, might cause outbreaks of anxiety or of obviously sexualized transference behavior in him, and would himself become manifestly upset, emotionally overinvolved.

At the same time, we found that other psychiatric residents were described in quite an opposite sort of way: they never lost their cool, were unruffled by affective outbursts and declarations of love or hate from their patients, and often did an excellent job of getting in their reports on time, seeing to their administrative duties, and being impartial in their handling of their entire wards. They were much better in these ways than the overidentifiers, who more obviously floundered, played favorites, and fell behind in routine duties though spending many more hours on the job. Let us call those who stayed at too great distance "fars" and those who got too close to patients "nears." Despite their virtues, the fars understood their patients less well, cared less about them, showed them less warmth, and affected them less one way or another. On the whole, the turbulent wards of the nears discharged more patients as significantly improved than the calm wards of the fars.

But here is my main point: by the end of their three years of training, many members of *both* groups had caught up with those lucky few who almost from the beginning seemed to know intuitively how to strike the right balance between closeness and distance, between overidentification and underidentification. Some people are naturals; but psychotherapy *can* be taught. Not to everyone, of course; even granting the requisite intelligence, moral integrity, and personal genuineness, some people's defenses seem too fragile to withstand constant interaction with emotionally disturbed people, while others' defenses seem too rigid to permit them to establish emotional communication of any depth with other people. I do not *know* that it is a matter of defenses, but that is not crucial for my point: when not too extreme, both kinds of behavior can be constructively changed.

I believe that we may get some help from developmental psychology for a way out of this hot-cold, near-far dilemma. First, almost any problem— surely this one—can be viewed as developmental. I encountered the nears and fars in a developmental context, for any kind of school is an attempt to guide a developmental process, psychiatric residencies and graduate programs in psychology pointedly included. If we have hots and colds among our scientific colleagues, they have *developed* into such, and in our roles as teachers we not only can but should accept the responsibility of guiding the development of future generations of psychological scientists so that they are not hampered by the drawbacks of hots and colds alike.

Second, in reading Piaget, I have been struck by the usefulness of his concept of *decentering* in aiding the comprehension of many kinds of developmental processes. At the very beginning of a child's construction of reality during his first year, he must make "the transition from an initial state in which everything is centered on the child's own body and actions to a 'decentered' state in which his body and actions assume their objective relationships with reference to all the other objects and events registered in the universe" (Piaget & Inhelder, 1969, p. 94). At many subsequent points in growth, strictly analogous decentering processes are again necessary. The name of the concept comes from Piaget's observation that a number of the classical perceptual illusions could be understood by a single hypothesis: when one element of a perceptual configuration is given especial attention, which usually means bringing it to the literal center of the visual field, it appears larger. The circular process involved contributes an important point to a psychology of values: what a person focuses on tends to appear more valuable, and what is valued tends to attract attention and thus to become central. This recognizably assimilative process thus contributes stability to the developmental process, and an important principle of growth is decentering—experiences that break into the positive feedback system just described.

Decentering takes place in four overlapping ways. First, since value is not the only determinant of attention, various kinds of experiences tend to bring what was peripheral into the center; so inappropriate overvaluing can be corrected by life experience. It is evident that an educator can plan her charge's environment in such a way as to combat natural centering processes, and "widen horizons." That can be expanded to a second point: by setting what was overvalued into a series of possible alternatives and by showing that they are equally valued by others with whom it is possible to identify oneself, the educator gives the contextual perspective that can help the student gain distance and "get outside" his hitherto unquestioned value system. Third, the same process is helped if what is implicit is made conscious and is thereby brought under voluntary control. Without attempting to examine your own value system and to formulate it explicitly, you will have great difficulty in preventing it from silently determining many judgments. This formulation actually covers two somewhat different cases, one in which the person can relatively easily become aware of nonconscious material (which is, in Freud's term, preconscious), and one in which it ordinarily requires the assistance of an expert therapist to help the person overcome resistances to awareness or defenses against it (when we say that the warded-off material is unconscious). Fourth, the person can be helped to decenter by discovering linkages between values he holds and various themes in his personal life—including accidents of his birth and residence, childhood experiences often of a traumatic nature, and aspects of his group identity. Sometimes a breadth of life experience is enough to teach the person that she need not be committed by others (e.g., "inheriting" parental political affiliations) or by her past (e.g., by her class position) but can make her own commitments once she has thought through all their ramifications. In other instances, to become free of the past—particularly repressed traumatic aspects of one's personal history—requires the expert assistance of a psychotherapist or psychoanalyst. On the whole, however, there are striking similarities between the processes of decentering and those of liberal education (Heath, 1968).

But decentering is only half of the story, for each achievement of gaining some distance and perspective makes possible a new centering of the world around the self without which the person would be disoriented and would lack a firm *grounding* in a developing sense of self, in free contact with his own feelings. The decentering process can overshoot, and then we see people seemingly without a "vital center," who characteristically feel paralyzed, dead, numb, or out of contact: they suffer from depersonalization or alienation from a sense of self, and derealization or loss of the sense of reality. Psychoanalysis as a therapy centers the analyzand intensely on a scrutiny of his own experience, in the service of achieving a greater ultimate degree of decentering—lessened egocentricity, with more capacity to love others and to deal effectively with the world of reality.[4]

To return to Piaget: in looking back on the long period of middle childhood during which the concrete operations of thought are attained, "we see the unfolding of a long, integrated process that may be characterized as a transition from subjective centering in all areas to a decentering that is at once cognitive, social, and moral. This process is all the more remarkable in that it reproduces and develops on a large scale at the level of thought what has already taken place on a small scale at the sensorimotor level" (Piaget & Inhelder, 1969, p. 128). And, I would add, in that it prefigures the same kind of changes at higher levels. Unfortunately, however, Piaget has not published any research on the processes involved in the education of scientists.

A reasonably close approximation exists in the work of Perry (1970), however. In studying patterns of intellectual and ethical development in Harvard and Radcliffe undergraduates over the course of their four years, Perry acknowledges his debt to Piaget's methods and theories alike, but produces something useful of his own.

The freshman often enters college holding a set of beliefs which Perry summarizes as basic dualism: a view of the world in simple, black-white terms. We are the good guys; the others are wrong and bad. Oversimplified, yes, but thanks to assimilation it is a relatively stable position, one that serves many people throughout their lives. College attacks it by bringing the freshman into contact with many more types of people than she is likely to have known before, from many backgrounds, and by exposing her to a multiplicity of ideas, opinions, and value systems. The very fact that her dualism has been unself-conscious and unexamined is an aspect of its centeredness, while the student's attempt to accommodate to the multiplicity of the college environment has a decentering effect. When the student

[4]My ideas about the nature and importance of decentering and grounding owe a good deal to discussions with Robert Jay Lifton in August 1974; see also Lifton (1976).

reaches the point of perceiving all knowledge and values as relative to a context, the decentering effect may cause her to lose all grounding, to flounder helplessly in a morass where there is nothing absolute to clutch. She may even attempt suicide. The way out, as Perry describes it, is seeing the necessity of getting an orientation by means of a personal commitment, exploring its implications, and affirming such a fealty to a personally satisfying set of beliefs and values. Notice how commitment is a process of recentering, which forms the ground for an affirmation of identity, but which also turns the student outward again with a new sense of responsibility. Firmly grounded in a sense of who she is, with continuity (through her commitment) to a socially shared set of conceptions among which values bulk large, the maturing person is now ready to function effectively in a relativistic world. Only now is she able to perceive other persons, things, and ideas with relative freedom from distortion by wish or fear.

I believe that there are important lessons here for us as educators. The development of scientists is too important a matter to be left to chance. Bronowski has shown us the nature of the value system implicit in scientific work and the urgency of helping the developing scientists to make a commitment to it, but Perry tells about a special problem of commitment in young scientists, which may throw some light on faulty developmental patterns. People who have marked talents for engineering or one of the sciences often enter college already committed, he says, and hardly ever seem to falter as they go through, seemingly imperturbed by the stressful impact of multiplicity. But their commitment is premature; it seems to shield them from the dangers of relativism, but at the cost of rigid, dogmatic outlooks. Too early commitment thus prevents a necessary process of decentering, and may very well be a characteristic of those cold scientists I described above who paradoxically seem to be too decentered where the hots are too centered in their personal value systems.

When we get down to particulars, developmental research is again helpful in showing how important it is to assess the stage to which any given person has grown, and not to believe that a monolithic educational program will be equally valuable for all students. Some of Kohlberg's colleagues (e.g., Turiel, 1966; Blatt, 1969) have shown that children can be helped to advance in their level of moral development through discussions of moral dilemmas, primarily by exposure to reasoning that is just one step above their own level. If the level of instruction is two or more steps above them, it has little or no effect.

The lesson is clear: we need appropriate means of diagnosing the developmental status of our students, with particular attention to the issue of commitment to science. The prematurely committed probably need exposure to a muliplicity of outlooks, a set-breaking plunge into relativism. Those whose commitment is as yet faltering and incomplete need help in extricating themselves from rudderlessness. All instruction should be informed with the necessity of helping students free themselves from egocentric naiveté by experiences that show the inadequacy of a too-centered outlook, but also by the need to help them find grounding in an enriched sense of self and in an appropriately considered commitment. Serious attention should be given to the possiblity of training in moral reasoning à la Kohlberg (1969); for in reading over Bronowski's discussion of the values of science I am struck by the need of mature scientists to function on Kohlberg's highest level—that of abstract principles like justice and truth—not just to help them develop ethical integrity, but to aid their scientific work itself.

Education, like other developmental processes, has no end, only new stages. All of us can profit from the attempt to decenter, to gain distance from our work and its presuppositions by looking at it from the standpoints of others—not just G. H. Mead's "generalized other," but the variety of communities and constituencies that make up our pluralistic society. Only thus can we hope to foresee some of what Merton called the "unanticipated consequences of purposive social acts," and look ahead to what may occur if we keep on acting as we have been acting. I think many of us have been prevented from doing so by a blind faith in scientific method as it was taught to us and in a superobjective conception of what scientific work is and should be. Let us critically re-examine these assumptions, and then look at the contrast between the nature of all too many psychologists' preoccupations and the glowering immensity of the social problems already looming over the horizon. If we do so, I believe that many of us will see the need for a new commitment—not only to the value system of science, but to the goal of directing our scientific work toward coping with disasters that threaten the survival not only of science but of all civilization, perhaps that of life itself.

Bibliography[1]
Robert R. Holt

1942

Holt, R. R. Level of aspiration as ego defense. *Psychological Bulletin,* 1942, *39,* 457 (Abstract).

1943

Sanford, F. H., & Holt, R. R. Psychological determinants of morale. *Journal of Abnormal and Social Psychology,* 1943, *38,* 93–95.

[Holt, R. R.] Contribution to Chapter 13. In E. G. Boring and M. Van de Water (Eds.), *Psychology for the fighting man.* Washington, D.C.: The Infantry Journal, 1943.

1945

Holt, R. R. Effects of ego-involvement upon levels of aspiration. *Psychiatry,* 1945, *8,* 299–317.

1946

Holt, R. R. Level of aspiration: Ambition or defense? *Journal of Experimental Psychology,* 1946, *36,* 398–416. (a)

Holt, R. R. *The TAT Newsletter,* from Vol. 1, No. 1 (September, 1946) to Vol. 5, No. 4 (Springs, 1952). (b) Vol. 3, No. 1 through Vol. 5, No. 4 reprinted in *Journal of Projective Techniques (Rorschach Research Exchange)* from 1949, *13* to 1952, *15.*

Maccoby, E. E., & Holt, R. R. How surveys are made. *Journal of Social Issues,* 1946, *2,* 45–57. Reprinted with minor modifications in T. Newcomb & E. Hartley (Eds.), *Readings in social psychology.* New York: Holt, 1947.

1947

Holt, R. R. Motivational factors in levels of aspiration. *Summaries of theses 1943–45.* Cambridge: Harvard University, 1947 (Abstract). (a)

[Holt, R. R.] The didactic curriculum. *Bulletin of The Menninger Clinic,* 1947, *11,* 123–134 (special issue on training in clinical psychology). (b)

1948

Bellak, L., & Holt, R. R. Somatotypes in relation to dementia praecox. *American Journal of Psychiatry,* 1948, *104,* 713–724. Reprinted in G. W. Lasker & F. P. Thieme (Eds.), *Yearbook of physical anthropology, 1948* (Vol. 4). New York: Viking Fund, 1949.

Holt, R. R. The assessment of psychiatric aptitude from the TAT. *American Psychologist,* 1948, *3,* 271 (Abstract).

Holt, R. R. Review of *The psychology of ego-involvements* by M. Sherif & H. Cantril. *American Journal of Psychiatry,* 1948, *104,* 749–750.

---

[1]A substantially complete bibliography through 1968 was included, with a curriculum vitae, in H. B. Molish, Great Man Award to Holt. *Journal of Projective Techniques and Personality Assessment,* 1969, *33,* 302–310.

Holt, R. R. Review of *The Thematic Apperception Test* by S. S. Tomkins. *Journal of Abnormal and Social Psychology,* 1948, *43,* 403–406.

1949

Holt, R. R. Review of *Projective methods* by L. K. Frank. *Journal of Abnormal and Social Psychology,* 1949, *44,* 140–142.

Holt, R. R. Review of *Four Picture Test* by D. J. van Lennep. *Rorschach Research Exchange,* 1949, *13,* 219–222.

Holt, R. R. Review of *Symonds Picture Story Test* by P. Symonds. *Rorschach Research Exchange,* 1949, *13,* 347–349.

Holt, R. R. Review of *Clinical application of psychological tests* by R. Schafer. *Journal of Abnormal and Social Psychology,* 1949, *44,* 294–296.

1950

Holt, R. R. Some statistical problems in clinical research. *Educational and Psychological Measurement,* 1950, *10,* 609–627. (a) Reprinted in S. J. Beck & H. B. Molish (Eds.), *Reflexes to intelligence* [entitled "What price quantification"]. New York: Basic Books, 1959.

Holt, R. R. An approach to the validation of the Szondi test through a systematic study of unreliability. *Journal of Projective Techniques,* 1950, *14,* 435–444. (b)

Luborsky, L. B., Holt, R. R., & Morrow, W. R. Interim report of the research project on the selection of medical men for psychiatric training. *Bulletin of the Menninger Clinic,* 1950, *14,* 92–101.

Holt, R. R. Review of *Studies in analytical psychology* by G. Adler. *Bulletin of the Menninger Clinic,* 1950, *14,* 149.

Holt, R. R. Review of *Varieties of delinquent youth* by W. H. Sheldon. *Journal of Abnormal and Social Psychology,* 1950, *45,* 790–795. Also reviewed in *Bulletin of The Menninger Clinic,* 1951, *15,* 72–73.

Holt, R. R. Review of *Schizophrenia and the MAPS test* by E. S. Shneidman. *Journal of Personality,* 1950, *18,* 385–387.

Holt, R. R. Review of *A manual for analysis of the Thematic Apperception Test: A method and technique for personality research* by B. Aron. *Journal of Projective Techniques,* 1950, *14,* 194–197.

Holt, R. R. Review of *Children's Apperception Test* by L. & S. S. Bellak. *Journal of Projective Techniques,* 1950, *14,* 198–199.

Holt, R. R. Review of *Projective techniques* by J. E. Bell. *Bulletin of The Menninger Clinic,* 1950, *14,* 183.

1951

Holt, R. R. The accuracy of self-evaluations: Its measurement and some of its personological correlates. *Journal of Consulting Psychology,* 1951, *15,* 95–101. (a)

Holt, R. R. The Thematic Apperception Test. In H. H. and G. L. Anderson (Eds.), *An introduction to projective techniques.* New York: Prentice-Hall, 1951. (b)

Holt, R. R. Psychological tests. In G. Devereux, *Reality and dream* (Part 3). New York: International Universities Press, 1951. (c)

Holt, R. R. An inductive method of analyzing defense of self-esteem. *Bulletin of The Menninger Clinic,* 1951, *15,* 6–15. (d)

Holt, R. R. [Untitled; an analysis of a TAT and MAPS test] In E. S. Shneidman *et al., Thematic test analysis* (Chap. 10). New York: Grune & Stratton, 1951. (e)

Holt, R. R. Our fears and what they do to us. *Menninger Quarterly,* 1951, *6,* 9–16. (f)

Holt, R. R. Review of *Psychodiagnosis* by S. Rosenzweig (with K. L. Kogan). *Journal of Projective Techniques,* 1951, *15,* 111–114.

1952

Holt, R. R., & Luborsky, L. Research in the selection of psychiatrists: A second interim report. *Bulletin of The Menninger Clinic,* 1952, *16,* 125–135.

Holt, R. R. The case of Jay: Interpretation of Jay's Thematic Apperception Test. *Journal of Projective Techniques,* 1952, *16,* 457–461.

Holt, R. R. Review of *Childhood and society* by E. H. Erikson. *Journal of Personality*, 1952, *21*, 149–153.

Holt, R. R. Review of *Personality* by D. C. McClelland. *Journal of Abnormal and Social Psychology*, 1952, *47*, 276–278.

Holt, R. R. Review of *Public opinion 1935—1946* by H. Cantril & M. Strunk. *Bulletin of The Menninger Clinic*, 1952, *16*, 75.

Holt, R. R. Review of *Statement on race* by A. Montagu. *Bulletin of The Menninger Clinic*, 1952, *16*, 110.

1953

Holt, R. R., Chotlos, J. W., & Scheerer, M. Publication problems in psychology. *American Psychologist*, 1953, *8*, 235–242.

Holt, R. R. Review of *The Travis-Johnston Projection Test* by L. E. Travis & J. J. Johnston. In O. K. Buros (Ed.), *The fourth mental measurements yearbook*. Highland Park, N.J.: Gryphon, 1953.

Holt, R. R. Review of *Group Projection Sketches for the study of small groups* by W. E. Henry and H. Guetzkow. In O. K. Buros (Ed.), *The fourth mental measurements yearbook*. Highland Park, N.J.: Gryphon, 1953.

Holt, R. R. Review of *Psychoanalysis as science* by E. Pumpian-Mindlin (Ed.), E. R. Hilgard, & L. Kubie. *Journal of Abnormal and Social Psychology*, 1953, *48*, 607–608.

1954

Holt, R. R. Implications of some contemporary personality theories for Rorschach rationale. In B. Klopfer, M. D. Ainsworth, W. G. Klopfer, & R. R. Holt, *Developments in the Rorschach technique: Vol. 1. Technique and theory*. New York: World Book Co., 1954.

Holt, R. R. Review of *The life and work of Sigmund Freud: Vol. 1. The formative years and the great discoveries, 1856–1900* by E. Jones. *Journal of Abnormal and Social Psychology*, 1954, *49*, 319–320.

1955

Holt, R. R. Problems in the use of sample surveys. In R. Kotinsky and H. L. Witmer (Eds.), *Community programs for mental health*. Cambridge; Harvard University Press, 1955.

Holt, R. R., & Luborsky, L. The selection of candidates for psychoanalytic training: On the use of interviews and psychological tests. *Journal of the American Psychoanalytic Association*, 1955, *3*, 666–681.

Holt, R. R. Review of *The origins of psycho-analysis. Letters to Wilhelm Fliess, drafts and notes: 1887–1902* by S. Freud (M. Bonaparte, A. Freud, & E. Kris, Eds.; translated by E. Mosbacher & J. Strachey). *Scientific Monthly*, 1955, *81*, 95–96.

1956

Holt, R. R. Rejoinder to Mayzner's review of Schafer's "Psychoanalytic interpretation in Rorschach testing." *Psychology Newsletter*, 1956, *7*, 47–50. (a)

Holt, R. R. Gauging primary and secondary processes in Rorschach responses. *Journal of Projective Techniques*, 1956, *20*, 14–25. (b)

Holt, R. R. Review of *The life and work of Sigmund Freud: Vol. 2. Years of maturity, 1901–1919* by E. Jones. *Scientific Monthly*, 1956, *82*, 270.

Holt, R. R. Review of *Energy and structure in psychoanalysis* by K. M. Colby. *Contemporary Psychology*, 1956, *1*, 227–229.

Holt, R. R. Review of *Psychoanalysis and psychotherapy: Developments in theory, technique, and training* by F. Alexander. *Science*, 1956, *124*, 444–445,

1957

Luborsky, L., & Holt, R. R. The selection of candidates for psychoanalytic training: Implications from research on the selection of psychiatric residents. *Journal of Clinical and Experimental Psychopathology*, 1957, *18*, 166–176.

1958

Holt, R. R. Clinical *and* statistical prediction: A reformulation and some new data. *Journal of Abnormal and Social Psychology*, 1958, *56*, 1–12. (a) Reprinted in M. Zax and G. Stricker

(Eds.), *The study of abnormal behavior: Selected readings*. New York: Macmillan, 1964; 2nd ed., 1969. Also in I. N. Mensh (Ed.), *Clinical psychology: Science and profession*. New York: Macmillan, 1966. Also in E. I. Megargee (Ed.), *Research in clinical assessment*. New York: Harper & Row, 1966.

Holt, R. R. Formal aspects of the TAT—A neglected resource. *Journal of Projective Techniques*, 1958, *22*, 163–172. (b) Also in Bobbs-Merrill Reprint Series in the Social Sciences, P-481, 1966.

Klein, G. S., Spence, D. P., Holt, R. R., & Gourevitch, S. Cognition without awareness: Subliminal influences upon conscious thought. *Journal of Abnormal and Social Psychology*, 1958, *57*, 255–266.

Goldberger, L., & Holt, R. R. Experimental interference with reality contact (perceptual isolation): Method and group results. *Journal of Nervous and Mental Disease*, 1958, *127*, 99–112.

Holt, R. R., & Luborsky, L. *Personality patterns of psychiatrists* (2 vols.). New York: Basic Books, 1958.

Holt, R. R. Review of *The life and work of Sigmund Freud: Vol. 3. The last phase, 1919–1939* by E. Jones. *Contemporary Psychology*, 1958, *3*, 145–148.

1959

Holt, R. R. Personality growth in psychiatric residents. *AMA Archives of Neurology and Psychiatry*, 1959, *81*, 203–215. (a)

Holt, R. R. Researchmanship, or how to write a dissertation in clinical psychology without really trying. *American Psychologist*, 1959, *14*, 151. (b) Reprinted in R. A. Baker (Ed.), *Psychology in the wry*. New York: Van Nostrand, 1963.

Holt, R. R. A comment on the Wiener-Nichols controversy. *Journal of Projective Techniques*, 1959, *23*, 377–378. (c)

Holt, R. R. Discussion remarks on "Further observations on the Poetzl phenomenon—A study of day residues" by Charles Fisher. *Psychoanalytic Quarterly*, 1959, *28*, 442. (d)

Holt, R. R. (with the collaboration and assistance of Joan Havel, Leo Goldberger, Anthony Philip, & Reeva Safrin). Manual for the scoring of primary process manifestations in Rorschach responses (7th ed.). New York: Research Center for Mental Health, New York University, 1959 (dittoed). (e)

Holt, R. R., & Goldberger, L. Personological correlates of reactions to perceptual isolation. USAF WADC Technical Reports, 1959, No. 59-735.

Holt, R. R. Review of *Ego psychology and the problem of adaptation* by H. Hartmann. *Contemporary Psychology*, 1959, *4*, 332–333.

Holt, R. R. Review of *Psychoanalytic interpretation in Rorschach testing* by R. Schafer. In J. Frosch & N. Ross (Eds.), *Annual Survey of Psychoanalysis*, 1959, *5*, 530–538.

1960

Holt, R. R., & Goldberger, L. Research on the effects of isolation on cognitive functioning. USAF WADC Technical Reports, 1960, No. 60-260.

Holt, R. R., & Havel, J. A method for assessing primary and secondary process in the Rorschach. In M. A. Rickers-Ovsiankina (Ed.), *Rorschach psychology*. New York: Wiley, 1960.

Klein, G. S., & Holt, R. R. Problems and issues in current studies of subliminal activation. In J. G. Peatman & E. L. Hartley (Eds.), *Festschrift for Gardner Murphy*. New York: Harper, 1960.

Holt, R. R. Discussion remarks on "The effect of dream deprivation and excess: An experimental demonstration of the necessity for dreaming" by William C. Dement and Charles Fisher. *Psychoanalytic Quarterly*, 1960, *29*, 608. (a)

Holt, R. R. Recent developments in psychoanalytic ego psychology and their implications for diagnostic testing. *Journal of Projective Techniques*, 1960, *24*, 254–266. (b)

Holt, R. R. Cognitive controls and primary processes. *Journal of Psychological Researches*, 1960, *4*, 105–112. (c)

Pine, F., & Holt, R. R. Creativity and primary process: A study of adaptive regression. *Journal of Abnormal and Social Psychology*, 1960, *61*, 370–379.

Holt, R. R. Review of *Great cases in psychoanalysis* by H. Greenwald (Ed.). *Journal of Psychological Studies*, 1960, *11*, 147–148.

1961

Goldberger, L., & Holt, R. R. Experimental interference with reality contact: Individual differences. In P. Solomon *et al.* (Eds.), *Sensory deprivation*. Cambridge: Harvard University Press, 1961. (a)

Goldberger, L., & Holt, R. R. Studies on the effects of perceptual alteration. USAF ASD Technical Reports, 1961, No. 61-416. (b)

Goldberger, L., & Holt, R. R. A comparison of isolation effects and their personality correlates in two divergent samples. USAF ASD Technical Reports, 1961, No. 61-417. (c)

Holt, R. R. The nature of TAT stories as cognitive products: A psychoanalytic approach. In J. Kagan & G. Lesser (Eds.), *Contemporary issues in thematic apperceptive methods*. Springfield, Ill.: Thomas, 1961. (a)

Holt, R. R. Clinical judgment as a disciplined inquiry. *Journal of Nervous and Mental Disease*, 1961, *133*, 369–382. (b) Bobbs-Merrill Reprint Series in the Social Sciences, P-480, 1966.

Holt, R. R., & Goldberger, L. Assessment of individual resistance to sensory alteration. In B. E. Flaherty (Ed.), *Psychophysiological aspects of space flight*. New York: Columbia University Press, 1961.

Holt, R. R. The president's column. *Newsletter, Division of Clinical Psychology, APA*, 1961, *14*(4), 5; 1962, *15*(1), 1–2; *15*(2), 4–5; *15*(3), 6–7.

Holt, R. R. Review of *Research in psychotherapy* by E. A. Rubinstein & M. B. Parloff (Eds.). *International Journal of Group Psychotherapy*, 1961, *11*, 96–98.

Holt, R. R. Review of *Memory and hypnotic age regression* by R. Reiff & M. Scheerer. *Journal of Nervous and Mental Disease*, 1961, *132*, 545–548.

1962

Holt, R. R., & Proshansky, H. Roles for psychologists in promoting peace. *SPSSI Newsletter*, June 1962, 1–4.

Holt, R. R. A critical examination of Freud's concept of bound vs. free cathexis. *Journal of the American Psychoanalytic Association*, 1962, *10*, 475–525. (a)

Holt, R. R. Individuality and generalization in the psychology of personality. *Journal of Personality*, 1962, *30*, 377–404. (b) Translated into Italian: Individualita e generalizzazione nella psicologia della personalita. *Bollettino di Psicologia Applicata*, N. 57-58, Giugno-Agosto 1963. Reprinted in F. H. Sanford & E. J. Capaldi (Eds.), *Advancing psychological science, Vol. 1: Philosophies, methods, and approaches*. Belmont, Calif.: Wadsworth, 1964. Also reprinted in E. Southwell & M. Merbaum (Eds.), *Personality: Readings in theory and research*. Belmont, Calif.: Wadsworth, 1964. Also in D. Byrne & M. L. Hamilton (Eds.), *Personality research: A book of readings*. New York: Prentice-Hall, 1966. Also, Bobbs-Merrill Reprint Series in the Social Sciences, P-482, 1966. Also abridged under the title, "The logic of the romantic point of view in personology," in T. Millon (Ed.), *Theories of psychopathology*. Philadelphia: W. B. Saunders, 1967, pp. 315–322. Also reprinted in J. O. Whittaker (Ed.), *Recent discoveries in psychology*. Philadelphia: W. B. Saunders, 1972.
Revised version: In R. S. Lazarus & E. M. Opton (Eds.), *Personality: Selected readings*. Penguin Modern Psychology UPS 9. Harmondsworth, England: Penguin Books, 1967.

Holt, R. R. A clinical-experimental strategy for research in personality. In S. Messick & J. Ross (Eds.), *Measurement in personality and cognition*. New York: Wiley, 1962. (c)

Holt, R. R. (with the collaboration and assistance of Joan Havel, Leo Goldberger, Anthony Philip, & Reeva Safrin). Manual for the scoring of primary process manifestations in Rorschach responses (8th ed.). New York: Research Center for Mental Health, New York University, 1962 (mimeographed). (d)

Holt, R. R. Review of *Thought reform and the psychology of totalism: A study of brainwashing in China* by R. J. Lifton. *Journal of Nervous and Mental Disease*, 1962, *134*, 292–296.

1963

Holt, R. R. Two influences on Freud's scientific thought: A fragment of intellectual biography. In R. W. White (Ed.), *The study of lives*. New York: Atherton Press, 1963. (a)

Holt, R. R. New directions in the training of psychotherapists [editorial]. *Journal of Nervous and Mental Disease*, 1963, *137*, 413–416. Also in *American Psychologist*, 1963, *18*, 677–679. (b)

Holt, R. R. (with the collaboration and assistance of Joan Havel, Leo Goldberger, Anthony Philip, & Reeva Safrin). Manual for the scoring of primary process manifestations in Rorschach responses (9th ed.). New York: Research Center for Mental Health, New York University, 1963 (mimeographed). (c)

1964

Holt, R. R. Forcible indoctrination and personality change. In P. Worchel & D. Byrne (Eds.), *Personality change*. New York: Wiley, 1964. (a)

Holt, R. R. Imagery: The return of the ostracized. *American Psychologist*, 1964, *19*, 254–264. (b) Reprinted in E. P. Torrance & W. F. White (Eds.), *Issues and advances in educational psychology: A book of readings*. Itasca, Ill.: F. E. Peacock, 1969. Also abridged in B. L. Kintz & J. L. Bruning (Eds.), *Research in psychology: Readings for the introductory course*. Glenview, Ill.: Scott, Foresman, 1970.

Holt, R. R. The emergence of cognitive psychology [book essay]. *Journal of the American Psychoanalytic Association*, 1964, *12*, 650–665. (c)

Holt, R. R. Competence on competence (Review of *Ego and reality in psychoanalytic theory: A proposal regarding independent ego energies* by R. W. White). *Contemporary Psychology*, 1964, *9*, 433–434.

Holt, R. R. Review of *The encyclopedia of mental health* by A. Deutsch & H. Fishman (Eds.). *American Journal of Orthopsychiatry*, 1964, *34*, 156–160.

1965

Holt, R. R. A review of some of Freud's biological assumptions and their influence on his theories. In N. S. Greenfield & W. C. Lewis (Eds.), *Psychoanalysis and current biological thought*. Madison: University of Wisconsin Press, 1965. (a)

Holt, R. R. Experimental methods in clinical psychology. In B. Wolman (Ed.), *Handbook of clinical psychology*. New York: McGraw-Hill, 1965. (b)

Holt, R. R. Ego autonomy re-evaluated. *International Journal of Psycho-Analysis*, 1965, *46*, 151–167. (c) Reprinted with critical evaluations by S. C. Miller, A. Namnum, B. B. Rubinstein, J. Sandler & W. G. Joffe, R. Schafer, H. Weiner, and the author's rejoinder [see 1967a], *International Journal of Psychiatry*, 1967, *3*, 481–536.

Holt, R. R. Freud's cognitive style. *American Imago*, 1965, *22*, 163–179. (d)

Holt, R. R. Psychotherapy as an autonomous profession: An alternative to the Clark Committee's proposal. In *Preconference materials prepared for the Conference on the Professional Preparation of Clinical Psychologists*. Washington, D.C.: American Psychological Association, 1965. (e) Also in E. L. Hoch, A. O. Ross, & C. L. Winder (Eds.), *Professional preparation of clinical psychologists*. Washington, D.C.: American Psychological Association, 1966.

1966

Holt, R. R. A brave beginning to an enormous task. Critical evaluation of "A methodological study of Freudian theory" by A. Kardiner, A. Karush, & L. Ovesey. *International Journal of Psychiatry*, 1966, *2*, 545–548. (a)

Holt, R. R. Measuring libidinal and aggressive motives and their controls by means of the Rorschach test. In D. Levine (Ed.), *Nebraska symposium on motivation, 1966*. Lincoln: University of Nebraska Press, 1966. (b) Reprinted in P. M. Lerner (Ed.), *Handbook of Rorschach scales*. New York: International Universities Press, 1975.

Holt, R. R. New Freudiana [review of four books]. *Contemporary Psychology*, 1966, *11*, 211–214.

1967

Holt, R. R. On freedom, autonomy, and the redirection of psychoanalytic theory: A rejoinder. *International Journal of Psychiatry,* 1967, *3,* 524–536 [see also 1965c, above]. (a)

Holt, R. R. (Ed.). Motives and thought: Psychoanalytic essays in memory of David Rapaport. *Psychological Issues,* 1967, *5,* 2/3 (Whole Nos. 18/19). (b)

Holt, R. R. David Rapaport: A memoir (September 30, 1911–December 14, 1960). In R. R. Holt (Ed.), Motives and thought. *Psychological Issues,* 1967, *5,* 2/3 (Whole Nos. 18/19). (c)

Holt, R. R. The development of the primary process: A structural view. In R. R. Holt (Ed.), Motives and thought. *Psychological Issues,* 1967, *5,* 2/3 (Whole Nos. 18/19). (d)

Holt, R. R. Beyond vitalism and mechanism: Freud's concept of psychic energy. In J. H. Masserman (Ed.), *Science and psychoanalysis, Vol. 11: Concepts of ego.* New York: Grune & Stratton, 1967. And in B. Wolman (Ed.), *Historical roots of contemporary psychology.* New York: Harper & Row, 1968. Abstract in *Psychiatric Spectator,* 1967, *4,* 16–17 (Sandoz publication). (e)

Holt, R. R. Discussion: On using experiential data in personality assessment (Symposium). *Journal of Projective Techniques and Personality Assessment,* 1967, *31*(4), 25–30. (f)

Holt, R. R. Diagnostic testing: Present status and future prospects. *Journal of Nervous and Mental Disease,* 1967, *144,* 444–465. (g)

1968

Holt, R. R. (Ed.). Revised edition of *Diagnostic psychological testing* by D. Rapaport, M. M. Gill, & R. Schafer. New York: International Universities Press, 1968. (a)

Holt, R. R. Freud, Sigmund. *International encyclopedia of the social sciences* (Vol. 6). New York: Macmillan and The Free Press, 1968. (b)

1969

Holt, R. R. Assessing personality. In I. L. Janis, G. F. Mahl, J. Kagan, & R. R. Holt, *Personality: Dynamics, development, and assessment* (Part 4). New York: Harcourt, Brace & World, 1969. (a)

Holt, R. R. Kubie's dream and its impact upon reality: Psychotherapy as an autonomous profession. *Journal of Nervous and Mental Disease,* 1969, *149,* 186–207. (b)

Holt, R. R. The lasting value of the unconscious, or Rabkin fails to Peirce Freud. Critical evaluation of "Is the unconscious necessary?" by Richard Rabkin. *International Journal of Psychiatry,* 1969, *8,* 585–589. (c)

Holt, R. R. (with the collaboration and assistance of Joan Havel, Leo Goldberger, Anthony Philip, Reeva Safrin, & Carol Eagle). Manual for the scoring of primary process manifestations in Rorschach responses (10th ed.). New York: Research Center for Mental Health, New York University, 1969 (mimeographed). (d)

1970

Holt, R. R. Yet another look at clinical and statistical prediction: Or, is clinical psychology worthwhile? *American Psychologist,* 1970, *25,* 337–349. (a)

Holt, R. R. On the interpersonal and intrapersonal consequences of expressing or not expressing anger. Discussion of paper, "Experimental investigations of hostility catharsis," by L. Berkowitz. *Journal of Consulting and Clinical Psychology,* 1970, *35,* 8–12. (b)

Holt, R. R. Artistic creativity and Rorschach measures of adaptive regression. In B. Klopfer, M. M. Meyer, & F. B. Brawer (Eds.), *Developments in the Rorschach technique, Vol. 3: Aspects of personality structure.* New York: Harcourt, Brace, Jovanovich, 1970. (c)

1971

Holt, R. R. Freud's two images of man. *Western Psychologist Monograph Series No. 2,* 1971, 5–25. (a)

Holt, R. R. Some neglected assumptions and problems in psychology's information crisis. *American Psychologist,* 1971, *26,* 331–334. (b)

Holt, R. R. *Assessing personality.* New York: Harcourt, Brace, Jovanovich, 1971 (paperback reprint of 1969a, above). (c)

Holt, R. R. (Ed.). *New horizon for psychotherapy: Autonomy as a profession.* New York: International Universities Press, 1971. (d)

Holt, R. R. Summary and prospect: The dawn of a new profession. In R. R. Holt (Ed.), *New horizon for psychotherapy*. New York: International Universities Press, 1971. (e)

Holt, R. R. In memoriam: George S. Klein. *Psychological Issues*, 1971, 7(3), v–vii. (f)

1972

Barr, H. B., Langs, R. J., Holt, R. R., Goldberger, L., & Klein, G. S. *LSD: Personality and experience*. New York: Wiley, 1972.

Holt, R. R. Freud's mechanistic and humanistic image of man. In R. R. Holt & E. Peterfreund (Eds.), *Psychoanalysis and Contemporary Science*, 1972, *1*, 3–24. (a)

Holt, R. R. On the nature and generality of mental imagery. In P. W. Sheehan (Ed.), *The function and nature of imagery*. New York: Academic Press, 1972. (b)

Holt, R. R. Should the psychotherapist prescribe the pills? Preferably not! *International Journal of Psychiatry*, 1972, *10*(4), 82–86. (c)

1973

Holt, R. R. *Methods of research in clinical psychology*. Morristown, N.J.: General Learning Press. 1973. (a)

[Holt, R. R.] Personality. In B. B. Wolman (Ed.), *Dictionary of behavioral science*. New York: Van Nostrand Reinhold, 1973. (b)

1974

Holt, R. R. On reading Freud. Introduction to *Abstracts of the Standard Edition of Freud*. New York: Jason Aronson, 1974. (a)

Holt, R. R. In retrospect: Response to the Distinguished Contributions Award, Division 12, APA. *Clinical Psychologist*, 1974, *28*, 1, 5–6. (b)

Holt, R. R. *The current status of psychoanalytic theory*. Behavioral Sciences Tape Library. Leonia, N.J.: Sigma Information, 1974. (c)

Holt, R. R. Review of *Measuring ego development* (2 vols.) by J. Loevinger, R. Wessler, & C. Redmore. *Journal of Nervous and Mental Disease*, 1974, *158*, 310–318.

1975

Holt, R. R. Clinical and statistical measurement and prediction: How *not* to survey its literature. *JSAS Catalog of Selected Documents in Psychology*, 1975, *5*, 178, MS No. 837. (a)

Holt, R. R. The past and future of ego psychology. *Psychoanalytic Quarterly*, 1975, *44*(4), 550–576. (b)

1976

Holt, R. R. Drive or wish? A reconsideration of the psychoanalytic theory of motivation. *Psychological Issues*, 1976, *9*(4, Whole No. 36). (a)

Holt, R. R. Freud's theory of the primary process—present status. In T. Shapiro (Ed.), *Psychoanalysis and Contemporary Science*, 1976, *5*, 61–99. (b)

1977

Holt, R. R. A method for assessing primary process manifestations and their control in Rorschach responses. In M. A. Rickers-Ovsiankina (Ed.), *Rorschach psychology*, rev. ed. New York: Krieger, 1977. (a)

Holt, R. R. Introduction to L. Afflerbach and M. Franck (Eds.), *The emerging field of sociobibliography: The collected essays of Ilse Bry*. Westport, Conn.: Greenwood Press, 1977. (b)

References[1]

Abraham, K. (1921). Contributions to the theory of the anal character. In *Selected papers*. New York: Basic Books, 1953.

Abraham, K. (1924). The influence of oral erotism on character formation. In *Selected papers*. New York: Basic Books, 1953.

Ackoff, R. L. *The design of social research.* Chicago: University of Chicago Press, 1953.

Allport, G. W. *Personality: A psychological interpretation.* New York: Holt, 1937.

Allport, G. W. *Pattern and growth in personality.* New York: Holt, Rinehart & Winston, 1961.

Allport, G. W. *Letters from Jenny.* New York: Harcourt, Brace & World, 1965.

Allport, G. W., & Odbert, H. S. Trait-names: A psycho-lexical study. *Psychological Monographs,* 1936, *47* (1, Whole No. 211).

Alper, T. G. Memory for completed and incompleted tasks as a function of personality: An analysis of group data. *Journal of Abnormal and Social Psychology,* 1946, *41,* 403–420.

American Psychiatric Association. *Diagnostic and statistical manual of mental disorders.* Washington, D.C.: Author, 1968.

American Psychological Association, Ad Hoc Committee on Ethical Standards in Psychological Research. *Ethical principles in the conduct of research with human participants.* Washington, D.C.: Author, 1973.

American Psychological Association. Ethical standards of psychologists. In *Biographical directory of the American Psychological Association.* Washington, D.C.: Author, 1975.

Argyris, C. Some unintended consequences of rigorous research. *Psychological Bulletin,* 1968, *70,,* 185–197.

Argyris, C. Problems and new directions for industrial psychology. In M.D. Dunnette (Ed.) *Handbook of industrial and organizational psychology.* Chicago: Rand McNally, 1976.

Arieti, S. *Interpretation of schizophrenia.* New York: Brunner Mazel, 1975.

Aserinsky, E., & Kleitman, N. Two types of ocular motility occurring in sleep. *Journal of Applied Physiology.* 1955, *8,* 1–10.

Ashton, S. G., & Goldberg, L. R. In response to Jackson's challenge: The comparative validity of personality scales constructed by the external (empirical) strategy and scales developed intuitively by experts, novices, and laymen. *Journal of Research in Personality,* 1973, *7,* 1–20.

Atkinson, J. W. (Ed.). *Motives in fantasy, action, and society: A method of assessment and study.* Princeton: Van Nostrand, 1958.

Auerbach, E. *Mimesis, the representation of reality in western literature.* Princeton: Princeton University Press, 1953.

---

[1]All references where R. R. Holt is the senior (or sole) author will be found in the personal bibliography, beginning on p. 303.

Auld, F., & Murray, E. J. Content analysis studies of psychotherapy. *Psychological Bulletin,* 1955, *52,* 377–395.

Bach, S. Symbolic associations to stimulus words in subliminal, supraliminal and incidental presentation. Unpublished doctoral dissertation. New York University, 1960.

Bach, S., & Klein, G. S. The effects of prolonged subliminal exposures of words. *American Psychologist,* 1957, *12,* 397–398.

Baldwin, A. L., Kalhorn, J., & Breese, F. H. Patterns of parent behavior. *Psychological Monographs,* 1945, *58,* 268.

Barber, B., & Fox, R. C. The case of the floppy-eared rabbits: An instance of serendipity gained and serendipity lost. *American Journal of Sociology,* 1958, *64,* 128–136.

Barr, H. B., Langs, R. J., Holt, R. R., Goldberger, L., & Klein, G. S. *LSD: Personality and experience.* New York: Wiley, 1972.

Barron, F. Some test correlates of response to psychotherapy. *Journal of Consulting Psychology,* 1953, *17,* 233–241. (b)

Bavelas, A. Communication patterns in problem-solving groups. In H. van Foerster (Ed.), *Cybernetics: Circular, causal and feedback mechanisms in biological and social systems.* New York: Josiah Macy, 1952.

Beach, F. A. The snark was a Boojum. *American Psychologist,* 1950, *5,* 115–124.

Beck, S. J. The science of personality: Nomothetic or idiographic? *Psychological Review,* 1953, *60,* 353–359.

Berelson, B. *Content analysis in communications research.* Glencoe, Ill.: Free Press, 1952.

Bergin, A. E. The evaluation of therapeutic outcomes. In A. E. Bergin & S. L. Garfield (Eds.), *Handbook of psychotherapy and behavior change: An empirical analysis.* New York: Wiley, 1971.

Bergin, A. E., & Garfield, S. L. (Eds.), *Handbook of psychotherapy and behavior change: An empirical analysis.* New York: Wiley, 1971.

Bergman, P. An experiment in filmed psychotherapy. In L. A. Gottschalk & A. H. Auerbach (Eds.), *Methods of research in psychotherapy.* New York: Appleton-Century-Crofts, 1966.

Betz, B., & Whitehorn, J. C. The relationship of the therapist to the outcome of therapy in schizophrenia. *Psychiatric Research Reports,* 1956, *5,* 89–105.

Bingham, W. Halo: Invalid and valid. *Journal of Applied Psychology,* 1939, *23,* 221–228.

Blalock, H. M. *Causal inferences in nonexperimental research.* New York: Norton, 1972.

Blatt, M. The effects of classroom discussion on the development of moral judgment. Unpublished doctoral dissertation, University of Chicago, 1969.

Blenkner, M. Predictive factors in the initial interview in family casework. *Social Science Review,* 1954, *28,* 65–73.

Block, J. *The Q-sort method in personality assessment and psychiatric research: A monograph.* Springfield, Ill.: C C Thomas, 1961.

Block, J. *The challenge of response sets.* New York: Appleton-Century-Crofts, 1965.

Block, J. H. Issues, problems, and pitfalls in assessing sex differences: A critical review of *The Psychology of Sex Differences. Merrill-Palmer Quarterly,* 1976, *22,* 4, 283–308.

Bloom, R. F., & Brundage, E. G. Prediction of success in elementary schools for enlisted personnel. In D. B. Stuit (Ed.), *Personnel research and test development in the Bureau of Naval Personnel.* Princeton: Princeton University Press, 1947.

Bobbitt, J. M., & Newman, S. H. Psychological activities at the United States Coast Guard Academy. *Psychological Bulletin,* 1944, *41,* 568–579.

Borden, H. G. Factors for predicting parole success. *Journal of the American Institute of Criminal Law and Criminology,* 1928, *19,* 328–336.

Boring, E. G. Human nature vs. sensation: William James and the psychology of the present. *American Journal of Psychology,* 1942, *55,* 310–327. Also in Boring's *Psychologist at large.* New York: Basic Books, 1961.

Boring, E. G. The nature and history of experimental control. *American Journal of Psychology,* 1954, *67,* 573–589.

Breuer, J., & Freud, S. (1895) Studies on hysteria. *Standard edition* (Vol. 2). London: Hogarth, 1955.

Bronowski, J. *Science and human values* (Rev. ed.). New York: Harper & Row, 1965.

Bruner, J. S. Going beyond the information given. In *Contemporary approaches to cognition.* Cambridge: Harvard University Press, 1957.

Brunswik, E. *Perception and the representative design of psychological experiments.* Berkeley: University of California Press, 1956.

Burgess, A. *A clockwork orange.* New York: Norton, 1963.

Burgess, E. W. Factors determining success or failure on parole. In A. A. Bruce (Ed.), *The workings of the indeterminate sentence law and the parole system in Illinois.* Springfield: Illinois State Board of Parole, 1928.

Burgess, E. W. An experiment in the standardization of the case-study method. *Sociometry,* 1941, *4,* 329–348.

Burgess, E. W., & Wallin, P. *Engagement and marriage.* Philadelphia: Lippincott, 1953.

Campbell, D. T. Factors relevant to the validity of experiments in social settings. *Psychological Bulletin,* 1957, *54,* 297–313.

Campbell, D. T. Reforms as experiments. *American Psychologist,* 1969, *24,* 409–429.

Campbell, D. T., & Stanley, J. C. *Experimental and quasi-experimental designs for research.* New York: Rand McNally, 1966.

Canfield, A. A. The "sten" scale: A modified C-scale. *Educational and Psychological Measurement,* 1951, *11,* 295–297.

Cartwright, D. P. Analysis of qualitative material. In L. Festinger & D. Katz (Eds.), *Research methods in the behavioral sciences.* New York: Dryden Press, 1953.

Cartwright, R. A comparison of the response to psychoanalytic and client-centered psychotherapy. In L. A. Gottschalk & A. H. Auerbach (Eds.), *Methods of research in psychotherapy.* New York: Appleton-Century-Crofts, 1966.

Cassotta, L., Feldstein, S., & Jaffe, J. AVTA: A device for automatic vocal transaction analysis. *Journal of the Experimental Analysis of Behavior,* 1964, *7,* 99–104.

Cattell, R. B., & Luborsky, L. B. P-technique demonstrated as a new clinical method for determining personality and symptom structure. *Journal of Genetic Psychology,* 1950, *42,* 3–24.

Chauncey, H. Personal communication. Reported by P. E. Meehl in *Clinical vs. statistical prediction.* Minneapolis: University of Minnesota Press, 1954.

Chein, I. *The science of behavior and the image of man.* New York: Basic Books, 1972.

Cliff, R. Validation of selection procedures in enlisted-to-officer programs. USN Bureau of Naval Personnel Technical Bulletin, 1958, No. 58-11.

Cochran, W. G., & Cox, G. M. *Experimental designs.* New York: Wiley, 1957.

Cochran, W. G., Mosteller, F., & Tukey, J. W. Statistical problems of the Kinsey Report. *Journal of the American Statistical Association,* 1953, *48,* 673–716.

Cohen, J. Multivariate methods in clinical psychology. In R. B. Cattell (Ed.), *Handbook for multivariate experimental psychology.* New York: Rand McNally, 1964.

Cohen, J. Some statistical issues in psychological research. In B. Wolman (Ed.), *Handbook of clinical psychology.* New York: McGraw-Hill, 1965.

Cohen, J. Multiple regression as a general data-analytic system. *Psychological Bulletin,* 1968, *70,* 426–443.

Cohen, J. *Statistical power analysis for the behavioral sciences.* New York: Academic Press, 1969.

Cohen, J., & Cohen, P. *Applied multiple regression: Correlation analysis for the behavioral sciences.* New York: Wiley, 1975.

Colby, K. M. *A skeptical psychoanalyst.* New York: Ronald, 1958.

Conrad, H. W., & Satter, G. A. Use of test scores and quality classification ratings in predicting success in electrician's mates school. Office of Social Research and Development Report No. 5667, Sept. 1945. Summarized in D. B. Stuit (Ed.), *Personnel research and test development in the Bureau of Naval Personnel.* Princeton: Princeton University Press, 1947.

Coombs, C. M. A theory of data. *Psychological Review*, 1960, *67*, 143–159.

Coyle, E. Counselor prediction of academic success. Unpublished doctoral dissertation, Columbia University, 1956.

Cronbach, L. J. A validation design for qualitative studies of personality. *Journal of Consulting Psychology*, 1948, *12*, 365–374.

Cronbach, L. J. Assessment of individual differences. In P. Farnsworth & Q. McNemar (Eds.), *Annual Review of Psychology*, 1956, *7*, 173–196.

Cronbach, L. J. The two disciplines of scientific psychology. *American Psychologist*, 1957, *12*, 671–684.

Cronbach, L. J. *Essentials of psychological testing* (2nd ed.). New York: Harper & Row, 1960.

Cronbach, L. J. Beyond the two disciplines of scientific psychology. *American Psychologist*, 1975, *30*, 116–127.

Cronbach, L. J., & Gleser, G. C. Assessing similarity between profiles. *Psychological Bulletin*, 1953, *50*, 456–473.

Cronbach, L. J., & Gleser, G. C. Processes affecting scores on "understanding of others" and "assumed similarity." *Psychological Bulletin*, 1955, *52*, 177–193.

Cronbach, L. J., & Gleser, G. C. *Psychological tests and personnel decisions*. Urbana: University of Illinois Press, 1957.

Dahl, H. A quantitative study of a psychoanalysis. In R. R. Holt & E. Peterfreund (Eds.), *Psychoanalysis and Contemporary Science*, 1972, *1*, 237–257.

Davidson, P. O., & Costello, C. G. *N = 1: Experimental studies of single cases*. New York: Van Nostrand Reinhold, 1969.

Dawes, R. M., & Corrigan, B. Linear models in decision making. *Psychological Bulletin*, 1974, *81*, 95–106.

Dement, W. The effect of dream deprivation. *Science*, 1960, *131*, 1705–1707.

Dement, W., & Kleitman, N. Cyclic variations in EEG during sleep and their relation to eye movements, body motility, and dreaming. *Electroencephalography and Clinical Neurophysiology*, 1957, *9*, 673–690. (a)

Deutsch, M. Evidence and inference in nuclear research. *Daedalus*, 1958, *87*, 88–98.

Dickens, C. *American notes for general circulation*. New York: Harper, 1842.

Dittman, A. T., & Llewellyn, L. G. The phonemic clause as a unit of speech decoding. *Journal of Personality and Social Psychology*, 1967, *6*, 341–349.

Doleys, R. J., & Renzaglia, G. A. Accuracy of student prediction of college grades. *Personnel Guidance Journal*, 1963, *41*, 528–530.

Dollard, J., Doob, L. W., Miller, N. E., Mowrer, O. H., & Sears, R. R. *Frustration and aggression*. New Haven: Yale University, 1938.

Donelson, E. *Personality: A scientific approach*. New York: Appleton-Century-Crofts, 1973.

Drucker, A. J. Predicting leadership ratings in the United States Army. *Educational and Psychological Measurement*, 1957, *17*, 240–263.

Dunham, H. W., & Meltzer, B. N. Predicting length of hospitalization of mental patients. *American Journal of Sociology*, 1946, *52*, 123–131.

Dunlap, J. W., & Wantman, M. J. An investigation of the interview as a technique for selecting aircraft pilots. Washington, D.C.: Civil Aeronautics Administration, 1944, Report No. 33.

Eagle, C. An investigation of individual consistencies in the manifestations of primary process. Unpublished doctoral dissertation, New York University, 1964.

Ebel, R. L. Estimation of the reliability of ratings. *Psychometrika*, 1951, *16*, 407–424.

Edwards, A. L. The social desirability hypothesis: Theoretical implications for personality measurement. In S. Messick & J. Ross (Eds.), *Measurement in personality and cognition*. New York: Wiley, 1962.

Edwards, A. L. *Experimental design in psychological research* (4th ed.). New York: Holt, Rinehart & Winston, 1972.

Edwards, W. The theory of decision making. *Psychological Bulletin*, 1954, *51*, 380–418.

Edwards, W., Guttentag, M., & Snapper, K. A decision-theoretic approach to evaluation research. In E. L. Struening & M. Guttentag (Eds.), *Handbook of evaluation research* (Vol. 1). Beverly Hills, Calif.: Sage, 1975.

Einstein, A. Ernst Mach. *Physikalische Zeitschrift,* 1916, *17,* 101–104.

Elstein, A. S. Clinical judgment: Psychological research and medical practice. *Science,* 1976, *194,* 696–700.

Endler, N S., Hunt, J. McV., & Rosenstein, A. J. An S-R inventory of anxiousness. *Psychological Monographs,* 1962, *76*(17, Whole No. 536).

Erikson, E. H. (1950) *Childhood and society* (2nd ed.). New York: Norton, 1963.

Erikson, E. H. The nature of clinical evidence. *Daedalus,* 1958, *87,* 65–87.

Erikson, E. H. Identity and the life cycle: Selected papers. *Psychological Issues,* 1959, *1*(1).

Erikson, E. H. *Insight and responsibility.* New York: Norton, 1964.

Erikson, E. H. *Identity, youth and crisis.* New York: Norton, 1968.

Eysenck, H. J. The effects of psychotherapy: An evaluation. *Journal of Consulting Psychology,* 1952, *16,* 319–324.

Eysenck, H. J. The science of personality: Nomothetic! *Psychological Review,* 1954, *61,* 339–342.

Eysenck, H. J. The effects of psychotherapy. *International Journal of Psychiatry,* 1965, *1,* 97–142.

Eysenck, H. J. *The effects of psychotherapy.* New York: International Universities Press, 1966.

Fenichel, O. *The psychoanalytic theory of neurosis.* New York: Norton, 1945.

Fiedler, F. E. A comparison of therapeutic relationships in psychoanalytic, non-directive, and Adlerian therapy. *Journal of Consulting Psychology,* 1950, *14,* 436–445.

Fisher, C. Dreams and perception: The role of preconscious and primary modes of perception in dream formation. *Journal of the American Psychoanalytic Association,* 1954, *2,* 389–445.

Fiske, D. W. *Measuring the concepts of personality.* Chicago: Aldine, 1971.

Fiske, D. W., Hunt, H. F., Luborsky, L., Orne, M. T., Parloff, M. B., Reiser, M. F., & Tuma, A. H. Planning of research on effectiveness of psychotherapy. *American Psychologist,* 1970, *25,* 727–737.

Fiss, H., Goldberg, F., & Klein, G. S. Effects of subliminal stimulation on imagery and discrimination. *Perceptual and Motor Skills,* 1963, *17,* 31–44.

Frank, J. *Persuasion and healing.* Baltimore, Md.: The Johns Hopkins Press, 1961.

Fredenthal, B. J. Repression: Toward establishment of an experimental paradigm. Unpublished doctoral dissertation, Wayne State University, 1966.

Freud, S. (1900a)[2] The interpretation of dreams. *Standard edition* (Vols. 4 & 5). London: Hogarth, 1953.

Freud, S. (1901b) The psychopathology of everyday life. *Standard edition* (Vol. 6). London: Hogarth, 1960.

Freud, S. (1908b) Character and anal erotism. *Standard edition* (Vol. 9). London: Hogarth, 1959.

Freud, S. (1937d) Constructions in analysis. *Standard edition* (Vol. 23). London: Hogarth, 1964.

Freud, S. (1940a) An outline of psychoanalysis. *Standard edition* (Vol. 23). London: Hogarth, 1964.

Gardner, R., Holzman, P. S., Klein, G. S., Linton, H. B., & Spence, D. P. Cognitive control: A study of individual consistencies in cognitive behavior. *Psychological Issues,* 1959, *1*(4).

Gendlin, E. Focusing. *Psychotherapy: Theory, Research and Practice,* 1969, *6,* 4–15.

Gill, M. M., Simon, J., Fink, G., Endicott, N. A., & Paul, I. H. Studies in audio-recorded psychoanalysis: I. General considerations. *Journal of the American Psychoanalytic Association,* 1968, *16,* 230–244.

Girshick, M. A. An elementary survey of statistical decision theory. *Review of Educational Research,* 1954, *24,* 448–466.

---

[2]Dates of original publication, with letters distinguishing items from the same year, are taken from the definitive Freud bibliography in Vol. 24 of *The Standard Edition of the Complete Psychological Works of Sigmund Freud.* London: Hogarth, 1974.

Glaser, D. A. A reconsideration of some parole prediction factors. *American Sociological Review,* 1954, *19,* 335–341.

Glaser, D. A., & Hangren, R. F. Predicting the adjustment of federal probationers. *National Probation and Parole Association Journal,* 1958, *4,* 258–267.

Glass, G. V. Primary, secondary, and meta-analysis of research. *Educational Researcher,* 1976, *5*(10), 3–8.

Goldberg, L. R. Seer over sign: The first "good" example? *Journal of Experimental Research in Personality,* 1968, *3,* 168–171. (a)

Goldberg, L. R. Simple models or simple processes? Some research on clinical judgments. *American Psychologist,* 1968, *23,* 483–496. (b)

Goldberg, L. R. Man vs. model of man: A rationale, plus some evidence, for a method of improving on clinical inferences. *Psychological Bulletin,* 1970, *73,* 422–432.

Goldberg, L. R. Some recent trends in personality assessment. *Journal of Personality Assessment,* 1972, *36,* 547–560.

Goldberg, L. R. Objective diagnostic tests and measures. *Annual Review of Psychology,* 1974, *25,* 343–366.

Goldberger, L. Reactions to perceptual isolation and Rorschach manifestations of the primary process. *Journal of Projective Techniques,* 1961, *25,* 287–303.

Goldberger, L., & Holt, R. R. A comparison of isolation effects and their personality correlates in two divergent samples. USAF ASD Technical Reports, 1961, No. 61-417.

Goldenberg, H. *Contemporary clinical psychology.* Monterey, Calif.: Brooks/Cole, 1973.

Gottschalk, L. A., & Auerbach, A. H. *Methods of research in psychotherapy.* New York: Appleton-Century-Crofts, 1966.

Gottschalk, L. A., & Gleser, G. C. *The measurement of psychological states through the content analysis of verbal behavior.* Berkeley: University of California Press, 1969.

Gough, H. G. Clinical versus statistical prediction in psychology. In L. Postman (Ed.), *Psychology in the making.* New York: Knopf, 1962.

Grebstein, L. Relative accuracy of actuarial prediction, experienced clinicians, and graduate students in a clinical judgment test. *Journal of Consulting Psychology,* 1963, *37,* 127–132.

Gregory, E. Evaluation of selection procedures for women naval officers. USN Bureau of Naval Personnel Technical Bulletin, 1956, No. 56-11.

Group for the Advancement of Psychiatry. *Some observations on controls in psychiatric research.* Washington, D.C.: Author, Report No. 42 (May, 1959).

Grummion, D. L., & Butler, J. M. Another failure to replicate Keet's study, "Two verbal techniques in a miniature counseling situation." *Journal of Abnormal and Social Psychology,* 1953, *48,* 597.

Guetzkow, H. Unitizing and categorizing problems in coding qualitative data. *Journal of Clinical Psychology,* 1950, *6,* 47–58.

Guilford, J. P. *The nature of human intelligence.* New York: McGraw-Hill, 1967.

Guttentag, M., & Struening, E. L. (Eds.). *Handbook of evaluation research* (Vol. 2). Beverly Hills, Calif: Sage, 1975.

Hadamard, J. *The psychology of invention in the mathematical field.* Princeton, N.J.: Princeton University Press, 1945.

Halbower, C. C. A comparison of actuarial versus clinical prediction to classes discriminated by the Minnesota Multiphasic Personality Inventory. Unpublished doctoral dissertation, University of Minnesota, 1955.

Hamlin, R. Predictability of institutional adjustment of reformatory inmates. *Journal of Juvenile Research,* 1934, *18,* 179–184.

Hammond, K. R., & Adelman, L. Science, values, and human judgment. *Science,* 1976, *194,* 389–396.

Harris, J. G. Judgmental versus mathematical prediction: An investigation by analogy of the clinical versus statistical controversy. *Behavioral Science,* 1963, *8,* 324–335.

Hartmann, H. Comments on the psychoanalytic theory of the ego. *Psychoanalytic Study of the Child*, 1950, *5*, 74–96.

Hase, H. D., & Goldberg, L. R. The comparative validity of different strategies of deriving personality inventory scales. *Psychological Bulletin*, 1967, *67*, 231–248.

Havens, L. L. Emil Kraepelin. *Journal of Nervous and Mental Disease*, 1965, *141*, 16–28.

Heath, D. H. *Explorations of maturity*. New York: Appleton-Century-Crofts, 1965.

Heath, D. H. *Growing up in college*. San Francisco: Jossey-Bass, 1968.

Hebb, D. O. The American revolution. *American Psychologist*, 1960, *15*, 735–745.

Heider, F. Social perception and phenomenal causality. *Psychological Review*, 1944, *51*, 358–374.

Heider, F. *The psychology of interpersonal relations*. New York: Wiley, 1958.

Heim, R. B. An attempt to repeat the Keet counseling-comparison experiment. Paper read at Western Psychological Association, San Jose, Calif., April, 1951.

Hilden, A. H. *Manual for Q-sort and random sets of personal concepts*. Webster Groves, Mo. (628 Clark Avenue): Author, 1954.

Hoch, E. L. *Experimental contributions to clinical psychology*. Belmont, Calif.: Brooks/Cole: 1971.

Hoffman, P. J. The paramorphic representation of clinical judgment. *Psychological Bulletin*, 1960, *57*, 116–131.

Hollingshead, A. B., & Redlich, F. C. *Social class and mental illness: A community study*. New York: Wiley, 1958.

Holsti, O. R. Content analysis. In G. Lindzey & E. Aronson (Eds.), *The handbook of social psychology* (Vol. 2). Reading, Mass.: Addison-Wesley, 1968.

Holsti, O. R. *Content analysis for the social sciences and the humanities*. Reading, Mass.: Addison-Wesley, 1969.

Holton, G. *Thematic origins of scientific thought: Kepler to Einstein*. Cambridge: Harvard University Press, 1973.

Holtzman, W. H., & Sells, S. B. Prediction of flying success by clinical analysis of test protocols. *Journal of Abnormal and Social Psychology*, 1954, *49*, 485–490.

Horn, D. A study of personality syndromes. *Character and Personality*, 1944, *12*, 257–274.

Horst, P., *et al.* The prediction of personal adjustment. *Social Science Research Council Bulletin*, 1941, No. 48.

Horwitz, M. Hostility and its management in classroom groups. In W. W. Charters, Jr., & N. L. Gage (Eds.), *Readings in the social psychology of education*. Rockleigh, N.J.: Allyn & Bacon, 1963.

Hovey, H. B., & Stauffacher, J. C. Intuitive versus objective prediction from a test. *Journal of Clinical Psychology*, 1953, *9*, 349–351.

Howe, E. S. Three-dimensional structure of ratings of exploratory responses shown by a semantic differential. *Psychological Reports*, 1964, *14*, 187–196.

Humphreys, L. G., *et al. Proceedings of the 1955 Invitation Conference on Testing Problems*. Princeton: Educational Testing Service, October 1955.

Husén, T. La validité des interviews par rapport à l'âge, au sexe et à la formation des interviewers. *Travail Humain*, 1954, *17*, 60–67.

Jahoda, M. *Current concepts of positive mental health*. New York: Basic Books, 1958.

Janis, I. L., Mahl, G. F., Kagan, J., & Holt, R. R. *Personality: Dynamics, development, and assessment*. New York: Harcourt, Brace & World, 1969.

Jones, E. *The life and work of Sigmund Freud* (Vol. 2). New York: Basic Books, 1955.

Kagan, J., & Moss, H. A. *Birth to maturity: A study of psychological development*. New York: Wiley, 1962.

Kaiser, H. In L. B. Fierman (Ed.), *Effective psychotherapy: The contribution of Hellmuth Kaiser*. New York: Free Press, 1965.

Kaplan, A. *The conduct of inquiry: Methodology for behavioral science*. San Francisco: Chandler, 1964.

Keet, C. D. Two verbal techniques in a miniature counseling situation. *Psychological Monographs*, 1948, *62* (7, Whole No. 294).

Kelly, E. L., & Fiske, D. W. The prediction of success in the VA training program in clinical psychology. *American Psychologist,* 1950, *5,* 395–406.

Kelly, E. L., & Fiske, D. W. *The prediction of performance in clinical psychology.* Ann Arbor: University of Michigan Press, 1951.

Kelly, E. L., & Goldberg, L. R. Correlates of later performance and specialization in psychology. *Psychological Monographs,* 1959, *73* (12, Whole No. 482).

Kelman, H. C. *A time to speak: On human values and social research.* San Francisco: Jossey-Bass, 1968.

Keniston, K. *The uncommitted.* New York: Harcourt, Brace & World, 1965.

Keniston, K. *Young radicals.* New York: Harcourt, Brace & World, 1968.

Kernberg, O., Burstein, E. D., Coyne, L., Appelbaum, A., Horwitz, L., & Voth, H. Psychotherapy and psychoanalysis: Final report of The Menninger Foundation's Psychotherapy Research Project. *Bulletin of The Menninger Clinic,* 1972, *36,* 1–276.

Kiesler, D. J. Basic methodologic issues implicit in psychotherapy process research. *American Journal of Psychotherapy,* 1966, *20,* 135–155.

Klein, G. S. Need and regulation. In M. R. Jones (Ed.), *Nebraska symposium on motivation, 1954.* Lincoln: University of Nebraska Press, 1954.

Klein, G. S. Perception, motives and personality: A clinical perspective. In J. L. McCary (Ed.), *Psychology of personality.* New York: Logos Press, 1956.

Klein, G. S. Cognitive control and motivation. In G. Lindzey (Ed.), Assessment of human motives. New York: Holt, Rinehart, Winston, 1958. Also in G. S. Klein, *Perception, motives and personality.* New York: Knopf, 1970.

Klein, G. S. *Perception, motives and personality.* New York: Knopf, 1970.

Klein, G. S., & Holt, R. R. Problems and issues in current studies of subliminal activation. In J. G. Peatman & E. L. Hartley (Eds.), *Festschrift for Gardner Murphy.* New York: Harper & Row, 1960.

Klein, G. S., Spence, D. P., Holt, R. R., & Gourevitch, S. Cognition without awareness: Subliminal influences upon conscious thought. *Journal of Abnormal and Social Psychology,* 1958, *57,* 255–266.

Kleinmuntz, B. MMPI decision rules for the identification of college maladjustment: A digital computer approach. *Psychological Monographs,* 1963, *77* (14, Whole No. 577).

Kleinmuntz, B. *Personality measurement: An introduction.* Homewood, Ill.: Dorsey Press, 1967.

Kohlberg, L. Stage and sequence: The cognitive-developmental approach to socialization. In D. Goslin (Ed.), *Handbook of socialization theory and research.* New York: Rand McNally, 1969.

Köhler, W. (1929) *Gestalt psychology.* New York: Liveright, 1947.

Korman, A. K. The prediction of managerial performance: A review. *Personnel Psychology,* 1968, *21,* 295–322.

Kubie, L. S. The pros and cons of a new profession: A doctorate in medical psychology. *Texas Reports on Biology and Medicine,* 1954, *12,* 692–737.

Kubie, L. S. A school of psychological medicine within the framework of a medical school and university. *Journal of Medical Education,* 1964, *39,* 476–480.

Kubie, L. S. The overall manpower problem and the creation of a new discipline: The nonmedical psychotherapist. In M. Klutch (Ed.), *Mental health manpower: Vol. 2. Recruitment, training, and utilization—a compilation of articles, surveys and a review of applicable literature.* Sacramento: California Department of Mental Hygiene, 1967.

Kuhn, T. *The structure of scientific revolutions.* Chicago: University of Chicago Press, 1962; rev. ed., 1970.

Laffal, J. *Pathological and normal language.* New York: Atherton, 1965.

Langer, S. K. *Philosophy in a new key.* Cambridge: Harvard University Press, 1951.

Langer, W. Sensorimotor learning. In H. A, Murray [*et. al.*]. *Explorations in personality.* New York: Oxford University Press, 1938.

Lasagna, L., & von Felsinger, J. M. The volunteer subject in research. *Science,* 1954, *120,* 359–361.

Lazarsfeld, P. F., & Barton, A. H. Qualitative measurement in the social sciences: Classification, typologies, and indices. In D. Lerner & H. D. Lasswell (Eds.), *The policy sciences.* Stanford, Calif.: Stanford University Press, 1951.

Leach, E. Levi-Strauss in the Garden of Eden: An examination of some recent developments in the analysis of myth. *Transactions of the New York Academy of Science,* 1961, *23,* 386–396.

Leary, T., & Gill, M. M. The dimensions and a measure of the process of psychotherapy: A system for the analysis of the content of clinical evaluations and patient-therapist verbalization. In E. A. Rubinstein & M. B. Parloff (Eds.), *Research in psychotherapy.* Washington, D.C.: American Psychological Association, 1959.

Lennard, H. L., & Bernstein, A. *The anatomy of psychotherapy.* New York: Columbia University Press, 1960.

Lepley, W. M., & Hadley, H. T. In J. P Guilford (ed.), *Printed classification tests* (Army Air Force Aviation Psychology Program Research Report, No. 5). Washington, D.C.: U.S. Government Printing Office, 1947.

Lerner, D. (Ed.) On evidence and inference. *Daedalus,* 1958, *87,* 4.

Levi-Strauss, C. The structural study of myth. In T. A. Sebeok (Ed.), *Myth: A symposium.* Philadelphia: American Folklore Society, 1955.

Levy, L. H. *Psychological interpretation.* New York: Holt, Rinehart & Winston, 1963.

Lewis, E. C., & MacKinney, A. C. Counselor vs. statistical prediction of job satisfaction in engineering. *Journal of Counseling Psychology,* 1961, *8,* 224–229.

Lifton, R. J. *Thought reform and the psychology of totalism.* New York: Norton, 1961.

Lifton, R. J. *Death in life: Survivors of Hiroshima.* New York: Random House, 1968.

Lifton, R. J. *The life of the self: Toward a new psychology.* New York: Simon & Schuster, 1976.

Lilly, J. C. Mental effects of physical restraints and of reduction of ordinary levels of physical stimuli on intact healthy persons. *Psychiatric Research Reports,* 1956, *5,* 1–9.

Lindzey, G. Seer versus sign. *Journal of Experimental Research in Personality,rmo65, 1,* 17–26. Also in E. I. Megargee (Ed.), *Research in clinical assessment.* New York: Harper & Row , 1966.

Lindzey, G., & Aronson, E. (Eds.). *The handbook of social psychology: Vol. 2. Research methods.* Reading, Mass.: Addison-Wesley, 1968.

Loevinger, J. Conflint of commitment in clinical research. *American Psychologist,* 1963, *18,* 241–251.

Loevinger, J. Measurement in clinical research. In B. Wolman (Ed.), *Handbook of clinical psychology.* New York: McGraw-Hill, 1965.

Loevinger, J. The meaning and measurement of ego development. *American Psychologist,* 1966, *21,* 195–206.

Loevinger, J. *Ego development: Conceptions and theories.* San Francisco: Jossey-Bass, 1976.

Loevinger, J., Wessler, R., & Redmore, C. *Measuring ego development* (2 vols.). San Francisco: Jossey-Bass, 1970.

Lorr, M., Klett, C. J., & McNair, D. M. *Syndromes of psychosis,* New York: Macmillan, 1963.

Lovell, V. R. The human use of personality tests: A dissenting view. *American Psychologist,* 1967, *22,* 383–393.

Luborsky, L. A note on Eysenck's article, "The effects of psychotherapy: An evaluation." *British Journal of Psychology,* 1954, *45,* 129–131.

Luborsky, L. Clinicians' judgments of mental health: A proposed scale. *Archives of General Psychiatry,* 1962, *17,* 407–417. (a)

Luborsky, L. The patient's personality and psychotherapeutic change. In H. H. Strupp & L. Luborsky (Eds,), *Research in psychotherapy* (Vol. 2). Washington, D.C.: American Psychological Association, 1962. (b)

Luborsky, L. Momentary forgetting during psychotherapy and psychoanalysis: A theory and research method. In R. R. Holt (Ed.), *Motives and thought.* New York: International Universities Press, 1967.

Luborsky, L., & Shevrin, H. Dreams and day-residues: A study of tbe Poetzl observation. *Bulletin of The Menninger Clinic,* 1956, *20,* 135–148.

Luborsky, L., & Spence, D. P. Quantitative research on psychoanalytic therapy. In A. E. Bergin & S. L. Garfield (Eds.), *Handbook of psychotherapy and behavior change: An empirical analysis.* New York: Wiley, 1971.

Luborsky, L., Holt, R. R., & Morrow, W. R. Interim report of the research project on the selection of medical men for psychiatric training. *Bulletin of The Menninger Clinic,* 1950, *14,* 92–101.

Lundberg, G. A. Case-studies vs. statistical methods—an issue based on misunderstanding. *Sociometry,* 1941, *4,* 379–383.

Maccoby, E., & Jacklin, C. *The psychology of sex differences.* Stanford, Calif.: Stanford University Press, 1974.

MacFarlane, J. W., Allen, L., & Honzik, M. *A developmental study of the behavior problems of normal children between 21 months and 14 years.* Berkeley: University of California Press, 1955.

Marquis, D. Research planning at the frontiers of science. *American Psychologist,* 1948, *3,* 430–438.

Marsden, G. Content-analysis studies of psychotherapy: 1954 through 1968. In A. E. Bergin & S. L. Garfield (Eds.), *Handbook of psychotherapy and behavior change: An empirical analysis.* New York: Wiley, 1971.

Masters, W. H., & Johnson, V. E. *Human sexual response.* New York: Little, Brown, 1966.

Matarazzo, J. D., Saslow, G., & Matarazzo, R. G. The interaction chronograph as an instrument for objective measurement of interaction patterns during interviews. *Journal of Psychology,* 1956, *41,* 347–367.

Mayer, J. Science without conscience. *American Scholar,* 1972, *41,* 265–268.

McArthur, C. Clinical versus actuarial prediction. In *Proceedings, 1955 Invitational Conference on Testing Problems.* Princeton: Educational Testing Service, 1956.

McClelland, D. C. *Personality.* New York: Dryden Press, 1951.

McClelland, D. C., Atkinson, J. W., Clark, R. A., & Lowell, E. L. *The achievement motive.* New York: Appleton-Century-Crofts, 1953.

McNemar, Q. *Psychological statistics.* New York: Wiley, 1949.

McReynolds, P. (Ed.). *Advances in psychological assessment* (Vol. m).. t. opalo Alto, Calif.: Science & Behavior Books, 1968.

Meehl, P. E. *Clinical vs. statistical prediction: A theoretical analysis and a review of the evidence.* Minneapolis: University of Minnesota Press, 1954.

Meehl, P. E. Clinical versus actuarial prediction. In *Proceedings, 1955 Invitational Conference on Testing Problems.* Princeton: Educational Testing Service, 1956. (a)

Meehl, P. E. Wanted—a good cookbook. *American Psychologist,* 1956, *11,* 263–272. (b)

Meehl, P. E. When shall we use our heads instead of the formula? *Journal of Counseling Psychology,* 1957, *4,* 268–273.

Meehl, P. E. A comparison of clinicians with five statistical methods of identifying psychotic MMPI profiles. *Journal of Counseling Psychology,* 1959, *6,* 102–109.

Meehl, P. E. Seer over sign: The first good example. *Journal of Experimental Research in Personality,* 1965, *1,* 27–32.

Meehl, P. E. A scientific, scholarly, nonresearch doctorate for clinical practitioners: Arguments pro and con. In R. R. Holt (Ed.), *New horizon for psychotherapy: Autonomy as a profession.* New York: International Universities Press, 1971.

Meehl, P. E. *Psychodiagnosis: Selected papers.* Minneapolis: University of Minnesota Press, 1973.

Meehl, P. E., & Dahlstrom, W. G. Objective configural rules for discriminating psychotic from neurotic MMPI profiles. *Journal of Consulting Psychology,* 1960, *24,* 375–387.

Meehl, P. E., & Rosen, A. Antecedent probability and the efficiency of psychometric signs, patterns, or cutting scores. *Psychological Bulletin,* 1955, *52,* 194–216.

Meehl, P. E., Tiedeman, D., & McArthur, C. Symposium on clinical and statistical prediction. *Journal of Counseling Psychology,* 1956, *3,* 168–171.

Melton, R. S. A comparison of clinical and actuarial methods of prediction with an assessment of the relative accuracy of different clinicians. Unpublished doctoral dissertation, University of Minnesota, 1952.

Meltzoff, J., & Kornreich, M. *Research in psychotherapy.* Chicago: Atherton Press, 1970.

Merrill, R. M. On Keet's study, "Two verbal techniques in a miniature counseling situation." *Journal of Abnormal and Social Psychology,* 1952, *47,* 722.

Messick, S., & Ross, J. (Eds.). *Mesuusuuurrurment in personality and cognition.* New York: Wiley, 1962.

Michotte, A. (1946) *The perception of causality.* New York: Basic Books, 1963.

Miller, J. G. Information input overload and psychopathology. *American Journal of Psychiatry,* 1960, *116,* 695–704.

Millon, T., & Diesenhaus, H. I. *Research methods in psychopathology.* New York: Wiley, 1972.

Mischel, W. *Personality and assessment.* New York: Wiley, 1968.

Mumford, L. *The myth of the machine: Vol. 2. The pentagon of power.* New York: Harcourt, Brace, Jovanovich, 1970.

Murphy, L. B. Coping devices and defense mechanisms in relation to autonomous ego functions. *Bulletin of the Menninger Clinic,* 1960, *24,* 144–153.

Murray, H. A., & Kluckhohn, C. Outline of a conception of personality. In C. Kluckhohn & H. A. Murray (Eds.), *Personality in nature, society, and culture.* New York: Knopf, 1949.

Murray, H. A. [*et al.*] *Explorations in personality.* New York: Oxford University Press, 1938.

Murray, H. A. [*et al.*] *Assessment of men.* New York: Rinehart, 1948.

Oskamp, S. The relationship of clinical experience and training methods to several criteria of clinical prediction. *Psychological Monographs,* 1962, *76*(28, Whole No. 547).

Owens, W. A., & Jewell, D. O. Personnel selection. *Annual Review of Psychology,* 1969, *20,* 419–446.

Parrish, J. A., Klieger, W. A., & Drucker, A. J. A self-description blank for officer candidate school applicants. U.S. Army Personnel Research Branch Report, 1954, No. 1091. Summarized in A. J. Drucker, Predicting leadership ratings in the United States Army. *Educational and Psychological Measurement,* 1957, *17,* 240–263.

Perry, W. G. *Forms of intellectual and ethical development in the college years.* New York: Holt, Rinehart & Winston, 1970.

Piaget, J., & Inhelder, B. *The psychology of the child.* New York: Basic Books, 1969.

Pierson, L. R. High school teacher prediction of college success. *Personnel Guidance Journal,* 1958, *37,* 142–145.

Pine, F., & Holt, R. R. Creativity and primary process: A study of adaptive regression. *Journal of Abnormal and Social Psychology,* 1960, *61,* 370–379.

Piotrowski, Z. Digital-computer interpretation of inkblot test data. *Psychiatric Quarterly,* 1964, *38,* 1–26.

Platt, J. R. What we must do. *Science,* 1969, *166,* 1115–1121.

Polansky, N. How shall a life-history be written? *Character and Personality,* 1941, *9,* 188–207.

Polanyi, M. (1958) *Personal knowledge: Towards a post-critical philosophy* (Rev. ed.). New York: Harper Torchbooks, 1964.

Pool, I. *Trends in content analysis.* Urbana: University of Illinois Press, 1959.

Pope, B., & Siegman, A. W. Interviewer warmth in relation to interviewee verbal behavior. *Journal of Consulting and Clinical Psychology,* 1968, *32,* 588–595.

Rapaport, D. The structure of psychoanalytic theory: A systematizing attempt. *Psychological Issues,* 1960, *2*(2, Whole No. 6).

Rapaport, D., Gill, M. M., & Schafer, R. *Diagnostic psychological testing* (Rev. ed., R. R. Holt, Ed.). New York: International Universities Press, 1968.

Rapoport, A. An essay on mind. In J. M. Scher (Ed.), *Theories of the mind.* Glencoe, Ill.: Free Press, 1962.

Reich, W. (1933) *Character analysis* (3rd ed.). New York: Orgone Institute Press, 1949.

Reichenbach, H. *Experience and prediction.* Chicago: University of Chicago Press, 1938.

Revel, J. F. *Without Marx or Jesus.* Garden City, N.Y.: Doubleday, 1971.

Rogers, C. R. The necessary and sufficient conditions of therapeutic personality change. *Journal of Consulting Psychology*, 1957, *21*, 95–103.

Rogers, C. R. A tentative scale for the measurement of process in psychotherapy. In E. A. Rubinstein and M. B. Parloff (Eds.), *Research in psychotherapy*. Washington, D. C.: American Psychological Association, 1959.

Rogers, C. R., & Dymond, R. *Psychotherapy and personality change*. Chicago: University of Chicago Press, 1954.

Rosen, N. A., & Van Horn, J. W. Selection of college scholarship students: Statistical vs. clinical methods. *Personnel Guidance Journal*, 1961, *40*, 150–154.

Roszak, T. *The making of a counterculture*. Garden City, N.Y.: Doubleday, 1969.

Rotter, J. B. *Social learning and clinical psychology*. Englewood Cliffs, N.J.: Prentice-Hall, 1954.

Sanford, F. H. Speech and personality: A comparative case study. *Character and Personality*, 1942, *10*, 169–198.

Sarbin, T. R. A contribution to the study of actuarial and statistical methods of prediction. *American Journal of Sociology*, 1943, *48*, 593–602.

Sarbin, T. R. The logic of prediction in psychology. *Psychological Review*, 1944, *51*, 210–228.

Sarbin, T. R., Taft, R., & Bailey, D. E. *Clinical inference and cognitive theory*. New York: Holt, Rinehart & Winston, 1960.

Sargent, H. D. Insight test prognosis in successful and unsuccessful rehabilitation of the blind. *Journal of Projective Techniques*, 1956, *20*, 429–441.

Sargent, H. D., Horwitz, L., Wallerstein, R. S., & Appelbaum, A. Prediction in psychotherapy research: A method for the transformation of clinical judgments into testable hypotheses. *Psychological Issues*, 1968, *6*(1, Whole No. 21).

Sarnoff, I. *Personality dynamics and development*. New York: Wiley, 1962.

Sawyer, J. Measurement *and* prediction, clinical *and* statistical. *Psychological Bulletin*, 1966, *66*, 178–200.

Schafer, R. Psychological tests in clinical research. *Journal of Consulting Psychology*, 1949, *13*, 328–334. Reprinted in R. P. Knight & C. R. Friedman (Eds.), *Psychoanalytic psychiatry and psychology: Vol. 1. Clinical and theoretical papers*. New York: International Universities Press, 1954.

Schafer, R. *Psychoanalytic interpretation in Rorschach testing*. New York: Grune & Stratton, 1954.

Schafer, R. How was this story told? *Journal of Projective Techniques*, 1958, *22*, 181–210. (a)

Schafer, R. Generative empathy in the treatment situation. *Psychoanalytic Quarterly*, 1959, *28*, 342–373. (b)

Schiedt, R. *Ein Beitrag zum Problem der Rückfalls-prognose*. (Doctoral dissertation) Munich: Münchner-Zeitungs-Verlag, 1936.

Schneider, A. J. N., Lagrone, C. W., Glueck, E. T., & Glueck, S. Prediction of behavior of civilian delinquents in the Armed Forces. *Mental Hygiene*, 1944, *28*, 456–475.

Sellars, C. G. The travail of slavery. In C. G. Sellars (Ed.), *The southerner as American*. Chapel Hill: University of North Carolina Press, 1960.

Selltiz, C., Wrightsman, L. S., & Cook, S. W. *Research methods in social relations* (3rd ed.). New York: Holt, Rinehart & Winston, 1976.

Shakow, D. The recorded psychoanalytic interview as an objective approach to research in psychoanalysis. *Psychoanalytic Quarterly*, 1960, *29*, 82–97.

Shapiro, A. K. Placebo effects in medicine, psychotherapy, and psychoanalysis. In A. E. Bergin & S. L. Garfield (Eds.), *Handbook of psychotherapy and behavior change: An empirical analysis*. New York: Wiley, 1971.

Shapiro, A., Goodenough, D. R., & Gryler, R. Dream recall as a function of method of awakening. *Psychosomatic Medicine*, 1963, *25*, 174–180.

Shapiro, D. *Neurotic styles*. New York: Basic Books, 1965.

Silverman, L. H. A study of the effects of subliminally presented aggressive stimuli on the production of pathological thinking in a nonpsychiatric population. *Journal of Nervous and Mental Disease*, 1965, *141*, 443–455.

Silverman, L. H. Drive stimulation and psychopathology: On the conditions under which drive-related external events evoke pathological reactions. In R. R. Holt & E. Peterfreund (Eds.), *Psychoanalysis and Contemporary Science*, 1972, *1*, 306–326.

Skinner, B. F. *Beyond freedom and dignity.* New York: Knopf, 1971.

Smith, G. J. W., Spence, D. P., & Klein, G. S. Subliminal effects of verbal stimuli. *Journal of Abnormal and Social Psychology*, 1959, *59*, 167–176.

Smith, H. N. (Ed.). *Mark Twain's Adventures of Huckleberry Finn.* Boston: Houghton Mifflin, 1958.

Smith, M. B. "Mental health" reconsidered: A special case of the problem of values in psychology. *American Psychologist*, 1961, *16*, 299–306. Also in M. B. Smith, *Social psychology and human values.* Chicago: Aldine, 1969.

Snyder, W. U. Some investigations of relationship in psychotherapy. In E. A. Rubinstein & M. B. Parloff (Eds.), *Research in psychotherapy.* Washington, D.C.: American Psychological Association, 1959.

Snyder, W. U. *Dependency in psychotherapy.* New York: Macmillan, 1963.

Social Science Research Council, Committee on Historiography. The social sciences in historical study: A report. *Social Science Research Council Bulletin* No. 64, 1954.

Spence, D. P. PL/1 programs for content analysis. *Behavioral Science*, 1969, *14*, 432–433.

Spence, D. P. Find, a PL/1 program for computing frequency of specific words and type token ratios in a series of texts. *Behavioral Science*, 1971, *16*, 511.

Spence, D. P., & Holland, B. The restricting effects of awareness: A paradox and an explanation. *Journal of Abnormal and Social Psychology*, 1962, *64*, 163–174.

Srole, L., Langner, T. S., Michael, S. T., Opler, M. K., & Rennie, T. A. *Mental health in the metropolis: The midtown Manhattan study* (Vol. 1). New York: McGraw-Hill, 1962.

Stephenson, W. *The study of behavior: Q-technique and its methodology.* Chicago: University of Chicago Press, 1953.

Stern, G. G., Stein, M. I., & Bloom, B. S. *Methods in personality assessment.* Glencoe, Ill.: Free Press, 1956.

Stone, P. J., Dunphy, D. C., Smith, M. S., & Ogilvie, D. M. *The General Inquirer: A computer approach to content analysis in the behavioral sciences.* Cambridge: MIT Press, 1966.

Strong, E. K., Jr., & Tucker, A. J. The use of vocational interest scores in planning a medical career. *Psychological Monographs*, 1952, *66*(9, Whole No. 341).

Struening, E. L., & Guttentag, M. (Eds.). *Handbook of evaluation research* (Vol. 1). Beverly Hills, Calif.: Sage, 1975.

Strupp, H. H. *Psychotherapists in action.* New York: Grune & Stratton, 1960.

Sydiaha, D. On the equivalence of clinical and statistical methods. *Journal of Applied Psychology*, 1959, *43*, 395–401.

Szasz, T. S. *The myth of mental illness.* New York: Hoeber-Harper, 1961.

Taft, R. The ability to judge people. *Psychological Bulletin*, 1955, *52*, 1–23.

Taylor, J. A., & Spence, K. W. The relationship of anxiety level to performance in serial learning. *Journal of Experimental Psychology*, 1952, *44*, 61–64.

Tomkins, S. S. *The Thematic Apperception Test: The theory and technique of interpretation.* New York: Grune & Stratton, 1947.

Tomkins, S. S., & Messick, S. (Eds.). *Computer simulation of personality: Frontier of psychological theory.* New York: Wiley, 1963.

Trankell, A. Erfarenheter av en method for uttagning av piloter till Scandinavian Airlines System. *Meddelanded från Flygoch Nävalmedicinska Namnden*, 1956, No. 1.

Trankell, A. The psychologist as an instrument of prediction. *Journal of Applied Psychology*, 1959, *43*, 170–175.

Truax, C. B., & Carkhuff, R. R. *Toward effective counseling and psychotherapy: Training and practice.* Chicago: Aldine, 1967.

Truax, C. B., & Mitchell, K. M. Research on certain therapist interpersonal skills in relation to process and outcome. In A. E. Bergin & S. L. Garfield (Eds.), *Handbook of psychotherapy and behavior change: An empirical analysis.* New York: Wiley, 1971.

Truesdell, A. B., & Bath, J. A. Clinical and actuarial predictions of academic survival and attrition. *Journal of Counseling Psychology,* 1956, 50–53.

Tukey, J. W. Discussion. *Journal of Clinical Psychology,* 1950, *6,* 61–74.

Turiel, E. An experimental test of the sequentiality of developmental stages in the child's moral judgment. *Journal of Personality and Social Psychology,* 1966, *3,* 611–618.

von Domarus, E. The specific laws of logic in schizophrenia. In J. S. Kasanin (Ed.), *Language and thought in schizophrenia.* Berkeley: University of California Press, 1944.

Wald, A. *Statistical decision functions.* New York: Wiley, 1950.

Wallerstein, R. S., Robbins, L. L., Sargent, H. D., & Luborsky, L. The psychotherapy research project of The Menninger Foundation. *Bulletin of The Menninger Clinic,* 1956, *20,* 221–278.

Watley, D. J., & Vance, F. L. Clinical versus actuarial prediction of college achievement and leadership activity. U.S. Office of Education, Cooperative Research Project No. 2202, September 1964, University of Minnesota.

Watson, J. D. *The double helix.* New York: New American Library, 1969.

Watson, P. D., DiMascio, A., Kanter, S. S., Suter, E., & Greenblatt, M. A note on the influence of climatic factors on psychophysiological investigations. *Psychosomatic Medicine,* 1957, *19,* 419–423.

Weiss, P. *The science of life: The living system—a system for living.* Mt. Kisco, N.Y.: Futura Publishing Co., 1973.

Weizenbaum, J. *Computer power and human reason: From judgment to calculation.* San Francisco: Freeman, 1976.

Westoff, C. F., Sagi, P. C., & Kelly, E. L. Fertility through twenty years of marriage: A study in predictive possibilities. *American Sociological Review,* 1958, *23,* 549–556.

White, R. W. *Lives in progress.* New York: Dryden, 1952.

Whitehead, A. N. (1925) *Science in the modern world* (Rev. ed.). New York: Mentor, 1952.

Wiens, A. N., Matarazzo, J. D., & Saslow, G. The interaction recorder: An electronic punched paper tape unit for recording speech behavior during interviews. *Journal of Clinical Psychology,* 1965, *21,* 142–145.

Wiggins, J. S. *Personality and prediction: Principles of personality assessment.* Reading, Mass.: Addison-Wesley, 1973.

Winer, B. J. *Statistical principles in experimental design* (2nd ed.). New York: McGraw-Hill, 1971.

Wirt, R. O. Actuarial prediction. *Journal of Consulting Psychology,* 1956, *20,* 123–124.

Witkin, H. A., Dyk, R. B., Faterson, H. F., Goodenough, D. R., & Karp, S. A. *Psychological differentiation: Studies of development.* New York: Wiley, 1962.

Wittenborn, J. R., & Holzberg, J. D. The generality of psychiatric syndromes. *Journal of Consulting Psychology,* 1951, *15,* 372–380.

Wittman, M. P. A scale for measuring prognosis in schizophrenic patients. *Elgin Papers,* 1941, *4,* 20–33.

Wittman, M. P., & Steinberg, L. Follow-up of an objective evaluation of prognosis in dementia praecox and manic-depressive psychoses. *Elgin Papers,* 1944, *5,* 216–227.

Wolman, B. B. (Ed.). *Handbook of clinical psychology.* New York: McGraw-Hill, 1965. (a)

Wolman, B. B. Schizophrenia and related disorders. In B. B. Wolman (Ed.), *Handbook of clinical psychology.* New York: McGraw-Hill, 1965. (b)

Yates, A. J. Symptoms and symptom substitution. *Psychological Review,* 1958, *65,* 371–374.

Name Index

Subject Index